MAR 2 6 2014

The Unknown
HENRY MILLER

The Unknown
HENRY MILLER

A SEEKER IN BIG SUR

ARTHUR HOYLE

Arcade Publishing • New York

First Edition

Arcade Publishing books may be purchased in bulk at special discounts for sales promotion, corporate gifts, fund-raising, or educational purposes. Special editions can also be created to specifications. For details, contact the Special Sales Department, Arcade Publishing, 307 West 36th Street, 11th Floor, New York, NY 10018 or arcade@skyhorsepublishing.com.

Arcade Publishing® is a registered trademark of Skyhorse Publishing, Inc.®, a Delaware corporation.

Visit our website at www.arcadepub.com.
Visit the author's website at arthurhoyle.com

10 9 8 7 6 5 4 3 2 1

Library of Congress Cataloging-in-Publication Data

Hoyle, Arthur, 1941–
  The Unknown Henry Miller : a Seeker in Big Sur / Arthur Hoyle.
     pages cm
  ISBN 978-1-61145-899-2 (hardback)
  1. Miller, Henry, 1891-1980. 2. Authors, American—20th century—Biography. 3. Big Sur (Calif.)—Biography. I. Title.
  PS3525.I5454Z696 2014
  813'.52—dc23
  [B]

                                        2013046530

Printed in the United States of America

For Adrien, who loves to read

and

In loving memory of Alex and Ricardo

"We whose names are hereunder written, being desirous to inhabit the town of Providence, do promise to submit ourselves, in active or passive obedience, to all such orders or agreements as shall be made for public good of the body, in an orderly way, by the major consent of the present inhabitants, masters of families incorporated together into a township, and others whom they shall admit unto the same, only in civil things."

—Roger Williams, compact for the founding of the colony of Providence in present-day Rhode Island, 1636

"A fitly born and bred race, growing up in right conditions of out-door as much as indoor harmony, activity and development, would probably, from and in those conditions, find it enough merely *to live*— and would, in their relations to the sky, air, water, trees, etc., and to the countless common shows, and in the fact of *life* itself, discover and achieve happiness—with Being suffused night and day by wholesome ecstasy, surpassing all the pleasures that wealth, amusement, and even gratified intellect, erudition, or the sense of art, can give."

—Walt Whitman

"I would say that it was on this rock—temporarily forgotten—that America was founded."

—Henry Miller

CONTENTS

INTRODUCTION

Why a new biography of Henry Miller, and why now?

Henry Miller is an undeservedly neglected American author. Although the publication of his "Paris" books in the 1960s caused a national sensation, he remains unread by most Americans. And yet, Henry Miller was unique among twentieth-century American authors for making his own life experiences—all of them, from the scatological to the sublime—the raw material of his books. His aim as a writer was to use language to transform these life experiences into art and, through art, to transform himself. Art became for him the means for reaching the highest level of human attainment, self-realization. In the history of American literature, only his idol Whitman sang such a song of himself. But today, while Whitman is a fixture in the literary pantheon, Miller is largely unknown, excluded from the academic canon, rarely taught in colleges and universities, remembered, if at all, as the author of banned books that broke through the American and British censorship barriers. Perhaps his very uniqueness, his willingness to parade naked before us, has marginalized him; he refuses to fit into any recognizable American tradition. Does he embarrass us? Or perhaps shame us?

This biography was written to reposition Miller for a new generation of readers. It revisits Miller's life and work to reveal the man and the artist at their point of intersection, language. The facts of Miller's life have been thoroughly chronicled in three previously published biographies. But the facts of Miller's life do not give us a true portrait of him. A true portrait emerges only when we witness Miller's imagination at work, practicing the alchemical transmutation of the dross of his everyday experience into the gold of art. Miller's alchemical apparatus was his mastery of the English language, which he used in a variety of styles and forms to express and reveal his complex and often contradictory character. It is as a stylist, a stylist of the self, that Miller distinguishes himself. No modern writer, not Faulkner, not Joyce, surpasses Miller's ability to create a new imaginative reality out of words.

My portrait of Miller is drawn from his mature years as a writer, because only when he found his voice with *Tropic of Cancer* does the real Henry Miller come into view. It begins with his breakout in Paris during the 1930s, when he wrote the books whose originality and brilliance made him celebrated in Europe and whose obscenity made him notorious in America. It ends with his final breakthrough to the broad American readership denied him by the censors, the US publication of the Tropics and his major autobiographical saga, *The Rosy Crucifixion*. I have blended passages from Miller texts with letters he wrote and received to expose the intersection between his life and his art. His own words, and the words of those who knew him intimately, are the flesh of my portrait. The facts of his life are merely the skeleton.

Twenty years have elapsed since the last biographies of Miller were published. During this period, his reputation in America has continued to languish. For many commentators, the time of his relevance for American readers, the 1960s, has passed. But to regard Miller merely as the author of largely censorable books whose achievement was to liberate our standards of what words are permissible to appear in print is to diminish him by turning him into a historical curiosity and to miss his true significance.

Henry Miller's voice and the message it carries—the message of self-liberation—are timeless. Although he writes in great detail about his life as an American living in the twentieth century, to locate him solely in conventional time and space and try to understand him in that context is to see him only partially. For Miller, the specifics of his time and place were merely a stepping-stone to a higher plane of reality, the realm of cosmic consciousness. Miller writes not as a citizen of America, or even the Earth, but as a member of the human race who inhabits the universe.

Miller distrusted biography and biographers because he believed their obsession with facts blinded them to the reality of the imagination, which he considered the only true reality. Nevertheless, he wrote several biographies himself: full-length studies of D. H. Lawrence and Arthur Rimbaud, shorter sketches of people, usually artists like himself, whom he admired. Commenting on *The World of Lawrence* he said, "The only way to do justice to a man like that, is to give another creation. Not *explain* him, but prove by writing about him that one has caught the flame he tried to pass on." And that is what I have tried to do.

The Unknown
HENRY MILLER

1

THE PARIS YEARS

"A Writer Is Born."

IN THE SPRING OF 1939, AS THE EUROPEAN POWERS PREPARED FOR WAR, the writer Henry Miller sat down to his typewriter in his Paris apartment at Villa Seurat and composed a five-page, single-spaced letter to his American friend Huntington Cairns. Miller, age forty-seven, had been living in Paris for nine years. He had come there in flight from a failed life in America in a desperate bid to find himself as a writer. Now, as he made preparations for what he hoped would be an extended sabbatical from writing, during which he intended to travel to Greece and points east, he decided to recapitulate for a trusted friend all that he had accomplished during the period of his voluntary exile from his homeland.

His choice of correspondent for this letter might at first glance seem odd. Huntington Cairns was a thirty-five-year-old lawyer who lived in Baltimore, Maryland, where he was a partner in a prominent law firm. In 1934, the same year Miller's controversial novel *Tropic of Cancer* was published in Paris, Cairns was appointed a special legal advisor to the Customs Bureau of the United States Treasury Department. In that capacity, he served as the official US censor, advising the bureau on the application of the obscenity standard under the Tariff Act of 1930. Miller's notorious novel had been seized by customs officials in 1934 and declared obscene by a US district court.

In addition to his professional training in the law, Cairns was also a serious student of literature who wrote essays and book reviews and cultivated relationships with leading literary figures of his day.

This probably explains why the critic H. L. Mencken, who wrote for the *Baltimore Sun*, had forwarded to Cairns the copy of *Cancer* he had received from Miller. Although the book was banned in the United States and in England, Miller sent copies to prominent writers and critics in both countries in an effort to establish the book's reputation as serious literature.

Informed by Mencken that Cairns had read and admired *Cancer*, Miller wrote to Cairns in May 1936 announcing the imminent publication of another controversial book, *Black Spring*, and offering to send it to him. A few months later, Cairns and his wife, Florence, were in Paris, and the two men met. Over the next several years, they corresponded frequently, primarily about strategies for obtaining reviews of Miller's work that could be used to rebut the charge of obscenity and give Miller access to the American publishing market. Cairns also made arrangements for a show of Miller's watercolors in Washington, DC. By the time Miller wrote Cairns in April 1939, he considered him to be one of only two Americans he could count as friends, the other being his boyhood Brooklyn chum, the painter Emil Schnellock.

Miller's letter to Cairns begins on a gloomy note. War now seems certain and his own future cloudy. Fearing German bombardment and invasion, he plans to leave France. He has accepted an invitation to visit the Greek island of Corfu and stay with his friend, the English writer Lawrence Durrell and his wife, Nancy. As usual, Miller is without funds and has had to cobble together his travel money from an assortment of friends, admirers, and advances on book sales. Worried that he may be separated from his personal papers, or even killed in a surprise air raid, he feels the need to produce for posterity a brief account of what the Paris years have meant to him as a writer and as a man.

To this end, Miller sketches first the years of his early manhood in Brooklyn and New York, years of restless questing and failed romantic relationships as he sought his true vocation. He describes his origins as a writer and his first halting attempts at novel writing, his false starts. As the formative influences on his world outlook and aesthetic sensibility, he identifies the anarchism of Emma Goldman, whom he met in California during his early wanderings; the doctrine of acceptance that he found in Zen Buddhism and the teachings of LaoTse; the uncompromising explorations of the human soul that he discovered in the works of Nietzsche and Dostoevsky; and the writings of Knut Hamsun and August Strindberg, which he admired greatly—all influences from the Old World of Europe and Asia. He then goes on to sum up his accomplishments as a writer during the decade that he has been living in Paris, emphasizing his debt to Anaïs Nin, who gave him both financial and emotional support as he wrote several of his major works. Finally, Miller concludes by peering into the future, anticipating his return to America as war erupts in Europe and predicting for himself a life isolated from the mainstream of American culture.

The letter thus provides a layered snapshot of Miller at the moment of his maturation as a writer, which is where the present account of his life begins. Describing his artistic birth, it outlines the material—his life story during his formative years—that will occupy him for much of the remainder of his writing career as he labors through his magnum opus, *The Rosy Crucifixion*, the story of his spiritual death and rebirth. The letter also contains the seeds of themes that Miller will treat in many of his essay collections in years to come. Before tracing the path that would eventually take Miller to Big Sur, let's explore in detail his self-portrait as a writer at this decisive juncture in his life.

MILLER DATES HIS ORIGINS AS A WRITER to September 1924 when, at the urging of his second wife, June, he quit his job as personnel manager of Western Union in order to write full time. But he tells Cairns that he actually began writing in 1912, when he was twenty-one and working in his father's tailor shop on Fifth Avenue in New York. His early writing took the form of long, humorous letters to friends, a practice he continued throughout his life. (Miller estimated in 1939 that he had already written twenty-five thousand letters to twenty-five hundred different people.) In 1922, when he was married to his first wife, Beatrice, and was the father of a two-year-old daughter named Barbara, Miller wrote his first book, *Clipped Wings*, a seventy-five-thousand-word novel about twelve messengers under his employ at Western Union. (The book was never published and the manuscript has been lost.)

During the period from 1924 to 1930, he wrote two other novels, *Moloch, or, This Gentile World*, and *Crazy Cock*, both of which he brought with him to Paris hoping to publish. *Crazy Cock* was turned down for publication and *Moloch* was lost. (Each of these works was published posthumously, *Crazy Cock* in 1991 and *Moloch* in 1992.) Listing his literary output since coming to Paris, he expresses regret that it isn't more. In the fifteen years since he began writing full time, he has never been able to earn a living from his work and only recently has gained acceptance for his shorter pieces from literary magazines, which, when they pay at all, pay a pittance.

Miller begins the list of his Paris books with *Tropic of Cancer*, his signature novel. "In 1931 I began *Tropic of Cancer* and wrote it over about three or four times . . . It was published in 1934. *Aller Retour New York* published in 1935 and *Black Spring* in 1936. Then *Max and the White Phagocytes* and now *Tropic of Capricorn, volume one*." He mentions several other works, some never finished, others never published, as well as *Hamlet*, his lengthy and tedious correspondence with Michael Fraenkel over Shakespeare's play that Fraenkel published in 1939 through his Carrefour Press.

All of the major works mentioned in the letter to Cairns were published by Jack Kahane through his Obelisk Press. Kahane was an Englishman who wrote erotica under a pen name and was publishing in partnership with a Frenchman who owned the press. The manuscript of *Tropic of Cancer* reached him through William Bradley, the preeminent agent for literary exiles living in Paris whose clients included Gertrude Stein, Ernest Hemingway, and F. Scott Fitzgerald. Kahane was thrilled when he read the manuscript, telling Miller, "I've been waiting a long time for a book like yours to fall into my hands. There's smut, there's titillation, and then there's what you've written: the most terrible, the most sordid, the most truthful book I've ever read. It makes Joyce's *Ulysses* taste like lemonade."

Tropic of Cancer, Miller's first published work, established his distinctive voice and style and immediately branded him as an outlaw writer. Like all of his Paris books, it opens a window onto his imagination and aesthetic sensibility at the time when, according to many critics of his work, he was at the height of his artistic powers, writing from the edge of the world with fierce disdain while boldly experimenting with form, style, and content. The novel chronicles the picaresque adventures of the narrator (Miller) as he wanders the streets of Paris encountering an odd assortment of eccentric characters that he presents in a tone of affectionate contempt for their pathetic attempts at living. All of the characters are based on people Miller knew and in many cases depended upon for his day-to-day survival.

The book begins with Boris (Michael Fraenkel), a small Jewish writer-philosopher who shared his apartment with Miller for a time and encouraged his writing. When Boris is introduced to us on the first page, he is lice-infested. Miller is shaving his friend's armpits, while Boris expounds on "the weather," his metaphor for the climate of the times. "The weather will continue bad," he says. "There will be more calamities, more death, more despair. The cancer of time is eating us away." Thus Miller sets up the terms for his presentation of modern life: on the one hand, it is a time of desperation and sickness of soul. But on the other hand, there are more pressing, immediate concerns that demand attention; Boris is lousy.

The novel swings between these two poles of absurdity: at one extreme the calamity of a corrupt civilization that time is eating away, at the other modern man, comically degraded, no longer even capable of heroic struggle and reduced to a slavish obedience to his basic instincts. Yet Miller will suggest that in his basic instincts man may yet find the path to individual salvation, a path that passes through a purifying cosmic howl that releases him from conventional attachments. Miller's own dilemma is to be the perpetual artist-outsider, whose insight into the debased world isolates him from it and from his fellow humans.

Miller combined the two facets of modern life, the individual and the societal, into the image of Paris as a whore. Only through the use of obscene language and imagery could he express the full extent of his rage against his dilemma (the artist-individual as perpetual outsider), which he saw as also the dilemma of modern man. Miller writes of his mistress city: "Paris is like a whore. From a distance she seems ravishing, you can't wait until you have her in your arms. And five minutes later you feel empty, disgusted with yourself. You feel tricked." A few pages later, he bores further into this image in a type of language that appears frequently in the novel and that gave censors the ammunition they needed to ban his book. "When I look down into the fucked-out cunt of [this] whore I feel the whole world beneath me, a world tottering and crumbling, a world used up and polished like a leper's skull. If there were a man who dared say all that he thought of this world there would not be left him a square foot of ground to stand on." Miller here acknowledges the isolation that his searing vision of the modern reality has brought, and he accepts it. "The task which the artist implicitly sets himself is to overthrow existing values, to make of the chaos about him an order which is his own, to sow strife and ferment so that by the emotional release those who are dead may be restored to life."

Having assumed the role of the artist-outsider who carries the burden of truth, Miller offers us an alternate image of woman, woman transformed by his imagination into an embodiment of a higher, cosmic reality that blots out the ugliness of the man-made world:

The earth is not an arid plateau of health and comfort, but a great sprawling female with velvet torso that swells and heaves with ocean billows; she squirms beneath a diadem of sweat and anguish. Naked and sexed, she rolls among the clouds in the violet light of the stars. All of her, from her generous breasts to her gleaming thighs, blazes with furious ardor. She moves among the seasons and the years with a grand whoopla that seizes the torso with paroxysmal fury, that shakes the cobwebs out of the sky; she subsides on her pivotal orbits with volcanic tremors . . . Love and hate, despair, pity, rage disgust—what are these amidst the fornications of the planets? What is war, disease, cruelty, terror, when night presents the ecstasy of myriad blazing suns? What is this chaff we chew in our sleep if it is not the remembrance of fang-whorl and star cluster.

It is to an awareness of this cosmic dimension, and the potential it brings for a higher form of life, that Miller wishes to lead us through his language. But he insists that we can arrive at this awareness only through facing and accepting the most fundamental aspects of our being. He says with Hermes Trismegistus and other great mystics, "as above, so below." And the great irony of Miller's work is that the path to personal transformation that he found through his gritty experiences on the debauched streets of Paris was labeled obscene by the society whose individual members were in such desperate need of transformation.

This irony was not lost on Huntington Cairns, who wrote to Miller after their meeting in Paris, "I know of no other writer in English who is more naturally a novelist or who writes with anything approaching your power." But Cairns had to advise Miller that the prevailing legal standard for obscenity in America would prevent *Cancer* being read by the very audience for which it was intended.

Miller's sexual relations, and those of his friends, are a constant preoccupation of the novel, second in importance only to his perpetual quest for food and shelter. Miller has countless affairs, casual encounters, and transactions with prostitutes, which he relates with cynical coarseness, and he describes with sardonic amusement the trysts and fornications of his friends, some of which he witnesses as a bemused spectator offering words of encouragement or consolation. The cumulative effect of these scenes, beyond their bawdy surface humor, is to expose the hopelessness of finding love in the modern world, and to expose it without sentimentality, in a spirit of jaunty irreverence, as though even to wish for genuine human contact or sincerity of feeling between a man and a woman is a waste of emotion and a sign of spiritual weakness. The only exception to this pattern is his treatment of his love for his second wife, June, who appears intermittently in the novel as Mona, making unannounced visits from New York that upset his equilibrium and deflate his clownish attitude toward life.

These sexual escapades of Miller's friends, devoid of any human affection or meaning, bitter in their characterization of women, mocking in their treatment of men, have their origins in Miller's personal life. As a youth, Miller hated his mother for her rigid conventionality, her harshness and humorlessness, her henpecking of his father, her abuse of his half-witted sister, Lauretta. His hatred of her never abated. To avoid being drafted into military service during World War One, Miller married his piano teacher, Beatrice Sylvas Wickens, an older woman, and had a daughter, Barbara, with her. As he writes in his letter to Cairns, "From the day we hitched up it was a running battle." When Miller met June, his second wife, in a dance hall on Broadway, he abandoned Beatrice and Barbara and avoided contact with them for over thirty years. He suffered torments at the hands of June, whose constant "appointments" with "male admirers" humiliated him and whose lesbian relationship with a woman she brought home one day to their Greenwich Village apartment unmanned him and made him feel like a fool. His interest in prostitutes, his tendency to degrade all women to the status of whore, is clarified in a letter he wrote to his lover Anaïs Nin in the summer of 1933: "One day I saw a whore sitting in a café . . . As I rounded the corner, leaving her out of sight, suddenly it occurred to me how this woman resembled three women—a composite. And who were they, do you think? June, my first wife, and my mother. . . What should I say was the chief ingredient of this composite? *Scorn.*"

Set against this "composite" is Miller's memory of his unfulfilled love for a beautiful girl in his Brooklyn neighborhood, Cora Seward. When he was eighteen, Miller used to stand in the street in front of her house at night, gazing at the light from her bedroom window, unable to work up the courage to walk to the front door and ring the bell. This lost love haunted him all his life and embedded itself in him as an unattainable ideal of woman against which all of his actual relationships paled.

Some of this yearning is conveyed in *Tropic of Cancer* through Miller's literary treatment of his wife June during her periodic surprise visits to Paris. He writes:

Mona has been away a long time and it's just today I'm meeting her at the Gare St. Lazare. Toward evening I'm standing there with my face squeezed between the bars but there's no Mona, and I read the cable over again but it doesn't help any. I go back to the Quarter and just the same I put away a hearty meal. Strolling past the Dôme a little later I see a pale, heavy face and burning eyes – and the little velvet suit that I always adore because under the soft velvet were always her warm breasts, the marble legs, cool, firm, muscular. She rises up out of a sea of faces and embraces me, embraces me passionately. . . I sit down beside her and she talks – a flood of talk. Wild, consumptive notes of hysteria, perversion, leprosy. I hear not a word because she is beautiful and I love her and now I am happy and willing to die.

But such idyllic moments are infrequent and do not last long. They go to her hotel, make love, and sleep together. In the early morning light Miller awakens and looks at her tenderly. Suddenly, he feels something crawling on his neck. He notices that Mona's hair is alive with bed bugs. She wakes with a shriek and they flee into the street without paying their bill. They are swept up in Miller's tawdry street life.

Later in the novel they part, perhaps for the final time. Miller is in genuine despair; his clownish mask has fallen away. "When I realize that she is gone, perhaps gone forever, a great void opens up and I feel that I am falling, falling, falling into deep, black space. And this is worse than tears, deeper than regret or pain or sorrow; it is the abyss into which Satan was plunged. There is no climbing back, no ray of light, no sound of human voice or touch of human hand."

This language shows another side of Miller the writer— serious, reflective, direct. The undercurrent of irony and disgust that runs through so many of the scenes in the novel ceases, and Miller exposes himself. The novel is dotted with such passages, in which Miller extemporizes on metaphysics, aesthetics, and the conditions of modern life. From these passages one can piece together a coherent picture of the philosophy of life underpinning *Tropic of Cancer*, and Miller's conception of the role and responsibility of the artist.

Miller's experiences growing up in New York during the first quarter of the twentieth century had left him a deeply unhappy man. He was at odds with the society around him, felt it to be mechanical, materialistic, and dehumanized by its addiction to "progress."

He sought, through his readings in Nietzsche, Dostoyevsky, Oswald Spengler, Henri Bergson, and Élie Faure, to arrive at an understanding of what he felt acutely as the modern malaise. He had come to the conclusion that Western civilization, in following the path blazed through history by man's reliance on reason, will, and intellect (mankind's supposedly higher faculties), had gone off in the wrong direction and cut man off from the most fundamental and powerful aspects of his being, emotions, instincts, and the unconscious. He believed that man could not become fully human unless his connection to these basic elements in himself was restored. Until this happened, society would continue to rot and decay, and its individual members would continue to live incompletely and in a state of chronic dissatisfaction. In the novel, Miller expressed this through the sexual dysfunctionality of his characters. Miller saw the signs of social collapse around him—the Depression, the approaching war—as evidence that the obliteration of civilization that was necessary if a true revolution in man's way of life was to occur was proceeding. Hence, the anarchic glee that is the dominant tone of *Cancer.*

Miller believed that only the individual could be saved from the fate that awaited mass man, a fate that he likened to a living death in which people mechanically lived their lives in obedience to ignorant and inhuman taboos. Social movements, political revolutions, only produced more of the same. For Miller, the way to individuation was through art, and it was the role of the artist to point the way for others by being an example of how to escape the prevailing system and achieve personal freedom. Miller's descent to a life without hope, a life without past or future, on the streets of Paris, was a demonstration of how far he was willing to go in order to be free. Others could follow, if they dared, and find their own Paris. But they would have to own the whore that she was.

Miller sees the artist as reaching another plane of being that he calls "inhuman." "Side by side with the human race," Miller writes, "there runs another race of beings, the inhuman ones, the race of artists who, goaded by unknown impulses, take the lifeless mass of humanity and by the fever and ferment with which they imbue it turn this soggy dough into bread and the bread into wine and the wine into song." Miller sees himself as a member of this "inhuman" race and rejoices in it: "Once I thought that to be human was the highest aim a man could have, but now I see that it was meant to destroy me. Today I am proud to say that I am *inhuman*, that I belong not to men and governments, that I have nothing to do with creeds and principles, that I have nothing to do with the creaking machinery of humanity—I belong to the earth!"

Miller's novel, *Tropic of Cancer*, is his song. At the outset of the book, Miller tells the reader what to expect: "This is not a book. This is libel, slander, defamation of character. This is not a book, in the ordinary sense of the word. No, this is a prolonged insult, a gob of spit in the face of Art, a kick in the pants to God, Man, Destiny, Time, Love, Beauty . . . what you will. I am going to sing for you, a little off key perhaps, but I will sing. I will sing while you croak, I will dance over your dirty corpse."

Tropic of Cancer, written in 1931 to 1932 and published in Paris in 1934, was banned in England and the United States until the early 1960s. But although Miller was denied for many years the readership and the money that this work finally brought him, he was happy to have written it because writing it made him into the artist that he so desperately wanted to become. His early letters from Paris to Emil Schnellock in New York declare his determination to make this book—his "Paris book"—his breakthrough as an artist. "I will explode in the Paris book. The hell with form, style, expression, and all those pseudo-paramount things which beguile the critics. I want to get myself across this time—and direct as a knife thrust."

A FEW MONTHS AFTER *TROPIC OF CANCER* WAS PUBLISHED, Miller traveled to New York. This trip produced the second book he mentions in his letter to Cairns, *Aller Retour New York* (Round Trip to New York). Miller went to New York in January 1935 in pursuit of his lover, Anaïs Nin, who had gone there in November to study and practice psychoanalysis with Otto Rank, her therapist. Miller had been under the impression that Nin was going to New York with her husband, Hugo, but a mix-up in letters she sent to the two of them (Miller got the letter intended for Hugo; Hugo got the letter intended for Miller) caused him to realize that Hugo was still in France and that she was deceiving him. Suspecting (correctly) that Nin was having an affair with Rank, Miller became frantically jealous and declared his intention to come to New York in order to press Nin to end her marriage to Hugo so they could live together.

Miller had a second motive for going to New York—promoting *Tropic of Cancer*. He had sent copies ahead to Nin for distribution to his friends there. He had also sent copies to John Dos Passos, Katherine Anne Porter, and Richard Osborn, a friend from Paris who was now living in Bridgeport, Connecticut, with his mother. And he had asked Osborn to obtain for him addresses of Carl Sandburg, Max Eastman, William Carlos Williams, Scott Fitzgerald, Edgar Lee Masters, Walter Winchell, and Al Jolson. He was worried that the book would be entirely overlooked in America, not only among general readers, but also even among important figures on America's literary and cultural scene.

After raising money from friends in Paris, Miller booked passage on the *Champlain*. Just before he departed, he received a letter from Anaïs Nin informing him that her husband, Hugo, was also on his way to join her in New York. Nin was setting up a potentially explosive situation that would undoubtedly provide good fodder for her diary. Thus the stage was set for Miller's return visit to his native land.

Aller Retour New York is in the form of a long letter to Alfred Perlès, another close friend whom Miller had caricatured in *Tropic of Cancer*. It was begun a short time before Miller returned to France in June 1935 and continued on board the Dutch vessel *Veendam* that brought him back to Europe. The volatility of his relationship with Nin combined with his frustration at finding *Cancer* largely ignored in America had put him in a foul mood, and he unleashed his venom on the city of New York, its people, its architecture, its food, its forms of diversion and entertainment, its deadly commercial animus.

As he does in Paris, Miller samples the life of New York by walking its streets. Here he is on 42nd Street "which has now become a public shithouse. Five burlesque houses in one block, and all of them Jewish, even the black-and-tan. In between are sandwich joints, penny arcades and movies at fifteen cents a crack . . . A continuous performance from eight in the morning to midnight; it slides before your eyes like a tide of shit. All these movie houses were once good theaters; now they are filled with chinks, wops, polaks, litvaks, mocks, croats, finns, etc. Now and then a half-witted hundred-percent American from Gallup or Terre Haute."

He reaches Broadway, which offers him an opportunity to caricature American women. "Walking down Broadway I noticed how lousy the street was with whores. Not the old bag-swingers of 1908 and '10, but young ones without stockings, lean, trim, racy ones with strips of monkey fur or skunk slung around their necks. They come bouncing out of the side streets with a cigarette to their lips and they stand a moment looking bewilderedly up and down the Appian Way. They look right through you, not graciously and invitingly and sexually and sensually, but with that boring, riveting eye like the acetylene torch on the car tracks at night. There is only one look the American woman can turn on, be she a whore or a duchess . . . It speaks of cold cash and speed and sanitary conditions."

Miller has often been accused of anti-Semitism and misogyny. His letter to Nin about whores, and his fatal early love for Cora Seward expose the psychic polarities he wrestled with all his life. His apparent anti-Semitism may have been nothing more than a literary pose, struck for its shock value. Miller has written elsewhere that he sometimes thinks of himself as a Jew. He also married a Jew (June), and for a time in Paris he lived with, was influenced by, and collaborated with a Jewish intellectual, Michael Fraenkel. His Paris publisher Jack Kahane was Jewish. He may disparage Jews because he regards them as a leading force in creating social institutions that he despises and rejects and because in his view Jews sustain the prevailing order. As he writes in the letter to Perlès, "The ambition of every industrious, self-respecting Jew is to become a member of the School for Social Science, or the John Reed Club, or the Rand School, or better still, all three at once. This gives him a knowledge of the world, keeps him *au courant*, with hot and cold water always on tap—get me?"

The ethnic slurs in Miller's description of 42nd Street are clearly a sword thrust at that most precious of American mythologies, the melting pot. Miller did not exclude his own lineage from this slander, writing at one point, "My family were entirely Nordic, which is to say, idiots." What these barbs have in common is their scorn for the notion of group pride. Miller insults not individuals but groups and representative types, as in the big spender, Jack Brent, who takes him out for a night on the town, poisons him with alcohol and cigar smoke, and ends up in a fight with a street prostitute and her pimp.

Miller also savages the envied life of well-to-do business executives who work in Manhattan and reside in fashionable suburbs, the characters who show up later in the fiction of John O'Hara, John Cheever, and John Updike. He describes with relish a weekend debauch that he joins at the invitation of "a big advertising director" who lives in Manhasset, Long Island. "The idea is—how to kill the weekend . . . They don't know what to do with themselves after a hard week at the office. They like to get undressed and dance . . . to change wives. To prime themselves for these frolics, the men descend to the advertising director's basement to watch pornographic films." Miller sardonically sums up his own role in the affair. "I made a hit because 'I was unconventional.' Some times, when you are regarded as being unconventional, it is embarrassing to be obliged to refuse a choice piece of ass—your host's wife, let us say, size 59 and round as a tub."

Back in the streets, Miller excoriates New York's architecture, taking particular aim at the Empire State Building, a symbol of everything that Americans value and that Miller despises. Loading his pen with burlesque exaggeration, Miller provides Perlès with some "facts" about the building: "Lingerie and toilet articles on the 227th floor; 8,765,492,583 visitors to the mooring mast since this building was erected; the janitors comprise a force slightly larger than the standing armies of Europe, and are equipped with hole proof socks and bullet-proof jock straps." With cruel irony he compares New York's Woolworth Building ("like a Nuremberg cheese") and the Singer Building—both monuments to commercialism—with the great cathedrals of Europe. This leads him into a total denunciation of America: "I notice that the great cathedrals of Europe never seem outmoded . . . They will inspire a hundred years from now, five hundred years from now, a thousand years from now—if the Germans haven't destroyed them. The feelings I have about America, about the whole continent—flora, fauna, architecture, peoples, customs—is this: *nothing vital was ever begun here . . . nothing of value . . .* Tomorrow the whole continent might sink into the sea—and what would be lost? Is there one priceless monument? One irreplaceable thing? Anything whose loss would create a feeling of real deprivation, such as the loss of Dante's great work, for example?"

Or Henry Miller's?

In May 1935 Nin and Hugo returned to France, and soon after Miller followed, booking passage on the *Veendam*. Back in France, visiting Nin at her home in Louveciennes, Miller pens a postscript to Perlès. "I can't help thinking again of America . . . In reality there is no America! There are just millions of things unrelated one to another, except as one part of a machine is related to another. To the parts themselves nothing seems new; only an old watch which has stopped ticking can gaze in wonder at a new and moving part."

Miller concludes the letter with a revealing aside to Perlès: "Well, Fred, how was that? I'm going to stop now and let you praise the shit out of me. Tell me what a genius I am—from America sent." Miller is the lost voice of his country.

BEFORE MILLER WROTE HIS LONG LETTER TO PERLÈS FROM NEW YORK, he had been at work on another book, *Black Spring*, which was published in 1936, again by Obelisk Press. Though *Black Spring* is called a novel, it is a novel only in the Miller sense. The book is actually a collection of ten short pieces, ranging in length from six to thirty-nine pages, written in different styles about a variety of subjects of interest to Miller. What holds the pieces together is Miller's central consciousness, his voice and attitudes.

The book reveals a great deal about Miller's state of mind after the publication of *Cancer*. Clearly, his belief in the artistic achievement of that book has emboldened him to push his stylistic experiments to extremes, and has confirmed for him that his great subject as a writer will be himself. The collection shows two sides of Miller the author—his deep antagonism toward his American roots that he desperately sought to escape by becoming an outsider, an adopted European, and his complete psychological disengagement from the cultural reality around him in order to explore, through language, his inner self.

Miller opens the book with a rumination on the Brooklyn neighborhood, "The Fourteenth Ward," that shaped his childhood and laid the foundation for the artist he would become. "I was born in the street and raised in the street . . . To be born in the street means to wander all your life, to be free. It means accident and incident, drama, movement. It means above all dream . . . In the street you learn what human beings really are; otherwise, or afterwards, you invent them. What is not in the open street is false, derived, that is to say, *literature*. Nothing of what is called 'adventure' ever approaches the flavor of the street."

Miller recalls the boyhood chums who shared the life of the streets with him. "Their names ring out like gold coins—Tom Fowler, Jim Buckley, Matt Owen, Rob Ramsey, Harry Martin, Johnny Dunne, to say nothing of Eddie Carney or the great Lester Reardon." Miller recounts his boyhood exploits, summoning up vivid sense memories of sights, sounds, and smells encountered in the streets. Then he remarks on the great change, the passing from innocence to experience, from the body to the mind. "Suddenly, walking down a street, be it real or be it a dream, one realizes for the first time that all this has passed forever and will live only in memory . . . All things, as we walk, splitting with us into myriad iridescent fragments. The great fragmentation of maturity . . . We live in the mind, in ideas, in fragments. We no longer drink in the wild outer music of the streets—we *remember* only."

This lost sense of life as a reality in which mind and body are unified Miller recovers through his discovery of Dostoevsky. "And then one day, as if suddenly the flesh came undone and the blood beneath the flesh had coalesced with the air, suddenly the whole world roars again and the very skeleton of the body melts like wax. Such a day it may be when first you encounter Dostoevski. You remember the smell of the tablecloth on which the book rests, you look down at the clock and it is only five minutes from eternity . . ." This encounter with a writer who examined the spiritual torments of his characters alerted Miller to the potential of language to free him from the cage of modern life: "Now every door of the cage is open and whichever way you walk is a straight line toward infinity."

Miller's father, Heinrich, owned a tailor shop on Fifth Avenue in Manhattan that catered to an upscale clientele. The writer Frank Harris and the actor John Barrymore were Heinrich's regular customers. Miller worked in the shop during the early years of his marriage to Beatrice, until the business foundered and Heinrich was reduced to hiring himself out to other tailors. Miller's droll, picaresque experiences working for his father form the basis of the longest piece in *Black Spring*, "The Tailor Shop."

Heinrich was an inept businessman and bon vivant whose fondness for leisurely lunches and early afternoon exits to a nearby hotel bar, combined with his readiness to extend credit to unreliable customers, kept the shop on shaky financial ground and eventually led to its closing. Miller describes with comic delight a bartering war that took place between Heinrich and Tom Moffatt, the owner of a restaurant Heinrich frequently patronized, and that typified his father's manner of doing business.

Moffatt had run up a considerable clothing debt he refused to pay until some imaginary "error" in the account statement had been straightened out. Despairing of collecting these past due bills, Heinrich settled on the strategy of dining extravagantly at Moffatt's restaurant, often "treating" the cronies who accompanied him, and then airily signing his name to the check when it was presented and telling the waiter to add it to his account. When Moffatt would bring in a statement on his next visit to the tailor shop, Heinrich would find an "error" on it and promise to pay as soon as the error had been rectified. Then he would pull out a fine pair of trousers or an expensive bolt of cloth for Moffatt's approval. Miller noted that sometimes his father would come back to work from one of his lunches and announce to his employees, "I just ate Moffatt's dinner jacket."

Miller obviously delighted in this low-grade scheming and fraud. Echoes of it may be found throughout *Tropic of Cancer* in Miller's descriptions of his survival tactics on the streets of Paris.

Though he might recall his father with wry affection, Miller was ashamed of his family, ashamed, horrified, and amused. His chaotic feelings about his family made it difficult for him to come to terms with them. In "The Tailor Shop," he describes a typical family gathering for a holiday celebration: "If it happened to be a Thanksgiving Day, or New Years or a birthday, or just any old excuse to get together, then off we'd trot, the whole family, to join the other freaks who made up the living family tree. It always seemed astounding to me how jolly they were in our family despite the calamities that were always threatening. Jolly in spite of everything. There was cancer, dropsy, cirrhosis of the liver, insanity, thievery, mendacity, buggery, incest, paralysis, tapeworms, abortions, triplets, idiots, drunkards, ne'er-do-wells, fanatics, sailors, tailors, watchmakers, scarlet fever, whooping cough, meningitis, running ears, chorea, stutterers, jailbirds, dreamers, storytellers, bartenders—and finally there was Uncle George and Tante Melia." This catalog of infirmities, woes, and aberrations presents Miller's family as a microcosmic reflection of the disease and degeneracy that he sees in the larger society. They are representative of the cancer that is eating the world.

Miller's empathy for his mentally disturbed Aunt Melia, his mother's older sister, as he unfolds her story and his role in it, are revealing of Miller's deeply held values. The Nietings, Louise Miller's family line, showed signs of being damaged stock going back at least as far as Henry's grandfather, Valentin Nieting. Valentin and his wife Emilie had seven children, three of whom died in infancy. Louise, the second-born, apparently had the most stable personality in the family and became manager of the household at a young age when her mother suffered a breakdown and her sister Emilia was beginning to show signs of her own instability. This may explain the autocratic manner in which Louise ruled Heinrich Miller's household, earning Henry's undying hatred.

When Emilia became a woman, her family was able to arrange a marriage for her and found her serial employment. But her husband left her for another woman, and she lost all her jobs. Then her husband hung himself. Emilia "went completely crazy . . . They found her eating her own dung. The day before that they found her sitting on the stove."

The family decided that Emilia was a danger to herself and to others and arranged to place her in an asylum. The task of bringing her there, without telling her where she was going, was given to Henry. "They said—*Henry, you take her to the asylum tomorrow. And don't tell them that we can afford to pay for her.*" Emilia went willingly with Miller because she trusted him. He reports that as they rode out to the country, "she's very tranquil and she calls the cows by their first name." But Miller is deeply troubled by Emilia's treatment and strongly disapproves of the family's decision to institutionalize her. "Why couldn't they make a place for her by the fire, let her sit there and dream, if that's what she wanted to do? Why must everybody *work*—even the saints and angels? Why must half-wits set a good example?"

As they approach the gate to the asylum, Emilia begins to tremble. Miller kisses her good-bye, and watches as the attendants lead her away. She looks back at him, "two great round eyes, full and black as the night, staring at me uncomprehendingly. No maniac can look that way. No idiot can look that way. Only an angel or a saint." Out of sight, Miller stops by a high wall, buries his head in arms, and weeps.

This story is rich in implications for Miller's life choices and writing. Miller refused to judge his "crazy" aunt by conventional standards that he believed to be even crazier. Her inability to adjust to the world around her, to be reliable and predictable and responsible (i.e., "normal"), he saw not as a sign of illness but of saintliness. Like his half-witted sister Lauretta, whom he also considered an innocent and an angel, Emilia's fate was evidence for Miller of the cruelty and inhumanity of a society that values conformity to its rules and taboos above all else. The fact that these values were being transmitted by his own family only heightened his disgust. Miller wanted no part of such a society. He would also be a saint and an outsider.

Miller found in art, in writing, his escape from personal history and his entrance into a self-created world, not unlike the innocent dream world that his Aunt Melia inhabited. Later in "The Tailor Shop" he declares, "My whole life is stretching out in an unbroken morning. I write from scratch each day. Each day a new world is created, separate and complete, and there I am among the constellations, a god so crazy about himself that he does nothing but sing and fashion new worlds."

The style that Miller found for the creation of this new, intensely imagined personal world was surrealism. Surrealism was a cultural and philosophical movement that developed in Europe in the aftermath of World War One. The movement was strongly influenced by the psychoanalytic theory and practice of Sigmund Freud, whose probes into the dream world of the unconscious opened up new vistas on reality that found expression in both painting and literature. The definition of surrealism offered by one of its founders, the writer André Breton—"pure psychic automatism, by which one proposes to express, either verbally, in writing, or by any other manner, the real functioning of thought, dictation of thought in the absence of all control exercised by reason, outside of all aesthetic and moral preoccupation"—accords well with the artistic temperament and social outlook of Henry Miller. As a resident of Paris, Miller had direct contact with the work of surrealist artists. He was profoundly affected by the filmmaking of the Spanish surrealists Luis Buñuel and Salvador Dalí, whose short films *Un Chien Andalou* and *L'Age d'Or* amazed him. Miller wrote an appreciation of Buñuel that was published in an English language journal issued in Paris, and made efforts to meet him. In a 1936 letter to his friend Lawrence Durrell, Miller explained his view of surrealism: "It's only an effort, at bottom, to return to the original vital source, which is in the solar plexus, or in the unconscious, or in the stars, if you like."

Surrealist passages occur throughout Miller's writing of the 1930s. Two of the most extended flights in this style appear in *Black Spring*, in the essays "Jabberwhorl Cronstadt" and "Into the Night Life."

One of Miller's survival strategies during his Paris years was to solicit meals from some of his more domesticated fellow American expatriates. He recruited seven providers, each of whom would serve him one substantial meal per week at their tables. In exchange, Miller would give them a watercolor, or wash the dishes, or simply entertain them with his conversation. One such friend was Walter Lowenfels, an American poet (Jewish) living in Paris with his wife and children, making ends meet as a rental agent for apartment owners. Lowenfels appears in *Tropic of Cancer* as Jabberwhorl Cronstadt, a name with echoes of Lewis Carroll's jabberwocky. The essay "Jabberwhorl Cronstadt" in *Black Spring* describes one of Miller's dinner visits to Lowenfels's home.

It begins with a description of Lowenfels's dwelling. "He lives in the back of a sunken garden, a sort of bosky glade shaded by whiffletrees and spinozas, by deodars and baobabs, a sort of queasy Buxtehude diapered with elytras and feluccas. You pass through a sentry box where the concierge twirls his mustache *con furioso* like in the last act of Ouida. They live on the third floor behind a mullioned belvedere filigreed with snaffled spaniels and sebaceous wens, with debentures and megrims hanging out to dry. Over the bell push it says: JABBERWHORL CRONSTADT, poet, musician, herbologist, weather man, linguist, oceanographer, old clothes, colloids."

This passage operates on several levels of nonsense. While the sounds and rhythms of the words create a pleasing musicality, the unfamiliarity of many of them, at least for the average reader, results in an initial unintelligibility. "Elytra," "whiffletree," "mullioned," just to name a few, are words that fall outside the vocabulary range of many if not most habitual readers, unless they are crossword puzzle fanatics. One is tempted to wonder if Miller is simply making them up. But a visit to the dictionary reveals that all of the words in this passage come from the English lexicon, though many of them are arcane, highly specialized, or being deliberately employed "incorrectly." The mixture of these usages produces a sense of benign chaos and confusion that violates the conventional rules of description and defies the reader's expectations of coherence.

"Into the Night Life" is a prolonged dream sequence that offers the reader few familiar reference points in external reality. It is a fluid journey through Miller's subconscious, and the longest sustained passage of surrealism that he wrote. The surreal quality comes not from the vocabulary that Miller employs—his diction has none of the eccentricities of "Jabberwhorl Cronstadt"—but rather from the grotesque and often violent imagery that pervades.

The passage moves randomly through a series of scenes, much as our dreams melt one into another. It begins in a room in a house, presumably Miller's boyhood home, where he is being tortured and tormented and finally wounded in the side, like Christ. It shifts abruptly to a hellish rush hour in New York during which Miller boards a trolley that takes him out into a desert. This may be a reference to a trip he took to California after he dropped out of college. Then he is riding a train somewhere in Germany but finds himself suddenly on the seashore at Coney Island. This stop on the dream journey gives the essay its subtitle, "A Coney Island of the Mind" (a title later borrowed by the Beat poet Lawrence Ferlinghetti).

The dream continues through a hotel room with a whore, a coffin factory, a cemetery, a hospital operating room where surgery is being performed on a child. Then it journeys back in time to pre-settlement America "where the tomahawk gleams, scalps fly, and out of the river bed there rolls a bright billowy cloud of blood." The savages disembowel Miller and yank his arms from their sockets. "The wind roars through my broken rectum, howls like sixty white lepers."

Finally, the dream ends on "the street of early sorrows," Miller's Brooklyn neighborhood, dominated by his mother: "Down the street of early sorrows comes the witch mother stalking the wind, her sails unfurled, her dress bulging with skulls. Terrified we flee the night, perusing the green album, its high décor of frontal legs, the bulging brow. From all the rotting stoops the hiss of snakes squirming in the bag, the cord tied, the bowels knotted. Blue flowers spotted like leopards, squashed, blood-sucked, the earth a vernal strain, gold, marrow, bright bone dust, three wings aloft and the march of the white horse, the ammonia eyes."

"Into the Night Life" can be viewed as an X-ray, in full color, of Miller's tormented psyche, a window onto the interior demons that haunted him and drove him as a writer. That Miller attached great significance to this piece is suggested by the fact that in 1947 he self-published a special edition of the text with illustrations by his Big Sur neighbor, the painter Bezalel Schatz.

Painting was Miller's second artistic love. The essay "The Angel Is My Watermark" in *Black Spring* explains the origins of his devotion to watercolor painting and describes his anarchic method of composition.

The essay gives an account of a watercolor that Miller paints on inspiration from a painting by a madman. Miller launches into his watercolor without plan or design, proceeding instinctively and impulsively. He begins to draw a horse, working from his memory of Etruscan horses he has seen on ceramics in the Louvre. But Miller, who has no formal training as a visual artist, is not a draughtsman, and the horse soon mutates into a zebra and finally is obliterated altogether as other shapes are formed by Miller's truant pencil. Miller is not dismayed by his inability to draw, to produce images that are representational. He glories in it. "When I get into a predicament of this sort I know that I can extricate myself when it comes time to apply the color. The drawing is simply the excuse for the color . . . My theory of painting is to get the drawing done with as quickly as possible and slap in the color. After all, I'm a colorist, not a draught horse." The same words might be used to describe Miller's theory of writing. He disdains the conventional mechanisms of fiction, such as story, plot, character development—the drawing—in order to free himself to be swept along by his associations, memories, and feelings—the color.

This creative process resembles Miller's description in a letter to Emil Schnellock of the wave of words that washes over him when in the heat of composition. He is writing to Schnellock from a Paris café: "I get so damned chock full of ideas that I am afraid they will dribble away before I get back to the machine . . . The tablecloth is paper, and I begin jotting down my notes at the far, upper, left-hand corner . . . The ideas are streaming out of me, exhaustless as a supply of radium."

MILLER HAD TWO MORE FULL-LENGTH BOOKS PUBLISHED while he was working in Paris: *Max and the White Phagocytes* in 1938 and *Tropic of Capricorn* in 1939. *Max* is another collection of short pieces. They were recollected and republished in 1939 in an American edition titled *The Cosmological Eye*. *The Cosmological Eye* was brought out by the American James Laughlin, who was publishing leading-edge writing through his *New Directions* imprint. It included nearly all the essays from *Max* as well as several from *Black Spring*. It was Miller's first book to be published in America, was widely reviewed, and gave Miller a foothold with American readers.

Max and the White Phagocytes is an important book because it contains a number of key statements of Miller's philosophy of life and his aims for himself as a writer and a human being. The writing here is less of a performance, less of a display of Miller's stylistic acrobatics, and more of plain speaking. Miller wants to make clear his credo.

Probably the most fundamental statement of Miller's theory of being, if he can be said to have one, is made in a review he writes of the film *Extase* by the Czech writer-director Gustav Machaty. While discussing the controversy the film has stirred up in the public, he makes a startling ontological declaration: "Beneath the public's hostility [to the film] is the grudging admission of the presence of a superior force, a disturbing force . . . It is a force . . . which resides in the solar plexus, an astral force which is located there behind the stomach in the great nexus of nerves which unite the upper and lower nerve centers."

What is important to Miller about the recognition of this "superior" physiological force buried deep in man's body is that it determines a radically different mode of living. "The rhythm dictated by this ganglia of nerves and blood-vessels is in direct opposition to the rhythm which we have set up through our tyranny of mind and will. This rhythm elevates to its former prestige and glory the hegemony of the instincts; it regards the mind as a tool. This is body rhythm, blood rhythm, as opposed to the masturbative rhythm of the intellect. The recognition of this rhythm involves not a new technique but a new way of living."

What is this new way of living? For Miller, it entails the celebration of self in the pursuit of personal individuation, at the expense of any sense of social responsibility or engagement. As he writes in another essay in the collection, "An Open Letter to Surrealists Everywhere," "The struggle is to synchronize the potential being with the actual being, to make a fruitful liaison between the man of yesterday and the man of tomorrow"—in short, to live fully in the present.

His belief in the supremacy of each individual's unique personal destiny over all other considerations leads Miller to reject social movements, collective action, useful employment, and concepts such as "the brotherhood of man." Thus he can say, "The brotherhood of man is a permanent delusion common to idealists everywhere in all epochs: it is a reduction to the least common denominator of intelligibility. It is what leads the masses to identify themselves with movie stars and megalomaniacs like Hitler and Mussolini." Consequently, "there is no scheme for universal liberation. Each man has to do this for himself."

Miller pointed to key historical figures as prototypes of actualized human beings. Among them were Jesus Christ, the Buddha, and D. H. Lawrence. And he acknowledges, "Such men have indeed been rare in the course of our western civilization." He quotes Lawrence: "Being alive constitutes an aristocracy which there is no getting beyond. He who is most alive, intrinsically, is king, whether men admit it or not."

For Miller, the path to individuation, to life, was art. Through art, man can explore the depths of his being, accept the truth of who he is, and point the way to individual freedom for others. "The role which the artist plays in society is to revive the primitive, anarchic instincts which have been sacrificed for the illusion of being in comfort." Referring to his own difficult existence in Paris, Miller says, "It is not the most comfortable life in the world but I know that it is life and I am not going to trade it for an anonymous life in the brotherhood of man." And so Miller declares, "I am my own leader and my own god. I make my own bibles. I believe in myself—that is my whole credo."

In *The Cosmological Eye*, Miller appends a biographical summary similar in content to the letter he wrote to Cairns. He is introducing himself for the first time to American readers. In this brief biography, he characterizes himself as a writer: "My aim, in writing, is to establish a greater REALITY. . . I am at bottom a metaphysical writer, and my use of drama and incident is only a device to posit something more profound."

To *The Cosmological Eye*, Miller adds a new essay, "Peace! It's Wonderful," in which he attempts to eliminate the distinction between his life and his art. "The art of living involves the act of creation . . . The artist should be able to be an artist all the time, and finally not be an artist at all, but a piece of art." How closely Miller approximated this ideal in his own life can be used to measure his success in becoming the great man that he wanted to be.

MILLER CONCLUDES HIS LIST OF PARIS TITLES FOR CAIRNS with *Tropic of Capricorn*. *Tropic of Capricorn* was the first in a cycle of novels that Miller wrote about his tumultuous marriage to June Smith/Mansfield (real name Juliette Smerth). He conceived of the cycle in 1927 while still living with June in Brooklyn and outlined it during a single twenty-four-hour period. He did not complete the cycle until 1959, with *Nexus*, written while he was living in Big Sur, California. *Capricorn* is a portrait of Miller's life in New York up until the time he first meets June in a Broadway dance hall. It covers much the same period as "The Tailor Shop" and "The Fourteenth Ward" but in greater detail. The book is rich in bawdy episodes and humorous characterizations, written in the jaunty, irreverent tone of *Tropic of Cancer*.

Miller had begun work on the "novel" shortly after completing *Tropic of Cancer* (he often worked on several books simultaneously), and in a letter to Anaïs Nin he distinguished between the two Tropics as follows: "For me, Cancer means the crab—the creature which could move in any direction. It is the sign in the zodiac for the poet—the halfway station in the round of realization. Opposite Cancer in the Zodiac is Capricorn, the house in which I am born, which is religious and represents renaissance in death. Cancer also means for me the disease of civilization, the extreme point of realization along the wrong path—hence the necessity to change one's course and begin all over again. Cancer then is the apogee of death in life, as Capricorn is of life in death. The two symbols are found in geography as tropics (which is another word for hieroglyphics), Cancer lying above the equator and Capricorn below. Myself am trying to walk the hair line which separates the two. The line is only imaginary—there is no boundary line to reality."

Apart from illustrating the metaphysical plane on which Miller was attempting to live his life, the passage shows his burgeoning interest in astrology. In 1936 he met Conrad Moricand, a famous Swiss astrologer living in Paris who cast Miller's horoscope. Miller wrote to his friend Emil Schnellock that he was studying astrology with Moricand and was amazed at the penetrating insights into his own character that astrology was giving him. "Am seriously studying astrology with Conrad Moricand who did my horoscope ... An immense world—startling revelations. Incredible accuracies. I see him once a week ..."[*]

---

[*] See Appendix B.

The first seventy pages of *Capricorn* amount to a prologue in which Miller sums up the significance of being born in New York and coming to maturity in America. It is a declaration of his inability, his refusal, to accommodate himself to a social environment that he found to be completely hostile to his own interests and needs. "The whole continent," he writes, "is sound asleep and in that sleep a grand nightmare is taking place . . . To be accepted and appreciated you must nullify yourself, make yourself indistinguishable from the herd. You may dream, if you dream alike. But if you dream something different you are not in America of America American . . . The moment you have a different thought you cease to be an American."

Miller admits that his separation from his native culture was a painful process: "Not to belong to something enduring is the last agony . . . I have slipped away to rejoin an older stream of consciousness, a race antecedent to the buffaloes, a race that will survive the buffalo."

At the outset of *Capricorn*, Miller positions himself as a man who has undergone a radical change, which he calls a death and resurrection— the death of his social self and his rebirth as an individual living outside of historical time. *Capricorn* tells the story of that change down to his meeting with the primary change agent, his second wife, June. The book is autobiographical but not chronological. It proceeds by association, recounting his boyhood in Brooklyn, his escapades with friends from the street, his love affairs, his marriage to Beatrice, his years working as the employment manager of Western Union ("The Cosmodemonic Telegraph Company"), a surreal journey through "The Land of Fuck," and finally his fateful meeting with Mara (June), the encounter that he credits with changing the direction of his life and making him into a writer. But *Capricorn* is only the beginning of the story of Miller's transformation from nobody to somebody. Miller would write three more "novels"—*Sexus* (1949), *Plexus* (1952), and *Nexus* (1959), collectively called *The Rosy Crucifixion*—totaling 1,462 pages before the story of his death and resurrection would be fully told.

IN THE FINAL SECTION OF HIS LETTER TO CAIRNS, MILLER sketches his plans for the future, lists the main intellectual influences that have contributed to his view of the world and his place in it, and again expresses his despair at the impending war.

Miller sees himself as at the end of a period of his life, "the end of the European period, perhaps." He intends to return to America, tour the country, and write a book he has been planning to be called *America, The Air-Conditioned Nightmare*. He is looking for a sanctuary in which to settle—"perhaps some remote, outlandish island . . . Easter Island, or the Caroline Islands." He expresses a desire to go to Northern India and Tibet but confesses, "I lack the courage for further hardships." Miller clearly is tired, tired of writing, tired of civilization.

Miller had been living with a sense of fatalism about his future as a writer for some time. A year earlier, he had written to Emil, "I've only got another ten years ahead of me, if I live. After that, I'll retire." Six months later, after the publication of *Tropic of Capricorn*, he wrote to Richard Osborn that he believed his writing career was coming to an end: "No more writing. I don't believe in it, beyond a certain point—beyond the development of the over-self, shall I say? I am almost ripe to quit now. I will quit in full plenitude." But his stated plan for a book about America shows that Miller has not yet reached "full plenitude."

Zen Buddhism heads the list of influences that have informed his view of reality, and he writes to Cairns, "I began as an anarchist at the age of twenty and to-day, with my readings of Zen Buddhism, I feel confirmed in all my youthful ideas about life and society. I am today even more of an anarchist than I was at twenty-one . . . I am liberated from all metaphysical speculation . . . This view of the universe is, in my opinion, the most sublime and illogical at the same time, and the most grandiose that I know of." Miller also mentions as key influences Nietzsche and Dostoevsky "who taught me to look at man nakedly."

In contemplating the crisis that envelops the world in the spring of 1939, Miller adopts his usual posture of disengagement and scorn. "I see no hope for Europe . . . I can't hang on here and wait for events to catch up with me. I am living far ahead of the European and the American. What they are fighting for I have relinquished long ago. I have no interest in politics or culture. The only relationship I acknowledge is with God. I swear allegiance to no government . . . I say that the world we have created is a mad world and I renounce it."

Miller concludes the letter with an acknowledgment of his debt to Anaïs Nin, and the importance of his friendships with Alfred Perlès and Lawrence Durrell. Nin was a crucial figure in Miller's personal and artistic development during his Paris years. Their relationship has been extensively analyzed and documented in biographies and publications of their letters. Nin served as Miller's muse, critic, financial and emotional supporter, lover, and confidante as he struggled through the early stages of his writing career in France. For a time, Miller trusted her completely with himself and revealed himself to her in all of his aspects: as a fellow artist, as a man, as a friend, and as a lover. He was a devoted admirer of her work, encouraged her writing, urged her to publish, and advocated for her.

They were introduced by Richard Osborn, who worked for her husband, Hugo, in the Paris branch of an American bank. The connecting link was a study of D. H. Lawrence that Nin had written. Osborn showed Miller the study, and after reading it, Miller told Osborn he wanted to meet her. She invited Miller to lunch at her home in Louveciennes outside Paris, and their relationship began.

It began as a literary friendship but soon broadened and deepened. Following a brief and miserable stint teaching English at a French school in Dijon, Miller returned to Paris and he and Nin became lovers. He had been sending her pages of *Cancer*, and her encouragement and perceptive comments gave him enormous confidence in this work. When June arrived on one of her surprise visits (she had heard from someone in New York that Miller and Nin were close), a complicated romantic triangle developed when Nin took June's part in her stormy relationship with Miller. But June soon recognized that Nin had supplanted her as Miller's muse, and after *Tropic of Cancer* was published she divorced Miller by proxy in Mexico.

Nin had done more than act as midwife to the birth of Miller's first significant book. When Jack Kahane stalled in bringing out the book from fear he would not be allowed to sell it, Nin provided the money needed to cover the printing costs. The fact that she obtained the money from another lover, her psychiatrist Otto Rank, only added spice to the story. Although their affair cooled as Miller, desperate to possess her, pressed her to leave her marriage, he never forgot his debt to her. He wrote to Cairns, "I owe nearly everything to one person—Anaïs Nin . . . Had I not met her, I would never have accomplished the little I did."

But Miller was indebted to others as well. His correspondence with Emil Schnellock was the beginning of "the Paris book." In his letters to Emil, Miller found his authentic voice, the voice that we hear in all the books he wrote during his Paris years. It is a voice that Miller can pitch in different keys—satiric, mocking, angry, lyrical, reflective, tortured, ranting—but it is a voice that is unmistakably Miller's own. Miller lifted whole passages from his letters to Emil and dropped them unchanged into *Tropic of Cancer*. He wrote Emil at one point, "I can't remember anymore what I said in my previous letters and what I put down in the manuscript of the book." Emil was Miller's first reader, a man he trusted completely and to whom he could reveal his authentic self.

Then there was Alfred Perlès. Perlès had been like a brother to Miller, giving him shelter, picking up tabs at cafés, sharing women, finding him jobs and writing assignments, clowning with him, and most importantly, believing in Miller's brilliance as a writer.

Miller was also indebted to Richard Osborn, who spontaneously shared his apartment with Miller, gave him "pin money," and introduced him to Anaïs Nin. Though Miller caricatured Osborn mercilessly in *Tropic of Cancer*, he sustained their friendship through correspondence, encouraged Osborn's own literary ambitions, and even published one of Osborn's poems in an issue of *The Booster*. Other expatriate Americans who sustained Miller with either food or encouragement or both were Michael Fraenkel, Walter Lowenfels, the sculptor Fred Kann, and Bertha and Joe Schrank, among others.

What had he accomplished in his Paris years? Most of all, he had found himself as a writer, and in doing that, he had found himself as a man. He knew who he was and what he believed, and he would yield to no one on the field of literature. In his personal life, he was still alone. He was in hiding from his daughter, Barbara, ashamed and contemptuous of his parents, divorced from June though not psychically free of her, and frustrated in his determined pursuit of Anaïs Nin. But what galled him the most was his inability to make any kind of living from what he did so devotedly and brilliantly—writing. Shortly after he arrived in Paris in 1930, he wrote to Emil, "I can't understand my failure. Somewhere there must be an audience waiting for my words. Where? Why does nobody want what I write?" And he concludes his letter to Cairns with the identical lament: "What gripes me more than anything is that in fifteen years of the highest consecration to the task I am still unable to earn my living as a writer."

It was true that Miller had gained scant recognition for his efforts. Though he had received appreciative letters for *Tropic of Cancer* from influential writers such as T. S. Eliot, Ezra Pound, Katherine Anne Porter and from Blaise Cendrars in France, and though Edmund Wilson in America had publicly acknowledged Miller's accomplishment, his iconoclasm and fierce criticism of the prevailing social order had marginalized him. When his shorter pieces were published—and they were—it was nearly always in obscure, avant-garde literary journals with small readerships and smaller payments to contributors. Miller was determined not to write for the market because to do so would have compromised his whole aim in writing, which was not to sell but to become a more fully actualized human being. What he wrote about his friend the painter Hans Reichel in *The Cosmological Eye* applied equally to himself: "the penalty for being different, for being an artist, is a cruel one."

2

INTERLUDE IN GREECE

"The Peace Which Passeth All Understanding"

SHORTLY AFTER HE WROTE HIS LETTER TO HUNTINGTON CAIRNS, MILLER left Paris to visit the other friend he had mentioned in the letter, Lawrence Durrell. Durrell brought Miller into a world—Greece—that changed his views about nature and pointed him in the direction of the next major period in his life, his years living in Big Sur, California.

The friendship between Miller and Durrell also began as a correspondence. Miller had sent a copy of *Cancer* to an American acquaintance, Barclay Hudson, who lived on the island of Corfu near Durrell. Hudson loaned his copy of the book to Durrell, who was bowled over by it and wrote Miller an enthusiastic letter of appreciation. "It's a howling triumph from the word go," he wrote. Miller wrote back, asking for samples of Durrell's writing, and the two men quickly became long distance soul mates, exchanging compliments and watercolors, engaging in metaphysical speculations, and sharing their views of the state of contemporary English literature. Through their correspondence, the two writers hatched schemes for setting up literary magazines (succeeding only with *The Booster/Delta*) and for obtaining favorable publicity for Miller's books that would change the perception held in America and England that they were obscene. In September 1937 the two men finally met during a trip Durrell and his wife, Nancy, made to Paris. The Durrells stayed near Miller in another apartment at Villa Seurat, and remained in Paris until April 1938.

Even before they met, Durrell had extended several invitations to Miller to visit him in Corfu. But Miller showed little interest in coming. He was immersed in his work, and did not hold the Greeks in high esteem, writing to Durrell at one point, "As for the Greeks, as for Athens, I am no great admirer of that venerable civilization." Miller would subsequently revise this opinion drastically in the book he wrote about his experiences in Greece, *The Colossus of Maroussi.*

Another strong opinion Miller held about himself was upended by his stay in Greece—his view of himself as a man of the city, a man born and raised in the streets. He had expressed these views not only in the *Tropics* and *Black Spring* but also in letters to Anaïs Nin. After returning to Paris in July 1933 from an excursion to the countryside, Miller wrote disgustedly to Nin, "Fed up with the little provincial towns, and with nature especially. I'm a man of the cities, sorry to say. I realize it now only too well." A day later, he wrote further, "I need the hum and roar, the excitement, life, change, diversion of a big city. I realize that it is for me what the sea is for a sailor." This attitude changed as result of Miller's travels in Greece, a change reflected in the new tone in Miller's voice as he speaks to us from the pages of *The Colossus of Maroussi.* It is likely that Miller's experiences in Greece prepared him to fall in love with the solitude and scenic grandeur of Big Sur when he visited it in 1944.

At the end of May 1939, Miller left Villa Seurat for good, heading south. He traveled through the Dordogne region, visiting the Lascaux caves and rhapsodizing over the culture of Cro-Magnon man. He stopped in Nice, and dropped into a casino in Monte Carlo, contemplating using the tables there to augment (or lose!) the small traveling stake he had raised from friends in Paris and the United States. On July 14 he sailed from Marseille on the French vessel *Théophile Gautier* and arrived in Piraeus, the port of Athens, on July 19.

What Miller found in Greece was an external landscape that corresponded to the inner state he had been creating in Paris through his writing, a state that he called "the synchronization of dream and reality." Buoyed by the euphoria he felt on completing the work he had set for himself in Paris, he was primed to enfold Greece in an embrace of love even before he sighted land. He has a shipboard conversation with a Greek medical student returning from Paris. They talk far into the night about one of Miller's favorite writers, Knut Hamsun. "There we were, a Greek and an American, with something in common, yet two vastly different beings. It was a splendid introduction to that world which was about to open before my eyes. I was already enamored of Greece, and the Greeks, before catching sight of the country."

The love affair continued as Miller disembarked in baking heat and found a hotel room in Athens. Late at night, he went for a walk in the park. "Seeing lovers sitting there in the dark drinking water, sitting there in peace and quiet and talking in low tones, gave me a wonderful feeling about the Greek character. The dust, the heat, the poverty, the bareness, the containedness of the people, and the water everywhere in little tumblers standing between the quiet, peaceful couples, gave me the feeling that there was something holy about the place, something nourishing and sustaining."

The next day Miller takes a night boat from Piraeus to Corfu. He feels light and free. "I had everything a man could desire, and I knew it . . . I had entered a marvelous new realm as a free man . . . Christ, I was happy."

His days on Corfu are an idyll. The Durrells live on a remote part of the island, away from town. Miller sleeps late, paints, swims nude in the sea, goes on camping trips. He does no writing, except letters. To Nin he writes happily, "I look like a beachcomber."

When the Greek army is mobilized, Corfu is evacuated out of fear of an Italian invasion. Miller goes to Athens with the Durrells, and there he meets George Katsimbalis, the colossus.

Katsimbalis is a larger than life figure who embodies Miller's ideal of the man whose life has become a work of art. What distinguishes him is his gift for storytelling. He lives to tell stories, and his life is a continuous story that he invents as he lives it. Like Miller, "he talked about himself because he himself was the most interesting person he knew . . . he could galvanize the dead with his talk." Here is Miller's description of him at their first meeting:

> He was a curious mixture of things to me on that first occasion;
> he had the general physique of a bull, the tenacity of a vulture,
> the agility of a leopard, the tenderness of a lamb, and the coyness
> of a dove. He had a curious overgrown head which fascinated

me and which, for some reason, I took to be singularly Athenian. His hands were rather small for his body, and overly delicate. He was a vital, powerful man, capable of brutal gestures and rough words, yet somehow conveying a sense of warmth which was soft and feminine. There was also a great element of the tragic in him which his adroit mimicry only enhanced. He was extremely sympathetic and at the same time ruthless as a boor. He seemed to be talking about himself all the time, but never egotistically.

Above all, what endears Katsimbalis to Miller is his zest for living, his enjoyment of food, drink, conversation, friendship, adventure—all on a Paul Bunyanesque scale. "Between great carnivorous gulps of food he would pound his chest like a gorilla before washing it down with a hogshead of *rezina.*" Later, he visits Katsimbalis at his home. The man has just woken from a nap and seems caught in the transitory state between dream and reality. He walks out onto the veranda, and words gush out of him, "a spread eagle performance about the clear atmosphere and the blue-violet hues that descend with the twilight, about ascending and descending varieties of monotony, about individualistic herbs and trees, about exotic fruits and inland voyages, about thyme and honey and the sap of arbutus which makes one drunk, about islanders and highlanders, about the men of the Peloponnesus . . ."

Katsimbalis's monologue is reminiscent of Miller's stream of consciousness flights in *Black Spring*, a similarity that may explain Miller's feeling of affinity for the man. The scene concludes with Miller mythologizing him: "The man who was talking had ceased to be of human size or proportions but had become a Colossus whose silhouette swooned backwards and forwards with the deep droning rhythm of his drug-laden phrases. He went on and on and on, unhurried, unruffled, inexhaustible, inextinguishable, a voice that had taken form and shape and substance, a figure that had outgrown its human frame, a silhouette whose reverberations rumbled in the depths of the distant mountain sides."

As war breaks out but Italy remains neutral, Miller returns alone to Corfu and relishes the solitude. Prophetically, he writes to Nin, "I feel that something good awaits me here. And if nothing else comes of it I shall at least learn the meaning of solitude. This may be a sort of training for a greater solitude later."

Much of the remainder of the book describes Miller's excursions to various archaeological sites throughout Greece, sometimes in company with Katsimbalis, the poet George Seferiades, or the Durrells, sometimes accompanied only by a taxi driver. Miller visits Nauplia, Poros, Epidaurus, Hydra, Mycenae, Crete, Corinth, Sparta, and Delphi. It is Epidaurus, an ancient healing center on the Peloponnesus, that makes the deepest and most lasting impression on Miller, because it holds the quality of life that he wants to carry inside himself.

"I never knew the meaning of peace until I arrived at Epidaurus . . . I am talking of course of the peace which passeth all understanding. There is no other kind . . . Our diseases are our attachments, be they habits, ideologies, ideals, principles, possessions, phobias, gods, cults, religions, what you please . . . At Epidaurus, in the stillness, in the great peace that came over me, I heard the heart of the world beat. I know what the cure is: it is to give up, to relinquish, to surrender, so that our little hearts may beat in unison with the great heart of the world . . . Epidaurus is merely a place symbol: the real place is in the heart, in every man's heart, if he will but stop and search it." In Greece Miller seems to have found principles of living that accorded with what in Zen Buddhism had attracted him as a young man.

Miller had no plans to leave Greece, but the war drove him out. In December 1939 his passport was invalidated by the American consul in Athens and he was ordered to return to America. The prospect dismayed him. He made one last tour of the Peloponnesus with the Durrells before leaving for New York on the *Exochorda* at the end of the month. From shipboard he wrote to Nin: "I don't see what more any country, any landscape, could offer over this experience. Not only does one feel integrated, harmonious, at one with all life but—one is silenced . . . And now, on the boat, in the midst of the American scene, I feel as though I am living with people who are not yet born, with monsters who escaped from the womb before their time."

Look out America, Henry Miller is coming home.

3

Adrift in America

"The Air-Conditioned Nightmare"

If Miller was dismayed and dispirited as he surveyed his fellow passengers on his return to America, his gloomy mood darkened even further as the *Exochorda* approached the United States coast for a stop at Boston harbor. "When I came up on deck to catch my first glimpse of the shore line I was immediately disappointed . . . The American coast looked bleak and uninviting to me . . . It was *home*, with all the ugly, evil sinister connotations which the word contains for a restless soul." The sight of the New York skyline only depressed him further. "To the image of stark, grim ugliness which Boston had created was added a familiar feeling of terror. Sailing around the Battery from one river to another, gliding close to the shore, night coming on, the streets dotted with scurrying insects, I felt as I had always felt about New York—that it is the most horrid place on God's earth."

Behind Miller's state of mind on this winter's day was a host of uncertainties about the life awaiting him. In returning to New York, no better off financially than when he had left ten years earlier, he was leaving behind him the protective cocoon he had spun around himself over the years in Paris—the fellow artists and expatriates who helped support him, the familiar streets and cafés that he loved, the complete freedom from responsibility to anything except his writing. His friends were now scattered around the globe—Durrell in Greece, Perlès in England, Fraenkel in Havana, Osborn in Connecticut, Fred Kann in Kansas City, the painter Hilaire Hiler in San Francisco.

Only Anaïs Nin was close at hand. She had returned to the United States while Miller was in Greece and was living in Manhattan.

What may have provoked Miller's "feeling of terror" were his tenuous relations with his own immediate family. He had had very little contact with his mother and father during his years of exile, and none at all with his ex-wife Beatrice and their daughter Barbara, now a young woman of twenty-one. During his return visit to New York in 1935, Miller had avoided contact with his parents. He rarely wrote to them, and had not sent them copies of any of his books. Late in 1937 Miller had received a pathetic letter from his father asking Henry to send him $3 a week for lunch and carfare. Miller, manifestly distressed at being unable to help him, wrote back explaining his own precarious circumstances but promising to send what he could. He particularly dreaded his mother's judgmental view of his failure to support himself through his writing. And he knew the content of his books, when it didn't mystify her, would horrify her conventional morality. As for Beatrice and Barbara, Miller's biggest fear was that should his ex-wife learn that he had returned to New York, she might pursue him for payment of back alimony and child support.

There were other uncertainties as well. Where would he live, and how would he support himself? He had developed a relationship with the publisher James Laughlin, who in 1936 had started New Directions, his publishing house devoted to avant-garde writing. Laughlin had been introduced to Miller's writing by Ezra Pound, with whom he had studied in Italy. Pound had handed Laughlin his copy of *Tropic of Cancer*, reportedly with the recommendation, "Here's one dirty book that's really good. You'd better read it." In 1936 New Directions published excerpts from *Aller Retour New York* and *Black Spring*. Subsequently, Miller and Laughlin corresponded about possible publication of *Tropic of Cancer*. In 1938, when Miller was trying to leave France because of the Munich Crisis, Laughlin cabled Miller $200 as an advance against royalties for *Cancer*. The two men were still discussing a New Directions edition of the book in 1939, with Miller cautioning Laughlin against the risks and offering to abort the deal. But as late as May 1939 Laughlin remained determined to issue the book. In the meantime, Laughlin had agreed to publish excerpts from

Tropic of Capricorn and to bring out selections from *Max and the White Phagocytes* and *Black Spring* under the title *The Cosmological Eye.*

These negotiations with Laughlin were important to Miller because he believed that his reputation and fortunes as a writer would be greatly enhanced if his banned works could be sold in the American market. The Obelisk Press edition of *Tropic of Cancer* had become Kahane's bestselling title and had already gone through five editions. English-speaking tourists passing through Paris eagerly sought the book. But Kahane had died suddenly in September 1939, and with the outbreak of war Miller's royalties from Obelisk had stopped. Thus American editions of the Tropics and *Black Spring* were a potential income stream for Miller if they could somehow be made to pass the obscenity test.

Miller remained in frequent correspondence with his friend Huntington Cairns on this issue. Cairns believed that overturning the obscenity ruling against Miller's books required a consensus among recognized American literary critics that Miller was a writer of serious literature, comparable in stature to James Joyce, whose novel *Ulysses* had been allowed into the United States, ironically on the grounds that not very many people would read it and it therefore posed no danger to the community. Cairns believed that a substantial body of criticism from respected academics and critics—not all of it necessarily favorable—would be needed as evidence in a court test to demonstrate that Miller was not simply a lowly pornographer. Cairns had been making efforts on Miller's behalf to obtain critical assessments of his books. In effect, Cairns was advocating a literary public relations campaign to change the perception of Miller as an outlaw author of smut.

In fact, Miller's work had been reviewed by a number of prominent American and English critics by the time he returned to the United States, and Miller had also received letters of admiration from well-known American writers who might be willing to testify for him. After *The Cosmological Eye* was published in November 1939, the book had been reviewed in over forty newspapers from coast to coast. Though the reviews were mixed, the majority were favorable, with some critics comparing Miller to Joyce and Lawrence, others calling him a "genius," "an artist of the first rank," "a satirist of Swiftian powers," and "the most extraordinary writer of his time." In its December 25, 1939, issue, the national news magazine *Time* devoted two columns to Miller and Laughlin in its "Books" section.

But the greatest and most significant uncertainty facing Miller as the *Exochorda* sailed into New York's harbor was his relationship with Anaïs Nin. As it played out, the arc of that relationship would be the major factor behind Miller's decision four years later to settle in Big Sur.

During his Paris years, Nin had been Miller's primary support— emotionally, artistically, and financially—a debt he openly acknowledged. Nin encouraged his writing, gave him money to live on from her household allowance, slept with him, and through all this gained intimate knowledge of his character. She had been the one to obtain the five thousand francs ($330) needed to cover the printing costs for *Tropic of Cancer* when Kahane began to stall publication. But soon after that, strains began to show in their relationship. Partly this was due to Miller's egocentricity and dependence, which Nin grew to resent, and partly it was due to her own chronic promiscuity and fondness for complex emotional drama that would keep her diary interesting.

Since beginning his affair with her in 1932, Miller had entertained the fantasy that she would leave her marriage to Hugo and become his life partner. In August 1932 Miller had spent a week living with Nin at her house in Louveciennes while Hugo was away on a business trip. After Hugo returned and Miller was back in Paris, he wrote her an impassioned letter setting forth his romantic vision of their future together: "Don't expect me to be sane any more. Don't let's be sensible. It was a marriage at Louveciennes—you can't dispute it . . . I say this is a wild dream—but it is this dream I want to realize. Life and literature combined, love the dynamo, you with your chameleon's soul giving me a thousand loves, being anchored always in no matter what storm, home wherever we are."

Nin quickly pulled away from Miller after receiving this "proposal," then tried to cast their relationship in a more realistic light. "I can make you much happier and give you much more and enrich you in every way far more deeply by staying *here* and giving you nothing to worry about except your work."

What Miller failed to recognize or admit was that Nin did not want to jeopardize the self-indulgent life she enjoyed in her marriage to Hugo. He also seemed oblivious to the fact that if she were to leave Hugo, his own source of support would disappear. For whatever reasons, Hugo tolerated Nin's promiscuous lifestyle, did not exhibit jealousy, and pretended to be ignorant of her clumsy deceptions. Miller was an exciting addition to the cast of characters who populated her diary, and he was a stimulating companion. He was brilliant, literary, unconventional, dependent on her, and extremely supportive of her writing. It never seems to have occurred to Miller to think through the practical consequences should Nin leave Hugo to live with him—how would they survive? how would he deal with her promiscuity?—or to perceive that he was only one of many buzzing flies that had flown into her web.

So despite the fractures that had appeared in their relationship, despite Nin's efforts to make it conform to her needs, despite the practical obstacles to their living together, Miller continued to cling to the fantasy of their making a life together somewhere in paradise. As he vacationed in Greece with the Durrells, he wrote her frequently in this vein, first suggesting that they move together some place in the American west, then proposing Mexico or Haiti, and finally urging her to join him in Greece on the supposition that the war would soon be over. What these appeals reveal about Miller is his profound emotional dependence on Nin, a dependence that blinded him to the true dynamics of their relationship and prevented him from evolving.

AS MILLER PREPARED TO DISEMBARK FROM THE *EXOCHORDA* in New York in mid-January 1940, he brought with him several literary goals. One was to explore with Cairns and Laughlin the US publication of the Tropics. Another was to resume work on his major opus, the *Capricorn* series—also known as *The Rosy Crucifixion*—that would tell the complete story of his Brooklyn years and his relationship with June. And a third was to tour America and write a book about what he saw and experienced. That he already had in mind the title "The Air-Conditioned Nightmare" suggests the tone and attitude that Miller was bringing to his proposed survey. In his preface to the book,

Miller explained the motive behind this undertaking. "I felt the need to effect a reconciliation with my native land. It was an urgent need because, unlike most prodigal sons, I was returning not with the intention of remaining in the bosom of the family but of wandering forth again, perhaps never to return. I wanted to have a last look at my country and leave it with a good taste in my mouth."

The words that stand out in this statement are "reconciliation" and "bosom of the family." They imply that the origins of Miller's alienation from his native country can be traced to his estrangement from his family. Family to Miller meant his parents, Louise and Heinrich, his daughter Barbara, his half-witted sister Lauretta, and his second wife, June. All these people lived in New York. With none of them had he had significant contact since the publication of *Cancer*. And none of them, excepting June, had any idea of the writer he had become or the kind of life he had been leading in Europe. Clearly, his feeling of alienation from his country was connected to his physical and emotional separation from his family. And yet, as he further wrote in the preface, he has no intention of confronting his past. "Back in the rat trap. I try to hide from my old friends; I don't want to relive the past with them because the past is full of wretched, sordid memories. My one thought is to get out of New York, to experience something genuinely American," as though his own experience is somehow not "genuinely American." This aspect of Miller's personality—his love/hate relationship with America—prompted a future critic, Kingsley Widmer, to write, "He is someone in complete flight from both himself and America. The further outside America and self he gets, the more American he becomes." So it is perhaps not surprising that after Miller came ashore, took a room at the Royalton Hotel in midtown Manhattan, and went to check for mail at the Gotham Book Mart, he requested owner Frances Steloff not to give out his address to members of his family. But that did not mean they were not in his thoughts. He did try to get in touch with June but was unable to locate her.

Nin did not meet Miller at the boat when it docked; she was ill with the flu. Subsequently, their relationship resumed basically unchanged. However, Nin was reevaluating it. She wrote in her diary on February 4, "I brood over my relationship to Henry. The last two afternoons he took me into bed. I responded fully, though there is no passion, no tenderness even. Henry is remote, dehumanized . . . Yet I can't break with Henry. There is a mystical relationship." The diary goes on to reveal that her erotic energies are being more fully and sat-isfyingly directed toward Gonzalo More, a lover from her Paris years who has, in company with his neurotic and chronically ill wife, left Paris to be with Nin in New York. Hugo will return from Europe in May, and so the complicated romantic web that Nin has designed in Paris will continue, and will continue to impact Miller.

Over the next ten months Miller's agent at Russell & Volkening, John Slocum, tried to arrange a publishing deal for Miller's American book. Miller had signed with Russell & Volkening the year before he left France. Slocum and Laughlin had met while students at Harvard, where Slocum edited the *Advocate*, a magazine that had published a piece by Miller. While waiting for Slocum to find a buyer, Miller moved back and forth between New York and Virginia, all the while working on several writing projects. His relationship with Nin con-tinued to be the central element of his life, as it would for the next four years.

In February Miller traveled to Virginia to visit Emil Schnellock, who taught art at a college in Fredericksburg. He stopped along the way in Washington, DC to meet with Cairns. They discussed pros-pects for publication of the Tropics, and Miller quickly conveyed to Laughlin Cairns's recommendation against trying to bring out the Tropics until there was a more substantial body of serious criticism about Miller's work.

Around this time, on his return from Virginia, Miller screwed up his courage and paid a visit to his parents' house in Brooklyn, an obli-gation he had been dreading. Stunned and horrified by the physical deterioration in his family and guilty over his years of neglect, Miller became a frequent visitor, often bearing gifts, and giving them money when he had it to give. He wrote an account of his efforts at reconcil-iation that was published in the 1944 collection *Sunday After The War* under the title "Reunion in Brooklyn." This narrative exposes the oppressive psychological atmosphere of the Miller household—the bullying, hypercritical Louise, the meek, long-suffering Heinrich, the religiously devout half-witted sister Lauretta. But it also reveals a compassionate side of Miller rarely seen in his discussions of his family.

Miller takes the Eighth Avenue subway, emerges into the familiar neighborhood, but immediately becomes lost. He describes his first sighting of his parents' house. "As I approached the gate I saw my father sitting in the arm chair by the window. The sight of him sitting there, waiting for me, gave me a terrible pang. It was as though he had been sitting there waiting all these years. I felt at once like a criminal, like a murderer.

"It was my sister who opened the iron gate. She had altered considerably, had shrunk and withered like a Chinese nut. My mother and father were standing at the threshold to greet me. They had aged terribly. For the space of a moment I had the uncomfortable sensation of gazing at two mummies who had been removed from the vault and galvanized into a semblance of life."

Miller embraces them all, whereupon his mother says, "Well Henry, how do we look to you?" At these words Miller breaks down in sobs and is overcome with feelings of guilt for having abandoned them. Then they go inside, and Miller records the conversation that ensues about his father's illness. Heinrich has prostate cancer and has lost control of his bladder. He relies on a catheter, and periodically he must go to the doctor to have his urinary tract and bladder flushed, a painful procedure. Louise, obsessed with thrift, insists that Heinrich delay these treatments for as long as possible because they cost $5, even though the delay intensifies the pain Heinrich experiences during the procedure. That his mother puts such a trifling sum ahead of his father's discomfort infuriates Miller, but in order not to provoke a row, he says nothing. Miller also learns that his mother has discontinued their phone service, leaving the house without communication to emergency services should Heinrich need them. These vignettes, slight as they are, expose the dysfunctional family dynamics that wounded Miller so deeply.

Intending to share some entertainment with Miller, his parents turn on the radio. Miller listens stoically, then later records his reaction.

"Suddenly the whole American scene, as it is portrayed over the radio, came flooding back—chewing gum, furniture polish, can openers, mineral waters, laxatives, ointments, corn cures, liver pills, insurance policies; the crooners with their eunuch-like voices; the comedians with their stale jokes; the puzzlers with their inane questions (how many matches in a cord of wood?); the Ford Sunday evening hour, the Bulova watch business, the xylophones, the quartets, the bugle calls, the roosters crowing, the canaries warbling, the chimes bringing tears, the songs of yesterday, the news fresh from the griddle, the facts, the facts, the facts . . . Here it was again, the same old stuff, and as I was soon to discover, more stupefying and stultifying than ever."

Following this, Miller's mother gives him a tour of the house, proudly showing off the new oil-burning furnace in the basement and the new refrigerator. Miller struggles to feign admiration for these "modern conveniences" whose worship fills him with contempt. The visit builds to a climactic moment as Miller says goodbye to them. "As I say, there was a blend of stupidity, criminality and hypocrisy in the atmosphere. By the time I was ready to leave my throat was sore from repressing my emotions. The climax came when, just as I was about to slip into my overcoat, my mother in a tearful voice came rushing up to me and, holding me by the arm, said: 'Oh, Henry, there's a thread on your coat!' A thread, by Jesus! That was the sort of thing she would give attention to! The way she uttered the word thread was as if she spied a leprous hand sticking out of my coat pocket. All her tenderness came out in removing that little white thread from my sleeve. Incredible—and disgusting! I embraced them in turn rapidly and fled out of the house."

Miller wept again as he returned to the subway. But his compassion for his father brought him back, bearing presents, and cigarettes and cash, which he gave stealthily to Heinrich when Louise was out of sight. The two men sat in the backyard reminiscing about old times or stationed themselves on the front porch where they could watch the neighbors coming and going.

During one such visit, which other relatives also attended, Miller slipped out of the house to take a solitary stroll and walked in a state somewhere between dreaming and waking. He is walking down a street he often dreamed about while in Paris. His description of this experience builds to a startling statement of the meaning and purpose of life.

> There were two realities which in walking through the street now began to fuse and form a composite living truth which, if I were to record faithfully, would live forever. But the most curious thing about this incident lies not in the fitting together of the dream street and the actual street but the discovery of a street I had never known, a street only a hand's throw away, which for some reason had escaped my attention as a child. This street, when I came upon it in the evening mist, had me gasping with joy and astonishment. Here was the street which corresponded exactly with that ideal street which, in my dream wanderings, I had vainly tried to find ... I realized as I pushed ecstatically forward that the joy and bliss which we experience in the profound depths of the dream—a joy and bliss which surpasses anything known in waking life—comes indubitably from the miraculous accord between desire and reality. When we come to the surface again this fusion, this harmony, which is the whole goal of life, either falls apart or else is only fitfully and feebly realized.

Though his reunion in Brooklyn shows Miller that nothing has really changed in his parents' household—the environment that shaped him as a child—he is able to affirm that he is changed through his ability to experience, if only fleetingly and intermittently, a transcendent reality in which two modes of consciousness, the cognitive and the intuitive, are fused. Miller pursued this state, which he had found in Greece and left there, for the rest of his life. It was his quest.

In March, he and Laughlin met for lunch. Laughlin informed Miller that to avoid jeopardizing the funding from his family for New Directions he would not try to publish *Cancer*. (Laughlin was heir to a Pittsburgh steel fortune. Miller never wrote about the obvious irony of this, and he seemed to understand Laughlin's position.) Laughlin proposed instead to publish another collection of essays as a way to enhance Miller's reputation. This collection, initially to be called

"The Enormous Womb" but published in 1941 under the title *Wisdom of the Heart*, gathered together a number of short pieces previously published in small international literary reviews and included two new essays that Miller wrote during his American tour. The book followed the now familiar pattern of alternating portraits of individuals, artists, and thinkers whom Miller admired—D. H. Lawrence, the British psychoanalyst E. Graham Howe, the philosopher Hermann Keyserling, the Jewish mystic Erich Gutkind, the French film actor Raimu—with opinion pieces on topics such as writing and death. Laughlin and Miller also discussed a contract that would give New Directions the rights to Miller's subsequent books.

Another writing project that materialized around this time was a proposal from a New York book dealer, Barnet Ruder, for Miller to write pornography at the rate of one dollar per page. The proposal originated from Roy Johnson, a wealthy Oklahoma oil millionaire (more irony) who had been commissioning pornography from prominent writers through Ruder for several years. Gershon Legman, a scholar and author of erotica who was planning to print an underground edition of *Cancer* (with Miller's consent), arranged a meeting between Miller and Ruder at the Gotham Book Mart. But Nin appeared at the meeting in Miller's stead and subsequently began writing pornography for hire. Miller did produce erotic works as a result of the proposal, *The World of Sex* (1941) and *Quiet Days in Clichy* (1956), but neither of them was strictly pornographic and did not meet Ruder's exacting standard. A third erotic work, *Opus Pistorum*, was attributed to Miller, but he denied authorship. Miller did not enjoy writing pornography. His writings on sexual behavior were never literal, and tended toward the comically absurd or the sublime.

In March Miller began living in an apartment in Manhattan belonging to Caresse Crosby, a friend of Nin whom he had met when she visited Nin in Paris. Caresse was a wealthy, much-married socialite and supporter of the arts whose principal residence was Hampton Manor, an estate in Bowling Green, Virginia. Miller was then writing *The Colossus of Maroussi*. In June Caresse introduced to Miller and Nin two young artists from the Midwest, John Dudley, a painter from Kenosha, Wisconsin, and Lafayette Young, a writer and aspiring publisher from Des Moines, Iowa. These young men were soliciting Caresse to provide financial backing for a periodical to be called *Generation*. They were both big Miller fans. Dudley was handsome, aristocratic (descended from the Earl of Dudley), and magnetic. Nin was smitten, and promptly began an affair with him. She recorded in her diary that she told Dudley, "You know, there is no more passion between Henry and me."

Early in July, Miller, Nin, John Dudley with his wife Flo, and Lafayette Young went to Hampton Manor to stay as guests of Caresse Crosby. Nin was in her element, hopping between Miller's bed and Dudley's bed, enlisting Caresse in her deceptive intrigues, and writing contemptuously about Dudley's wife in her diary. Miller stayed at Hampton Manor throughout the summer, completing *Colossus*. In September he signed a contract with the publisher Doubleday, Doran for the American book, a deal that had been set up by Slocum. The publisher agreed to advance Miller $500 against royalties, his biggest presale to date.

Meanwhile, Miller's relations with Laughlin had deteriorated badly. In April Laughlin had sent Miller a letter with a small royalty check ($41) from sales of *New Directions 1939*, a collection that included excerpts from *Tropic of Capricorn*. He explained his accounting system, and told Miller that more royalties would be forthcoming. Then he alarmed Miller by speculating that the time for Miller to obtain copyrights in the United States for *Tropic of Cancer*, *Black Spring*, and *Tropic of Capricorn* may have lapsed. He cited a law that states that a work written in English but published outside the United States must be reprinted in the US within six months of the date of foreign publication in order to be copyrighted here. According to Laughlin's reading of the statute, none of Miller's work published by Obelisk Press could be copyrighted in the United States. Laughlin accused Miller of showing poor business judgment in his arrangement with Obelisk and jeopardizing his access to American publishers. He also informed Miller that before New Directions could bring out *Wisdom of the Heart*, and before he could advance Miller royalties for that book, he must receive permission from Obelisk to publish selections from *Black Spring* and *Max and the White Phagocytes*.

Miller sent Laughlin an angry reply, accusing him of being "stingy," raising objections to the terms of their recently drafted publishing contract, defending Obelisk Press, which, he pointed out, published him when no one else would, and finally threatening to break off entirely with New Directions.

Laughlin wrote back immediately and tried to mollify Miller. He explained the difficulty he faced in trying to get Miller's work into bookstores. "You know people don't want good books. They want bad books . . . Henry, in almost every store I went into—all over this country, hundreds of them—they had never heard of you and didn't give a damn." Clearly, Laughlin respected Miller as a writer and wanted to bring out his work. Laughlin had written a promotional blurb for Miller in the Gotham Book Mart catalog *We Moderns* that was both accurate and flattering. "Miller's books defy the conventional structure of the novel. An artist in the instinctive sense, he lets the patterns of life dictate the forms of his work. Broadly talented, he has done brilliant work in the fields of narrative, satire, humor, metaphysical and aesthetic speculation, and surrealism." Nevertheless, in July when Miller submitted pages from *Colossus* for consideration, Laughlin turned the book down, further widening the breach between them.

There was also trouble afoot in the Hampton Manor menagerie. Salvador Dalí and his wife had arrived. Tension developed between Miller and the painter, and also between Nin and Dalí's wife. French was being spoken, which excluded Dudley and his wife from the conversation. When Nin spoke Spanish to Dalí, she made his wife jealous. Dudley had run out of money, and Caresse decided not to back his periodical. She went to Reno to divorce her husband, Bert. Nin's ardor for Dudley had cooled; her affections had swung back to Gonzalo, and she returned to New York to be with him. Miller also departed to prepare for his tour. While Caresse remained in Reno to establish Nevada residency, Bert made a surprise visit to Hampton Manor in the dead of night and threw out the Dalís. The Dudleys left for Kenosha. (Lafayette Young had already returned to Des Moines.) And so *la vie bohème* in Virginia came to an end.

Back in New York, Miller gave the completed manuscript of *Colossus* to John Slocum and made preparations for his American tour. With money from the advance, he bought a used 1932 Buick and took driving lessons (he had never driven a car). He also asked Abe Rattner, a painter he had met in Paris, to accompany him and produce illustrations for the text. He may also have wanted a companion to share driving duties with him. Miller's eyesight was poor and he was a jittery driver. Although Doubleday nixed the idea of illustrations as being too costly, Rattner decided to go with Miller anyway, at least for part of the trip. The two men set out on October 24, 1940, for what was to become, for Miller, a yearlong odyssey.

Miller continued to see Nin in the days before their departure. She wrote in her diary, "The night before last I slept with Henry—who clings to me. He is preparing to leave for a tour of America." Her words suggest the apprehension that Miller felt at the prospect of parting from her for an extended period of time.

MILLER'S AMERICAN TOUR was carried out in stages that corresponded roughly to regions of the country: the South, the industrial Northeast, the Midwest, the Plains and the Southwest, California. The book that resulted from these travels was not a narrative. It was a composite portrait, eclectic and episodic, drawn from Miller's impressions of people, places, and incidents, expressing recurrent Miller themes and prejudices, and held together by Miller's familiar presence and tone of voice. With few exceptions, Miller was critical of the American way of life, but he was also awed by the natural splendor of the continent. As usual, his greatest enthusiasms were for exceptional individuals he encountered, and his most scathing criticisms were directed at materialism and the absence of beauty in the man-made environment. At one point in his journey, as he was working on the book, he wrote to Nin: "I am not trying to give a picture of America as it is—that has been done by others. I am just giving my own personal reaction to the scene."

Miller wrote frequently to Nin over the course of the trip. She was his lifeline, both financially and emotionally. The advance from Doubleday, Doran was used up quickly in purchasing the car, paying for driving lessons, and other basic expenses. Miller was traveling on $5 a day, with which he paid for meals, hotel rooms, gasoline, and car repairs. Nin cabled him money throughout the trip. But she also recorded in her diary, and occasionally in a letter, her growing resentment at this burden. To obtain the funds she sent to Miller, she wrote pornography for Barnet Ruder's client. This took its toll on her.

Miller and Rattner drove out of New York City through the Holland Tunnel, with Miller behind the wheel, headed for Pennsylvania and Virginia. The noise, the confinement, the speed, the maze of choices when the tunnel spit them out on the other side of the river rattled Miller, and he quickly changed places with Rattner. In the notebook that Miller kept throughout the trip, he likened the experience to a painting by Hieronymus Bosch. He admires the bucolic setting of the Amish farms they ride past but is chilled by the sight of the "fanatical expressions" he sees on the faces of the Amish. This contrast between his feelings about the land and his feelings for the people who live on it becomes a frequent theme in his letters to Nin and in the book. From Richmond, Virginia, he writes to Nin, "The contrast between the earth and the people who inhabit it is tremendous. Nowhere else is it so marked, I imagine, as in America." In another letter he writes, "I can't say enough about the country itself—it's beautiful . . . But the life is nil." Miller sees small-town American life revolving around the drugstore, with its endless array of products: "Life centers in drugstores which are lit up with fluorescent lights and crowded with a million useless objects. Surrealistic, if you can detach yourself."

When Miller reached Boswell's Tavern, Virginia, on November 13, he was out of money and asked Nin to send him airfare so he could return to New York for his parents' wedding anniversary. She complied, and Miller spent a week in New York, leaving Rattner with the car in Asheville, North Carolina. Nin was just then fending off John Dudley, who had come east to see her.

In early December, Miller rejoined Rattner in Asheville and they resumed their tour of the South, stopping in Charleston, South Carolina, which delighted Miller: "Charleston is simply marvelous . . . Like walking around in Paris again. Could live here if I wanted to. Has all the atmosphere I crave—and a fine climate, fine sky." This comment suggests another motive for Miller's tour, that he is looking for a place to settle, hopefully with Nin. In another letter written to

Nin at about this time he says, "The thing that appeals to me now is a quiet spot—a sacred spot—such as I saw in Greece."

Miller and Rattner returned to New York for the Christmas holidays and stayed two weeks. After Miller left again to resume his journey, Nin recorded her impression of him in her diary. "Henry left yesterday. I always feel it—it hurts me—He seems frail—and he lost the joy he found in Greece. He is not happy—He is forcing himself to write—to travel."

After Rattner rejoined Miller in Charleston they drove into Florida. What Miller found there caused him to change his itinerary. They pulled into Jacksonville and Miller was appalled. He wrote to Nin, "The picture one gets at Jacksonville is depressing. It's just like it was 15 years ago—only worse. Something disgusting and unappetizing. The uprooted lost souls of America milling around in a rabbit stew."

Miller had been to Jacksonville during his Brooklyn years with June. He had gone there during a real estate boom, hoping for a quick score. As usual, he was without funds and tried to sleep on a park bench. He was rudely awakened by blows from a policeman's billy club and ushered out of the park. He had been drawn back to the scene of this humiliation. Rattner took a photo of him sitting on a park bench with his overcoat draped over him like a blanket.

The Jacksonville stopover, and the memory behind it, yielded an essay in *The Air-Conditioned Nightmare* entitled "Vive La France." It gave Miller occasion to make a comparison between the small city parks in America and those in France. This initial comparison led, in typical Miller fashion, to a reverie about his travels in France that culminates in an account of another stopover he made, this one on his way to Greece, when, acting on an impulse, he took a side trip to a small medieval town, Sarlat. There, browsing in a bookstore window, he saw a book he wanted on the seer Nostradamus but could not afford. The proprietor of the bookstore noticed Miller's interest in the book and invited him for a drink in a bistro. The two men spent the evening together, first dining in a restaurant, then walking about the town, whose historical secrets were known to Miller's host. In the center of the town, a gay festival that had brought the children of Sarlat into the streets was under way. Miller describes the climax of this encounter: "We had walked back towards the ancient wall of the city into the very heart and bowels of the Middle Ages. At times he had to take my hand and lead me because the narrow, twisting lanes lay in absolute darkness. Once in such a lane he felt his way along the wall with his hand and, having come to the right spot, he lit a match and asked me to rub my hand over the woodwork of a huge portal. By lighting match after match we managed to examine the whole door, a procedure which made that door live in my memory as no other door does ... My eyes were brimming with tears. The past was alive again; it lived in every façade, every portal, every crevice, in the very stones under our feet." Of course, at the conclusion of their evening together, the bookstore proprietor makes a gift to Miller of the book he had seen in the window.

This episode discloses the values—warm hospitality, respect for a living past rich in a history shared by all—that underlay Miller's state of mind as he surveyed the American scene. Jacksonville, Florida, was a universe away from Sarlat, France, and would never be its equal.

Although by the time he reached Florida Miller had not yet begun writing *The Air-Conditioned Nightmare*, the impressions he was forming and the comments about America that he was making in his notebook and in his letters to Nin began to give him concern that the book would be turned down by Doubleday, Doran. He had written to Nin from Atlanta, "I'm beginning to think that when I write the book it will be so distasteful to D.D. & Co. that they will refuse to publish it. I don't need any ugly words to make the picture I now have. It will be unpalatable even in the finest language. If I were a Czar I'd wipe the whole population out—leaving just Indians and Negroes."

This expectation persisted as the trip wore on and Miller's initial impressions deepened. It was a cause of serious concern to Miller, on two counts. If the manuscript were to be rejected, he would have to return the $500 advance, a major sum for Miller. And if he was feeling so negatively about the country, why write the book at all?

Exiting Florida, Miller and Rattner drove along the Gulf Coast toward New Orleans, where they planned to visit a friend of Rattner who owned a former plantation in the town of New Iberia. Miller's mood brightened with expectation as they drove through the Deep

South amid signs of an older, unchanging way of life. He noted cheer-
fully in a letter to Nin mailed from Mobile, Alabama, "Just saw a cart
drawn by a bullock. The Deep South! Feeling bully today."

Miller romanticized the Deep South for its slow, sensuous way of
life and its continuity with a rich, highly cultured past. When writing
about his stay at "The Shadows," the plantation owned by Rattner's
friend Weeks Hall, Miller extolled the virtues of the old slave culture:
"All through the South I had been made aware again and again of
the magnificence of a recent past. The days of the great plantations
bequeathed to the brief and bleak pattern of our American life a
color and warmth suggestive, in certain ways, of that lurid, violent
epoch in Europe known as the Renaissance." Acknowledging that
this "magnificence" was purchased at the expense of the slave labor
of black people, Miller attempted to repay them by calling them the
true owners of the land. "The Negro is anchored to the soil; his way
of life has changed hardly at all since the great debacle. He is the real
owner of the land, despite all titular changes of possession." Small
consolation to one-mule tenant farmers scratching out a subsistence
living from the soil.

Miller also took delight in the physical pleasures he experienced
in the lush Louisiana landscape. In a letter to Nin written from New
Orleans after his stay at "The Shadows," Miller describes a walk he
took: "Today I walked along the levee, thru swamps and forests, at
once desolate, wild and hallucinatory . . . I went through a bamboo
grove, the bamboo shooting up to about fifteen feet or so. Marvelous
unreal sensation, of light and shadow, of rosy-cream earth, of jungle
and spaciousness, of filtered powdered light, of silence, of unworldly
colors. Saw crocodiles sleeping like stone, their tails hanging immo-
bile as rock in the still swamp water which had turned green and gray
like the bodies of the crocodiles—a frozen scum with frozen beasts
of antediluvian times . . . Wild geese flying overhead, fish of all kinds
below, stud bulls standing quietly grazing, exotic plants and grasses of
all kinds, and mosquitoes, mosquitoes."

Miller also found in the Deep South rare congenial types: vital
individuals passionate about their interests who embody Miller's
ideal man because they have made themselves into "artists of life."

Two such are Weeks Hall of "The Shadows" and Dr. Marion Souchon, a Creole living in New Orleans who is both a distinguished surgeon and a skilled painter. Miller devoted essays to each of these men in *The Air-Conditioned Nightmare*.

Weeks Hall was a man who dedicated his life to maintaining his family's estate and leading visitors on tours. Eccentric, fanatical, a recovered alcoholic and former painter whose arm was smashed in an accident, Hall spent his days researching obscure details about the history of "The Shadows" that he could share with visitors. Miller approvingly repeats the story of how Hall, during his drinking days, once ordered his servants to clean the house from top to bottom in twenty-four hours. He then went to bed. When he awoke, he discovered that the cleaning crew had scrubbed clean a door that had been autographed by famous visitors to the plantation. Hall tracked down the addresses of all the signers, then shipped the door from one to the other in order to recover their signatures, a project that took years to complete. Miller remarks, "This hunger of his touched me deeply. He was a man who knew no stint . . . He was an artist to his finger-tips, no doubt about that . . . He was in search of something which eluded all definition . . . He had transformed the house and grounds, through his passion for creation, into one of the most distinctive pieces of art which America can boast of. He was living and breathing in his own masterpiece . . ."

It is Weeks Hall who introduces Miller and Rattner to Dr. Souchon. When they meet him at his New Orleans office, Souchon is seventy years old, and has been painting for only ten years, while continuing his medical practice. He paints in his office in his free time. His work has been exhibited in a New York gallery and, according to Miller, "there is no question, especially in the opinion of other estimable artists, that he is a serious artist whose work is growing more and more important day by day, improving with a celerity that is astounding." After studying some of his paintings, Miller calls him "an instinctivist" who has been influenced by Van Gogh, Toulouse-Lautrec, Matisse, and Gauguin, among other masters. Miller situates him in the great tradition of European art. But quite apart from the quality of Souchon's paintings, what impresses Miller about the man is his passionate commitment to the medium. When Souchon says to Miller, "This thing called paint is a soul-stirring, brain-twisting, time-absorbing, all-exacting something which monopolizes one's whole being and eventually transcends all other interests," Miller writes approvingly, "that is what I wanted to hear."

Souchon is an exemplar of the man who has devoted himself fully to the task of living well. This is a type of human being that Miller rarely encounters in America, a deficiency that he attributes to the country's failure to appreciate the value of art and of artists. "There is no doubt in my mind that art comes last in the things of life which preoccupy us. The young man who shows signs of becoming an artist is looked upon as a crackpot, or else as a lazy, worthless encumbrance. He has to follow his inspiration at the cost of starvation, humiliation and ridicule. He can earn a living at his calling only by producing the kind of art which he despises." This is surely the son of Louise Miller speaking.

The pleasures that Miller experienced in Louisiana with Weeks Hall and Dr. Souchon only served to deepen his sense that the life most Americans had made for themselves in their homeland was barren, shallow, and lacking in vitality. Of New Orleans he writes, "It is the most congenial city in America that I know of and it is due in large part, I believe, to the fact that here at last on this bleak continent the sensual pleasures assume the importance which they deserve. It is the only city in America where, after a lingering meal accompanied by good wine and good talk, one can stroll at random through the French Quarter and feel like a civilized human being." Thus Miller can say about Souchon's paintings, "It is the same with Dr. Souchon's paintings as with the whole atmosphere of Louisiana— it is American and it is not American." The culture of Louisiana is an anomaly in American life. And it won't last. Miller's forecast for the future of New Orleans is bleak: "At the rate we are going, in another hundred years or so there will be scarcely a trace or evidence on this continent of the only culture we have been able to produce—the rich slave culture of the South . . . When the beautiful French Quarter is no more, when every link with the past is destroyed, there will be the clean sterile office buildings, the hideous monuments and public buildings, the oil wells, the smokestacks, the air ports, the jails, the lunatic asylums, the charity hospitals, the bread lines, the gray shacks of the colored people, the bright tin lizzies, the stream-lined trains, the tinned food products, the drug stores, the Neon-lit shop windows to inspire the artist to paint. *Or*, what is more likely, persuade him to commit suicide." Miller's dark pessimism about where the "progress" of the industrial North was taking the country was one note among many others that Miller suspected would give cause for Doubleday, Doran to reject *The Air-Conditioned Nightmare*.

After the ten-day stay in New Orleans and New Iberia, Miller drove on alone. Rattner had returned to New York for an exhibition of his paintings and did not rejoin the tour. When Miller reached Natchez, Mississippi, he received word that his father was dying from prostate cancer, and he wired Nin for the $30 plane fare. He arrived in New York two hours after his father's death. Nin noted in her diary, "I feel Henry's pain with him. The father—like Henry—Because he was like Henry I sent him cigarettes, magazines pocket money. He was so humble and gentle." Nin felt tenderly toward Henry during this painful time for him. "He seems so small—so delicate," she wrote. "I look at his wrists."

Miller remained in New York for nearly a month. He saw Nin frequently. They met for lunch and went to bed at his hotel. She softened toward him, remarking about him in her diary, "Henry's first act of protectiveness was for his father. His first act of human responsibility. He was wonderful to his father, visited him, brought him presents, wrote to him." Then she discloses that she has offered herself to him: "Today I said to him: when you return, if you still want to marry me—we will get a place and live together. I will leave Hugo."

This stunning reversal of Nin's attitude toward Miller is hard to understand. Perhaps, seeing how lost and vulnerable he seemed, her maternal impulses overcame her better judgment. Perhaps she sensed that Miller realized, deep down, that a marital relationship between them would never work out and wanted him to be the one to acknowledge this. At any rate, Miller seems to have been taken aback by her "proposal." She recorded that his response was doubt: "Henry said, 'I thought you could not separate.'" She wrote no further about this conversation, and Miller never referred to it in his correspondence with her.

At the beginning of March Miller resumed his journey, traveling now by train through the Northeast and Midwest, heading for Natchez where he had left his car. He passed through Pittsburgh, Cleveland, and Detroit, then stopped for a few days in Chicago. What he saw in these heavily industrialized cities horrified him and provoked him to begin writing *The Air-Conditioned Nightmare*. Up to this point, he had only made notes in a travel journal. On March 3 he wrote to Nin from Cleveland. "Just got here after spending the night in Pittsburgh—a hell hole . . . The whole journey today through Penn. and Ohio was like a ride thru an Inferno. I got such a kick out of it that I'm going to start the American book tonight from this point—the center of industrialism, the sink of democracy. It's almost beyond words—so grim, so black, so terrible. Like the planet Vulcan, if there is one." From Detroit he wrote again. "This trip thru the industrial regions gives the full impact of the real spirit of America, which is barbarous to the nth degree . . . When Slocum gets these pages I have a feeling Doubleday will not want the book. I'm not doing it purposely. I just can't hold back any longer."

In Chicago, Miller met with Ben Abramson, the proprietor of the Argus Bookshop, who intended to publish an edition of *The World of Sex* and who had also agreed to sell copies of the underground edition of *Tropic of Cancer* being published in New York through the efforts of Gershon Legman. Abramson showed Miller around the city, and it was on one of their walking tours that Miller came upon the slogan "Good News! God is Love!" written in letters ten feet high on the side of a run-down house. This saying, so pregnant with irony for Miller as he looked around him at the squalid neighborhood, became the title of his opening essay in *The Air-Conditioned Nightmare*. It was Miller's frontal assault on the American scene. A sampling of his observations:

> "Chicago's South Side . . . is like a vast, unorganized lunatic asylum. Nothing can flourish here but vice and disease."
> "There are kinds and degrees of suffering; the worst, in my opinion, is the sort one encounters in the very heart of progress."

"Wherever there is industry there is ugliness, misery, oppression, gloom and despair."

"The most terrible thing about America is that there is no escape from the treadmill which we have created."

"Everything that was of beauty, significance or promise has been destroyed and buried in the avalanche of false progress."

"Walt Disney . . . he's the master of the nightmare."

Miller's mood becomes apocalyptic as he contemplates the future of his country. "When the destruction brought about by war is complete another sort of destruction will set in. And it will be far more drastic, far more terrible than the destruction we are now witnessing. And the fires will rage until the very foundations of this present world crumble. Then we shall see who has life, the life more abundant. Then we shall see whether the ability to make money and the ability to survive are one and the same. Then we shall see the meaning of true wealth."

The rage running through this wishful prophecy is clearly fueled by Miller's frustration at his inability to earn a living from the fruits of his own "industry," the writing of books. His poverty, his refusal to get on the treadmill, have forced him to seek another kind of "abundance"—spiritual wealth. But his anger is a sign of resentment, and resentment does not accord well with his own doctrine of acceptance, evolved during his Paris years and confirmed by his experience of Greece. Nin perceived this about Miller and his American tour in an entry she wrote in her diary in May, while Miller was relaxing and enjoying the Grand Canyon. "Henry's adventure is a destructive, catastrophic one—a wasted sacrifice—for he is creating nothing out of his trip through America, he is only spitting in its eye, like a preacher on an endless sermon casting it to hell, etc."

AFTER A BRIEF SIDE EXCURSION TO VISIT THE DUDLEYS IN KENOSHA, Wisconsin, Miller continued on by train to Natchez, where he recovered his car and resumed the drive west. But nothing that he saw or experienced on the remainder of his trip would alter the fundamental attitudes about America that had formed during the first six months.

He continued to extol the beauties of the American landscape. He was particularly delighted by the beauty of the desert plateaus of the Southwest: the "huge rectangle which embraces parts of four states— Utah, Colorado, New Mexico, and Arizona—and which is nothing but enchantment, sorcery, illusionismus, phantasmagoria. Perhaps the secret of the American continent is contained in this wild, forbidding and partially unexplored territory." But he continued to deplore the culture that the white man had made from the land and its resources. After gazing in awe at the Grand Canyon, Miller writes: "Why is it that in America the great works of art are all Nature's doing? There were skyscrapers, to be sure, and the dams and bridges and the concrete highways. All utilitarian. Nowhere in America is there anything comparable to the cathedrals of Europe, the temples of Asia and Egypt—enduring monuments created out of faith and love and passion. No exaltation, no fervor, no zeal—except to increase business, facilitate transportation, enlarge the domain of ruthless exploitation."

The only exception to this "schizophrenia" Miller encounters is a community in the Ozarks that he passed through early in April. He recorded his stop here in his travel journal, but did not include it in *The Air-Conditioned Nightmare*: "Arrived about 6pm. Walk in dusk. First sign of genuine old wooden homes in America—looking beautiful in honest poverty and simplicity. The old covered wells! The types—so friendly & gracious. Gentle like the earth itself. Here is the face of America—at its best. Great peace, great character. Even food has improved—substantial and well cooked. This is the *heart* of America. And, like Greece, everything in right scale—man-sized."

As he drove west, Miller also continued to nurse the hope that Nin would join him, and that they could eventually make their way to Mexico together. For her part, Nin seemed to be receptive to this. The problem, as always, was money. In March, she wrote in her diary that she wanted to join Henry in Natchez but lacked the funds. This conundrum had been repeated at various stages of Miller's trip, always with the same result—nothing. And so it continued until Nin finally made a decisive break from Miller.

Miller's Mexico fantasy may have been fed from several sources. He had never been to Mexico, nor did he know any Mexicans. He may have been influenced by D. H. Lawrence, who had written two books about the pre-Columbian culture in Mexico, *The Plumed Serpent* and *Mornings in Mexico*. His friend Michael Fraenkel had moved to Mexico from Havana and was publishing from there. And Lafayette Young was making plans to go to Mexico to set up a publishing enterprise that would bring out the Tropics and *Black Spring*. That Miller had not really given Mexico serious thought is revealed in a letter he wrote to Nin from Albuquerque: "After this tour, Mexico surely. The more I hear about it, the better it sounds. I got shaved by a Mexican barber yesterday who was just down there ..." Mexico was more a state of mind than a likely resting place for the nomadic Miller. It represented escape from the American milieu that he loathed. And living there would be cheap.

Miller arrived in Hollywood on May 12, 1941, and settled in for what would become a three-month stay. During this period his relationship with Nin began to deteriorate again, but he found a publisher for *The Colossus of Maroussi* and he saw Big Sur for the first time.

Miller's agent and other literary contacts in New York had provided him with entrée into the creative community that swarmed around the motion picture industry. Miller was flattered to discover that his work was known to the scriptwriters, directors, and actors he met, many of whom asked him to autograph copies of his books. But when he was offered a job writing scripts at $200 a week, he turned it down, contemptuously. He wrote to Nin: "Had an offer of a job doing script work here, but promptly refused. Terrible world here—the movies I mean. Hollow as sawdust. The real men are the technicians—they are really geniuses. It's all technique. The human element is just nil."

At the time that Miller rejected the job offer, he was feeling, for him, flush. He had received $100 from the sale of his essay on Weeks Hall to *Town & Country* magazine. Another magazine sale had brought in $25. And Laughlin had promised him another $100 for *Wisdom of the Heart*. Additionally, he was expecting a payment from Ben Abramson for *The World of Sex*. So his immediate need for cash was met. And Miller never looked beyond his immediate needs. But when Nin received Miller's letter, she was furious. All through the winter and spring, Miller had been encouraging her to join him;

the obstacle had always been lack of money. Now Miller had been offered a solution to the money problem and he had turned it down. This to Nin was a sign that he was not serious about making a life with her and freeing her from his dependence. Meanwhile, she was continuing to churn out pornography so she would have money to send to Miller when he needed it. She wrote in her diary, "Henry is in Hollywood and refused to do script writing at $200 a week . . . I expect this. He does not want to sacrifice himself to free me . . . He merely thinks he does not want to be driven, compelled, forced—lose his liberty. He does not ever tell himself it will unburden Anaïs. No child ever thinks of unburdening the mother."

Although he disliked the movie industry, Miller found the Southern California lifestyle and climate congenial and decided to extend his stay. He was writing *The Air-Conditioned Nightmare*. Early in June, he received an offer from William Roth, a small independent publisher who operated Colt Press in San Francisco, to bring out *The Colossus of Maroussi*. He moved into the garage apartment of a screenwriter he had met and began taking Spanish lessons, presumably in preparation for "Mexico." Toward the end of June Miller made a trip to San Francisco to meet Roth and finalize the contract for *Colossus*. On the way back he drove down the coast from Monterey and saw Big Sur for the first time. He wrote to Nin, "This last trip was marvelous. I almost got the feeling I had in Greece—except that here nothing is *sacred*."

Miller remained in California until September so that he could proof the galleys of *Colossus*. He had given up plans to complete his motor tour of America, convinced that the publisher would reject the book he was writing. He intended to sell the Buick and use the proceeds to return to New York by train, but the sale fell through and he ended up driving back through Nevada, Utah, Wyoming, Nebraska, Iowa, Indiana, and Ohio with stop-offs in Kenosha and Chicago. As Miller headed east, Nin wrote in her diary, "Henry is slowly traveling back, but I wish he were not coming. I feel separated from him." Miller arrived back in New York City on October 9. Approximately two months later Doubleday, Doran rejected his manuscript. He abandoned the book until the end of the war, when Laughlin brought it out at New Directions.

OVER THE NEXT TWO AND A HALF YEARS MILLER continued to founder in his attempt to stabilize his life, obtain a dependable income, and find a hospitable environment in which to live and write. His relationship with Nin persisted, but his financial dependence on her and his insensitivity to her needs finally wore her down, and she broke with him. About the time that this happened, the door to Big Sur opened, and Miller walked through it into the next stage of his life.

Miller was penniless when he returned to New York from his American tour. His only asset was his car, which he had no use for in the city and tried to sell. Caresse Crosby again offered him the use of her Manhattan apartment. He took up residence there and began work on *Sexus*, the first volume of *The Rosy Crucifixion* trilogy that would occupy him on and off throughout his Big Sur years. He tried to raise money by selling his notebooks; he wrote letters of appeal to friends and editors seeking gifts and writing assignments. But his main source of support continued to be Nin. He once asked her for fifty cents, a request she felt was designed to make her feel guilty at the extent of his poverty. She came to regard him as a helpless child and she as the enabling mother, and questioned whether this form of relationship was healthy for either of them. She wrote in her diary in November: "I can see in Henry the inability to grasp the reality of money. It is so much like the process of a child becoming aware of the evil in the world, duties, etc. . . . In freeing him, protecting him, I have nurtured both his dream and his weakness . . ." She viewed Miller's carefully developed "mystical detachment" not as a sign of wisdom but as evidence of his dysfunctionality. "There is great confusion in Henry between the detachment, the mystical personality, the cosmic attitude, and the schizophrenic Henry who is always not wholly present in his experience. It is not the sage's removal, but the unrelatedness of the schizophrenic." Nevertheless, she continues to feel sorry for him and to help him. "I see him fragile, bowed."

Nin also took a critical view of Miller's writing during this period. Of the American book she comments, "It is insincere and forced. The writing is bad. It is self-conscious. There is no new Henry, but a bewildered one, only his defects." And she sees *The Rosy Crucifixion* project as regressive. "He is only writing to fill the void of one

American life, compared merely of *reflections* of our life in Paris, sad echoes of a *finished* experience."

Meanwhile, Nin's own life was moving in directions that increased her distance from Miller. She had purchased a used press and some type and was using them to print her own work, a project that excited her and gave her a sense of her own power. Her husband Hugo had become an artist, an engraver who had a successful show of his engravings shortly after Miller's return. Nin was continuing her love affair with Edward Graeffe, a singer whom she had met in a bar in Provincetown, Massachusetts, and whom she has nicknamed Chinchilito. And her relationship with Gonzalo More had involved her in revolutionary politics and made her briefly sympathetic to communism. In the face of all this, Miller's fantasies that they would somehow make their way to Mexico to enjoy the fruits of paradise seem delusional.

It did not take long for Miller to realize that he had come to a dead end in New York. In December he wrote to Cairns that he had to beg for food on Christmas Day. He asked Cairns for help in finding work—"anything but writing or critical work"—then immediately rescinded the request, writing that "someone has come to the rescue." In June 1942 he received a letter from Gilbert Neiman, a writer and professor he had met and briefly stayed with in Los Angeles, offering him rent-free accommodations at a house in Beverly Glen, close to the University of California. Miller unhesitatingly accepted, writing to Cairns on the eve of his departure, "Am going to look for a job in the movies. That's the only way to get to Mexico, it seems."

Miller took the train from New York to Los Angeles and set up house in a residence next door to the Neimans. He liked the setting—"big front yard and a piece of mountain in back covered with trees and flowers"—and his hosts—"everybody very hospitable and affable"—but complained about a lack of privacy and space in which to work. He spent considerable time in the outdoors, sunning and swimming at the beach, and soon recovered his vitality. He had been provided with entrée into a Hollywood literary agency by Slocum and was optimistic that he would soon obtain work as a screenwriter. He expressed his buoyancy in a letter he wrote to Emil Schnellock in the fall of 1942. "Today has been the most perfect day

I've ever known in America. A bright blue sunlight over the dry hills, reminding me powerfully of Greece. At night too it is like Greece—the most brilliant starlight, the planets burning like lamps."

But Miller now found the doors of Hollywood closed to him. Perhaps word had gotten around that a year earlier he had turned down an offer of work. Perhaps Miller was unable to conceal the contempt he felt for the whole Hollywood scene. In May, shortly before he left New York, he had written a letter to an agent—a letter never sent—that did not bode well for his chances. He tells the agent: "I'm willing to manufacture any kind of shit they want, if it will help to entertain and relax the already demoralized American public. If you want to bother to read some of my work . . ." Miller did not have the political skills to play the Hollywood game, and he knew it. He was baffled by the vague assurances and empty promises that are standard currency in the movie industry. In August he wrote to Nin, "The terrible thing to witness here is the disgust which everyone has for the work he is doing. It's so completely a money-mad world—and nothing more. (And yet you mustn't say that that's all you care about. You are supposed to pretend great interest. And I'm very poor at that.)" A week later he wrote her again, reporting on a dinner party he attended at which he met the composer Igor Stravinsky. "One thing stands out like lightning. Everybody who comes out here comes to sell his soul." By September, Miller had given up hope of finding employment as a screenwriter. He wrote to Eleanor Howard, the wife of an erotica collector whom he had met in Chicago through Abramson, that he had lost all desire to work in movies. His only contribution to the industry was a treatment he wrote on speculation based on the novel *The Maurizius Case* by Jakob Wassermann. A producer who had obtained rights to the novel paid Miller $100 for the treatment, but the project went nowhere.

Discouraged, Miller wrote a long plaintive letter to Nin describing his predicament. "I am at the point where I am questioning my role, of writer. I have doubts about its importance. It begins to look more and more like a luxury . . . I'm congenitally incapable of writing anything I don't believe in. This may be an excuse, but I don't honestly think so. I have tried. It never works. Then a worse thing happens. When I do nothing I find I like it immensely. One can do nothing here because the surroundings are themselves sufficient. That was what I discovered in Greece ... Always I have the forlorn wish that there might be a way of living here with you. It's terrible to think that you have the right place and the right person, but can never bring them together."

Nin, reading this, struggled with her feeling of protectiveness toward him and her wish to be free of him. She was now sending him money that she earned from her press. But she wrote in her diary: "I can't live in Hollywood ... What I should write to Henry is that I no longer love him except as a child—and that I will continue to take care of him *as a mother*—and thus free him to live how he pleases. *Can I do this? That is the truth*—can I say it?"

Sensing that he is losing Nin, Miller wrote her that he intends to return to New York and find work there. Nin has become physically exhausted from the strain of managing her complex life with its overlapping intrigues. She is on the verge of a breakdown and does not want Miller to return. When she receives a letter from him suggesting that she remain in New York only because she needs its cultural background, Nin writes and then sends the letter that opens the final rupture between them. "Your passivity has created my struggle. I don't want you to return ... You think your way of life is wisdom— but it isn't. It's the way of life permitted to those who are protected by someone else's struggle ... I shall continue to keep you. I have always wanted you fulfilled—I have my own plans and it won't be Hollywood ... This separation has been going on since you went to Greece. You would feel much happier if I became a child like you, joined you and repeated your life with June for I repeat to you, I'm as helpless as you in regard to money and it is Hugo who has guarded us both. What you want me to do is destructive—to join you and become blind with you. You ran away to Greece. At that time your trip was a break from me, and your unsolvable problem. We broke physically and emotionally. You found you could live without me—I did too. It became clearer and clearer that the only bond left was a mother and child one."

Miller abandoned the idea of returning to New York, but told Nin he would find work in California, even if he has to take a job in a defense plant, so that she will no longer need to support him. But instead of finding work, Miller sent out begging letters to everyone in his address book. Nin aptly remarked that he was turning from dependence on her to dependence on the world.

After the rupture with Nin, Miller drifted, like a boat cut loose from its mooring. His begging letter brought surprising results: gifts of cash and supplies, orders for watercolors, a reviewing assignment, and a $200 loan from the National Institute of Arts and Letters. He picked up his brush and resumed painting watercolors. Attilio Bowinkel, proprietor of an artists' supply store in nearby Westwood, took a liking to Miller, gave him free supplies, and displayed Miller's watercolors in his store window. Bowinkel's other customers, many of them people working in the movie business, began to buy Miller's work and soon he developed a considerable local reputation as a painter. Miller wrote his painter friend Emil Schnellock about his deepening interest in the watercolor medium: "Did I ever tell you that between tones of any color I find gaps which it seems impossible to fill in? Especially in the blues. Between ultramarine and cobalt or cerulean or Prussian blue there are gaps which seem impossible to bridge. I'm naively amazed by this—just as I am when I see the spectrum. Colors seem to come in bands. I'm always looking for the right blue—and never find it. Then, too, I notice that making one's own green—by mixing all kinds of blues with all kinds of yellows—is fascinating and much more interesting than squeezing the right shade out of a tube."

WHEN THE NEIMANS LEFT FOR NORTHERN CALIFORNIA, where Gilbert had found work, Miller wrote to John Dudley and invited him to stay with him in the Beverly Glen house. Dudley's marriage had collapsed after his brief but torrid affair with Nin. Nin recorded in her diary in February 1942 that Dudley had suffered a nervous breakdown and his wife Flo had attempted suicide with a pair of scissors. Dudley, now divorced, eagerly came west and the two painters turned the Beverly Glen residence into an art studio and gallery, inviting friends and neighbors to view their work.

A frequent visitor, the Danish painter Knud Merrild, described their living arrangement. "The place was furnished with just the bare necessities. Miller occupied the front room. He had only a small table, which had to be cleared of writing or water-color materials before each meal, the materials to be placed on the couch and then moved back again after the meal—slightly annoying, I should think—a book case, two chairs and a couch which also served as his bed. But then, greater work has been done in attics than in castles ... Dudley's room had just a bed, a dresser and one chair. You may wonder where, in this Spartan set-up, a writer might keep his writing material, his manuscripts, correspondence, and such like. Why, in the kitchen drawers, of course. The drawers served as a primitive filing cabinet. In their meager circumstances it was impossible to fill the drawers with groceries anyway, so why not put them to use? Very appropriate, I thought. A kitchen is a storage place for edible food—why not for spiritual as well?"

Miller did very little writing during this period. His time was taken up with an extensive correspondence and with his painting, which was now his chief means of support. In February he received a commission to review a short biography of the Danish philosopher Soren Kierkegaard. The review was published in the May 10, 1943, issue of the *New Republic*.

In the spring, Miller met a young Greek woman, Sevasty Koutsaftis, with whom he quickly fell in love. He had been introduced to her by Lawrence Clark Powell, the librarian at UCLA. Miller had met Powell in France when they both were teaching at the same school in Dijon, and their relationship resumed when Miller moved to Beverly Glen, where Powell was a neighbor. Powell introduced Miller to Sevasty as a potential translator of *The Colossus of Maroussi*. Sevasty was a poet, and soon after meeting her Miller wrote to Emil Schnellock that he was "head over heels" in love with her. Miller's passion for Sevasty inspired "O Lake of Light," his only published poem.* By July, he reported to Schnellock, the affair had become "all consuming," but it came to a sudden end when Sevasty wrote him a letter stating her wish to be only his friend. Dejected, Miller wrote again to Schnellock in September: "My Greek idyll is all over. Have been thru hell—but am now out of

---

* See Appendix C.

it and writing about it. Recently all my love affairs come to naught."
In November an obviously lonely Miller wrote to Abe Rattner about
his desire for a companion—"a simple peasant woman, or a negress or
an Indian, would do. Just something female around—to sleep with, to
cook, to look at, to talk to. I don't give a shit whether I'm in love or not."
Miller, demoralized by his failures with women, was looking for a squaw.

As the year drew to a close, Miller prepared for an exhibition
of his watercolors at the American Gallery of Contemporary Art
on Hollywood Boulevard. Miller rounded up paintings owned by
friends around the country and added them to his inventory of new
work. All in all more than sixty of Miller's paintings were put on
display. A number sold before the exhibition had even opened. There
were plans for additional exhibitions in Santa Barbara, New York,
and London. Miller had become a painter and was generating more
income from his watercolors than from his books.

But he was still begging. In December, "Another Open Letter"
was published in the *New Republic*. In it Miller defended his appeals
for support and attacked the censoring mentality that prevented his
major works from being issued in the United States and giving him an
income. He also rather disingenuously asserted that he could easily find
work writing scripts for the movie industry, quoting a casual remark
made by a studio executive that "the door is wide open," but refused to
prostitute himself. This open letter was read by a fellow artist, the sculptor Jean Varda, who promptly invited Miller to come and stay with him
in Monterey. After Miller's show in Santa Barbara had closed, he went to
Monterey as the guest of Varda and his wife, Virginia, also an artist. One
day, Varda drove Miller down to Big Sur to meet Lynda Sargent, a friend
of Varda who was writing a novel. She lived in a cabin overlooking the
sea. Sargent had an unoccupied room in her cabin, and offered it to
Miller for as long as he wished to stay. Miller decided to accept the offer.

Before leaving for Monterey, Miller wrote Nin a touching letter in which he acknowledged his responsibility for their falling-out
and expressed his continuing devotion to her. The letter shows that
Miller saw himself as entering a new phase of his life, much as he had
felt when he wrote to Cairns from Paris in 1939. As Miller writes to
Nin, his tone is deferential, even humble. "It has been hard to write

you, knowing that you preferred silence. Well, I am about to leave here now, for an extended vacation. I may never return to this place. I have no definite plans—only an urge to get out and relax. The experiences lived through here were of enormous value to me. By a strange irony of fate I was put in a situation which enabled me to realize, as I never could have before, just how I must have appeared in your eyes. It makes your stature even grander. I learned the lesson. Everything (I think) that you wished me to do I have done. I went through a veritable ordeal, for which I am most thankful. I hope your own struggles have proved as fruitful. I would like to know, if you care to tell me. All my strength came from the example you set me. There is no one on this earth I venerate more than you."

As he prepared to settle in Big Sur, Miller wrote Nin again, offering words of encouragement for her own work. And he said about Big Sur: "I have much work to finish and am seeking peace and isolation. I am completely out of the world there. The stores are 35 miles away. I have no car. Depend on mailman to bring food—mail twice a week. Precisely what I want." He concluded this letter with the plaintive words, "I hope you do not mind if I write to you now and then."

4

SETTLING IN BIG SUR

"This Is Heaven Enough."

MILLER HAD LEFT LOS ANGELES FOR MONTEREY WITHOUT DEFINITE plans. His intention, declared in a letter to an acquaintance just before his departure, was to take a vacation of "five, six, or seven weeks," then try to figure out a way to get to Mexico. He set out on the road in mid-February, a homeless fifty-two-year-old hitchhiker with seven dollars in his pocket, and reached Big Sur in early March, after staying in Monterey with the Vardas. But after living as Lynda Sargent's guest in a cabin above the sea for several weeks, he decided to remain longer, and Lynda arranged for him to move to a one-room shack on Partington Ridge used as a weekend getaway by a former boyfriend from Carmel, Keith Evans, then serving in the US Army. Rent was ten dollars per month, payment optional.

Shortly before moving into this cabin, Miller wrote to Nin describing the powerful appeal of Big Sur. "I am living with nature more and more, and this Big Sur country (where I have been now for two months) is truly tremendous. There are only about 25 people on this mail route. Back from the coast, over the mountains, there is an absolute emptiness. It is almost as forbidding as Tibet, and it fascinates me. I should like to go back in there and live for a time quite alone. But I would need a horse and an axe and a few other things I have never used. I am a little terrified of it." This romantic fantasy of himself as a hardy pioneer surviving alone in the wilderness would no doubt have amused Miller's new neighbors on Partington Ridge, who soon discovered his comical ineptitude with even the most rudimentary demands of carpentry, plumbing, and gardening—the essential skills needed for survival in Big Sur.

The nomadic Miller had decided to settle, at least temporarily, in one of the most dramatic and inspirational meetings of land and sea in North America, if not the world. Big Sur (so named by the Spaniards, referring to it as the "big south") was formed approximately two million years ago by enormous tectonic forces that pushed together the earth's North American and Pacific plates, thrusting abruptly up from the coastline a steep mountain range. The collision of these two plates created a narrow band of jagged coastline, scalloped with small irregular shaped coves and bays, backed by the steeply rising wall of the Santa Lucia mountain range, which ascends to heights of nearly six thousand feet. The region extends one hundred miles from the Carmel River in the north to the San Carpoforo Creek in the south above San Luis Obispo. Its location in one of the earth's few Mediterranean climate zones, when combined with its rugged topography and unique geological features, created the conditions for producing what Miller called "a Paradise."

The region's startling beauty and ecological diversity offered Miller sensuous and spiritual delights that equaled, if they did not surpass, what he had experienced during his visit to Greece five years before. When he arrived in March, the slopes of the Santa Lucia Mountains were cloaked in a mantle of green from the winter rains, while the higher peaks of the range were likely still capped with snow. Splashes of color may have started to appear on the landscape from early blooming flowers such as sky lupines, shooting stars, and buttercups. From the windows of Lynda Sargent's cabin Miller could look down the long winding ribbon of the coastline dotted with small coves and see streams emptying into the Pacific. When he went for walks along the cliffs, he could hear the pounding of the surf against the rocks below, the barking of basking seals and sea lions, and the songs of wrentits, thrashers, and sparrows. Scents from the fragrant shrubs and herbs that grow among the coastal scrub mingled with the odor of kelp and sea spray as he strolled, while above him hawks, kestrels, and eagles soared, hunting for the small rodents and reptiles hidden in the brush. At night, the stillness of the earth under the vast canopy of glittering stars created a sacred domain, far removed from the noise and bustle of any town or city.

Miller was an urban man, born and raised in the city. He believed in the vitality of the streets, a vitality that nourished his early writing, giving him both material and an outlook. But now Miller was seeking the tranquility offered by nature, and he found it in Big Sur. Shortly after arriving, Miller read the novel *The Stranger* by Big Sur resident Lillian Bos Ross, who lived on Partington Ridge. He wrote her a letter of appreciation for the book, which "has made me feel to home." Several years later, writing the preface to a French edition of *The Stranger*, Miller was more effusive in his appreciation of Big Sur: "It is a region where extremes meet, where one is always conscious of weather, of space, of grandeur and of eloquent silence. Many people remark that it is a landscape in which the masculine and feminine elements are perfectly blended. It is a Paradise which is constantly challenging one to live at one's highest level or go down in conflict and defeat . . . Often I say to myself, especially when the clouds pile up in the north and the sea is churning with whitecaps and the grain bends low under the wind: 'This is the California that man dreamed of years ago, this is the Pacific that Balboa looked out on from the Peak of Darien, this is the face of the world as the Creator intended it to look. How wonderful is the earth and the creatures which inhabit it! This is Heaven enough. Why ask for more?' "

This passage suggests that Miller found in Big Sur the possibility of reconnection to the impulse that brought the first Europeans to the American continent in search of "the fresh green breast of a new world," a world that had existed before the spread of commerce, industrialism, and urbanization formed the America that Miller loathed, "the air-conditioned nightmare." In fact, Big Sur had experienced three distinct waves of settlement before he arrived, and his coming was part of a transition to a fourth wave that had begun with the completion of Highway 1 between San Luis Obispo and Monterey in 1937.

The earliest inhabitants of the region were Native Americans who established small villages on a site near what is now Cambria in approximately 6,000 BC. They were a Stone Age people who survived by hunting, fishing, and gathering edible plants. Three separate aboriginal groups with distinct languages occupied the Big Sur region: the Ohlone in the north, the Esselen in the center, and the Salinan in the south.

The first reported sighting of Big Sur by a European occurred in 1542, when Juan Cabrillo sailed up the coast and discovered Monterey and Carmel bays. In 1600, another Spaniard, Sebastian Vizcaino, surveyed the bays, but no settlement took place. The Portola Expedition came north from San Diego in 1769, but was forced inland by the mountains and bypassed Big Sur. Portola returned a year later and was joined by Father Junipero Serra, who arrived in Monterey Bay by sea and established a mission. Thus began the mission period, during which the natives were converted to Christianity, taught agriculture, and made to labor on the mission lands. The native population soon began to decline because of exposure to European diseases such as smallpox and measles, and their emigration from the missions soon followed.

In 1822 Mexico seceded from Spain. Four years later, the governor of Alta California emancipated many of the Indians and made them Mexican citizens. Then in 1833 the Secularization Act transferred mission lands to the public domain. The lands were given to Mexican citizens as grants, initiating the Rancho period of occupation. Two of the grants fell within Big Sur, the 8,949-acre Rancho El Sur in the Point Sur area, granted to Juan Bautista Alvarado in 1834, and the 8,876-acre Rancho San Jose y Sur Chiquito, which extended from the Carmel River to Palo Colorado Canyon and is now partially incorporated in Garrapata State Park. The Rancho El Sur is still a working ranch today.

After California gained statehood in 1850 and gold was discovered, a new wave of settlement began. Homesteaders moved into Big Sur to claim 160-acre parcels. At first they survived as the natives had done, through foraging, but gradually agriculture was introduced. Livestock was raised, orchards planted, gardens cultivated. Big Sur remained isolated, connected to Monterey in the north by a wagon trail and to communities in the south by horse trails. The early settlers of Big Sur were pioneers who gave their names to many of the canyons and ridges that have become familiar landmarks in the area: the Pfeiffers, the Posts, Tom Slate, Jim Anderson, Sam Trotter, the Plasketts, the Prewitts, and the Partingtons, who settled on the ridge named after them in 1874.

The opening of the highway brought a new wave of visitors, some of whom decided to remain there or build second homes. They were artists, writers, musicians, philosophers. Miller joined this wave and unintentionally became one of its leaders. During this transition period, the region's economy shifted from extraction industries like logging and mining to tourism services.

When Miller moved into Keith Evans's cabin on Partington Ridge, his neighbors included Sam and Nancy Hopkins (from the prominent San Francisco Hopkins family), Harrydick and Lillian Bos Ross, Nicholas Roosevelt (a musician and cousin to FDR) and his wife Tirzah, Frank and Walter Trotter (craftsmen, descendents of an early pioneer), Maud Oakes, a cultural anthropologist, Jaime de Angulo, a wild and brilliant man who operated a cattle ranch when he was not undertaking linguistic studies of western Native Americans, and Jean Wharton, a theosophist and cousin of James Laughlin. A human mosaic existed on Partington Ridge and throughout Big Sur that seemed to echo the region's ecological diversity and complexity.

ALTHOUGH MILLER WAS NOW GEOGRAPHICALLY ISOLATED and a stranger in a small rural community, he was not without allies or resources for his most important goals: the continuation of his writing and the advancement of his literary reputation in America. While still living in Beverly Glen, Miller had been approached on separate occasions by three young men who wanted to aid him in disseminating his work. They all had been deeply affected by Miller's work as well as by his life example. Over the next few years, Miller would spend considerable time and energy advising and assisting these young "acolytes" in publishing and distributing his writing. All three were aspiring artists, and all were pacifists who, in one way or another, had been psychologically and emotionally damaged by the war. They were drawn to Miller by his rebellious voice and by his insistence that the individual must seek meaning and freedom on his own terms, outside conventional society.

The most important of these men for his tangible contribution to Miller's literary reputation was Bern Porter, a young physicist with an interest in art and writing. Porter came from a poor but respectable East Coast family. He had been raised in a small township near Houlton, Maine. His father was a skilled craftsman who worked as a handyman; his mother took in boarders to supplement the family's income. A brilliant student, Porter had won a scholarship to do graduate studies in science at Brown University but had been forced to withdraw when he was discovered stealing money from students' lockers in the men's gymnasium. He made restitution through money earned from menial jobs, and a forgiving professor recommended him for a job at the Acheson Colloids Corporation in New York, a position that he obtained.

While on a business trip to Paris in 1937, he attended one of Gertrude Stein's salons, where he met Michael Fraenkel. Fraenkel introduced Porter to Miller, and soon he had acquired a copy of *Tropic of Cancer.* At the time of his first meeting with Miller, Porter was working as a research physicist. But from an early age, he had shown a strong interest in the arts, and he was searching for ways to fuse his scientific and artistic inclinations, to put science in the service of creativity rather than commerce and war.

In 1940, Porter was drafted and assigned to the Physics Department at Princeton, where experiments for the separation of uranium were under way. He met Einstein and J. Robert Oppenheimer, then a professor of physics at UC Berkeley.

Porter soon found himself involved in the Manhattan Project. He underwent intense security scrutiny—constant surveillance and interrogation by the FBI over his frequent association with writers and artists. According to his biographer, James Schevill, this experience left Porter distrustful of people and accentuated the feelings of being an outsider that he had carried with him as a struggling scholarship student at Brown.

Porter was sent by the Department of Defense to work at a laboratory in Berkeley that had been chosen to develop the technology for the separation of uranium isotopes. Then he was transferred to Oak Ridge, Tennessee, where a massive high-security industrial plant had been built. Porter began corresponding with Miller, then living at Beverly Glen, and visited him there late in 1943, before Miller departed for Monterey and Big Sur. They discussed a series of publishing ventures that Porter wished to undertake on Miller's behalf and agreed on a series of titles, beginning with a collection of Miller's letters to Emil Schnellock that Miller had been pushing Emil to bring out even before he left France. Miller had written essay-length letters to Emil about his own watercolors and European painters. The book was to be oversized, printed on high-quality paper, and would include black-and-white reproductions of nine Miller watercolors. It would be called *Semblance of a Devoted Past*, a phrase Porter had found in one of Miller's books.

Other titles they agreed upon were a pamphlet *Murder the Murderer* expressing Miller's views on war, a collection of Miller's "begging letters" to be called *The Plight of the Creative Artist in the United States of America, Henry Miller Miscellanea*, a collection of short early fugitive pieces, *Varda: The Master Builder, Henry Miller: A Chronology and Bibliography*, and *Escholia*, a collection of Miller's watercolors. As these projects moved along, Miller also raised other possibilities with Porter, including his own *Black Spring* and Nin's diary. Additionally, Porter launched a "secret" project, a collection of Miller tributes by friends and admirers to be titled *The Happy Rock*, a sobriquet given him by Lawrence Durrell.

Out of respect for his contract with James Laughlin, Miller insisted that Porter get clearance to proceed with these projects. When Laughlin raised no objection, Porter sprang into action. It did not seem to trouble Miller that Porter had no publishing or bibliographic experience, and that his only financial resource was his government salary. As they firmed up their arrangement, Miller wrote to Porter: "I like your enthusiasm and your sense of reality—your executiveness. You're a doer. Damned few of my friends are. They're all dreamers. I think we can do some very interesting things together."

Another acolyte who entered Miller's circle around this time was George Leite, a young radical from Berkeley who was about to launch a literary magazine with the forlorn title *New Rejections*. The son of a Portuguese immigrant who had become a missionary, Leite had been expelled from UC Berkeley for refusing to enroll in a required defense course. Leite supported his wife, Nancy, and their small daughter by driving a taxi. He had started a small experimental writing group in Berkeley that he used to introduce students to Miller's work.

Leite knew Porter, and had read some of Miller's letters to Emil at Porter's house in Berkeley. He wrote Miller that he wanted to publish one of the letters in his next issue of the magazine, which he had decided to retitle *Circle*. When Miller agreed to submit material to *Circle*, Leite grew bolder. He proposed bringing out a collection of letters written to Miller by readers of the Tropics. He also asked Miller if he would obtain a copy of Nin's diary for him to read. He expressed interest in publishing *Tropic of Cancer*. While suggesting these ambitious projects to Miller, Leite declared he had no financial interest in publishing Miller's work, "but I do want to see Henry Miller's books on the shelves of every public library. The people are in need of them." This was just the combination of principled impracticality and worship that Miller could not resist. When Miller sent Leite his letters to Emil for possible publication, Leite was overwhelmed and opened wide the spigot of adulation. "You swell Henry to heights I have never before seen except in dreams," he wrote Miller. "You tower and obscure those other giants who have lived before. You have become whole and *real* in the way Christ must have been to the apostles." If Miller raised an eyebrow at this froth, he did not remonstrate. He wrote to Nin about Porter and Leite: "I know they are making quite a cult of me—I can't help that—it's the writing that causes it." By May of 1944, when it was clear that Miller intended to remain in Big Sur for a while, Leite moved his family down there to be near the man whom he now considered to be a father figure, writing to him, "You have helped me more than anyone I have ever known, you have given me the faith to be myself, to continue being what I know I am."

The third "apostle" who presented himself to Miller around this time was Judson Crews, an aspiring writer from Waco, Texas. Crews, like Leite and Porter, was attracted by Miller's anarchism and pacifism. He had become aware of Miller's writing while an undergraduate at Baylor University, where he started a literary magazine called *Vers Libre*. Crews came from a Southern Bible Belt family struggling to survive in the Depression. His father, a nurseryman who had put Crews to work in his fields at age nine, committed suicide in 1936. Crews began collecting Miller's work and Miller became for him, as he had for Leite, a surrogate father figure.

After graduating from Baylor in 1941 with a double major in English and Sociology, Crews started work on a masters degree, then enlisted in the army in 1942 as a noncombatant medic. He became ill with a gastrointestinal inflammation that made him unable to sleep at night and was hospitalized. The army shuttled him from base to base, never adequately treating his illness. During this time, he corresponded with Miller, who offered him sympathy, advice, and encouragement and answered Crews's questions about the availability of Miller's banned books, which Crews was eager to collect and disseminate through a small bookstore he operated from Waco called Motive Book Shop.

In December 1943 Crews visited Miller in Beverly Glen while on a three-day pass from a military camp in Beaumont. Meeting Miller became a turning point in Crews's life, as it had been for Leite. Writing to Miller from camp after the visit, Crews said, "Meeting you in December brought me a more thorough acceptance of myself than anything ever had before. I'll simply never be the same again." To show his appreciation, Crews declared that he wanted to help Miller circulate his books through Motive.

Before leaving for Monterey, Miller connected Crews to Leite and Porter, and asked Crews to assist Porter with the bibliography. He also tried to touch Crews for some cash, offering to sell him personal items at a price to be determined by Crews. (Relics for sale!) They continued to correspond, mostly about publishing suggestions from Miller, for Crews also operated a small press through Motive. When Crews was given a medical discharge from the army in April, Miller invited him to come to Big Sur. But instead, Crews returned to Waco to finish his masters degree at Baylor, which he completed with a literary analysis of Southern writers that was titled *Southern Temper* and earned him honors. Miller read the thesis and praised it in a letter to Crews. In the following year, after Miller repeated his invitation, Crews came to Big Sur, walking the thirty miles from Monterey in the dead of night and knocking on the cabin door of another Miller devotee and helper, Emil White.

Emil, like Miller and his other Big Sur recruits, was a refugee from twentieth-century civilization. Born and raised in Central Europe, Emil and his family fled to Vienna at the onset of World War One. There Emil ran away from home to escape the strictures of his rigid Orthodox Jewish father and settled for a time in Budapest, where he joined a communist movement. He drifted, first to Switzerland, then to Paris. In 1922 he emigrated to New York, changing his name from Wieselmann to White. He survived on the streets, working briefly as messenger for Western Union under Miller's supervision. His poor command of English made him unsuitable for the job, and he took a position as assistant steward on a passenger liner bound for Buenos Aires. He discarded this job as well after one voyage and moved to Chicago with a girlfriend who was studying English and Psychology at the university.

Emil became a voracious reader, with a preference for political radicals and literary iconoclasts. He worked in a Chicago bookshop and participated in Marxist political groups, for whom he organized lectures and debates and gave readings on political theory.

Emil's first contact with Miller's work was *The Cosmological Eye*. The book was passed to him by a member of an anti-totalitarian political group that he had joined. The book struck a chord with him, and he began reading it aloud to groups and then passing the hat to take up a collection for the author. The funds were handed over to Ben Abramson, owner of the Argus Bookshop, who transmitted them to Miller with a note explaining who had collected them.

Emil met Miller by chance on Michigan Avenue in Chicago while Miller was returning to New York from his American tour. He walked up to him and embraced him. Then he invited Miller to his apartment for lunch and brought along two young ladies to keep them company. After this meeting, Miller and White corresponded regularly, and Emil continued to send him proceeds from readings of Miller's books.

In August 1943, to avoid the draft, Emil left Chicago for a laboring job on the Alaska Yukon Highway. When Emil's nine-month commitment ended, Miller invited him to come and live in Big Sur. Emil made his way to Monterey, where he visited Jean Varda, and then rode the mail truck down the coast to Miller's mailbox on the highway below Partington Ridge. He remained in Big Sur for the rest of his life, and bequeathed his home on Highway 1 to the Henry Miller Memorial Library.

The recruits who gathered around Miller at the start of his Big Sur years shared many traits. They were rootless and disenfranchised men, misfits who could not or would not adapt to mainstream American life. They were opposed to war and scarred by their experiences of it. An inadequate family life had left all of them in search of a father figure. They all harbored aspirations of becoming artists in their own right, like their exemplar Miller. Miller's message of contempt for the direction of western civilization, his insistence on the need for self-transformation as the only escape from the trap of modern life, resonated with each of these men and made them eager disciples. All of them remarked that their encounter with Miller through his writing had changed their lives. Emil too, when he wrote about Miller in his autobiography, declared, "Little did I know when I first held his books that the man would change my life." But Emil's role in Miller's life would become both more enduring and more personal than that of any of the other lost souls who made pilgrimages to Big Sur in search of renewal and purpose.

THERE IS A SENSE IN WHICH MILLER, living alone in a small cabin halfway up a mountainside without electricity, a telephone, or a car, thirty miles from the nearest town, was as isolated from American life in Big Sur as he had been in Paris, if not more so. But as he had done in France, Miller built a community of supporters through whom he could pursue his goals as a writer and obtain the assistance he needed to survive from day to day on his scant resources. In Paris, his mainstays of support were Anaïs Nin and Alfred Perlès, who sheltered him, gave him money, found work for him, and encouraged his writing. A wider circle of friends and fellow artists—Richard Osborn, Michael Fraenkel, Walter Lowenfels, Fred Kann—often provided him with meals and a place to sleep when he was too broke to afford a hotel room or a café. Miller never forgot his debt to these people. He wrote about them in his books, and he remained in correspondence with many of them for years afterward.

A similar pattern unfolded in Big Sur. He enlisted Porter, Leite, and Crews to help him grow his reading public and his literary reputation in America. For, despite his protestations to the contrary, despite his bitterness at being unable to earn even a subsistence income from his writing, Miller wanted deeply to be taken seriously as a writer, and he wanted his banned Paris books to be published in his own country.

Miller also needed help with his day-to-day survival and upkeep. Maintaining the cabin, keeping himself supplied with firewood, water, and food required hours of chores each day, and Miller was not used to heavy work. He depended upon the mailman, who came down the coast three days a week, to bring him provisions which then had to be lugged up the hill on foot, a two-mile round trip. Then there was his correspondence, averaging seventy-five to one hundred letters per week from readers and friends, most of which Miller felt obligated to answer. He also needed time to paint watercolors, which he either sold or used as barter for needed services and supplies. All these responsibilities left him little time for his main work, writing.

But Emil White came to his rescue. Quickly sensing that his friend was overwhelmed, he took upon himself the role of jack-of-all-trades in Miller's service. "I realized that one of the best services I could render Henry was to lend him my hands," White wrote in his autobiography. "Away from the typewriter his hands were useless. I chopped wood for him; I learned basic carpentry and made things (such as the little cart Henry used to haul his laundry, mail and groceries up the one-mile hill to his home); I answered his mountains of mail when the correspondence became too demanding of his time. Henry needed me! I was his man Friday, his confidant, his facilitator. I was always available to help."

As Miller settled into Big Sur in the spring of 1944, he wrote a letter to his friend Huntington Cairns, summing up his circumstances, much as he had done when he was about to leave France for Greece. After complaining to Cairns about the lack of support from "many of my so-called friends" (was this a sly reference to Cairns's reluctance to speak out publicly in support of Miller's banned books?), he launched into encomiums for his new circle of supporters.

There is my new friend and publisher Bern Porter, about whom you shall read in the last Open Letter I wrote for that book he is bringing out called *The Plight of the Creative Artist in the U.S.A.* Let him stand as a model for publishers for all time!

There is George T. Leite, another new-found friend, who edits out of his own pocket a little magazine called *Circle* at Berkeley, California. George Leite has a wife and child and works as a taxi driver a few days a week. Out of this he sends me royal gifts every now and then, always at a crucial moment, for he has a nose for my needs. In addition he does things for me which my oldest friends would never dream of doing. He can find the time though he has less time than nearly any one I know.

There is Emil White, an Austrian refugee who ekes out a living at one thing and another. Not only does he send me handsome sums out of his meager earnings, from time to time, but now and then he gathers his friends together, reads to them from my work, and then passes the hat around for me. That's what I call a friend!

And here, lest I close this letter without mentioning his name, let me add instantly the name of Judson C. Crews of Waco, Texas. His name should be written up in gold!

Another ally whom Miller neglected to mention was James Laughlin, the man who was publishing Miller's work through New Directions, providing him with advances, and sending him quarterly royalty checks. After their falling-out over the publishing contract that Laughlin had offered him, Miller attacked Laughlin in an open letter he submitted to the *New Republic* for failing to bring out any of Miller's banned books. "A great many people think him to be my champion and benefactor. Nothing could be further from the truth," Miller wrote rather nastily. But the reality was that Laughlin did want to challenge the censorship of Miller's books (he had been arrested while an undergraduate at Harvard for publishing an excerpt from one of the Tropics in the university literary magazine), but he feared losing his family's financial backing for New Directions if he went too far and drew notoriety to the Laughlin name. Laughlin admired Miller's writing, but he was also a businessman trying to build New Directions. He needed to be prudent to protect himself as well as the other authors he was publishing. Miller subsequently backed away from his slight, writing to Laughlin in December 1943, "All that belongs in the past." Laughlin quickly wrote back, "Many thanks for the footnote explaining that we have made up." After receiving this letter, Miller wrote to Cairns: "Laughlin has changed from a demon into an angel." By April, Miller felt fully reconciled to Laughlin, writing, "I feel very fine about our having settled our differences. We'll never see eye to eye, I know, but we can have faith in one another." Miller was then assembling the collection of short essays that Laughlin would bring out later in the year under the title *Sunday After the War*. After reading the manuscript, Laughlin wrote to Miller, "You know you are really quite a writer. I mean apart from what you say, just the style is sometimes quite overwhelming. I marvel at the limpidity you attain, the way rather difficult ideas just FLOAT out without any effort."

Laughlin, unlike Miller's "new friends," was an experienced publisher who understood the book market. He wanted to build the reputation of his authors over the long haul, and he was in agreement with Huntington Cairns that the best chance of lifting the ban on Miller's Paris books was to position Miller in the public mind as a serious writer who chose to write candidly about sex. The indiscriminate publishing of Miller's New Directions rejects by men who lacked both Laughlin's business experience and his considerable financial resources (in addition to New Directions, he owned a ski lodge in Alta, Utah) would, over time, result in financial setbacks for Porter, Leite, and Crews and erode their relationship with Miller.

As Miller worked to set up conditions for living and writing in Big Sur, he had other unmet needs. The most pressing was his need for cash to cover his basic living expenses. The money he received from the sale of his watercolors and royalties on his books from New Directions was neither dependable nor adequate. There were no opportunities for employment in Big Sur, and if there had been, Miller would in all likelihood not have pursued them. Instead, he resorted to a measure that had brought surprisingly good results while he was living in Beverly Glen: the begging letter. In April he sent a letter to his closest friends and allies in the United States, asking them to provide him with the funds he would need to place an ad in several literary magazines. The ad would solicit support from a patron willing to provide him with a one-year stipend of $2,500, payable in fifty weekly installments of $50. The ad would promise that Miller would use the stipend to move to Mexico for a year, where he would complete his magnum opus, the novel about his Brooklyn years and his marriage to June Mansfield that he had laid out in a twenty-four-hour burst of inspiration in 1927. *Tropic of Capricorn* had been the first novel in this personal saga. The remainder of the story, to be called *The Rosy Crucifixion*, would be written in three volumes: *Sexus*, *Plexus*, and *Nexus*. Miller, perhaps to reassure himself that his struggles as a writer would not go on forever, declared in this letter, "Once I have finished the books in question I do not care whether I write another book or not." Miller sent the letter to a select group of friends, most of whom lacked either the motive or the means to send him money.

But miraculously, within a month, Miller had an offer, and a backup prospect as well. An artist in California who wished to remain anonymous and used the pseudonym "Harry Kovarr" (a sound pun on the French words for green beans, *haricots verts*) offered to send Miller $200 for twelve months, and threw in the final $100 to cover the costs of his travel to Mexico. And Huntington Cairns wrote that he might have a patron willing to grant Miller's request. Miller's benefactor sent him $300 as a first installment: $200 for living expenses and $100 to get him to Mexico. He (or she) also informed Miller that he was an artist and had borrowed the money he was sending Miller. He asked Miller to notify him if he received other offers of help.

Miller immediately revised the terms of the loan. In another letter to Cairns, he explained how he planned to use the funds. He would not be going to Mexico, as promised. He would send $100 per month of his stipend to Anaïs Nin in partial repayment of his long-standing debt to her, and to enable her to publish her diary. (Having set up her own press, Nin was self-publishing.) Of the remaining $100, he planned to send $50 per month to Harry Herschkowitz, a merchant seaman who lived in New York, aspired to be a writer, and, before he had even met Miller, had been sending him three dollars a week from his salary.

This windfall clearly stirred Miller's own philanthropic impulses. He wrote Herschkowitz a long letter outlining schemes to obtain financial help for two struggling artists in New York: the African American painter Beauford Delaney, whom Miller had met through Herschkowitz, and the writer Kenneth Patchen, who was suffering from ill health. He offered to split any income he received from sales of his watercolors at two upcoming shows in Washington, DC, and London with Delaney. And he said he intended to ask John Dudley to send Patchen $500 that Dudley owed Miller. Both of these gestures came to naught, but they indicated how strongly Miller identified with the struggles of other artists whom he admired and knew.

But Miller soon lost his own good fortune. Within three months, "Harry Kovarr" got wind of how his patronage of Miller was being used and ceased his payments. To add insult to injury, Nin complained to Miller that he valued Herschkowitz's literary talent almost as much as hers. And Huntington Cairns reported that his potential patron had been hospitalized and could not be approached.

Harry Herschkowitz played a significant role in helping Miller satisfy another of his unmet needs in Big Sur, his desire for a female companion. Pickings were slim in the sparsely populated rural community, and Miller's spartan lifestyle offered limited appeal. After the collapse of his relationship with Nin and the failure of his suit for Sevasty Koutsaftis in Los Angeles, Miller had become despondent about his numerous ill-fated love affairs. Writing to Herschkowitz about his romantic frustrations, Miller remarked, "I guess my malady now is that I am continually falling in love with my daughter." Miller, now in his early fifties, has not forgotten his adolescent crush on Cora Seward.

Miller needed a multifaceted woman who could serve as mistress, housekeeper, and secretary. He contemplated placing a personals ad in the *Saturday Review of Literature*, then thought better of it. Instead, in another form of begging, he put out discreet inquiries to friends and acquaintances in New York. One of them, a woman named Janice Pelham, connected him to June Lancaster, a twenty-six-year-old dancer and artists' model who was trying to build a career teaching a new style of modeling that was based on movement rather than static posing. A correspondence between Miller and June ensued, during which June revealed herself to be a rather coy but intelligent young lady who admired Miller's writing and had her own strong opinions about the degeneration of western civilization. "White people as a race are steadily deteriorating physically, it seems to me, with their lack of sufficient muscular exercise due to their passion for machines, 'labor saving' devices, etc.," she wrote Miller in one of her letters, sounding a note that surely resonated with the author of *The Air-Conditioned Nightmare*. Although Miller courted her through the mail using all of his considerable powers of persuasion, June resisted his invitation to come west and sample life with him in Big Sur. She insisted that she wished to remain independent in order to pursue her own artistic ambitions. She was focused on a presentation of her modeling theory that she was scheduled to deliver at Columbia University in May and refused to be distracted from her purpose. In another letter, she told Miller that she was not the companion he was looking for. "Your letters make it very plain that you are in need of someone to fulfill the longings you have so eloquently expressed—(and practical needs too) someone to cook for you and mend your socks . . . You must understand and accept the fact that I am married to my art and will not yield for anything standing in the way of my work." This response only further inflamed Miller's passion. It did not help her argument that June had sent Miller a nude photograph of herself in a dancing pose.

Desperate to overcome June's resistance, Miller enlisted Harry Herschkowitz as pander to plead his case. After obtaining June's permission to give Herschkowitz her address and phone number, Miller put Herschkowitz on the scent. Herschkowitz called on June, seduced her, and then reported the results to Miller in a sequence that is straight out of *Tropic of Cancer*. He assured Miller that June's resistance was breaking down. "Ignore the returned letters. That was before I convinced her. Only a Jew could have handled this situation. You chose the right man for the job."

As Herschkowitz predicted, June changed her mind. After making her presentation at Columbia at the beginning of May, June telegrammed Miller that she was coming west. Herschkowitz covered his tracks in another letter to Miller, characterizing June as a narcissist who couldn't cook and was married to a soldier fighting in the war. He assured Miller that if June did not work out, he could recruit replacements. "If June fails (I can't see how) and if Edia [a backup] fails I will line up some more females. I'll have a string waiting in line from New York to Big Sur."

June arrived in Monterey in mid-May, a few days after Emil had come in from Alaska. Lynda Sargent drove Miller and Emil up to Monterey for a celebratory meeting at Jean Varda's Red Barn. Within three months, June was gone, dismayed by the primitive conditions and completely out of place in an environment that could not even supply her with the electricity she needed to play her dancing records. Near the end of his life, Miller fondly recalled his days with June Lancaster in a short essay titled "The Mail Order Bride":

> She had a good heart, a good soul, that girl. Unfortunately, the chemistry wasn't right for a long-lasting relationship. One day I came upon her unexpectedly in the forest. She was swinging through the trees like a circus acrobat in her leotards. A whole other aspect of her personality was revealed to me at that moment. The night before she left Big Sur she danced all night for me. She did magical dances, mystical, exotic dances from all over the world that nearly made me fall in love with her again and again and again.

LETTERS—TO FRIENDS AND SUPPORTERS, TO PUBLISHERS, TO AGENTS, to strangers, to fellow writers—played a central role in Henry Miller's development and survival as a writer. Corresponding with Bern Porter in the spring of 1944 about their various publishing projects, Miller appended a note about his letter writing that identified it as the source of his career. "My apprenticeship as a writer came about through the voluminous letters I wrote from as far back as I can remember. Certainly began when I was seventeen, after finishing high school. The earliest important correspondence was with my oldest friend Stanley J. Borowski of 'the old neighborhood' (the 14th Ward) Brooklyn, known as Williamsburg." The letters he wrote to Emil Schnellock from Paris during the early 1930s contained the seeds of his breakout novel *Tropic of Cancer*. Many passages in *Cancer* were lifted whole from these letters to Emil. Cut off from the outside world in Big Sur, Miller used letters as his lifeline. He promoted himself and his books, he bartered and begged for the means of survival, and he responded to the inquiries and appreciations of his readers through the mail.

To a few select correspondents, whom Miller trusted and regarded as his artistic peers, Miller wrote letters about his deepest concerns and ambitions as an author. The most important of these correspondents were Anaïs Nin, Lawrence Durrell, Alfred Perlès, and Wallace Fowlie. These writers Miller considered as his spiritual counterparts, artists whose judgments of his work he valued and whose confidences he shared. With Durrell and Perlès far away in a Europe engulfed by war, and with his relationship to Nin cooled by their rupture, Miller initiated a correspondence with Wallace Fowlie, a man whom he quickly came to regard as a confessor and spiritual advisor, roles Miller usually reserved for himself.

Fowlie was a professor of French literature who taught at Yale University. He had published an essay entitled "Narcissus" in *View* that prompted Miller to write him expressing his admiration. Fowlie, who had read and admired *Tropic of Cancer* and was trying to obtain a copy of *Tropic of Capricorn* for the Yale library, was flattered, and responded enthusiastically. He told Miller that his book *Clowns and Angels* was about to be published, and that he was writing a book about love to be called *The Clown's Grail*. Miller, who regarded himself as a clown and often painted himself in that guise, was intrigued. He urged Fowlie to stay in touch, saying, "I feel drawn to you," and offered to send him a watercolor as a gift.

Soon Miller was revealing to Fowlie his deepest concerns and desires as an artist. In January, barely two months after their correspondence began, Miller wrote: "What is coming over me strongly these last few years—due to very definite reasons, due largely to certain meetings with other men [here he may have been thinking of George Katsimbalis]—is the realization that the decalage between the writer and the artist must be overcome. I have no respect for the artist, however great, who does not practice his art in living . . . I think, though, I lack the supreme courage here. I feel that the artist in me is getting the better of the man. This is *one* of my problems."

This letter restates a theme that preoccupied Miller throughout his writing career: his desire to fuse art and reality. Miller knew that he had yet to achieve this state of grace, that for him his art remained a substitute for reality, a means of reaching states of being he could not reach simply by living.

To demonstrate his appreciation for Fowlie as a friend and fellow writer, Miller offered help in getting Fowlie's books published. He referred Fowlie to his British agent, Patience Ross, and urged Laughlin to read the manuscript of *The Clown's Grail*. Fowlie revealed his interest in writing a book on Rimbaud, a writer who greatly interested Miller. It is fair to say that during this period of Miller's life, Fowlie had replaced Nin as Miller's most intimate literary confidant. With his Big Sur support system now in place, Miller was ready to resume his central task, exploring and revealing himself through his writing.

5

A Writer in Big Sur

"My Own Star Is Rising."

What was the state of Miller's literary reputation as he began his sojourn in Big Sur and prepared to pick up his pen? Although Miller often expressed disdain for the opinions of editors, publishers, and critics—writing to his agent, John Slocum, a few months after his return from Greece, "I don't believe there exists such a public as the editors and publishers imagine"—in letters to friends and supporters like Huntington Cairns and Lawrence Durrell he revealed his sensitivity to being overlooked, undervalued, or misunderstood by the critics. And when a favorable notice or assessment appeared, he spread the word among his network and sent out copies, if he had them. Clearly, it mattered to Miller what the reading public thought of him.

The problem Miller faced was that much of the public perception of him was based on hearsay rather than direct experience of his work, due to the fact that the works that had generated the most admiration and discussion by critics, the "Paris" books, were largely unavailable to the general reader in the United States and England. Even in France, where the Tropics and *Black Spring* were readily available, they were available only in English, which meant that the French reading public was as much in the dark about them as were the English and the Americans.

This situation was all the more frustrating for Miller because, among the literati who were able to obtain copies of Miller's banned books and reviewed them in the major American and English literary organs, Miller's writing was widely admired and respected.

Miller's idol, the French writer Blaise Cendrars, had bestowed his blessing on *Tropic of Cancer* in a brief French review that appeared shortly after the novel was issued in Paris. In 1938, the eminent American critic Edmund Wilson wrote a favorable review of the novel in the *New Republic*, lauding Miller for producing "the most remarkable book which, as far as my reading goes, has come from [the Left Bank] in many years. *Tropic of Cancer* is a good piece of writing; and it has also a sort of historical importance." A year later, reviewing *Tropic of Capricorn* in the *Nation*, Paul Rosenfeld called Miller "a free and important author" and remarked the "grand qualities" of his prose style. "His prose at its most characteristic is elevated in pitch, lyrical, dithyrambic. The sometimes brutal style is prevalently high-colored; spare, but in many instances precious and magnificent." In 1940, Herbert Muller wrote an assessment of Miller for the *Kenyon Review* based on his readings of the Tropics, *Black Spring*, and *Max and the White Phagocytes*. Comparing Miller favorably to D. H. Lawrence and Thomas Wolfe, Muller observed, "Few writers today seem so intensely alive." Muller downplayed Miller's obscenity: "It is usually hearty and healthy, often a source of rich humor, never merely pornographic . . ."

Philip Rahv underscored the problem of forming an accurate opinion of Miller's work when he wrote in the *New Republic* in 1941 that Miller should be judged on the basis of his Paris books. Rahv saw Miller as a "desperado" whose extreme estrangement from society "makes of him a natural anarchist" and "biographer of the hobo-intellectual." Alfred Kazin, in his seminal study of American literature, *On Native Grounds*, linked Miller to Faulkner and Thomas Wolfe, characterizing them as "the epic recorders of demoralization and collapse, specialists in doom."

Miller also had supporters and admirers among the literary elite of England. George Orwell in an essay titled "Inside the Whale" (an allusion to Miller's search for the "cosmic womb") published in 1940, noted Miller's voice and use of ordinary English. "English is treated as a spoken language, but spoken *without fear*, i.e., without fear of rhetoric or of the unusual or poetical word . . . It is a flowing, swelling prose, a prose with rhythms in it, something quite different from the flat cautious statements and snack-bar dialects that are now in fashion." Miller's voice he found "a friendly American voice, with no humbug in it, no moral purpose, merely an implicit assumption that we are all alike." Orwell praised Miller as "the only imaginative prose-writer of the slightest value who has appeared among the English speaking races for some years past."

Sir Herbert Read, "England's leading critic," found Miller's body of work "possibly the most significant contribution to the literature of our time... He is never obscene for obscenity's sake—there is 'effort' about his obscenity—it is all part of the process of realization, a natural conse-quence of his devastating honesty, and also of his vitality, his *joie de vivre*."

The most profound and penetrating evaluation of Miller at this stage of his life and career was written by the English poet and critic Nicholas Moore. His monograph, entitled simply *Henry Miller*, was published in 1943. He viewed Miller not simply as a writer, but as "a WHOLE man," a man who celebrates life in all its manifestations and contradictions, whose view of man's experience is essentially pos-itive and affirmative despite the degradations he exposes and ridicules. "What he is concerned with is the heart of man, his mind, and his soul, and anything else he may possess - - - his inner possessions ... And it is because he is so alive to all these things that Miller is such a great writer and such a great man." Moore saw Miller breaking through to a new kind of novel with *Tropic of Cancer,* a novel whose form was organic, not artificial, structured like a jazz improvisation rather than around a contrived plot, imitating the random stream of life, embracing all, accepting all. Moore lamented the fact that Miller's most important books were not readily available to the ordinary reader. "For he is a common man himself, and he speaks in the language of the common man, a language that in its full richness is not permitted in print... It is unfortunate that for this reason his best books cannot be published either in America, the country of his birth, or in this country."

Miller was so pleased with Moore's estimate of him that he alerted his friends to the existence of the monograph and urged them to order it from the London publisher or from the Gotham Book Mart in New York, which had bought three hundred copies.

But the existence of a body of favorable criticism of Miller's work in the United States and England did not help Miller reach his intended audience, did not spread his vision of an alternative approach to the problems of living in the modern world, an approach based on self-transformation. The books by Miller that were available to the man and woman in the street—*The Cosmological Eye, The Colossus of Maroussi*, and *Wisdom of the Heart*—were not Miller at full strength. They offered a milder, more temperate Miller, Miller in his more didactic mode. And although these books were widely reviewed in many metropolitan newspapers as well as in literary periodicals like *The New Yorker* and *Partisan Review*, the reviewers invariably compared them with the banned books, whetting readers' appetites for products they could not obtain. Sales of the New Directions releases were small and yielded a meager royalty stream for Miller. It was no wonder that Miller vented his frustration in a letter sent from Big Sur to his friend and Beverly Glen neighbor Lawrence Powell, the UCLA librarian: "Wonderful country, America. Fucks you up at every turn."

BEFORE LEAVING BEVERLY GLEN FOR THE CENTRAL COAST EARLY IN 1944, Miller had set in motion an ambitious program of writing and publishing that would occupy him throughout most of the year. He was orchestrating a campaign to get his work, both his writing and his painting, to as wide an audience in America and England as he could, absent the support of any major publishing houses. His two primary agents in this campaign were James Laughlin and Bern Porter, but he was also getting assistance from George Leite for publishing short articles and advertisements for forthcoming books in *Circle*, and from Judson Crews in distributing copies of his books. And when Emil White arrived in Big Sur in May, he collaborated with Porter and Leite in assembling and circulating Miller's work.

Laughlin had Miller working on several projects. He had advanced $350 for *Sunday After the War*, the new collection of Miller's writing that would include three fragments from his major work in progress, *The Rosy Crucifixion*, as well as a number of short pieces previously published in small periodicals like *Circle*. He had also agreed to publish *The Air-Conditioned Nightmare* if Doubleday & Doran would relinquish their rights, which they did in August. And Laughlin had raised the possibility of issuing *Black Spring* (with illustrations by Abe

Rattner), if another New Directions title, *Les Chants de Maldoror* by the Comte de Lautréamont, passed the censor. Laughlin was also encouraging Miller to undertake a translation of the French poet Arthur Rimbaud's *Season in Hell.* Finally, Laughlin said that if Colt Press was financially unable to bring out a second edition of *The Colossus of Maroussi*, he would publish it through New Directions.

Additionally, plans were afoot by Ben Abramson of Argus Bookshop in Chicago to issue *Aller Retour New York* and a black-market edition of *Tropic of Capricorn* (a project that was aborted when the printer lost his nerve and melted all the type). As for his painting, Miller had two watercolor shows scheduled, one in Washington, DC, being organized by Caresse Crosby, to be followed by another in London organized by Miller's editor there, M. J. Tambimuttu. And Miller had arranged for two printers from Fullerton, California— George Barrows and Norman Holve—to produce an expensive ($50) four-color book of his watercolors accompanied by his text *The* "The Angel Is My Watermark." Only twenty copies of this book were printed in January before Barrows-Holve broke up.

These multiple projects—some of which required Miller to write, some to paint, others to coordinate through his correspondence—kept him working at a frantic pace throughout the spring and summer of his first year in Big Sur.

During the spring Miller was trying to finish the manuscript for *The Air-Conditioned Nightmare* while Laughlin pressed him to assemble the pieces for *Sunday After the War.* At the same time, Porter badgered him to produce a new article for *The Plight of the Creative Artist in the United States of America* (the collection of Miller's begging letters that lamented America's neglect of its artists), and to write an antiwar statement that Porter intended to issue as a pamphlet for sale at $1.25. He also needed Miller's help in selecting fragments from his letters to Emil Schnellock that dealt with watercolor painting and in choosing Miller watercolors for black and white reproduction in *Semblance of a Devoted Past.* And when Miller learned about the tribute book in March (Fowlie had inadvertently tipped him off), he suggested contributors and wrote to introduce them to Porter. He had also, before "Harry Kovarr" cut him off, urged Porter to approach Anaïs Nin with a proposal to bring out her diary using her $100 share of his $200 monthly stipend. The demands on his time were extraordinary. It was no wonder that early in July he wrote to Laughlin, "I'm right down to bone and muscle."

By then he had completed *Sunday After the War*, which New Directions published in August, and his antiwar tract, *Murder the Murderer*, which Porter issued in October.

Sunday After the War offered readers a medley of pieces that showed the range of styles and subjects of the mature Miller. These selections are built around the major themes found in his earlier work that continue to preoccupy him: his belief in the sanctity and limitless potential of the individual; his insistence on imagination expressed through art as the means to individual growth through the apprehension of reality; his conviction that Western civilization, especially in its American form, stifles the life of the imagination and substitutes for it the living death of "security" through material comfort; his belief that Western civilization is therefore doomed and his prediction that from its collapse a new kind of man, capable of living in harmony with himself and with the cosmos, will emerge; his view of himself, and a sparse few other "aristocrats of the spirit" whom he identifies, as the forerunners of this new planetary being.

In the fragments from *The Rosy Crucifixion* that he selected for inclusion in *Sunday After the War*, Miller declares his credo as a writer: his belief that the act of writing, by engaging his imagination, frees him from "his false way of life" and brings him to a state of realization in which he feels at one with the world. "Through art then one finally establishes contact with reality: that is the great discovery . . . The world has *not* to be put in order: the world *is* order incarnate. It is for us to put ourselves in unison with this order, to know what is the world order in contradistinction to the wishful thinking orders which we seek to impose.on one another. . . The great joy of the artist is to become aware of a higher order of things, to recognize by the compulsive and spontaneous manipulation of his own impulses the resemblance between human creations and what is called 'divine creations' " [sic].

Miller believed that every man has the potential to discover and activate this "divine" capacity, and that it is every man's responsibility to do this, to find himself. "Every man, when he gets quiet, when he becomes desperately honest with himself, is capable of uttering profound truths. We all derive from the same source." His ultimate goal, Miller declares, and the goal of every great artist, is not merely to create art but to live imaginatively. "We are all guilty of crime," Miller writes, "the great crime of not living life to the full. But we are all potentially free ... Imagination is everything. Imagination is the voice of daring. If there is anything godlike about God, it is that He has dared to imagine everything." The reason that Miller loathes work, the activity that would bind him to society, is that it stifles the life of the imagination. While many artists might consider the making of their art to be "work," Miller refuses to place it in that category. "Work, it seemed to me even at the threshold of life, is an activity reserved for the dullard. It is the very opposite of creation, which is play, and which just because it has no raison d'être other than itself is the supreme motivating power in life. . . The world would only begin to get something of value from me the moment I stopped being a serious member of society and became—*myself*."

In *Sunday After the War* Miller revives his argument with America, so unsparingly expressed in *The Air-Conditioned Nightmare*, as an environment that is inhospitable to art, to artists, to the life of the imagination, in short, to life itself as Miller believes it should be lived. Miller had been invited by his friend Parker Tyler to write the preface to Tyler's book on the American movie industry, *Hollywood's Hallucination*. When Tyler's publisher rejected the preface, Miller included it in *Sunday After the War*. Miller sees in Hollywood films a reflection of the vapidity and emptiness of American life. He calls the newsreel voice "the anonymous voice of the anonymous herd ... The peculiar feature of this news voice is that no matter what it narrates it never loses its toneless luster ... To glide from the fall of Paris to the latest metal clip garter not the slightest modulation is demanded."

Miller praises Tyler's criticism of the industry because "it overleaps the subject and indicts not only the sponsors and producers of this form of entertainment, indicts not only the audience which suffers it to be, but levels an unanswerable condemnation at our whole way of life."

In "A Death Letter to Emil" Miller tells his Brooklyn friend, "I am a man of the old world, a seed that was transplanted by the wind and could not blossom in the Africa of America . . . My soul is not an economic soul, as is the fashion in souls today. . . I could not exist among the sanitary, sterile instruments of the economic soul. . . America can have no Renaissance until it has tasted death. I have had my Renaissance."

The personal death that Miller refers to here is the death of his Brooklyn self, the self that was married to Beatrice, fathered Barbara, and worked as the employment manager for Western Union. This was the self that June Mansfield eradicated through the torments that Miller revealed in another of *The Rosy Crucifixion* fragments published in *Sunday After the War*, an account that leaves him completely humiliated, barking like a dog. Because Miller believes that individual destiny is the key to social evolution, he insists that society must undergo its own form of death before rebirth into a higher plane of existence can occur. In the essay "Of Art and the Future," he predicts an apocalyptic end to Western civilization and the emergence of a new cultural pattern from the East. "Before the present conflict is terminated it is altogether likely that we shall see un-leashed the deadly secret weapon so often hinted at on all sides. . . [And] that the men of science will be coerced into yielding up the secret now in their possession I have no doubt." This prediction—borne out when the United States dropped two atomic bombs on the civilian population of Japan—showed that Miller understood the virulent direction that Western civilization was taking through its elevation of the machine over the human. Miller foresaw a chaotic future marked by widespread revolution and mass slaughter, followed by the rise of nations in the east, China, and India. "Then, and only then, will the embryonic man of the new order appear, the man who has no feeling of class, caste, color or country, the man who has no need of possessions, no use for money, no archaic prejudices about the sanctity of the home or of marriage with its accompanying treadmill of divorce. A totally new conception of individuality will be born, one in which the collective life is the dominant note. In short, for the first time since the dawn of history, men will serve one another, first out of an enlightened self-interest, and finally out of a greater conception of love."

If this new man resembled Henry Miller—unemployed, twice-divorced, father of a child he abandoned, isolated from the American mainstream in his Big Sur cabin—he was not the only road to the future. There was also D. H. Lawrence.

Miller had not abandoned his intention, initiated by Jack Kahane as a positioning strategy for the publication of *Tropic of Cancer*, to produce a study of D. H. Lawrence. In *Sunday After the War*, Miller published "Shadowy Monomania," an essay compiled from notes on Lawrence he had made in Paris. In this essay, Miller heralds Lawrence as the prototype of the "new man," the man who can lead humanity into the future by his example. Miller is, by implication, a counterpart to Lawrence, if not his successor. Miller begins by using Lawrence to clarify the meaning of obscenity, a label that continued to haunt Miller's writing and his career. Referring to *Lady Chatterley's Lover*, Miller observes, "The book is obscene and there is no justification for it. Because it requires none. And the miracles of Jesus are obscene. Because there is no justification for them either. Life is miraculous and obscene, and neither is there any justification for life . . . In its obscenity lies its great purity, its miraculous, its sacred quality." Underlying this doctrine is Miller's belief that modern man has lost contact with his true self because he denies and suppresses his deepest instincts and desires, which provide the energy and stimulation for his imagination. He saw Lawrence as an artist who sought to free man from his fear of the instinctual, sensuous life. This fear man has passed down through history in institutions, such as the church, that have codified behavior based on a set of ideals. Miller sees this inherited fear as the root of modern man's alienation. "The evil of modern times lies precisely in this, that men cannot have any real, true relationship with their fellow men. There is sterility, an atrophy, of the affective self. Man's sensuous nature is blighted at the roots."

Miller saw Lawrence, and perhaps himself, as a man who had become a scapegoat in the service of mankind by providing an example of the sacrifice needed to achieve personal fulfillment. "Through the saviors we have life, because through them we cast out corruption, rid ourselves of the devastating sense of guilt, of sin, and of responsibility."

Apart from restating Miller's belief in the central role that art plays in the well-lived life, *Sunday After the War* also extends a helping hand to his benefactress and former lover Anaïs Nin. The collection reproduces two letters he wrote in 1933 expressing his admiration for her diaries as "A tremendous revelation of the evolution of an artist."

MILLER REGARDED WAR AS THE ULTIMATE EXPRESSION OF ANTI-LIFE. His unequivocal opposition had drawn to him a number of young men, some of them aspiring artists, as literary helpers. One of them, Bern Porter, urged him to issue a statement of his position. Not surprisingly, Miller's views on war reflect his belief in the inviolability of the individual human conscience and his condemnation of mass movements. War results because men surrender their individuality to the will of the herd, a herd that is manipulated to pursue the interests of a privileged few.

Murder the Murderer, a pamphlet issued by Porter in one thousand copies and sold for $1.25, has two parts. Part I, "An Open Letter to Fred Perlès," was written in 1941 but never sent. It was Miller's response to a letter from Perlès, who had moved to England, become a British citizen, and joined the army, in which Perlès faulted Miller for his "detachment" in taking his American tour while his country was at war. Miller replies that the ultimate authority of the individual conscience justifies his detachment from state-sanctioned mass murder.

Miller's argument against involvement in the war effort is based on his belief that wars are fought to advance the economic interests of a vested few whose will to power denies the individual his freedom of choice. "It is the minority which sponsors war, and this minority always represents the vested interests . . . The vast majority of people in the world to-day not only believe but know the sole reason for war, in this day and age, is economic rivalry." Miller insists on the right of the individual to obey his own conscience and refuse involvement in war. "What I protest against, and what I will never admit to be right, is forcing a man against his will and his conscience to sacrifice his life for a cause which he does not believe in."

Miller asserts that his detachment, far from being a fault, is actually the highest form of virtue, practiced by the world's greatest spiritual

leaders. "The figures who have most influenced the world all practiced detachment: I mean men like Lao tse, Gautama the Buddha, Jesus
Christ, St. Francis of Assisi, and such like." Miller traces his own detachment to his stay in Greece. "The visit fortified me inwardly to a degree
beyond anything I had ever known before . . . In Greece I came to
grips with myself and made my peace with the world . . . I succeeded in
detaching myself completely . . . I finally became a citizen of the world."

Miller made this supranationalism into an ideal world order that
would come about only through the effort of each individual to
become free, to self-actualize. "There can be no civilized effort until
the organism embodying the ideal becomes world-wide. . . The fact
that we are all alike before God has to be demonstrated in practice."

In Part I of *Murder the Murderer* Miller defends his detachment
and disengagement from the war on the principle of individual freedom. In Part II, he argues for the supremacy of individual freedom,
whether of conscience or of expression, over state authority and
implies that militarism and censorship of his work emanate from the
same repressive animus that dominates American life. He cites distinguished American thinkers such as Thoreau and Supreme Court
Justice Louis Brandeis in support of his position. Thoreau: "There
will never be a really free and enlightened state until the state comes
to recognize the individual as a higher and independent power, from
which all its own power and authority are derived, and treats him
accordingly." Brandeis: "No danger flowing from free speech can be
deemed clear and present, unless the incidence of evil apprehended
is so imminent that it may befall before there is opportunity for full
discussion. Only an emergency can justify repression. Such must be
the rule if authority is to be reconciled with freedom."

Miller sees America's willingness to go to war and its willingness
to censor free speech as driven by a deeply rooted impulse toward
conformity and control that springs from greed and fear. "We are paying now for the crimes committed by our ancestors. Our forefathers
when first they came to this country, were hailed as gods. To our dis-
grace, they behaved as demons. They asked for gold instead of grace . . .
We have emphasized gold instead of opportunity . . . Power and riches,
not for all Americans—that would be bad enough!—but for the few."

Miller refuses to participate in a society that suppresses individual liberty. He accepts his role as an outsider, one of a small number of people, like Thoreau, or Lawrence, or Christ, whose ability to self-govern eliminates their need for, or obligation to, society. "Men of good will need no government to regulate their affairs. In every age there is a very small minority which lives without thought of, or desire for, government . . . They lie outside the cultural pattern of the times . . . They are evolved beings." Miller views himself as being among the spiritually elite of his day, a man in possession of himself, an adept who is attuned to a higher moral order than the vast majority of men. And until all men become adept at living war will not cease. Christ is Miller's touchstone. "The Christian world has welcomed every excuse to fight in the name of Christ who came to bring peace on earth. There can be no end to this repetitious pattern until each and every one of us become as Christ, until belief and devotion transform our words into deeds and thus make of myth reality." In these words are echoes of Miller's oft-stated wish to create art not through language but through living, to make his life a work of art.

Though *Sunday After the War* was not widely reviewed in the American press—only five metropolitan newspapers took notice of it—it did receive favorable and insightful commentary from three distinguished critics who were following Miller's career. Edmund Wilson, writing in *The New Yorker*, found the book "very representative of Miller and full of interpretations, visions, impressions, of a kind that no one else is writing." He compared Miller's prose to the writing of Thomas De Quincey and John Ruskin. Nicola Chiaromonte, reviewing for the *New Republic*, praised Miller's humanism. "I don't know any other writer who has succeeded in completely humanizing the writer as character, stripping him of any special prestige, making of him a true Everyman who wins his laurels, if any, only in actual competition with other individuals for the possession of human qualities and for the enjoyment of whatever there is to be enjoyed in life."

But it was Miller's friend Wallace Fowlie who offered the most penetrating assessment of Miller the writer. He called Miller "a leading example of a special kind of writer produced only by our age. I mean the writer who is essentially seer and prophet, whose immediate ancestor was Rimbaud and whose leading exponent was D. H. Lawrence. The prophet and the visionary is the man who daily lives the metaphysical problems of his age . . . The metaphysical torment of today which Miller seems to feel the most persistently is the loss throughout the world of the great fact of living."

But if *Sunday After the War* did not bring Miller to many new readers, it did, through a strange turn of fate, provide the link to a major new chapter in his life, marriage and fatherhood.

BY MID-AUGUST 1944, the mood of euphoria that had settled on Miller as he arranged his new life in Big Sur had faded, and he was again restless, writing to friends of his intention to return to Europe as soon as the war ended. He seems to have been badly disheartened by the rapid failure of his relationship with his mail-order lover, June Lancaster, who departed early in August after staying with him little more than two months. He wrote despondently to Fowlie, "It didn't pan out. We remain good friends, however (which means there was no passion in it). This morning I made a rapid mental summary of all the failures of heart I've met with—a shockingly big list. Yet nothing seems more important to me than love, unless it be truth. I also feel I shall be leaving here in another month or two. Where to I don't know yet."

Later in the month he wrote in a similar vein to Emil Schnellock. "My great problem now is time. Don't have enough time in one day to do all I have to do. Especially since I am alone again, keeping house, cooking, washing, hauling, etc. . . . And Bern with his proofs and his questionnaires! . . . If I see that the war will end suddenly, and if I don't go to Mexico, I will jump to Fredericksburg and pay you a long visit—before hopping a boat to England. I think I can live in Europe on my English royalties." That Miller was contemplating living among the English, whom he loathed and who had humiliated him when he tried to enter their country without adequate funds, shows the depths to which his spirits had sunk.

As the reference to "Bern" suggests, Miller's relationship with Porter had begun to fray. Already, the impracticality of Porter's publishing "Ponzi scheme," whereby proceeds of one publication would pay for the printing of the next, was becoming apparent. In

July Porter wrote Miller with the news that he had used up all his funds in the preparations for bringing out *Semblance of a Devoted Past* and had gone into debt. He also informed Miller that printing of the book was being held up because the printer was balking at some of Miller's language. Miller offered to forego all his royalties from Porter's publishing projects until his debts were paid, and he fumed about efforts by printers and even paper manufacturers to censor his words. He also attempted to help Porter financially by giving him watercolors he could sell for his own pocket.

Meanwhile, friction had developed among Miller's little band of disciples. Porter, a frequent visitor to Big Sur over the summer, and Leite, who had moved to Anderson Creek with his family to be near Miller, were feuding over editorial control of *Circle*. And Emil White, jealous of his position as Miller's right hand, was distrustful of Porter and refused to cooperate with him. Miller had also been receiving complaints from his friends who had offered to write essays for *The Happy Rock* about Porter's peremptory manner with them. Miller was also annoyed by Porter's often mysterious whereabouts, caused by his involvement with the Manhattan Project. By early October, Miller's patience had worn thin. He wrote to Porter, "Don't want to hear any more about books until I see them in the flesh." Porter's unsuitability for the complex publishing ventures he had offered to undertake on Miller's behalf was remarked in correspondence between Ben Abramson and Lawrence Powell. Powell had expressed to Abramson his concern that Porter was not a competent bibliographer. Abramson agreed, calling Miller "a babe" for getting involved with Porter. He wrote to Powell in September, "Porter seems to be a pleasant but rather unreliable person. I have never met him, but it seems to me that he is undertaking things that are far beyond his financial power."

At this time, Miller was preparing to travel east to visit his mother. In September he had received word that she was suffering from cancer and would have to undergo an operation. Miller left for New York on a trip that would last three months and profoundly change the direction of his life.

6

Marriage and Family

"A Wonderful New Period"

Miller found on his arrival in New York that his mother was not as ill as he had feared, and he took the opportunity to visit a number of his East Coast friends. He wrote a note to Anaïs Nin, but her chilly reply discouraged him from seeing her. Within a week of arriving he met, through his pander Harry Herschkowitz, Janina Martha Lepska, the woman who would become his third wife and mother of two of his children.

Lepska was a twenty-two-year-old college student who had graduated from Bryn Mawr in June. A brilliant scholar, she had won a fellowship to study philosophy at Yale University and was preparing to move to New Haven from her home in New Jersey when she met Miller. Lepska and her sister, Helene, frequented the artistic scene in Greenwich Village, where Helene had met Harry Herschkowitz. Herschkowitz had read to Lepska one of *The Rosy Crucifixion* excerpts from *Sunday After the War*. Herschkowitz reported to Miller that Lepska had wept at Miller's description of his dog's life with June Mansfield, whereupon Herschkowitz gave her the copy of the book as well as a watercolor Miller had sent him. She had previously heard of Miller from Paul Weiss, one of her professors at Bryn Mawr, who owned a copy of *Tropic of Cancer*, corresponded with Miller, and occasionally sent him money.

When Miller arrived in New York, Herschkowitz arranged a dinner date with the two sisters. Lepska, thirty-one years Miller's junior, was smitten by his intellectual brilliance, his iconoclasm, and his apparently romantic life in Big Sur. Miller had been invited by Paul Weiss to visit him at Bryn Mawr, and he asked Lepska to join him. Their romance quickly blossomed. After the Bryn Mawr visit, Lepska returned home to pack for her year at Yale, and Miller went to Virginia to stay as the guest of Caresse Crosby. He and Lepska stayed in touch by telegram. By October 11, Miller had decided he wanted Lepska as his mate. He wrote to Fowlie at Yale, "I may take Lepska with me to California. It's come to that already. Here I put my whole trust and confidence in you. I wish her no harm. I want to open new worlds for her. But, should you feel I am doing her an injury, I give you permission to dissuade her—in the name of God."

Fowlie did not intervene, and Miller moved forward with his plans. He had scheduled visits to Richard Osborn in Bridgeport, Connecticut, and to Professor Herbert West at Dartmouth, where he gave a talk to a boisterous and somewhat unfriendly audience angered by his pacifist views. Through Fowlie, he had been invited by Henri Peyre, Chairman of Yale's French Department, to meet with a group of graduate students. During this visit, Miller asked Lepska to marry him and come with him to California.

This was a momentous decision for Lepska because she feared the impact on her family, and especially on her father, should she give up her fellowship and abandon her studies. Her family had emigrated from Poland, where her father had been a career military officer actively involved in the country's nationalist movement. He had rebuilt their lives in America and held out high hopes for his daughters' futures. Lepska especially seemed on a path to fulfill his dreams for them. When Miller proposed to her, she asked him to wait until she had completed her studies. But when Miller said, "It's now or never, Lepska," she resigned her fellowship, went to New York to stay with her sister, and broke the news to her father and mother. Her father was devastated and never forgave Miller.

Looking back on her decision sixty-four years later, Lepska said, "I was naïve. My knowledge came from books, not experience. It was Miller's books, his writings, that entrapped me. I could play a part in that. Miller described the magical beauty of Big Sur. I was in love with him, and saw only what I wanted to see."

Miller took Lepska to Fredericksburg to meet Emil Schnellock. They planned to marry before they returned to California, and Miller wrote again to Fowlie, asking for his blessing on their union, which Fowlie bestowed. They also spent time in Washington, DC, as guests of Caresse Crosby, during which Cairns arranged for Miller to give readings from *Black Spring* and *Tropic of Capricorn* at the Library of Congress.

In December, they traveled west by train to Boulder, Colorado, where they stayed for a month as guests of Gilbert and Margaret Neiman. Gilbert had obtained a position as professor of Spanish at the University of Colorado. Miller and Lepska were married on December 18, with Gilbert serving as their witness. Miller was elated as he prepared to leave Boulder for Big Sur with Lepska in tow. He wrote to Fowlie again early in January, "I feel a wonderful new period opening up. Also, a great change in my style. To the joyous, the imaginative, the world of dream and truth and reality, in the best sense. I long to 'dispatch' that program I laid out [the plan formed in 1927 to tell the story of his marriage to June Mansfield in *The Rosy Crucifixion*] and get to the new level—the 'open' level, I'd call it. I'm sick of dragging my old (unreal) carcass around, in novels." Miller was ready to shed a skin, to take another step toward the objective of turning his life into art.

During the next two years, Miller consolidated his position in Big Sur. His life took on a semblance of normalcy, thanks in great part to Lepska, who brought order and structure into their home. Miller became a family man again, bought property for the first time, and saw his European audience expand significantly after the liberation of France at the end of the war. However, his readership and reputation in America continued to lag significantly behind Europe. He made no headway against the censorship of his Paris books, sales of his New Directions titles were slow, and money for the basic necessities of his household was in short supply. A substantial sum of royalties had accumulated in his Paris account thanks to brisk sales of the Tropics and *Black Spring* to American servicemen, but the French exchange laws prevented his agents in France from converting his francs to dollars and sending funds to Miller. He continued to rely on sales of his watercolors, charitable donations of cash, food, and supplies from friends and well-wishers to supplement his meager royalty payments from Laughlin. His publishing ventures with Porter, Leite, and Crews had only succeeded in putting these amateur publishers into debt, and Miller eventually broke with each of them. Laughlin too revealed to Miller that New Directions was barely breaking even and paid him no salary.

In February 1945, as he settled into Keith Evans's cabin on Partington Ridge with Lepska, Miller wrote contentedly to Lawrence Durrell about his new life circumstances. "I have a wonderful cabin, you know, dirt cheap—ten dollars a month. I have a young wife (21), a baby on the way probably, food in the larder, wine a discretion, hot sulphur baths down the road, books galore, a phonograph coming, a radio also coming, good kerosene lamps, a wood stove, an open fireplace, a shower, and plenty of sun, and of course the Pacific Ocean, which is always empty . . . This is the first good break I've had since I'm living in America. I open the door in the morning, look towards the sun rising over the mountains, and then bless the whole world, birds, flowers and beasts included. After I have moved my bowels I take the hound for a walk. Then a stint of writing, then lunch, then a siesta, then watercolors, then correspondence, then a book, then a fuck, then a nap, then dinner, and so to bed early and all's well except when I visit the dentist now and then."

Lepska enabled Miller to enjoy this simple but comfortable routine that freed him from many of the chores that would otherwise have deprived him of writing time. After breakfast, Miller would ascend the road to the home of their neighbor, Jean Wharton, who had offered Miller a room to use as a writing studio. Lepska maintained the household, cutting firewood, keeping a fire going twenty-four hours, heating water for the shower, cooking on the wood-burning stove. Every Monday, Wednesday, and Friday she would walk the mile down Partington Ridge to the highway to collect groceries from Jake the postman, who brought them from Monterey. She would return with their parcels and Miller's correspondence, much of which she now answered—incurring the jealousy of Miller's erstwhile amanuensis, Emil White. She walked six miles to the hot springs at Murphy's (now Esalen) to do their laundry. She became skilled at putting three meals on the table every day without the convenience of a refrigerator, a pantry, or a nearby grocery store. Miller would return to their house for lunch, after which he would resume writing or, if mail had arrived, go through the letters hoping for checks. He answered mail from his regular correspondents: Alfred Perlès, Lawrence Durrell, Emil Schnellock, the Neimans, Abe Rattner, and all his publishers. The Millers entertained frequently in the evening—the Vardas, Lynda Sargent, Jean Wharton—and hosted occasional visitors, including Frieda Lawrence and her lover Angelo, and Laughlin, who fell in love with Big Sur and asked Miller to be on the lookout for a property he might buy.

Miller's writing projects at this time included continuing work on his major opus, *The Rosy Crucifixion*, and an essay on the French symbolist poet Arthur Rimbaud that he was writing for Laughlin. By his own account, Miller had first been exposed to Rimbaud in 1927 when he was living in a ménage à trios in Brooklyn with June and her lesbian lover, Jean Kronski, whom Miller detested. Kronski was immersed in Rimbaud, a fact that gave Miller reason not to read him. Then in 1943, while living in Beverly Glen with John Dudley, Miller read a translation of Rimbaud's *A Season in Hell* as well as Enid Starkie's biography of the poet and "was overwhelmed, tongue-tied. It seemed to me that I had never read of a more accursed existence than Rimbaud's. I forgot completely about my own sufferings, which far outweighed his."

A year later, Miller was corresponding with Wallace Fowlie about Fowlie's intent to write a study of Rimbaud and suggested that Fowlie submit his manuscript to Laughlin. Encouraged by Laughlin, Miller had also begun work on the translation of *Une Saison en Enfer* that he had been contemplating. But he found himself unequal to the task of translating Rimbaud's verse ("Words like *charité, esprit*, etc. slay me. How to render them?" he writes Fowlie), and decided to undertake a critical study of Rimbaud instead.

Miller was drawn to Rimbaud as a counterpart, a fellow seer who carried a vision of an alternate reality that could only be reached through art but that he longed to experience in life. Miller saw many parallels between Rimbaud's life and artistic mission and his own. His study of Rimbaud is therefore useful not so much for what it tells us about Rimbaud as for what it reveals about Miller's perceptions of himself as an artist and a man at this stage of his life.

Miller wrote his Rimbaud study in two parts. Part I was completed in July 1945 and published a year later in *New Directions 9*, an annual anthology of writing selected by Laughlin. Part II was completed in May 1946 and published in 1949 in *New Directions 11*. The two essays were subsequently combined, arranged in reverse order, and published by New Directions in 1956 as *The Time of the Assassins*, a phrase borrowed from Rimbaud. Throughout the essays, Miller emphasizes his affinity for Rimbaud. "Why is it, I ask myself, that I adore Rimbaud above all other writers? . . . In Rimbaud I see myself as in a mirror." His purpose in performing the study, he tells us, "is to indicate certain affinities, analogies, correspondences and repercussions." What follows is a catalogue of similarities between the doomed poet and Miller that comprises an exercise in self-analysis through which Miller discloses his essential characteristics as man and artist.

The central link between them is their relationship to their mothers. Both of them suffered under the strictures of cold, puritanical mothers who denied them affection and imposed on them values and expectations drawn from a bourgeois society they grew to despise and reject. "Like Madame Rimbaud, my mother was the Northern type, cold, critical, proud, unforgiving, and puritanical . . . My natural temperament was that of a kind, joyous, open-hearted individual— as a youngster, I was often referred to as 'an angel.' But the demon of revolt had taken possession of me at a very early age. It was my mother who implanted it in me. It was against her, against all that she represented, that I directed my uncontrollable energy."

Miller's sense of alienation from his mother led to his complete rejection of the world she inhabited and the values she espoused. His life became a repudiation of all that she stood for. "Like Rimbaud, I too began at an early age to cry: 'Death to God!' It was death to everything which the parents endorsed or approved of . . . Like Rimbaud, I hated the place I was born in; I will hate it till my dying day. My earliest impulse is to break loose from the home, from the city I detest, from the country and its citizens with whom I find nothing in common."

Later in the essay, after pointing out many other similarities between him and Rimbaud that flowed from their estrangement from the mother, Miller describes the devastating consequences of this loss. On both of them the devouring mother inflicted a wound that permanently damaged their capacity to love. Miller describes how, following Rimbaud's death, his mother denied her son the honor of a ceremonial funeral. "What a mother! The very incarnation of stupidity, bigotry, pride and stubbornness. It was she who thrust him out into the world, she who denied him, betrayed him, persecuted him . . . She even robbed him of that privilege which every Frenchman craves—the pleasure of having a good funeral . . . His revolt from her tyranny and stupidity converted him into a solitary. His affective nature completely maimed, he was forever incapable of giving or receiving love. He knew only how to oppose will to will As the revolutionary, he seeks desperately for an ideal society in which he can staunch the wound of separation. This is the mortal wound from which he never recovers." Miller links this rupture from the mother to his own inability to feel a connection, an otherness, with the world around him. The missing mother becomes "the gnawing secret [that] continues to eat me away . . . And what is the nature of this secret? I can only say it has to do with the mothers. I feel that it was the same with Lawrence and with Rimbaud. All the rebelliousness which I share with them derives from this problem, which as nearly as I can express it, means the search for one's true link with humanity. One finds it neither in the personal life nor in the collective life, if one is of this type. One is unadaptable to the point of madness."

Miller traces many other traits that he shares with Rimbaud to this rift from the mother. Both men despised their native land and the shared values of its citizens, and both became nomads who wandered for many years in search of a home (Miller was fifty-three when he settled in Big Sur; Rimbaud ran away from home at age sixteen and wandered Europe and the Middle East for ten years before settling in Aden, Yemen); at an early age both men suffered disappointments in love with "the girl with violet eyes" from which they never fully recovered; both men had a loathing for work and held a variety of unsatisfying menial jobs; both men struggled with tormenting intimate relationships that yielded major artistic works; both men went to Paris to seek their literary fortunes. And significantly for Miller, who believed in the existence of a brotherhood of spiritual adepts spanning the ages, Rimbaud died six weeks before Miller's birth.

Miller also found many points of similarity to Rimbaud as an artist and a thinker. Both men rejected traditional literary forms and language and sought a new vocabulary and framework to express their vision. Both men exhibited in their work a fascination with aspects of life regarded by conventional society as seamy or sordid—prostitutes, outcasts, and misfits in the social realm, instinctual drives and body processes in the personal realm—and employed shock and outrage to jolt their readers into awareness. They shared a belief that the prevailing order of society was doomed and would collapse under the weight of its falseness and corruption, and they both discounted the efficacy of political or social reform efforts to bring about meaningful change. They saw individual transformation as the only path to renewal and regarded the artist as the medium for bringing to other men a vision of an alternate reality that is the true reality. Both men rejected scientific rationalism and its belief in the inevitability of "progress" in favor of a mystical, intuitive wisdom that stressed acceptance of the world's plurality and ultimate mystery. Both men regarded themselves as seers, belonging to a higher order of being closer to the angels. Both men celebrated the imagination as the gateway to a higher, truer reality.

Although Miller remarks on the numerous similarities of temperament, background and artistic mission between himself and Rimbaud, it is the difference between them that is most revealing of Miller's character and fate. Rimbaud, having discovered his identity as a poet during a brief but brilliant period of creativity that began when he ran away to Paris at age sixteen, renounced his calling at age twenty-one and spent the remainder of his life struggling to survive in distant and inhospitable lands on the Arabian desert. Having found himself in art, he scornfully turned his back on it. Miller's path was just the opposite. Miller wandered in the desert of Brooklyn until he was nearly forty, struggling to find himself as a writer, working at jobs he loathed, abandoning his first wife and daughter, suffering unspeakable humiliations at the hands of his second wife, June. He was reborn as an artist in Paris with *Tropic of Cancer*. Although he often spoke of wanting to pass from literature into life, as Rimbaud had unsuccessfully attempted, he never put down his pen (or his brush) until he died. Miller remarks his divergence from the path that Rimbaud followed: "Rimbaud experienced his great crisis when he was eighteen, at which moment in his life he had reached the edge of madness; from this point on his life is an unending desert. I reached mine at the age of thirty-six, which is the age at which Rimbaud dies. From this point on my life begins to blossom. Rimbaud turned from literature to life; I did the reverse."

Miller's Rimbaud essay temporarily bruised his relationship with Wallace Fowlie, the man Miller called "friend, mentor, guide, consoler, confessor." Fowlie had sent the manuscript of his own Rimbaud study to Laughlin months before Miller completed his essay, but Laughlin had been slow to read it. In May 1945 Laughlin wrote to Miller that he was reading Fowlie's manuscript but having trouble getting through it. "Tried again last night to finish the ms but couldn't stick it." After Miller sent Laughlin his Rimbaud essay two months later, Laughlin wrote him again, enclosing a check for $100. "I'm almost sorry now I took Fowlie's book on Rimbaud. Your piece is better I think, though shorter."

In January 1946 Miller wrote to Fowlie informing him that Laughlin intended to publish Miller's essay "When Do Angels Cease to Resemble Themselves?: A Study of Rimbaud" in *New Directions 9*. The news upset Fowlie. He wondered how Miller, aware that Laughlin had Fowlie's manuscript under consideration, could have preempted him. "The fact that you turned in the manuscript before my book appeared has certainly made Laughlin regret having accepted mine." Miller was defensive. He assured Fowlie that he had not meant to trump Fowlie's book. He had written the essay only because he had failed in his attempt to translate *Une Saison en Enfer*. As if to reassure Fowlie that he and Laughlin have not betrayed him, Miller launched into an attack on all his publishers. "It's true you have a just grievance against Laughlin. No one realizes it more than I. I wish you knew what my experience has been—with him, with Kahane, with Fraenkel, with Argus, with 'the devoted B.P.' You would understand what makes a man's hair turn white ahead of time." But once Fowlie had read Miller's essay, as he did in February, his anger at Miller dissolved. "It makes no difference when or whether mine appears. [Your essay] has moved me almost more than anything else you have written."

At the same time that Miller was working on his Rimbaud piece, he received a letter from his French publisher, Maurice Girodias, Jack Kahane's son, who had taken over Obelisk Press following the death of his father. Girodias had taken his mother's maiden name during the war to conceal his Jewish ancestry from the Nazis. With Paris flooded with US servicemen, sales of Miller's banned books were brisk (it was reported that servicemen were stuffing their duffel bags with copies of *Tropic of Cancer*), and Girodias wanted to take advantage of the momentum to bring out French editions of the Tropics and *Black Spring*. Miller had been getting mail from American soldiers telling him that his books were prominently displayed in Paris bookstores and letting him know that they were sending copies to wives, friends, and sweethearts in the United States. Miller wrote to Cairns wondering "about the present attitude of the censor." He noted that favorable reviews of his books had been accumulating in America and England and asked Cairns for his opinion about "what must happen to set things in motion?" He alerted Cairns to an essay he had recently completed on censorship that was about to be published in *Tricolor* as "Obscenity and the Law of Reflection."

In this essay Miller argues that obscenity is an essential ingredient of the creative act; it is censored by an ignorant public afraid of the artist's vision. Obscenity exists not in the work of art, but in the mind of the censor, who projects onto it his terror of the dark mysteries that underlie creation. "Nothing could be regarded as obscene, I feel, if men were living out their inmost desires." The suppression of these desires Miller sees as a prime cause of the impulse toward war. "The sordid qualities imputed to the enemy are always those which we recognize as our own and therefore rise to slay, because only through projection do we realize the enormity and horror of them. Man tries as in a dream to kill the enemy in himself."

Up to the time of writing this essay, Miller had been trying to play the censorship game according to the rules laid down by Cairns—that "obscene" content can only be considered socially acceptable if it occurs in works of high artistic merit—which he did by striving to accumulate a body of critical opinion that, favorable or unfavorable, treated his work as serious literature. He now dismisses this standard as irrelevant as he defends the right of the artist to include all aspects of human experience in his work. "Its [obscenity's] purpose is to awaken, to usher in a sense of reality. [The person who is awakened is the artist himself.] And once awake, he is no longer concerned with the world of sleep; he walks in the light and, like a mirror, reflects his illumination in every act. Once this vantage point is reached, how trifling and remote seem the accusations of the moralist. How senseless the debate as to whether the work in question was of high literary merit or not!"

Miller is not sanguine that the artists' prerogative will prevail over conventional morality as expressed in standards of "decency." "The politician, the soldier, the industrialist, the technician, all those in short who cater to immediate needs, to creative comforts, to transitory and illusory passions and prejudices, will take precedence over the artist." Miller views the war as proof that it is society itself that is obscene. "Fear, guilt and murder—these constitute the real triumvirate which rules our lives. *What is obscene then?* The whole fabric of life as we know it today."

After promising to read Miller's article, Cairns gave Miller his usual cautious reply to the question of how "to set things in motion," brushing Miller off with the excuse that "the censorship business is a complicated matter, too full of ramifications for me to set out in a letter." It appears that much as Cairns may have personally admired Miller as a writer and believed in his right to publish the Paris books in America, he did not want to go on the record for Miller and possibly jeopardize his career as a government lawyer. Shortly after their exchange over censorship, Cairns wrote Miller to warn him that he had been attacked in an article published in the left wing Jewish journal *New Currents.*

The article, titled "Odyssey of a Stool Pigeon," had been written by Albert E. Kahn, an activist political journalist and avowed Marxist. Kahn had coauthored several books with inflammatory titles such as *Sabotage! The Secret War Against America, The Plot Against the Peace: A*

Warning to the Nation, and *The Great Conspiracy: The Secret War Against Soviet Russia* that attacked Nazi sympathizers and collaborators and defended Soviet Russia and Josef Stalin.

Kahn had encountered Miller during Miller's visit to Dartmouth College in November 1944. Kahn was an alumnus of the college and sat in on the talks that Miller gave to students there at the invitation of Miller's staunch admirer Professor Herbert West. Inflamed by Miller's lack of patriotism and war zeal, Kahn pounced on several of Miller's statements, finding in them evidence of Miller's Nazi sympathies and treasonable collaboration. He accused Miller of being "a fascist, anti-Semitic propagandist and a former labor spy." The evidence that Kahn offered in support of these slanderous allegations consisted of quotes from several of Miller's books as well as statements that Kahn alleged Miller had made to the Dartmouth students, including a group of apprentice seamen and midshipmen.

Kahn wrote that Miller had said, "The Nazis are no different than you are. They're fighting for the same things you're fighting for . . . You're in uniform not because you want to be but because there's an authority that forces you to be." Then, pointing out Miller's German ancestry in the classic inquisitor's tactic of guilt by association, Kahn offered this remark as proof that Miller was a Nazi sympathizer, calling it "treasonable propaganda." Similarly, Kahn, a Jew, found evidence of Miller's anti-Semitism in Miller's largely sympathetic portrait of the long-suffering Jew Max in *The Cosmological Eye* by taking out of context Miller's remark, "If I were a Jew I would tie a rope around my neck and jump overboard." Lost on Kahn is the conceit that Max is a foil for Miller's own suffering and misery as he struggles to survive in Paris while writing *Tropic of Cancer* and *Tropic of Capricorn.* As evidence that Miller is a labor spy, Kahn cited Miller's years of employment at Western Union, which, as Miller relates in *Tropic of Capricorn,* initially hired him to report on its employees' job performance, then promoted him to Employment Manager, a job he loathed.

Miller must have viewed Kahn's article as confirmation that he was indeed living in "the time of the assassins." In the aftermath of the article, members of the FBI visited Herbert West at Dartmouth. Miller wrote to Cairns that the FBI had begun reading his books (!) and had come to Big

Sur on several occasions to question Miller about his friends. Investigators from the FBI questioned West and others who had attended Miller's talk and came to the conclusion that Miller had never made the remarks Kahn attributed to him. Although Miller considered Kahn's article "scurrilous, libelous and defamatory," he took no legal action against either Kahn or *New Currents*. Miller was not combative and regarded the US justice system as just another corrupt American institution, dispensing not justice but revenge (see Miller's essay *Maurizius Forever* for his observations on "justice"). He closed the matter in a letter to Cairns with the sign-off "Q.E.D." It was clear that Miller saw the article as representative of the treatment meted out to anyone who questioned or challenged conventional thinking in the paranoid environment fostered by war.

In an interesting footnote to the incident, the inquisitor Kahn was subsequently interrogated by the Senate Judiciary Committee, which was investigating "Communist Activity in Mass Communications" under the authority of the Internal Security Act of 1950. The committee pilloried Kahn as "a leading member of the Communist party U.S.A. specializing in the field of producing anti-American and pro-Soviet propaganda." He was imprisoned for six months for withholding from the government the manuscript of *False Witness*, an account by a government informant of his dishonest testimony before the Judiciary Committee. Miller must have chuckled when he read of Kahn's fate. The ultimate irony is that both Miller and Kahn were ardent advocates of peace. But Miller, unlike Kahn, put no faith in politics, insisting that each individual had to find his own way to peace.

DURING 1945 A NUMBER OF BERN PORTER'S PUBLISHING PROJECTS came to fruition. In May, *Semblance of a Devoted Past*, the collection of Miller's letters about watercolor painting written to Emil Schnellock from Paris, was published. In June, Porter brought out *Henry Miller Miscellanea*, a collection of fugitive pieces from Miller's Brooklyn years, and also issued *Varda: The Master Builder*, a forty-page pamphlet containing a text previously published in *Circle*. Nineteen forty-five also saw the publication of *The Happy Rock*, Porter's edition of tributes to Miller by friends, critics, and admirers.

Each of these publications sank Porter deeper into debt. Porter printed 1,650 copies of *Semblance of a Devoted Past*, but had only 561 copies of the seventy-four-page book bound. They sold for the rather high price of $7.50. Porter later tried to sell the unbound sheets to other publishers, including Laughlin, who admired the book, but Porter held fast to an unrealistic asking price and got no sale. The sheets were subsequently accidentally destroyed. *Henry Miller Miscellanea* was another overpriced book. Only sixty-two pages long, it was offered for sale at $7.50 in an edition of five hundred copies, most of which were remaindered. Porter printed three thousand copies of *The Happy Rock* and bound seven hundred and fifty copies in 1945 priced at $7.50. By March of 1946, only 213 copies of the book had been sold and Porter reported to Miller that he was $3,000 in debt on their various projects. Responding to Porter's complaints of indebtedness on his behalf, Miller suggested that Porter solicit loans from wealthy patrons on their mailing list, as though exchanging one debt for another would somehow solve Porter's problem. Lawrence Durrell, who had contributed an article to *The Happy Rock*, called the book "a wretched affair—quite unworthy of its object. What a talent you have for attracting the immortality hunters, the moral crooks, to you. How freely you let them feed on your own flesh." Laughlin was no kinder, writing of Porter that he "did you a great deal of harm with his absurd little editions that irritated the trade no end. They hate such petty items."

The subjects of these and other books that were published in 1945 show Miller's preoccupation with painting and his reverence for artists like himself who struggled against poverty and neglect while remaining true to their artistic vision. In the letters to Emil collected in *Semblance of a Devoted Past*, Miller writes about the joy of creation that is the artist's ultimate reward and urges Emil to partake of this joy in his own work. "If there is not enough joy in painting, for its own sake, then better not do it. Choose something else. Because the tangible rewards are meager. It is only the inner riches that matter, and you have to want that bitterly, desperately, to sacrifice your whole life for it." In another letter, he likens the spirit that animates him to "the Holy Ghost, the living clue inside me, which demands obedience." This letter, written from Clichy in

1933 where he was living with Alfred Perlès, also contains an eerily accurate forecast of his settlement in Big Sur. "Some day I am going to own a few feet of earth somewhere and put a house over it. Just one big room will do, with a stove and a basin of water, a huge desk, a bookcase and an easel. Then life can go rolling by, and what floats in through my door will be sufficient for me." Six years later, as he was about to leave Europe, he wrote to Emil: "I find myself wanting two things strongly—a fine natural life in the open air, with vigorous exercise, ruggedness, etc., and the most rarified spiritual sort of life at the same time."

Miller also had published in 1945 three other essays about artist friends. Besides *Varda: The Master Builder*, there was *Knud Merrild: Holiday in Paint*, about the painter who had been a frequent visitor at Miller's residence in Beverly Glen, which *Circle* published in a limited edition of two hundred copies, and *The Amazing and Invariable Beauford Delaney*. This booklet, which included several photographs of Delaney in addition to Miller's text, was published by the Alicat Bookshop in Yonkers, New York.

As fall approached, Miller's thoughts turned to Lepska and their child, due to arrive in late October. Money worries were now pressing in on him again. Keith Evans was returning to Big Sur from his war service and intended to resume use of his cabin. The Millers had been asked to move out by Christmas. Miller's neighbor, Jean Wharton, offered to sell Miller property on Partington Ridge on which he could build a house, but he had no money. When Laughlin, who was preparing to publish *The Air-Conditioned Nightmare*, wrote Miller in September that he was optimistic about sales of Miller's books now that the war was over, Miller promptly wrote back asking for a loan against future royalties that would enable him to buy the Wharton property. Laughlin kindly wrote back, "Now don't worry about raising that money. If every other resort fails, I'll manage to find it for you somehow. I can always sell something if it comes to that." Miller also put out a feeler to Huntington Cairns, who was still on the lookout for a possible patron for Miller. He wrote Cairns that he had "roughly $10,000 by the current exchange" credited to his royalty account in Paris but could not access the money. Cairns wrote back that a potential patron he had been courting on Miller's behalf had turned him down and he would have to start over.

Early in October Lepska went to Berkeley to wait out her confinement in the care of George and Nancy Leite. Miller made arrangements to move his family to the abandoned convict shack at Anderson Creek that the Leites had recently vacated. Anderson Creek was a bohemian enclave south of Partingon Ridge where Emil White, Judson Crews, and the Neimans also lived. At the end of October, the baby now overdue, Miller joined Lepska in Berkeley to wait for the birth. Anxious to resume work on *The Rosy Crucifixion*, he expressed to Fowlie his feeling of being hemmed in by circumstances. "We have only one big room. We have visitors every few days—who stay overnite. I go mad some times trying to concentrate." Of the baby he wrote, "No, I shan't baptize baby a Catholic. [Fowlie, a Catholic, had been named godfather to the child.] I want it to have no education of any kind—if possible." This remark set the stage for major child-rearing differences between him and Lepska that would play out over the remainder of their marriage.

On November 19, 1945, Lepska delivered a girl at Alta Bates Hospital in Berkeley. The Millers named the child Valentine, after Henry's maternal grandfather, Valentin Nieting. (Miller's middle name was Valentine; June had always called him "Val.") Lepska remained in Berkeley for several weeks after the birth while Miller readied their new home at Anderson Creek.

Lepska described conditions in the shack they occupied as even more primitive than Evans's cabin on Partington Ridge. It was a one-room cabin with bath, but it had no heat source. Stairs dropped down to a small alcove used as a kitchen. One wall of the cabin had floor-to-ceiling glass that gave a view out to the Pacific Ocean. Jean Varda, worried about the baby's health, brought them a Franklin stove that he modified to provide more heat. The community donated a bed, dishes, and a carpet, and Dan Harris, a painter friend from Monterey, made a cradle for Val. Varda also built a small platform outside the "kitchen" as a play area for Val. In lieu of a refrigerator or icebox, Lepska kept their food fresh in coolers stored in the hillside. Miller turned an unused cabin at the edge of the cliff into his writing studio.

Despite the hardship and the new responsibility, Miller was in a good mood as the new year began. He described the cabin in a letter to Emil Schnellock and his studio in a letter to Durrell. To Schnellock he wrote, "The place looks quite beautiful—after about $100 of repairs, the donation of rugs, chairs, round table, phono, records, etc. The ceiling + walls are all white and the doors + window sashes blue. The kitchen is yellow. It looks like a doll's house." From his studio he wrote to Durrell, "Now I am at the ocean, right over it, writing you from a little hut which is my studio, the first real isolated studio I ever knew. It's marvelous. Nothing but sky, ocean and cliffs and mountains. Waves pounding under my feet—like dynamite."

Around this time Miller appears to have undergone a mystical experience that put him in possession of a profound truth that he was unable, or unwilling, to put into words. He wrote to Fowlie about it not long after moving into his new residence at Anderson Creek. "I said I would write to you about the life of Jesus after the resurrection—the period of forty days, was it, between the resurrection and the ascension. But the more I think about it the more I feel that it is important not to communicate what I think I have learned—a most tremendous truth—but to live my life in the light of it. I didn't come by this truth alone, I must tell you. Though for some time now I have been preparing myself to receive it, so to speak. By one of those strange coincidences I find corroboration, perhaps the kind few would see or accept, in Krishnamurti's words and actions. I found it again in the life of Milarepa, the Tibetan poet-saint. When you strike it several times in succession, and from such different sources, you are bound to take notice."

In the same letter, Miller expressed his gratitude for having settled in Big Sur. "I get up with the dawn these days. Am out on the road watching it come over the hills as I walk beside the sea. There is here a quality of the eternal which I have felt nowhere else except in Greece. It is most fortunate I chose this place to live in. Now it seems as though I shall be able to own a few acres of land and a house. From this anchorage I hope to sally forth into the world now and then by plane—I mean to Europe, Asia and Africa. But it does begin to seem as tho' I'd found 'home' at last. Maybe I've just found myself."

If nothing else, this letter to Fowlie shows the perception gap separating Miller the Big Sur mystic and spiritualist from an American reading public conditioned to think of him as a renegade pornographer, and the difficulty Miller faced in bridging this gap, given the elusiveness of the mystical underpinnings of his writing. Miller was reminded of the barriers separating him from American readers by the unfavorable reviews that greeted *The Air-Conditioned Nightmare*, which Laughlin had published in December. Laughlin had written Miller in January to express his optimism about sales of this book and other Miller titles. "I think the time is about come when we have enough bookstore support to make commercial advertising begin to pay off. It's like blowing into a hundred gallon vat if the stores aren't interested in following it up by carrying stock and pushing the customers. But I think now they realize you are saleable. It's been a long pull."

A few days after Laughlin sent this letter, *The Air-Conditioned Nightmare* received unfavorable reviews from Bernard DeVoto in *The New York Times* and Philip Wylie in *Saturday Review*, and Laughlin quickly changed his tune. "Sales of *The Air-Conditioned Nightmare* have been very badly hit by the adverse reviews of DeVoto, Prescott and Wylie," he wrote in February. "It is boobs like that who mould literary opinion. All the local stores have stopped ordering." In another sign that Miller was making small headway in the American market, he ended his relationship with his American literary agency, Russell & Volkening, in July. Miller had written Henry Volkening that he believed he would not be producing any work that could be published in America, excepting his New Directions titles, and he could deal with foreign agents himself. Volkening agreed that Miller had no further need of his services and the relationship was terminated amicably. Miller's agent at Russell & Volkening, John Slocum, who had already left the firm, wrote to Lawrence Powell a few months later that he believed Miller should not be living in America. "Tell him also that if he wishes to continue growing, he ought to get the hell out of Southern California and go back to Paris, or Athens, where he will be surrounded by adults. His most recent work is not his best."

But if Miller was finding peace and ease in Big Sur despite the continued resistance to his work, his tranquility was being purchased at the expense of Lepska's happiness and well-being. To all of the challenges she had faced maintaining the Miller household on Partington Ridge was now added the responsibility of caring for an infant whose father retreated for long hours each day to his writing studio and posted signs on its door saying, "Leave me in peace." Fortunately for Lepska, there were neighbors with young children living nearby who offered companionship for her and Val. The Neimans had moved into the former Anderson Creek dining hall with their daughter, Arianne, and the painter Ephraim Doner, his wife, Rosa, and daughter, Natasha, lived near Murphy's Hot Springs, where Lepska went almost daily to wash Val's diapers. Lepska and Margaret Neiman planted a vegetable garden and grew lettuce, parsley, mint, corn, and string beans. But Miller's isolation and intense concentration on his work—he was immersed in *Sexus*, volume one of *The Rosy Crucifixion*—left Lepska feeling unappreciated and neglected. She said that she was overwhelmed by her responsibilities and tasks and frustrated by Miller's lack of interest in her needs, especially her need for his affection. Tension arose between them over money— Lepska was ashamed of Miller's sense of entitlement and appeals for charity—and over parenting, Lepska insisting on structure and limits, Miller's belief in "freedom" disposing him to be indulgent.

MILLER BROKE OFF HIS RELATIONSHIP WITH BERN PORTER in 1946 in disgust with Porter's "miserliness." In January, Porter wrote Miller from Berkeley informing him that he planned to marry soon and live abroad for five years, either in Argentina or France. He had no idea how he would finance this new lifestyle. Summarizing the projects they had mapped out at Beverly Glen in 1943—publishing manuscripts, compiling a bibliography, assembling a book of tributes, establishing a foundation to support writers, writing a book about Miller, starting a collection of Miller material at a major library—he noted that all but two had been realized. (Porter had arranged with Lawrence Powell to establish a Miller collection at UCLA and was donating his own papers as a companion collection.) He held out hope that the writers' foundation might somehow come to pass. Porter closed his letter with the rueful observation, "We both realize, by now, the sheer folly of publishing without money. Only a fool would do what I have done."

Miller had been pressing Porter to provide authors' copies of *The Happy Rock* to all the contributors, most of whom were Miller friends whose articles Miller had helped Porter solicit. Porter now informed Miller that only George Leite and Gilbert Neiman had received free copies of the book. Several other contributors—Knud Merrild, Paul Weiss, Emil Schnellock, Herbert West, Thomas Gilbert, and Richard Osborn—had purchased copies. None of the other contributors, twenty-five in all, had received copies. Miller was disappointed to learn this, and in his reply urged Porter to provide them with copies, and to subtract the cost of doing this from any future royalties due him. Porter responded by itemizing expenses and revenue that showed the book to be $1,400 in the red and noted that he had never promised free copies to the contributors. Oblivious to the effect his refusal was having on Miller, Porter proposed staying with Miller for a while ("sleeping bags") while he gathered material for a book. Miller, incensed, wrote back, "Doesn't ordinary decency dictate what to do?" and vetoed the visit. Porter replied that it would cost him $110 to send out free copies to all the contributors and said he did not have the money, whereupon Miller severed their relationship and said he would purchase contributor copies himself and send them out.

Over the next three years, Miller and Porter continued to correspond about disposition of the unsold copies of Porter's books and pamphlets. At the suggestion of Lawrence Powell, they were given away to libraries in Europe. In 1960 Porter wrote Miller from his home in Maine proposing to reprint some of the titles he had published in the 1940s. He admitted to Miller that he had no money to finance the project.

If Miller was still struggling to get his works into the hands of readers in America, demand for his books, especially the banned books, continued strong in Europe. Miller's French publisher, Maurice Girodias, encouraged by continuing sales of the Tropics to American GIs, pressed ahead with the French translations. *Tropique du Cancer* was published in December 1945, followed by *Printemps Noir* in February 1946 and *Tropique du Capricorne* in July. Sales of these titles were stimulated when a French moral crusader, Daniel Parker, president of the Cartel d'Action Sociale et Morale, registered a complaint against the publishers and the author on charges of pornography. A committee was formed to judge whether the works in question were pornographic, and a counter committee, whose members included prominent French writers such as Albert Camus, André Gide, and Jean-Paul Sartre, was formed to defend Miller and his publishers. The ensuing scandal, which became known as *l'affaire Miller* in France, greatly enhanced Miller's reputation and visibility in Europe and boosted sales of his books. The trial dragged on for months until the French government, embarrassed by the public outcry against censorship of Miller, dismissed Parker's complaint. Girodias subsequently sued him.

Laughlin saw opportunity for his own titles in Miller's growing notoriety in Europe. He wrote Miller in June of his "desire to help in any way possible to get you published in every language of the globe." He suggested that Miller work through a foreign rights agent, Max Pfeffer, who had over twenty years experience in international publishing. But Miller, perhaps mindful of his time-consuming experience with Bern Porter, elected not to deal directly with another agent and granted foreign rights for all his New Directions titles to Laughlin. Laughlin then put Pfeffer to work arranging publishing deals for *Wisdom of the Heart, Sunday After the War, The Air-Conditioned Nightmare, The Cosmological Eye,* and *The Colossus of Maroussi* in all countries except France and England. Miller was especially interested in seeing his works published in Germany, Austria, Switzerland, Russia, Spain, all of South America, Holland, Sweden, Yugoslavia, South Africa, and India. He had already entered into a publishing agreement with Arnoldo Mondadori in Italy and had received queries from publishers in Norway and Denmark. Girodias continued to hold French rights, and Nicholson and Watson published Miller in England. Miller was on his way to becoming an internationally recognized author, yet he remained a marginal figure in his own country.

Despite the many demands on his attention at this time—his writing, his family, his dealings with publishers, his intention to buy property, his attempt to secure his French royalties—Miller found time to take up the cause of George Dibbern. Dibbern was a German writer and adventurer who was interned at a concentration camp for Germans on Somes Island, New Zealand. Dibbern had left Germany in 1930, abandoning his wife and four children to their fate under Nazism, to sail to New Zealand on a thirty-two-foot boat named the *Te Rapunga*. He was seeking to reconnect with a Maori woman, Mother Rangi, whom he regarded as his spiritual mother. After a five-year sea voyage, accompanied by his mate Gunter, Dibbern reached New Zealand to find that Mother Rangi was dead. When the war broke out he was imprisoned on account of his German origin. He wrote a book about his adventure, titled *Quest*, that Miller read and then reviewed in *Circle*. He also wrote to Dibbern to express his admiration for Dibbern's courage and independence, and to offer support. He wrote Cairns to inquire whether anything could be done by the US government to secure Dibbern's release. Cairns wrote back suggesting that Miller approach the British government through Alfred Perlès. When Dibbern was about to be released from prison in December 1945, Miller sent out a "Dear Friend" letter to his personal mailing list offering copies of *Quest* for sale, with $1.50 from every copy sold to be sent to Dibbern to enable him to resume his journey on the *Te Rapunga*. He also encouraged people to send money, food, clothes, or equipment for Dibbern's use. Miller took it upon himself to solicit aid for Dibbern's wife and children, who were suffering the extreme deprivations of postwar Germany. Miller wrote to Perlès, who was then in Germany as part of the Occupation, asking if he could obtain relief for Dibbern's family. Perlès wrote back with the warning that Dibbern's wife should not try to contact him.

Dibbern was one of those quixotic figures who attracted Miller by his fierce independence and unshakeable commitment to "a higher ideal of human behavior." He was a fellow "aristocrat of the spirit" whom Miller identified with and promoted because, like Miller, he refused to march in lock step with the mass of mankind. Dibbern, rejecting nationalism, had made himself "a citizen of the world," sailing the *Te Rapunga* under a flag of his own invention and issuing his own passport. "What would happen," Miller wonders in his review of *Quest*, "if all who preached the brotherhood of man followed suit? How long would the stupid barriers and restrictions of nationality hold?" Miller saw Dibbern as an exemplar, a man who "puts words into act. In this he approaches the religious figures." He likened Dibbern to "our own Thoreau. These men are far ahead of society; their tragedy is that they are condemned to wait for others to catch up . . . Dibbern makes us realize *how much* life may be enjoyed even on the fringes of society." Miller, perched at the edge of the continent in a remote community cut off from the mainstream of American life, must have been thinking of himself when he wrote those words. Big Sur was Miller's *Te Rapunga*, and Dibbern's quest was his own. Miller defended Dibbern's choices as the choices of a man who was seeking, as was Miller, a better way to live. "He is striving desperately to participate, to be at one with his fellow man, but on the best of terms, i.e., on the terms of his own best self."

BY THE END OF 1946 MILLER was ready to move his family into their new home on Partington Ridge. Jean Wharton had executed a deed of sale for $5,000 for property including a house and garage on land bordered by Partington Ridge Road, to Henry Miller and Lepska Miller in joint tenancy. Miller's recently acquired French agent, Michael Hoffman, had sent Miller two installments of royalties that had accumulated in France during the war years. A $2,000 payment in April followed by another $2,000 in September had enabled Miller to make the purchase. In December, Hoffman wrote with the unsettling news that he was having difficulty collecting monies due Miller from Girodias, who was avoiding him.

In May, Miller had finished a draft of *Sexus* and had sent it to Herbert West for review, after which it was to be forwarded to Emil Schnellock. He had also assembled a collection of short pieces for volume two of *The Air-Conditioned Nightmare*, which Laughlin intended to bring out in 1947 under the title *Remember to Remember*. Laughlin had gone to Europe in October to look after his international publishing ventures and wrote Miller from a Paris in the throes of *l'affaire Miller*. "You are the rage in France. Every little bookstore—even railway kiosks—has your French books and things are buzzing . . . No telling how many books may be sold if Girodias can print them."

Though worries about money persisted, Miller had good reason to feel a sense of accomplishment as he began life as a first-time homeowner at age fifty-five. He wrote proudly to Durrell in February 1947, "I'm sitting in the new studio this morning and it's raining like hell here. It's an old garage, transformed. The house, one large room with a little annex for the baby, is quite simple and beautiful, almost Japanese in its austerity. I have 2½ acres, not five, as I once thought. And it's mostly hillside—but no matter. I bought the view— sea, wind, air, sky, stars, not land. Have enough to grow all the vegetables for twenty people . . . The baby is now walking. She's adorable. Jabbers away in her own tongue—has the gift of gab, I see."

7

A YEAR OF CRISIS

"Almost More Than I Can Bear"

MILLER'S FIRST TWO YEARS IN HIS NEW HOME WERE A TIME OF TRIALS and crises. Money worries, attacks in the press, distress over his ex-wife June's condition, and a disastrous houseguest piled troubles on him. Worst of all, his marriage to Lepska, little more than two years old, was foundering. But in spite of these difficulties, Miller had a productive year as a writer. Three new titles were issued in 1947, and he completed a fourth book that was published early in 1948. As well, he made progress on his major project, *The Rosy Crucifixion*, revising volume one (*Sexus*) and starting work on volume two (*Plexus*).

Money worries were uppermost in Miller's mind as the new year began. Miller was used to living a hand to mouth existence. He had been doing it since 1924 when he left his position as employment manager for Western Union and vowed never again to hold a job. He survived by begging, borrowing, selling or bartering his watercolors, and cashing royalty checks or book advances from Laughlin at infrequent intervals. Miller had developed a philosophical attitude about his poverty. He regarded it as a condition of the artistic purity of his writing that he valued above all else. Because his writing was largely autobiographical, to violate that purity was to violate himself. But when he learned in the spring of 1947 that a small fortune had accumulated in his French royalty account, his perspective on money changed.

In May Hoffman wrote Miller with the news that almost $40,000—a fabulous sum—was due him from Maurice Girodias, but that the Exchange Control Bureau in Paris, which was operating on a quota system, had no funds to authorize payments to American authors in dollars. Hoffman had suggested that Miller come to France, take his royalties in francs, and either live on them or invest them in French property. Another suggestion had been that Miller appoint an agent to purchase French paintings that could be shipped to America and resold at a profit. But Miller was not interested in pursuing any of these options. Perhaps, newly settled on Partington Ridge in his own home, he did not wish to become uprooted again. As his correspondence shows, he also did not want to be any more distracted from the task of completing *The Rosy Crucifixion* than he already was.

The funds that had accumulated in Miller's royalty account with Girodias were the fruits of his artistic labors over a period of fifteen years. It was "pure" money, earned by his own standard of integrity. That he could not get access to it owing to circumstances beyond his control put him in a state of perpetual frustration. Before he was aware of his royalty wealth, Miller had adopted the mystical view that, because he was in tune with the cosmos and the cosmos is essentially benevolent, the cosmos would take care of his basic needs. His begging letters were simply his way of letting the cosmos know that he was in need. But now that millions of francs were sitting in an account he could not tap, he felt deprived.

Hoffman was doing all in his power to get Miller's money out of France. He had first to collect the francs from Girodias, then obtain a copyright credit from the French Exchange Office for the United States that would enable him to convert the francs into dollars. Hoffman, who reported frequently to Miller on his collection efforts, ran into difficulties on both fronts.

In December 1946, Hoffman had written Miller that he was owed 300,000 francs (about $2,500) in royalties from Girodias for September, October, and November but that Girodias, who had just bought a house, was avoiding him. The following March, Hoffman reported that Girodias had paid two hundred fifty thousand francs (about $2,100) on account, and had promised another five hundred thousand (about $4,200) by the end of the month. However, Hoffman was unable to send Miller any money because copyright credits for the United States were "exhausted for the present moment." That these circumstances were putting Miller under considerable stress was reflected in an angry letter he wrote to George Leite around this time in regards to Leite's publishing efforts on Miller's behalf. "You're getting as bad as Bern. You put out the records [Miller had made recordings of readings that Leite sold through his newly opened gallery *daliel's* in Berkeley] to help me build the house. The house is up and paid for. Never a cent out of you. Yes, once—excuse me. . . Aren't you just a dreamer? You raised lots of money to start this and that—all very vital—*yes, for George.*" Leite wrote back immediately itemizing all his debts and telling Miller that he and his family were living on $100 a month.

Hoffman's May accounting showed the impact of *l'affaire Miller* on Miller's fortunes in France. The French edition of *Tropique du Capricorne* had sold 110,000 copies. A second printing of 30,000 copies was soon to be issued. *Max and the White Phagocytes* had sold out a first printing of 25,000 copies, and 5,000 copies of a second printing of an equal number had also been sold. English editions of all Miller's books published in France were sold out. Perlès, who had visited Paris in April, wrote to Miller, "Joey, you're famous." All told, Miller had accumulated nearly five million francs (about $40,000) in royalties. However, the entire allowance for copyright credits to the United States was only $45,000. This was why Hoffman urged Miller to come to France to collect his royalties in francs before they were devalued, as seemed likely.

Miller was at a loss what to do. He wrote to Cairns in June summarizing his situation. "Little hope is offered me as to when I will receive my money. This is quite a blow to me, as you can imagine. In the first place, I never dreamed that the sum owed me represented such a staggering figure . . . But to know that it is there and yet unseizable is maddening. Particularly since I am deep in debt, having banked from month to month on monies being sent me from France." Miller wondered whether Cairns, through his government connections, might be able to suggest a way for him to retrieve his funds. He told Cairns that he did not want to go to France because he was about to resume work on *The Rosy Crucifixion*, "a long hard job which may take me two or three years, and I don't want to get up and travel suddenly." Cairns, not surprisingly, wrote back that no one he had spoken to in Washington knew much about French currency exchange laws, and suggested that Miller try to find an American importer who would be willing to use Miller's francs to purchase merchandise in France, then reimburse Miller in dollars at a favorable exchange rate. Miller did not pursue this avenue. Instead, he sought help from the French consul in San Francisco. The royalty issue dragged on for years, with Miller sporadically receiving payments when Hoffman was able to extract francs from Girodias.

Miller's money problems were compounded by his decision to invite his longtime Paris friend, the astrologer Conrad Moricand, to come to America and live with him and Lepska in Big Sur. This decision had disastrous consequences for their friendship, and further damaged Miller's already strained marriage with Lepska. The Miller-Moricand story has been told in detail by Karl Orend in *The Brotherhood of Fools and Simpletons*, published by Alyscamps Press in 2005, and by Miller himself in *A Devil in Paradise*. What follows is based largely on their accounts, supplemented by information obtained from my own interviews with Lepska and letters Miller wrote to Durrell, Laughlin, and Cairns.

Conrad Moricand was a renowned European astrologer whom Miller met in Paris in 1936 through Anaïs Nin. A member of a wealthy Swiss family living in Paris (his father was a baron), Moricand circulated among well-known French artists whom he dazzled with astonishing powers of character analysis based on readings of their horoscopes. "When it came to reading personalities," Miller wrote, "Moricand impressed one as possessing certain powers of divination." By the time Miller met him, Moricand had been deprived of his substantial private income by a scheming older brother and was living in a modest hotel room, supporting himself by casting horoscopes and teaching astrology. A dedicated student of occult religions, he spent his days doing research at the Bibliothèque Nationale and his evenings peddling his services in cafés and salons. Miller's first impressions of Moricand, as recorded in *A Devil in Paradise*, "were not altogether favorable. The man seemed somber, didactic, opinionated, self-centered. A fatalistic quality pervaded his whole being." Perhaps more ominously, Miller didn't like how Moricand smelled. "There was an odor about him which I could not help but be aware of. It was a mélange of bay rum, wet ashes, and *tabac gris*, tinctured with a dash of some elusive, elegant perfume. Later these would resolve themselves into one unmistakable scent—the aroma of death."

Nin commissioned Moricand to cast Miller's horoscope in July 1936, and Miller was astonished by Moricand's accurate penetration of his character [see Appendix B]. He quickly opened himself to Moricand's influence, much as he later did in his relationship with Wallace Fowlie. "What we had in common was the basic nature of the Capricorn," Miller remarked. "Philosophers. Inquisitors. Sorcerers. Hermits. Gravediggers. Beggars." Moricand was five years Miller's senior and deeply read in the occult lore that attracted Miller. It was Moricand who urged Miller to read two of Balzac's most spiritual novels, *Seraphita* and *Louis Lambert*, books that would greatly influence Miller's thought. In *A Devil in Paradise*, Miller credits Moricand's gift of *Seraphita* with inclining him toward inviting the astrologer to Big Sur. "Had it not been for *Seraphita* I doubt very much that my adventure with Moricand would have terminated in the manner it did." When Miller left France in 1939, he considered Moricand one of three Frenchmen he could call a friend.

As Miller left for Greece, he worried about Moricand's future under war conditions. The services he provided to the bohemian café society of Paris were unlikely to be in demand by occupying Germans. Miller wrote Moricand from the *Exochorda* in December 1939, then sent him small sums of money from New York. Their last prewar contact occurred in June 1940.

Then, shortly after moving into his new home on Partington Ridge in the winter of 1947, Miller received a large envelope from "an Italian princess" that enclosed a letter from Moricand, who had moved to a small village in Switzerland after the war. Moricand described himself as destitute and in ill health. Miller immediately wrote back, suggesting that Moricand come to America to live as his guest in Big Sur. Miller promised to take care of Moricand for the rest of his life, if necessary, and to cover his travel expenses. At the same time, he warned Moricand that his marital situation was turbulent and that the accommodations he could offer on Partington Ridge were spartan: a tiny room without bath adjoining Miller's writing studio, lit by a kerosene lamp and heated by a small oil burner.

Miller then investigated the procedures required to obtain a visitor's visa for Moricand and pondered how to raise the money for his voyage. He wrote to Cairns for legal advice and asked Durrell to loan him money. Durrell suggested that Miller give Moricand access to francs in Miller's royalty account, a suggestion that Miller—somewhat curiously, given his determination to help Moricand—did not act upon. Instead he instructed Laughlin to send Moricand the $500 due Miller from royalties in his New Directions account. Laughlin notified Miller in early September that he had wired the funds to Moricand, adding the wry comment, "You certainly are good to your friends." Around this same time, Miller informed Moricand that Lepska had gone to Monterey to live with friends, leaving Valentine in his care, then, missing her daughter, had decided to return to give the marriage another chance. By the time Moricand arrived in December, she was pregnant again. The child, a boy named Henry Tony, was born August 28, 1948.

Moricand sailed from Southampton for New York on December 18, 1947, and arrived in San Francisco shortly before Christmas. He was met at the airport by Miller's friend, the painter Bezalel "Lilik" Schatz, who had him paged in French. A few days later, Schatz drove Moricand down the coast to Miller's house. It was dark when they arrived. The two men tearfully embraced, then Miller showed Moricand to his quarters. "The little studio I had turned over to him to sleep and work in was about half the size of his attic room in the Hotel Modial [Moricand's Paris residence]. It was just big enough to hold a cot, a writing table, a chiffonier. When the two oil lamps were lit it gave off a glow. A Van Gogh would have found it charming."

After only a few weeks, it was apparent that Moricand was ill suited to life in Big Sur and would not last. Lepska described him as "a dandy": cultivated, intelligent, used to the good life of the Paris cafés, and completely out of place in the primitive conditions on Partington Ridge. He made no effort to adapt, requesting Yardley soap and aftershave lotion when Lepska went to shop, and complaining about the one-course meals she prepared. Because he spoke very little English, he was isolated from the Big Sur community, able to converse freely only with Miller, who was working in his studio most of the day. He gave Lepska French lessons, but his flirtatious manner with her, brought on perhaps by his observation of the evident tension between the Millers, irritated his host. The Millers were also distressed to discover that Moricand drew child pornography for sale and was servicing the appetites of a client who lived in Pebble Beach. On top of everything else, Moricand developed a serious skin disease, St. Anthony's Fire, or erysipelas, which plagued him with itching. He further upset the Millers by illegally importing codeine from France for relief of the tormenting symptoms.

But, according to Lepska, what really turned Miller against Moricand was his antagonism toward their daughter, Valentine, on whom Miller doted. "He seemed to have no use for children," Miller observed. "They annoyed him, unless they were extremely well behaved. As with most people who stress behavior, being well behaved meant keeping out of sight and reach." Moricand made no secret of the fact that he believed Valentine to be a spoiled child. "She ought to be disciplined," he would say. "It's not good for a child to receive so much attention." Once, when Moricand pushed away Val's hand as she was about to touch a piece of his breakfast toast, Miller exploded at him in anger. Not long after, Miller declared, "He's gotta go, Lepska. I can't take it anymore."

An unusually severe winter intensified Moricand's misery. Miller seemed to revel in his guest's suffering. "With the coming of the first good rain he began to grow despondent. It's true that his cell was tiny, that water leaked through the roof and windows, that the sow bugs and other bugs took over, that they dropped on his bed when he was asleep, that to keep warm he had to use an ill-smelling oil stove which consumed what little oxygen remained after he had sealed up all the cracks and crevices, stuffed the space beneath the door with sacking, shut all the windows tight, and so on. It's true that it was a winter in which we got more than our usual share of rain, a winter in which the storms broke with fury and lasted for days on end . . . Meanwhile the itch continued to plague him. Every time he came down for meals he rolled up the sleeves or the legs of his trousers to show us the ravages it had made. His flesh was by now a mass of running sores. Had I been in his boots I would have put a bullet through my brain."

Miller summoned a physician to examine Moricand. He concluded that Moricand wanted to be unwell, and there was no medicine that could cure him. As Miller escorted the doctor to his car, the man urged Miller to get rid of Moricand. "You might as well have a leper living with you. . . He doesn't want to get well. What he wants is sympathy, attention. He's not a man, he's a child. A spoiled child."

Soon Miller was treating Moricand like a character from *Tropic of Cancer*—foul, diseased, ludicrous. One evening at dinner Moricand described his flight to Switzerland at the end of the war. Miller recapitulates in ghoulish detail: "With a valise in each hand he marches on from place to place, shaking with fever, parched with thirst, dizzy, dopey, desperate. Above the cannonade he can hear his empty guts rattling. The bullets whiz overhead, the stinking dead lie in heaps everywhere, the hospitals are overcrowded, the fruit trees bare, the houses demolished, the roads filled with homeless, sick, crippled, wounded, forlorn, abandoned souls. Every man for himself! War! War! And there he is floundering around in the midst of it: a Swiss neutral with a passport and an empty belly. Now and then an American soldier flings him a cigarette. But no Yardley's talc. No toilet paper. No perfumed soap. And with it all he's got the itch. Not only the itch, but lice. Not only lice, but scurvy." The longer Moricand stays, the deeper becomes Miller's loathing for him.

In the midst of the narrative, Miller vents about his own itch—his marriage. "I too was suffering from the itch, only it was an itch one couldn't get at, an itch that didn't manifest itself bodily . . . Every day of my life I was fighting a corpse, a ghost, a cancer that had taken possession of my mind and that ravaged me more than any bodily affliction possibly could. Every day I had to meet and battle anew with the person I had chosen as a mate, chosen as one who would appreciate 'the good life' and share it with me. And from the very beginning it had been nothing but hell—hell and torment. To make it worse, the neighbors regarded her as a model creature—so spry, so lively, so generous, so warm. Such a good little mother, such an excellent housewife, such a perfect hostess!" The passage puts one in mind of Robert Browning's poem, *My Last Duchess*.

One day in March, barely three months after his arrival, Moricand told Miller he was miserable in Big Sur and wanted to leave. He begged Miller to take him to a hospital where he could receive treatment for his itch. Miller summoned Lilik Schatz from San Francisco to drive them. Once at the hospital, Miller witnessed the doctor examining Moricand. "Without a stitch he looks lamentable. Like a broken down nag. It's not merely that he's pot bellied, full of sores and scabs, but that his skin has an unhealthy look, is spotted like tobacco leaf, has no oil, no elasticity, no glow. He looks like one of those derelicts one sees in the washroom of the Mills Hotel, like a bum that has just crawled out of a flophouse on the Bowery. His flesh seems never to have been in contact with air and sun; it looks half-smoked."

Miller put Moricand up at a hotel in Monterey and continued to subsidize him when he moved to San Francisco. He paid Moricand's hotel bills and gave him spending money while he tried to arrange passage back to France through his friend Raoul Bertrand, the French consul. But Moricand balked at leaving unless Miller would give him $1,000 to cushion his transition. Miller refused. Moricand then initiated a letter writing campaign attacking Miller's character. Miller ceased communicating with him and left him to sort for himself. Moricand was eventually arrested by US Immigration authorities in the fall of 1949 and deported. He died five years later in Paris, but not before publishing further attacks on Miller in France. Miller retaliated after Moricand's death with *A Devil in Paradise*, published in 1956.

From this experience Miller took away the lesson that it was a mistake to play the Good Samaritan. "Never, never again, would I make the mistake of trying to solve someone's problems for him. How deceptive to think that by means of a little self-sacrifice one can help another overcome his difficulties."

Moricand was not the only "cause" that preoccupied Miller during this period. He continued his efforts to obtain the release of royalties due George Dibbern for *Quest* and to send aid to Dibbern's family in Germany. He must have seen in Dibbern's dilemma a reflection of his own problem retrieving the francs due him. Dibbern was still in New Zealand where he had fathered a child with his mistress, Eileen Norris. Through Cairns, Miller obtained the assistance of a lawyer, George Middleton, in the Department of Justice who agreed to take up Dibbern's claim. Five hundred and fifty dollars were due him.

In August 1947 Miller received word from his ex-wife June that she had been abandoned by her husband, Stratford Corbett, and was destitute, living in a miserable apartment in New York on a tiny welfare stipend that left her no money for food after she had paid her rent and utilities. Her weight had dropped to seventy-five pounds and her teeth were falling out from calcium deprivation. Through her physician, his old Brooklyn chum Emil Conason, he learned that she had briefly been a mental patient at Pilgrim State Hospital. Miller sent her small sums after that and arranged for Irving Stettner, a New York friend of Michael Fraenkel he had met in San Francisco, to look in on her from time to time. Miller was also sending money from his infrequent French royalty payments to Anaïs Nin to enable her to publish her diary. Given all these strains on his time and finances, it was no wonder that Miller had written to Emil at the beginning of September 1947, "I've got all sorts of demands made on me now— almost more than I can bear. No work done for two weeks. Just about getting Moricand over—a terrific job that. Then Anaïs asks for money. And now June, I learn, is destitute and ill (probably cancer), deserted by her husband Corbett." It seems not to have occurred to Miller that he had brought on himself the "demands" overwhelming him. Alfred Perlès, now a civilian back in England, became alarmed about Miller's state of mind and wrote to him in January. "I'm worried about you, Joey, you sound discouraged and depressed . . . You must be terribly overworked . . . You still ought to have quite a lot of money in Paris, so why don't you just pack up and come over here with Lepska for a few months? Bring the baby along too, or if this is impossible, leave her in charge of Moricand or somebody . . ."

In September 1947, Nin paid a brief visit to Miller in Big Sur while on a motor tour of America with Paul Mathiesen, a teenage traveling companion she had brought with her from New York. She remarked on the tension between Miller and Lepska, and Lepska's evident unhappiness, in her diary. She and Mathiesen went to the Miller home for lunch.

Lepska appeared. She was blond, sturdy, attractive, but spoke little. There was tension between them . . . It seemed to me that Henry was demanding an expansiveness and warmth which was not there. Lepska was silent, but affable in a closed-in way.

He criticized her. He was embarrassed. Why? I was concerned about Lepska. Knowing Henry I was sure she was young and insecure, and that he would never know how to give a woman confidence in herself. It would be no concern of his, her doubts, fears, her lack of confidence. I was sure he had praised me with exaggerations. The atmosphere was not relaxed. . .

When I stepped onto the terrace in front of the cottage Lepska suddenly and impulsively made a gesture of affection, and said with great intensity, "Anaïs, I love you, and if ever you need me, or need anything, let me know." We embraced, suddenly, spontaneously. There was in her gesture a mixture of distress and desperation, and if I had stayed I am sure we would have reached the confidences which her silence earlier seemed to withhold.

It is not difficult to imagine the source of Lepska's unhappiness. She had given up her promising future as an academic and alienated her family in order to marry Miller and become his helpmate. Once arrived in Big Sur, she found herself coping with extremely challenging living conditions in an isolated and unfamiliar community. She made the best of her circumstances, but her efforts and contributions seemed unappreciated by Miller, who treated her like the squaw he had said he was seeking in his 1943 letter to Abe Rattner from Beverly Glen. As if their life in Big Sur were not difficult enough, Miller impulsively piled on more difficulties with his impractical scheme to rescue Moricand, his missionary fervor for the Dibberns, and his dispensing of charity out of their meager resources to a former wife and a former lover. These unwise indulgences by Miller could only have deepened her sense that he took her and their marriage for granted, that his personal priorities lay elsewhere. The frustration that she felt was known only to Margaret Neiman, her closest friend in Big Sur, and to Harrydick Ross, a neighbor, who urged her to leave Miller.

WHILE MILLER WRESTLED WITH HIS VARIOUS DOMESTIC PROBLEMS, he came under attack in the national media. In April 1947, *Harper's Magazine* published an 8,000-word essay written by Mildred Edie

Brady that fingered Miller as the spiritual leader of a decadent West Coast bohemia and the founder of a "new cult of sex and anarchy" based on the writings of Emma Goldman and Wilhelm Reich. Brady, an economist and freelance writer from Berkeley, had been brought down to Big Sur along with her husband, an economics professor, by the astrologer Chester Arthur to meet Miller. Miller apparently took an instant dislike to the Bradys, and when he broke out a bottle of wine, offered a glass to the astrologer but none to the economists. Mildred was incensed. Miller speculated that she wrote the article to avenge this slight.

According to Brady's article, a "new bohemia" had sprung up on the West Coast in the aftermath of World War Two. Its members were disillusioned young intellectuals and artists, men like George Leite, Judson Crews, and Bern Porter, who were attracted to the anti-authoritarian philosophy they discovered in the writings of Henry Miller and Wilhelm Reich. The intellectual hub of this movement was to be found in the cafés and avant-garde bookstores of Berkeley and San Francisco. Leite's and Porter's *Circle* was their literary organ; Wilhelm Reich's *Function of the Orgasm* was "the most widely read and frequently quoted writing in this group." The philosophy the group shared was "a combination of anarchism and certain concepts related to psychoanalysis . . . holding on the one hand that you must abandon the church, the state, and the family (even if you do it, as James Joyce preached, 'by treachery, cunning, and exile'); and on the other offering sex as the source of individual salvation in a collective world that's going to hell . . . The core of the philosophy of this new bohemia rests in the sexual thesis, from which their anarchism stems . . . In other words, you are very much all right if you are orgastically potent."

Brady identified Miller as the seed from which this movement sprouted on the West Coast. "Miller's shack down in the Big Sur was the goal of many a cultural pilgrim . . . These disciples came to see him because he had written and published a booklet, through a local publisher [Bern Porter], called *Murder the Murderers*. It was outspokenly pacifistic—and he published it during the war. He thus became for the conscientious objectors a symbol of literary courage and the only writer of any standing at all who dared to write what they felt . . . They read his uncensored books and from them imbibed an engaging potpourri of mysticism, egoism, sexualism, surrealism, and anarchism." Brady compares Miller's extreme individualism to "the subjective absolutism of the famed Stephan George circle in pre-Hitler Germany," and tags Miller a "neo-fascist."

Brady's article attacked Miller as much by innuendo as by fact. It's true that Miller viewed himself as an anarchist. It's true that he held mystical beliefs. It's true that he was opposed to war and expressed his opposition fearlessly. It's true that a number of young men wounded psychically and spiritually by the war attached themselves to him as a father figure. (It's not true that he subscribed to the sexual theories of Wilhelm Reich. He told his friend Walker Winslow that he had never read *The Function of the Orgasm* and had no interest in Reich or his theories.) Brady, with her sneering tone, tried to demonize Miller by turning these "facts" into evidence of depravity. She called Miller a pornographer and implied that free love abounded in "the new bohemia," with Miller as orgy maestro, smashing the values of home and country that hold society together. She gave his insistence on "love" as the solution to the problem of living well a carnal dimension that distorts Miller's intent. She spoke in the voice of a conventional American intellectual frightened by Miller's determined iconoclasm and marginalized lifestyle. Brady's attack coincided with a period of political hysteria in the United States expressed through the workings of the ponderously titled House Committee on Un-American Activities and especially its investigations into subversives and communists in the motion picture industry that resulted, shamefully, in the Hollywood blacklist.

James Laughlin thought the article libelous and wrote to Lepska urging Miller to sue *Harper's*. He was certain that *Harper's* would settle and offered the services of Julien Cornell, New Directions' attorney. But Miller, preoccupied with Moricand, Dibbern, and his marital difficulties, and against litigation on principle anyway, had no interest. However, Kenneth Rexroth, whom Brady referred to in the article as a communist, did use the services of Cornell to sue her. And, proving that there is no such thing as bad publicity, Laughlin told Miller in May that Brady's article had stimulated sales of his books.

Brady's article spawned other attacks on Miller and his "cult." In May, Hearst's *San Francisco Examiner* published a series of four articles by Clint Mosher "exposing" Miller's "Cult of Hatred in the Carmel Mountains." And in its August 16, 1947, issue the *Saturday Review* published an article by Associate Editor Harrison Smith that credited Brady with unearthing "our new Bohemia" with Henry Miller as its prophet:"the hermit prophet, the mountain, a new bible, primitive sex worship, and total anarchy!"These warped views of Miller published in mainstream American media demonstrate how wide was the gap between the writer Henry Miller and American readers, and the fear that separated them. And they prefigured the bitter censorship battles that would erupt after publication of his banned books in the 1960s.

The consequences of these perceptions for Miller's battle against censorship of his Paris books were evident in a report generated by the Commission on Freedom of the Press in 1947. The commission had been formed by Robert Hutchins, president of the University of Chicago, at the instigation of Henry Luce, publisher of *Time* and *Fortune*, to address ways in which the communications industries—newspapers, periodicals, books, radio, motion pictures, television—could fulfill their social purpose more effectively. Huntington Cairns, in his capacity as official US censor, was invited to speak on issues arising from application of the obscenity statutes of the Tariff Act of 1930. Cairns wrote to Miller in June to inform him that, "I spoke at some length on your books, and outlined the problems they presented under the Federal censorship statute."

Cairns pointed out to the commission that there are "those who look upon censorship in its entirety as futile and vexatious." But he noted, "There is no likelihood whatever that the present obscenity statutes will be repealed." He admitted that the process of defining what is obscene is arbitrary because it involves "drawing a line . . . If the line must be drawn—and in practical politics the task is inescapable—we can draw it around only pornography with the largest possibility of minimum damage and maximum effectiveness." Cairns defined as the essential characteristic of obscenity its quality of being hidden. Under this definition a work is obscene because it brings into public view "sexual stimulants" that, according to common standards of decency, should remain private. Of course, bringing out into the open what society wants to hide was exactly Miller's purpose in writing his banned books. Cairns acknowledged this conundrum as he took up the issue of Miller's books before the commission, and the commission report, written by Zechariah Chafee Jr., summarizes the problem Miller faced as one not even his good friend the censor could solve. Inescapably, in the view of the commission—a group that included unimpeachable community standard-bearers such as Archibald MacLeish, Reinhold Niebuhr, and Arthur Schlesinger—Miller was the writer of obscene books.

> Another troublesome example consists in the writings of Henry Miller, an American expatriate in Paris. If you admit that obscenity exists at all, then he is obscene. Yet some people say that he is our number-one novelist. If Mr. Cairns applied the *Ulysses* test [the author's intent to write an esoteric work, not a work of pornography], Miller's works would probably be admitted, for they clearly display the literary impulse as contrasted with pornographic intent. But the test of the effect of the book "as a whole," which is habitually used, does not save Miller's books, *because they are obscene as a whole* [italics mine]. The proviso is of no benefit to him because favorable reviews by French critics are not the kind of recognition of merit which the Legal Adviser [Cairns] is willing to accept. It has been suggested as a possible way out, that Mr. Cairns could build up an American critical opinion *ad hoc* for a previously banned book by submitting the newly arrived copy to some persons in whose judgment he had confidence. He did this for Henry Miller, but it did not help Miller. Mr. Cairns has given much thought to the perplexities of the Miller case and has always ended by excluding his books. In drawing the line of obscenity, Mr. Cairns must keep an eventual court proceeding in mind.

It did not help Miller shed the "obscene" label being attached to his work that even his staunchest defenders and supporters approvingly regarded some of his writing as obscene. Wallace Fowlie had written in 1944 that Miller's obscenity was necessary "to redirect the American consciousness of evil. The obscenity in Miller's two *Tropics* is a form of medication and catharsis, an extroversion needed after all the books of puritanical foreboding." And in the same year as the commission report, Miller's Dartmouth friend Herbert West published the essay "The Strange Case of Henry Miller," in which he interpreted Miller's obscenity as "insisting on creating the truth." The problem was that American society needed to accept, not Miller's books, but the reality of obscenity in their everyday lives. As the obscenity issue continued to percolate, Miller was busy revising the book that some would consider his most inexcusably obscene, *Sexus*.

Despite these trials and tribulations in his domestic and business affairs, Miller managed to publish four new titles in 1947 and 1948. In April 1947 Miller and his friend Bezalel Schatz self-published an eighty-six-page oversized art book titled *Into the Night Life*. The text was taken from Miller's surreal improvisation on Freud's phrase that was first published in *Black Spring* and subsequently offered to American readers by James Laughlin in *The Cosmological Eye*. Schatz provided illustrations to accompany the text, which Miller wrote out by hand for this special edition. Text and illustrations were then reproduced through a four-color silkscreen process at a cost of $3,500. The result—more a "work of art" than a book—was handsome, unique (the screens were destroyed after eight hundred copies had been printed), expensive ($100 per copy), and completely impractical (Laughlin, while giving Miller permission to use the text, advised against the project, certain that Miller would have a hard time finding buyers). At the end of March Miller sent out one of his "Dear Friend" letters announcing the sale of the first one hundred copies. Recipients of the letter included William Carlos Williams, Gore Vidal, Igor Stravinsky, Isaac Stern, William Saroyan, Pierre Matisse, Frieda Lawrence, and Aldous Huxley, in addition to Miller stalwarts Emil Schnellock, Abe Rattner, Herbert West, Caresse Crosby, and Huntington Cairns.

In July the book was featured in an exhibition on "Creative Collaboration" at the San Francisco Museum of Art. Schatz and Miller attended the exhibition (so did Irving Stettner, who met Miller there), and their friend Beniamino Bufano wrote a review, reporting that "Mr. and Mrs. Will Rogers were the first ones to buy a copy of the book." Bufano also announced that André Breton, "poet laureate of the new regime," had arranged for "an insignificant French bookseller" to purchase one hundred copies of the book. But despite the promotion and publicity, the book sold slowly, as Laughlin had warned. Of the eight hundred sets of pages printed in 1947, less than two hundred were bound. Miller stored the unbound sheets in a closet, where approximately four hundred sets were destroyed by "rats and fungus." In 1977, thirty years after their original publication date, Miller was still trying to peddle the book. He bound one hundred and ninety copies for an exhibit that opened in April 1978 in Tel Aviv, where Schatz then lived. The book has become a collector's item. Copies now sell on Amazon for around $1,000.

In June 1947 the Alicat Bookshop Press in Yonkers, New York, published *Of, By and About Henry Miller*, a collection of short, previously published essays and reviews of Miller's work by prominent American literary critics. The collection also included reviews Miller had written, appreciations of contemporary artists such as Max Ernst and Albert Cossery. The book appears to have been conceived by its publisher, Oscar Baradinsky, as a reputation builder for Miller along the lines of *The Happy Rock*, but less obviously self-serving. It brought together favorable assessments of Miller's work by respected critics writing in prominent journals, such as Paul Rosenfeld (*Nation*), Nicola Chiaromonte (*New Republic*), and Wallace Fowlie (*Accent*). These reviews, while recognizing Miller's artistry with language and his exuberance for life, also pointed up the difficulty that Miller faced overcoming the "obscenity" label. Rosenfeld praised Miller as a stylist but faulted *Tropic of Cancer* for being "often obscene to the verge of pornography" and lamented that *Tropic of Capricorn* contains "a load of partially inevitable, mainly superfluous obscenity." Fowlie, perhaps Miller's most perceptive and understanding critic, acknowledged Miller's obscenity, but dismissed it as nothing more than a device.

In November 1947, New Directions published *Remember to Remember*, subtitled "volume 2 of The Air-Conditioned Nightmare." The book serves up a familiar medley of Miller subjects and concerns: profiles of Miller's artist friends, satirical assaults on the American way of life, discourses on war and censorship, and, notably, a long nostalgic hymn to his years in France and their transformative power in his life.

During the summer of 1946 as Miller selected essays for inclusion, he and Laughlin had debated over the title of this book. Mindful of the poor reviews that had slowed sales of *The Air-Conditioned Nightmare*, Laughlin wanted a fresh title. Miller suggested calling the book *The Egg in Its Prison*, an ugly title that Laughlin quickly rejected, suggesting instead the equally awkward *The Electrified Rat-Race*. They finally settled on the title essay "Remember to Remember," and in December of that year Laughlin wrote approvingly to Miller from Europe. "You really do have a wonderful style. And now the overall architecture of your philosophy begins to shape up before me."

Miller's "philosophy," if there was one, centered on the meaning of being an artist and the artist's role in society, issues that had occupied Miller's thoughts from his earliest attempts at writing and that had become paramount concerns with the publication of *Tropic of Cancer* and its subsequent censorship in America and England. These concerns obviously guided Miller's selection of essays for *Remember to Remember*. They also animate his little clown fable, *The Smile at the Foot of the Ladder*, completed in the summer of 1947 and published in March 1948.

Miller's preface to *Remember to Remember* anticipates the themes that will be developed in the essays that follow. On the one hand there are "people to whom I wish to pay homage": artists like himself who have made their art the center of their lives, usually at the cost of considerable personal suffering and material deprivation. On the other hand there is America, the culture in which these artists attempt to function and which they hope to awaken and enliven through their art. This America Miller finds spiritually and culturally defective. "America is full of places," he writes. "Empty places. And all these empty places are crowded. Just jammed with empty souls. All at loose ends, all seeking diversion. As though the chief object of existence were to forget." The artist's responsibility is first to himself, to remember his own humanity and its source in nature, and second to his fellow man, to society, to serve as an example of what it means to be human and thereby to inspire others to remember their common humanity.

Only when the individuals who comprise society manifest their humanity in their everyday lives will man live harmoniously on the planet.

Miller included portraits of five artists in *Remember to Remember*
(six if you include his fond recollections of Alfred Perlès in the title
essay). He profiled three painters, a theater director, and a sculptor.
All were friends of Miller whom he admired both for their work
and for their personal qualities. Jean Varda—"The Master Builder"
who introduced Miller to Big Sur—was a Greek from Smyrna who
turned the detritus of civilization into art. "There is one thing that is
anathema to Varda," Miller informs us, "and that is waste . . . He takes
delight in plundering the refuse heaps and from the plunder creating
veritable mansions of light and joy." For this quality, this ability to
transform what is ugly and discarded into something useful and beautiful, Miller sanctifies Varda. "Once he dreamt of becoming a monk.
He did not know then that he was already a saint." Miller tells Varda,
"You are the monk of paint. With every picture you make you teach
renunciation. You mint only what is pure. You are the metaphysician
of space and color."

The African American painter Beauford Delaney is called by
Miller "amazing and invariable," for he embodies the same principle of transformation that Miller found in Varda. Miller had been
introduced to Delaney by their mutual friend, Harry Herschkowitz.
Delaney lived in a miserable unheated studio in Greenwich Village
while he struggled to earn a living from his painting, leading Miller
to deplore the conditions under which the artist had to work: "Logic,
our crazy logic, dictates that the environment of the creative individual must be composed of all the ugly, painful, discordant and diseased
elements of life. To prove his genius the artist must transform these
elements into durable symbols of beauty, goodness, truth and light."
Delaney is the prototype of the pure artist who sacrifices all to his
medium. "For twenty-five years all he has demanded of the world
is permission to paint . . . He never curses his lot because he has
never for a moment questioned his fate." Delaney too is sanctified
by Miller because of his unwavering commitment to his art. "In his
most amazing, most invariable state of beatitude, Brother Beauford
is himself the summum and optimum of all the solar energies and

radiances combined . . . So Beauford, sitting at 181 Greene Street, breathing slowly, evenly, gently, deliberately, sets in motion the universal brotherhood of man, the white sisterhood of doves and angels, and the great serpentine constellation of birds, beasts and flowers, all caracoling towards the sun in color, peace and harmony."

In "A Bodhisattva Artist" Miller pays tribute to his friend Abe Rattner, whom he met during the 1930s while living in Paris and who subsequently accompanied him on the first part of his American tour. Rattner is another prototypical artist, a kind of superman. "He works indefatigably because he loves what he is doing. He would ask nothing better than that his working day be doubled. . .This is the way of the true artist beyond all doubt, for the real artist is all creation, all energy, all impulse, all enthusiasm. He is a sun whose central fires never cease to blaze. He radiates warmth, courage, hope, because in himself he is the essence of these attributes." Miller extols painting as the highest art form:"The man who takes up painting, who pursues it with his whole heart and soul, *must* be a joyous individual. Myself I have always regarded it as the happiest medium to work in. It is a medium which seems to sharpen the psyche and restore the whole being."

Rattner too has made his life a sacrifice, a rosy crucifixion. He is a "Bodhisattva artist," because "having attained grace and freedom, having realized himself, [he] elects to remain in the realm of painting in order to inspire other artists . . . His life is all devotion, all consecration . . . If I were asked to say what Rattner immortalizes I should say Color, the color of the rose which blossoms on the cross."

Jasper Deeter was the director of the Hedgerow Theatre in Moylan, Pennsylvania. Miller met him while visiting his friend Paul Weiss at Bryn Mawr with Lepska in 1944. He saw in Deeter not only an artist in the highest sense of the word, but also a leader of a community of artists. The Hedgerow Theatre thus became for Miller a tiny model of what American society could become were it to fulfill its potential as a true democracy. Miller lauds Deeter as "the type of American whom I like to think of as being a true representative of the New World, a sort of forerunner to the democratic man of whom Whitman sang . . . Deeter epitomizes certain rare qualities which have come to be regarded as purely American."To illustrate his concept of the "pure American," Miller cites a widely known actor. "Gary Cooper comes nearer to personifying this sort of individual than anyone I can think of, especially in certain roles which he has made famous."

What makes the Hedgerow Theatre fit Miller's utopian model is that it is without hierarchy. There are no "stars" and no "bit players." Each member of the company does what is required to carry out the production at hand, regardless of whether it be performing the lead role or helping to change the set between scenes. In this sense, it is a purely democratic community and passes Miller's test of complete equality and complete responsibility for each individual. There is no need for the superstructure of a "state," because the community is self-governing. "I speak of the Hedgerow group as a little self-governing community because it is just that—and seldom do we see self-government," Miller writes. "The fact that any group, no matter where, no matter how small, can give the illusion of such an ultimate, means to me that it is possible to realize this condition of the human family on a universal scale."

The phrase "self-governing" is a *double entendre* in that it suggests both a self-sufficient individual exercising self-control and a group of such individuals cooperating as a community.

Beniamino Bufano—"the man of hard materials"—was a sculptor and arts activist who had been a member of the San Francisco Arts Commission. He was also for a time a resident of Big Sur. Miller wrote about Bufano because the sculptor's experience with officialdom in San Francisco illustrated Miller's belief that America not only failed to appreciate and support its artists, it often abused them and their work, as it had done with his banned books, all of which were seized and destroyed if discovered by the authorities.

Bufano is another of Miller's meta-beings, made exceptional by his artistry and his determination to share his art with the public. "In one being he combines dreamer, worker, athlete, gladiator, adventurer, monk, saint, and statesman." Bufano created large sculptural works intended for display in public places, pieces "imposing enough to dominate whole cities . . . eloquent enough to stand alone in the midst of a desert . . ." Many of these pieces had been lost, mutilated, or consigned to storage while in public custody. For his protests against the city's mistreatment of his work, Bufano was sentenced to ten days in jail. Bufano thus became for Miller another example of the neglected, unappreciated, vilified artist in America, and a symptom of a diseased civilization. "We are more desperate than the boldest among us dares to imagine," Miller concludes. "We are dry and barren, joyless, sick at heart, sick in mind; we are being stifled and smothered by our creature comforts, by our fear of change, our fear of adventure, but above all, by our fear of ideas. What we crave is a life of 'gilt-edge security.' And we are getting it. We are embalming ourselves."

The notion of America as a dry, barren, joyless place bereft of ideas or culture Miller developed at length in a critique of American bread in "The Staff of Life." The sterility of American white bread that he found served everywhere on his American tour in 1941 Miller took as symptomatic of the emptiness pervading American life. "You can travel fifty thousand miles in America without once tasting a piece of good bread . . . Why? Because the very core of life is contaminated. If [Americans] knew what good bread was they would not have such wonderful machines on which they lavish all their time, energy and affection . . . They have lost their taste for life. For enjoyment. For good conversation. For everything worthwhile, to put it briefly. What do I find wrong with America? Everything." By contrast, in the France that Miller lovingly recalls in the essay "Remember to Remember," everywhere "there is good food, drink and conversation." And each individual is a distinct character. "There was never that nondescript quality about them which is so annihilating here in America."

The only exception to this universal incidence of unpalatable American bread occurs in Jewish delicatessens. "A Jewish sandwich contains more food value than an eighty-five cent meal in the ordinary American restaurant . . . The desire to survive has made the Jews keen about preserving the staff of life."

The way to obtain good bread in America, Miller suggests, is to bake your own. This metaphoric advice reiterates Miller's belief that it is up to us as individuals to take full responsibility for the quality of our lives, whether measured by the bread we eat, the work we perform, the friendships we cultivate, or our metaphysical relationship to reality.

Miller also took up his quarrel with America in his essay on Abe Rattner. Recollecting their tour of America, Miller wrote, "Whenever there was a bit of life, a bit of leisure, a bit of real conversation, a bit of decent food, a glass of good wine, a moment of forgetfulness, of ease, cheer, tolerance and wisdom, we thought of Europe. But how often was that? Almost never." Miller believed that America has fallen from its Golden Age. "In the early part of the Nineteenth Century this country produced a flock of men who might truly be called cultured men. They were individuals, men of rounded vision, democrats in the real sense of the word. They were aristocratic spirits; they had links with the men of Europe. Today they stand out as anomalies. Uniformity and conformity, these dominate the spirit of the present-day American."

If there is an inconsistency in holding up Gary Cooper—an American innocent, freed from the European tradition—as the archetype of the democratic American, while simultaneously yearning for the lost culture of Europe, Miller was untroubled by it. Given that he perceived a decline in the American character over the course of the country's history, Miller foresaw a bleak American future, ever more materially comfortable and technologically advanced, ever more spiritually empty. "This is the beginning of a black cycle," Miller gloomily predicted. "The color is gray. The taste is neutral. Passion is dead. The future holds no promise except more war, more destruction, more catastrophe." The root of the problem is in the American soul: "The American in general is not seeking beauty, peace, well-being . . . At heart he is very much like those men who first invaded the continent, a plunderer. Not only is he exploiting the country's natural resources, but he is also exploiting his fellow man." In the face of this ongoing desecration of what Miller considered to be the essential values of a meaningful life, Miller seeks and finds an alternate reality in art, and he imbues art and artists with an almost supranatural power to give life religious significance.

The dilemma of choosing between art and life that engaged Miller in his writing and in his personal life was the central issue of *The Smile at the Foot of the Ladder*, a slender fable that Miller wrote about a circus clown who grows weary of his ability to make people laugh.

Edwin Corle, a well-known Western author, wrote a flattering estimate of Miller as an introduction to the book. He selected a passage from *Wisdom of the Heart* to convey the religious dimension of Miller's belief in the supreme value of art. "When we have rid ourselves of the suicidal mania for a beyond we shall begin the life of here and now which is reality and which is sufficient unto itself. We shall have no need for art or religion because we shall be in ourselves a work of art." In his epilogue to *Smile* Miller identifies the clown as a being in whom life and art are fused. "A clown is a poet in action. He is the story which he enacts. It is the same story over and over—adoration, devotion, crucifixion. 'A Rosy Crucifixion' *bien entendu*." Miller identifies with the clown hero of the fable; the story of Auguste's struggle to choose between art and life is Miller's struggle. He writes, "When I was graduating from High School, they had asked me what I had intended to be and I had said—'a clown . . .' And later on I discovered to my surprise that my most intimate friends looked upon me as a clown." To the reader familiar with Miller's writing about the artist and society, it comes as no surprise when, at the end of *Smile*, after Auguste has accepted himself as a clown and found bliss, he is destroyed while idling in a public park by a club-wielding policeman (a likely reference to Miller's arrest for sleeping overnight in a public park in Jacksonville, Florida, while married to June). But Auguste dies with a "seraphic smile" on his face, and Miller remarks, "When Auguste becomes himself life begins—and not just for Auguste, but for all mankind."

THE AMERICAN CRITICS PAID SCANT ATTENTION TO MILLER'S output during this period. And among those who did give him notice opinion was divided. Because of its limited distribution, *Into the Night Life* was "reviewed" only by Beniamino Bufano. But his article reads more like a press release than a critical assessment. It appeared in *What's Doing*, a Monterey Peninsula events guide. *Remember to Remember* was reviewed only by *The New York Times* and the *San Francisco Chronicle* in the daily press. A few prominent periodicals also gave it space. Anne Fremantle, writing in *Commonweal*, took a favorable view of Miller, finding him, despite his evident dislike of his native land, a "valiant American [who] has a faith Walt Whitman would have envied." Charles Glicksberg, in *Southwest Review*, remarked that the "sex-inspired and sex-obsessed" Henry Miller had "turned preacher and prophet, seriously bent on saving the world from destruction." He also noted an apparent waning of Miller's creative powers since *The Cosmological Eye*. And he observed that "the passionate vehemence with which he decries the evil conditions in this country argues an inverted kind of love." But Charles Rolo in an essay on the American avant-garde that appeared in *Tomorrow*—a literary journal that had also published Miller's work—deplored "the hysterical infantilism of Henry Miller. He has turned out a staggering quantity of perverse nonsense, pointless obscenity and pretentious hokum. A fair-sized chunk of it, along with a few of the better things, is assembled in *Remember to Remember* . . . No living writer can deliver himself of clichés with so portentous an air of revelation." Opinion was also divided on *Smile*, but *Time* pronounced Miller the last writer in a great tradition. One of Miller's fans, the religious thinker Alan Watts, wrote Miller a letter of appreciation for *Remember to Remember*, congratulating him for having "things to say in your studies of Varda, Delaney and Rattner which are really profound" and telling Miller, "I agree with your general depiction of our 'air-conditioned nightmare'."

Although Miller's work from this period (1947–48) was not extensively reviewed, it did receive attention from prominent national publications. And it was clear from the reviews, whether favorable or unfavorable, that Miller was being treated as a serious writer. The charge of obscenity that had been leveled against the Paris books could not be applied to Miller's American output. It would seem that the criteria laid out by Huntington Cairns for lifting the ban on Miller's books were being met. But a test case in San Francisco and the publication of *Sexus* in France showed that Miller's battle with the censors was far from over.

8

THE ROSY CRUCIFIXION

"This Bloody Business of Censorship"

IN FEBRUARY 1949, FIVE YEARS AFTER COMING TO BIG SUR WITH THE intention of completing his major autobiographical opus, *The Rosy Crucifixion*, Miller sent to his agent in France the manuscript of *Sexus*, book one of the projected trilogy about his tortured and transforming relationship with his second wife, June Mansfield. The idea for this epic work had been germinating in Miller for over twenty years, since an evening in 1927 when, in a fever of inspiration, he had written extensive notes outlining its form and content. He had drawn from this well of material in *Tropic of Capricorn* but had not plumbed its depths.

Miller regarded the completion of this work as a crucial and necessary step in his evolution as an artist and human being. He was writing the book to exhume his past, to purify himself of it so that he could live more fully and completely in the present. He had often expressed to friends the hope that completing *The Rosy Crucifixion* might liberate him from the need to write and enable him to join the ranks of those who had mastered "the art of living." When he reported to Durrell that he had finished *Sexus* and was halfway through *Plexus*, he anticipated the moment when he would be free of the need to tell the story of his life. "Then I am off into the blue ... Joy through work hereafter. No more compulsion. I will be emptied."

Miller had been working on *The Rosy Crucifixion* intermittently since returning to the United States from Europe at the start of the war. In March 1949, Miller wrote to Durrell that he had drafted *Sexus* in about six months during the first half of 1942 at the conclusion of his American tour, when it became apparent that Doubleday & Doran would not publish *The Air-Conditioned Nightmare. Sunday After the War*, published in 1944, contained three fragments from *Sexus*, giving American readers a sampling of several of its infrequent "sanitary" passages. In the spring of 1946, Miller sent the manuscript to Herb West and Emil Schnellock for review. In February 1948, while Moricand was still his houseguest, Miller wrote to Laughlin, "I'm now at page 1,100 of the R.C. I believe I could write 3,000 pages as easily as 2,000 now . . . When this book comes out it will be like dropping an atom bomb on the literary world. I only hope I will live to complete it. I am exhausted."

Sexus is formed around Miller's relationship with June ("Mara"/"Mona") during the period of their courtship, a time when Miller was married to his first wife, Beatrice ("Maude"), and support ing her and their daughter, Barbara, by working as the employment manager for Western Union ("The Cosmodemonic Telegraph Company"). The book covers approximately one year, beginning with their meeting at a Broadway dance hall in the summer of 1923 and ending shortly after their hasty marriage at City Hall in Hoboken, New Jersey, on June 1, 1924. (Beatrice divorced Miller on December 21, 1923, after surprising Miller and June naked in bed in the Millers' home, witnesses in tow.)

In structure the "novel," if it can be called that, is picaresque, episodes succeeding one another in an apparently random order, usually triggered by Miller's memories and associations. The book has frequent digressions and digressions within digressions as Miller, the narrator, allows himself to drift from one thought or recollection to another. The narrative structure thus resembles a river, with the Miller-Mona relationship as the central channel, and Miller's recollections of his past life, portraits of characters he meets or remembers, commentary on social conditions in New York and America, and discourses on metaphysics forming smaller streams that flow into the main river. Structurally, *Sexus* bears comparison with Mark Twain's novel *Adventures of Huckleberry Finn*: Miller's memory stream and the figures borne on it like the mighty Mississippi and the cast of scoundrels and con men it floods into the lives of Huck and Jim. There is a further resemblance between Miller's hyperbolic, expressionistic style and Twain's frequent resort to the tall tale to embellish his narrative and define character.

The irrational flow of episodes in *Sexus* is meant to approximate the chaos of life. Underlying them is Miller's relentless quest for food, shelter, and sex. Miller is at pains to pursue the satisfaction of these basic needs in a pose of gay abandon. No situation, no matter how sordid, no sexual encounter, no matter how debauched and devoid of human affection or warmth, no panhandling, no matter how humiliating, can disturb the serenity of Miller's complacent acceptance and approval. Only when commenting on the soulless conditions of life in the megalopolis and the emptiness of its inhabitants, or when discoursing on art as a liberating force—the path of escape from the nightmare—does Miller's voice become serious. Otherwise he models Swift and Petronius, satirizing both himself and the world he inhabits.

As are nearly all of Miller's books, *Sexus* is a potpourri of the author's interests, friends, experiences, and beliefs. At its core is Miller himself in all his complexity, variability, vulgarity, and linguistic brilliance. The book is above all a portrait of Miller. And the Miller of *Sexus* is libidinous, a man gladly, joyously in thrall to his instincts, and especially to the demands of his penis.

What distinguishes *Sexus* is the frequency and extent of its sexual episodes and the significance that accumulates from their repetition. In *Sexus* Miller raises sex to an epic dimension, as though he is deliberately flaunting those very qualities of writing that have kept his most important books, the Paris books, out of the hands of American readers.

Ironically, the most lascivious and extended descriptions of sex in *Sexus* are given over to Miller's numerous couplings with his despised and forsaken first wife and mother of his child. Maude represents the bankruptcy of the conventional bourgeois life in which he finds himself trapped. He describes their home: "We were living then in a morbidly respectable neighborhood, occupying the parlor floor and basement of a lugubrious brownstone house. From time to time I had tried to write but the gloom which my wife created around her was too much for me. Only once did I succeed in breaking the spell which she had cast over the place; that was during a high fever which lasted for several days when I refused to see a doctor, refused to take any medicine, refused to take any nourishment. . . I lived several lives in the few days that it lasted. That was my sole vacation in the sepulcher which is called home."

Maude is prudish about sex, ashamed of her body and genitals. Although she enjoys the sexual act, she cannot face this aspect of herself consciously. She has lost connection with the instinctual life that Miller insists must be restored. Miller must play an elaborate charade with her in which she pretends to be asleep while they make love. "Must sneak up on her, slip it in while she's dreaming," Miller writes. "Must do it in my sleep like or she'll be insulted."

But no sooner has Miller disclosed to Maude that he has fallen in love with Mara than Maude discards her inhibitions about sex and becomes an ardent partner. Miller describes their subsequent coupling in graphic but comically hyperbolic language that is typical of the many sex scenes in the book. "She was making some sort of wheeling motion in the dark. Her legs came down over my shoulders and her crotch was up against my lips. I slid her ass over my head, like you'd raise a pail of milk to slake a lazy thirst, and I drank and chewed and guzzled like a buzzard. She was so deep in heat that her teeth were clamped dangerously around the head of my cock. In that frantic, teary passion she had worked herself up to I had a fear that she might sink her teeth in deep, bite the end of it clean off. I had to tickle her to make her release her jaws."

Maude has abandoned herself to her instincts and surrendered her mind. "She crouched on all fours like a she-animal, quivering and whinnying with undisguised pleasure. Not a human word out of her, not a sign that she knew any language except this block-and-tackle-subgum-one-ton-blow-the-whistle sort."

The undercurrent of playful humor in this scene, the rendering of the sexual act as grotesquely acrobatic and farcical, devoid of grace or dignity, removes it from the realm of the obscene and turns it into satire. By carrying his descriptions of sex to expressionistic extremes, Miller mocks the entire apparatus of "decency" and "propriety" that supports censorship. Later in the book, after Miller has moved out to live with Mona and Maude has filed for divorce, Miller makes regular visits to his previous home on the pretext of seeing his daughter. But the real purpose of these visits is sex with Maude. During one of them, they are joined by Elsie, a young woman who lodges upstairs, and a three-way orgy ensues. It too begins on a comic note:

> "Whew, it's hot!" said Elsie.
>
> "Take your dress off, if you like," said Maude. "I'm taking this off," and suiting action to word she slipped out of the wrap and stood naked before us.
>
> The next moment we were all stark naked.
>
> "It's wonderful not to be jealous anymore," said Maude very simply.

The three lovers play records, fiddle with each other, and drink wine. Maude declares, "I've never been so happy." The orgy goes on for pages, in all innocence.

Miller links the energy released in the sex act to the energy that fuels creative work. He remarks on this connection after one of his numerous trysts with Maude.

> I observed with the keenest pleasure how my mind was sparking, how it radiated energy in every direction. This was the sort of ebullience and *élan* I prayed for when I felt the desire to write. I used to sit down and wait for this to happen. But it never did happen—not this way. It happened afterwards, sometimes when I had left the machine and gone for a walk. Yes, suddenly it would come on, like an attack, pell-mell, from every direction, a veritable inundation, an avalanche—and there was I, helpless, miles away from the typewriter, not a piece of paper in my pocket. Sometimes I would start for the house on the trot, not running too fast because it would peter out, but easy like, just as in fucking—when you tell yourself to take it easy, don't think about it, that's it, in and out, cool detached, trying to pretend to yourself that it's your prick that's fucking and not you. Exactly the same procedure. Jog along, steady, hold it, don't think about the typewriter or how far it is to the house, just easy, steady-like, that's it . . .

Penis and pen.

If the libido was for Miller the seat of both sexual and creative energy, then Mara/Mona was for Miller the artist's bride and fecundator, a being who embodied the endless mystery of life that it was the artist's task to penetrate. The most beautifully lyrical passages in *Sexus* are dedicated to Mona and the power she held over Miller's imagination. During a long passage on "the creative life" as the means of escape from time, history, and personality, Miller renders Mara/Mona as an elusive phantom whose essence can never be grasped, whose bottomless mystery fires his imagination and brings forth hallucinatory prose:

> Studying her morsel by morsel, feet, hands, hair, lips, ears, breasts, traveling from navel to mouth and from mouth to eyes, the woman I fell upon, clawed, bit, suffocated with kisses, the woman who had been Mara and was now Mona, who had been and would be other names, other persons, other assemblages of appendages, was no more accessible, penetrable, than a cool statue in a forgotten garden of a lost continent. . . Haunting nights when, filled with creation, I saw nothing but her eyes and in those eyes, rising like bubbling pools of lava, phantoms came to the surface, faded, vanished, reappeared, bringing dread, apprehension, fear, mystery. Night after night, from words to dreams, to flesh, to phantoms. Possession and depossession. The flowers of the moon, the broad-backed palms of jungle growth, the baying of bloodhounds, the frail white body of a child, the lava bubbles, the rallentando of the snowflakes, the floorless bottom where smoke blooms into flesh. And what is flesh but moon? and what is moon but night? Night is longing, longing, longing, beyond all endurance.

"Think of *us!*" she said that night when she turned and flew up the steps rapidly. And it was as if I could think of nothing else. We two and the stairs ascending infinitely.

WHEN MILLER SENT THE MANUSCRIPT OF *SEXUS* TO HIS AGENT IN PARIS, he asked Hoffman whether the book should be given to Girodias to publish or to another French publisher, such as Denoel or Gallimard. Girodias's continuing financial difficulties were pinching Miller. He wrote to Fowlie at about the same time that he was "flat broke" and bartering for food. Laughlin, who had agreed a year earlier to send Miller $150 per month as an advance against his New Directions royalties, had reduced the monthly payment to $125 because of declining sales. Hoffman reported that Girodias still owed Miller 3,619,964 francs (about $10,350), but that his bankruptcy, which had occurred in June 1948, made payments in the near term doubtful. Nevertheless, Hoffman advised Miller to give *Sexus* to Girodias but to draw up a special contract that would obligate Girodias to pay Miller royalties for the entire edition on the date of publication. Laughlin, who at this time was aggressively promoting Miller's books to publishers in France, Germany, Italy, and Switzerland, urged Miller to give *Sexus* to another publisher. But Miller remained loyal to Girodias despite his unreliability, and Girodias published *Sexus* in an edition of three thousand copies in August 1949. The book was clothbound, and sold in a deluxe edition for two thousand francs ($5.60), a high price in France.

As Miller had predicted, the book caused an immediate explosion. The first reaction came from an unexpected quarter, Miller's literary soul mate Lawrence Durrell. A month before Girodias issued *Sexus*, Durrell had published in the British periodical *Horizon* an appreciation of Miller. Durrell praised Miller as a writer in the tradition of Whitman and Melville whose aim in writing was not to master a literary form but rather "to make use of his art in order to grow by it, in order to expand the domains of his own sensibility . . . What he has to offer us is the vicarious triumph of *finding ourselves* in reading him." For Miller, "the object of creation is not only to produce 'works of art' but to become more and more oneself in doing so." He likened Miller to D. H. Lawrence as a writer "who values art as a method of self-realization, not as an end in itself."

Durrell had not yet read *Sexus* when he wrote this essay, but he took up the issue of Miller's "obscenity" as Miller employed it in the Tropics and defended it in his essay "Obscenity and the Law of Reflection." After chiding Anglo-Saxon readers for being "emotionally stunted" and prone to "over-value obscenity," Durrell quoted Miller's justification of the obscenity in his work—"It's purpose is to awaken, to usher in a sense of reality"—and concluded that "the use of obscenity, then, has something like a religious function for Miller." After sketching Miller's career and acknowledging his defects—"there is much that is careless, ill-judged, rash, splenetic, shapeless, over-stated"—Durrell rendered the "considered opinion" that "judged by his best work he is already among the greatest contemporary writers."

But when he read *Sexus* early in September, Durrell became alarmed for his friend's reputation. He wrote Miller immediately from Belgrade, where he was attached to the British Legation, to convey to Miller his "bitter disappointment" in the book owing to its "moral vulgarity." Conceding that the book "contains some of your very best writing to date," Durrell scolded Miller for being undisciplined and sloppy. "These silly, meaningless scenes which have no raison d'être, no humour, just childish explosions of obscenity—what a pity . . . But the strange thing is that the book gives very little feeling of real passion . . . This book needs taking apart and regluing. The obscenity in it is really unworthy of you." A few days later, Durrell followed up this letter with an urgent telegram: "*SEXUS* DISGRACEFULLY BAD WILL COMPLETELY RUIN REPUTATION UNLESS WITHDRAWN REVISED."

Miller's reply to Durrell was gracious and accepting. He made no apologies for *Sexus*, declaring, "I am writing exactly what I want to write and the way I want to do it." He explained his purpose: "I am trying to reproduce in words a block of my life which to me has the utmost significance—every bit of it . . . The paramount thing is for me to get it out of my system—and in doing so to reveal what I was and am." He assured Durrell that he harbored no ill will toward him and encouraged him to be honest in his criticism. "You are to feel at liberty to baste hell out of me to all and sundry. I will understand that you are doing it out of love for me."

After Miller sent off this reply, he received another telegram from Durrell, apologizing, followed by a letter in which, while not altering his view of *Sexus*, he asked Miller to forgive him for being "ill-tempered" and "waspish" in his criticism. Durrell had been asked to review *Sexus* for *Horizon* and a number of other periodicals, and had not muted his objections to the book. Alfred Perlès, who had obtained a copy of *Sexus* during a visit to Paris and then had read Durrell's review, wrote to Durrell taking him to task for faulting the book. Durrell enclosed Perlès's letter, adding that he agreed with every word of it. Perlès also wrote to Miller declaring his support of Miller's aims and accomplishment with *Sexus*. There the matter ended, with no apparent harm done to the Durrell-Miller friendship.

But Durrell's was not the only negative response to *Sexus* from the critics. Chesley Saroyan, writing in *Points*, an English language review published in Paris, asserted that the writing in *Sexus* had fallen below the standard of the Tropics. "One feels a tiredness and lack of creative conviction in the present work which is the very antithesis of Miller himself. He seems now often to be writing more from literary habit than literary necessity." Saroyan, unlike Durrell, was not offended by the extensive obscenity in *Sexus* but saw in Miller's emphasis on sex a warped sense of reality. "In *Sexus*, sex is no longer a part of reality, but almost the sum total of reality—the sex act now practically the one end and object of all life—sex itself raised to the status of a belief—a way of life—a morality—a religion. It is as though Miller actually believes that man is capable of copulating his way through the riddles of the universe." Miller, when he read this review, suspected it had been written by Durrell using a pen name, and wrote to the editor. He received a reply from Mr. Saroyan himself.

Unfavorable criticism was only the beginning of the problems brought on by *Sexus*. The book was clearly testing the limits of French tolerance. Given the high level of interest in Miller's work owing to *l'affaire Miller*, Girodias had initially planned a first edition of twelve thousand copies. But a major French distributor, Hachette, had backed out of handling the book, even though it was in English, and Girodias was forced to sell it by subscription in the deluxe edition. In January 1950, Hoffman wrote to Miller expressing his doubt that a French-language version of *Sexus* could be published in France. Later in the month, Hoffman reported that Girodias had, without authorization, published a "purged" and "unpurged" edition of the French translation of *Sexus* and that the police had seized the unpurged version and were bringing an action against Girodias. Hoffman proposed to bring suit against Girodias for copyright infringement, and in February Miller wrote back giving his consent. The upshot was that Girodias was prosecuted, fined, and imprisoned. In December, the Ministry of the Interior banned sales of *Sexus* in France in any language.

These developments complicated Miller's plans to have *Plexus*, book two of *The Rosy Crucifixion*, published in France. Miller had completed the manuscript of *Plexus* in September 1949 but had held off sending it to France because of his uncertainty over who should publish it. Girodias's legal and financial problems, and his unreliability, caused Hoffman to recommend that *Plexus* be offered to Edmond Buchet, who owned the publishing house Correa. Miller agreed to this, on the condition that Girodias give his permission. Despite Girodias's poor business practices, Miller remained loyal to him. He wrote to his Belgian friend Pierre Lesdain, "He never does anything swiftly or smoothly . . . He is a born procrastinator . . . and I loathe procrastinators . . . But when I get his letter of apology and 'defense', I feel ashamed of myself. At heart he means well." Correa agreed to bring out *Plexus* if Miller would trim a five-page passage that Correa's editor Maurice Nadeau believed was censorable. Surprisingly, Miller agreed to the cut.

France was not the only front on which censorship battles over Miller's books were being fought at this time. In the spring of 1949, J. Murray Luck, a professor of biochemistry at Stanford University, purchased a copy of *Tropic of Cancer* and a copy of *Tropic of Capricorn* while in Paris and mailed them to his address in Palo Alto, California. The books were seized by US Customs at the port of entry in San Francisco and on June 24, 1949, the United States Attorney filed a libel claim against the books under authority of Section 305 of the Tariff Act of 1930, "praying" that the United States District Court authorize their "forfeiture and destruction." Prior to the libel action, Professor Luck "gave" the books to Ernest J. Besig, executive director of the American Civil Liberties Union of Northern California. Besig, acting as claimant, filed an answer to the libel in which he alleged that the books were not subject to seizure and should be returned. In effect, Luck and Besig had set up a test of whether the Tropics were obscene under US law.

Besig retained George Olshausen, a San Francisco attorney, to represent him, and in March 1950 Olshausen wrote to Miller asking for the names of critics or professors who could testify to the literary quality of the Tropics. Olshausen was pursuing a defense strategy that accorded with Huntington Cairns's belief that the Tropics could only overcome the charge of obscenity if they were the subject of serious discussion by acknowledged literary experts. Miller cooperated with Olshausen, suggesting Edmund Wilson, H. L. Mencken, Herbert West, Wallace Fowlie, Alfred Kazin, Philip Rahv, and Herbert Read. But in a letter he wrote to Laughlin about the case, Miller expressed his pessimism about the outcome and his resignation to the will of the public. "I have the feeling that only by assisting the censors make the [banned books] difficult to get will we finally create in the general public a desire to do something about this bloody business of censorship." Was Miller here expressing his Whitmanesque faith in the fundamental good sense of the common man? Or was he simply counting on the prurient interest of the ordinary American? Miller told Laughlin he would not become a party to the fight but lamented, "I am probably the only author in America who suffers because of censorship regulations."

To buttress his "literary merit" defense, Olshausen developed a questionnaire to be used to take depositions from nineteen literary experts in the United States and Europe and asked the court to admit the depositions as evidence. The US Attorney opposed their admission on the ground that the obscenity of the books could be determined from the books themselves without the necessity of expert testimony. Judge Louis Goodman announced that he would read the two books before ruling. Then, citing the opinion of Judge Augustus Hand in the *Ulysses* case—"the proper test of whether a given book is obscene is its dominant effect"—Goodman ruled that the Tropics were obscene. "Both books are replete with long passages that are filthy and revolting," the jurist wrote, "and that tend to excite lustful thoughts and desires. While the books also have passages, and indeed chapters, that may be said to be of literary merit, the obscene portions have no literary value; they are directly, completely and wholly filthy and obscene and have no reasonable relation to any literary concept inherent in the Books' theme." Goodman then wondered rhetorically if Besig would be comfortable "reading the innumerable filthy passages in the books to young people of his acquaintance." He ruled against the admission of expert testimony as being "wholly irrelevant and immaterial."

Miller saw the futility of proceeding if a judge could set himself up as the sole authority on the literary merit of a book and wondered if Cairns had been wrong in emphasizing the importance of critical opinion. Olshausen predicted that Goodman would rule in favor of the government at the trial scheduled for the following year but pointed out that his decision on the depositions would be useful for an appeal, if Besig were willing to pursue one. Perhaps anticipating this, at the trial Goodman admitted into evidence eighteen published reviews of Miller's work, fifteen letters and two affidavits of critics. The US Attorney submitted one book review (by Philip Rahv) and a letter from a professor of English at San Francisco State College. But the court, in declaring its opinion that the Tropics are obscene, disregarded expert testimony. Clearly, the sensibilities of Judge Goodman were deeply offended by the two books. In justifying his opinion, Goodman wrote, "The many obscene passages in the books have such evil stench that to include them here in footnotes would make this opinion pornographic. For example, there are several passages where the female sexual organs are referred to in such detailed vulgar language as to create nausea in the reader. If this be important literature, then the dignity of the human person and the stability of the family unit, which are the cornerstone of our system of our society, are lost to us."

This last remark goes to the heart of the fear that kept Miller's Paris books beyond the reach of American readers. Judge Goodman did experience the painful awakening that Miller's brutal frankness was meant to provoke; but he experienced it as nausea because it threatened the prevailing value system that he was sworn to protect. Miller was in a cul-de-sac. The values he was challenging appeared to be impregnable. Although Besig agreed to an appeal, the Ninth Circuit Court of Appeals upheld Goodman's ruling in a decision issued on October 23, 1953. Its reasoning was also founded on belief in a prevailing standard of decency that the Tropics violated.

One of the letters that Olshausen submitted to the court as evidence that all of Miller's writing, regardless of its content, has literary merit, came from a Dutch critic, Jan den Haan, of The Hague. His observations are among the most perceptive ever written about Miller and vividly reveal the unbridgeable chasm separating Miller from the conventional mind that Judge Goodman represented and enforced with his decision. "In my considered opinion—and I know the 'Tropics' from before the war—they certainly belong to the world of literature. I think they reach farther. I do not believe that 'literature' is the first thing in life. The utmost goal is to be oneself, to be whole, to be 'integer'. During the struggle for an inner freedom, which is the only thing that matters, Miller produced the 'Tropics' and only in that sense, they are more than literature, and nothing less than gospel. In that sense alone Miller is a preacher, showing every individual the road to a personal peace and a real freedom, without deceiving him about the fierceness of the struggle. Regardless of all conventions, all hypocrisy, all tabus, Miller fights against the inertia of the masses, without giving way to them. There can be no question about his integrity."

Another casualty of the censorship wars was *Black Spring*. For several years, Laughlin had been seeking a way to publish *Black Spring* in America. His strategy was to bring it out in an expensive deluxe edition with illustrations by a prominent artist so that it could be presented as a specialized art book intended primarily for collectors. The presumption was that this marketing approach would inoculate the book against the charge that it would tend to corrupt the minds of young readers. Miller had suggested Abe Rattner instead of Fernand Léger for the illustrations and insisted that if he agreed, Laughlin pay him well. When Rattner turned down the project, Laughlin suggested the French painter Dubuffet. But in July 1948, Miller began to question the wisdom of trying to publish *Black Spring* in the United States. He still thought Rattner should be the illustrator but worried about the potential legal consequences for him and for Rattner should the government decide to prosecute. There was the risk of a jail sentence for both the author and the publisher. "It isn't vital to me that it be brought out here, or the Tropics either," Miller wrote to Laughlin. "The sale of the English language copies in Europe is ample." Laughlin was persistent, and continued to push the project. "I am pretty well convinced that if we bring out *Black Spring* at $25.00 or $50.00, with deluxe illustrations by Chagall or somebody like that, we are not going to have any trouble about the contents." He wrote to Chagall but received no reply. In March 1949, while in Paris, Laughlin met with Chagall and was told that he could not undertake the project for three years. Back in the United States in April, he again approached Rattner, but Rattner, mourning the death of his wife, did not reply. Laughlin remained determined to break through the censorship barrier. "Sooner or later, we have got to get started on doing something about your books which have been denied publication in this country." In July Rattner agreed to do the illustrations. A month later Miller vetoed the project, saying that Rattner's $1,000 fee was too low and expressing his fear of being prosecuted. Laughlin agreed to postpone the project. *Black Spring* was not published in the United States until Grove Press brought it out in 1963.

IN OCTOBER 1950 MILLER sent the manuscript of *Plexus* to Michael Hoffman. There had been an interval of several years between the completion of *Sexus* (1942) and the completion of *Plexus* (1949), and Miller's voice had mellowed, become softer and more reflective as he wrote the second volume of his trilogy. The book continues Miller's account of his relationship with Mona and his early attempts to establish himself as a writer. In its formlessness it is similar to *Sexus*, a mosaic of reminiscences, character sketches, and metaphysical discourses linked by the narrative of his erratic and unpredictable life with Mona.

At the outset of the book Miller and Mona move into an elegant apartment in a well-to-do Brooklyn neighborhood they cannot afford. Although Miller worries initially about their extravagance, he gives himself over to Mona's assurances that they will manage if he just leaves all the details to her. His job is to write. Miller fatalistically agrees, knowing that Mona lives in a fantasy world but willing to drift in it with her and accept the consequences. Of her talent for fictionalizing her existence, Miller writes somewhat admiringly, "In the realm of make believe she was thoroughly at home. She not only believed her own stories, she acted as if the fact that she had related them were proof of their veracity."

Mona tries to support them through a combination of gold digging from "admirers" and a series of jobs hostessing and waitressing in Greenwich Village nightclubs and cafés. Miller spends hours at the New York Public Library researching arcane subjects that he turns into unpublishable essays. When the rejection slips pile up, they resort to printing "mezzotints" of Miller's prose experiments that Mona peddles door to door as her own. As their fortunes decline, they move to increasingly shabby quarters, often lodging and freeloading with friends nearly as impoverished as they are. At one point Miller borrows money from his parents so that he and Mona can open a speakeasy in the Village. The clientele is drawn from the pool of Mona's "gentlemen friends" and Miller's pals. Soon the patrons are eating and drinking on credit. After the speakeasy folds, Miller goes on a wild goose chase to Florida with his buddies Ned and O'Mara hoping to cash in on the real estate boom. Miller survives on handouts for several weeks, then returns to New York and moves in with his parents. Mona too is now living with her family. And so it goes, a dizzying spiral of futility and failure. Through it all Miller keeps writing, but only once does he sell an article, and it was never published.

Although he has vowed never to work again (writing is not working; it is creation/play), Miller reaches such a point of desperation that he takes a job selling encyclopedias. At this juncture in the story, Mona introduces him to Claude, a young man of mysterious origins who appears to have powers of divination. He tells Miller that he is about to enter a difficult period. "You're ashamed of your better self," he says, and predicts, "You'll soon be put to the test." He also gives Miller a glimpse of a higher plane of existence that is open to all. "There are only two classes in this world—*and in every world*—the quick and the dead. For those who cultivate the spirit nothing is impossible . . . There is only one thing, *spirit*. It's all, everything, and when you realize it you're it. *There is* and *you are*—that's it in a nutshell."

Not long after this mystical encounter, Miller's test begins. Mona has befriended a psychotic woman she meets at the restaurant where she works. Soon Miller finds himself marginalized, as Mona attends to Anastasia's endless needs and demands. Mona is often away all night nursing Anastasia through her various physical and mental crises. Miller finds solace in reading Oswald Spengler's *Decline of the West*, which had been given to him one evening by a patron at the speakeasy. Miller finds in Spengler's account of the deterioration of Western civilization a counterpart to the disintegration of his own life. He remarks, "For many a year I had been aware that I was participating in a general decline." But in this failure—his own, and society's—Miller discovers the path to becoming a new man, the path to rebirth. He writes, "The gulf between the dawn man, who participated mystically, and contemporary man, who is unable to communicate except through sterile intellect, can only be bridged by a new type of man. The man with a cosmic consciousness . . . From the earliest times the 'few' have been attempting to break through. Some undoubtedly have broken through—and will remain forever outside the rat trap." Miller was striving to become one of the "few."

Miller closes *Plexus* with an explanation of the meaning of "The Rosy Crucifixion." The phrase refers both to the occult seventeenth-century secret society founded by Christian Rosenkreuz and to Miller's own personal Calvary, suffered with Mona. He confesses: "Once I thought that I had been wounded as no man ever had. Because I felt thus I vowed to write this book. But long before I began the book the wound had healed. Since I had sworn to fulfill my task I reopened the horrible wound . . . Suffering *is* unnecessary. But one has to suffer before he is able to realize that this is so. It is only then, moreover, that the true significance of human suffering becomes clear. At the last desperate moment—when one can suffer no more!—something happens which is in the nature of a miracle. The great open wound which was draining the blood of life closes up, the organism blossoms like a rose. One is 'free' at last."

But ahead of Miller still lay the test, taken up in the third and final book of *The Rosy Crucifixion*, *Nexus*, a book that Miller postponed writing until 1958.

Although Correa and Miller reached an agreement on *Plexus* in May 1951 and Miller collected a royalty advance, publication of the book in English was delayed until 1953 because of continuing financial and legal complications rooted in Girodias's bankruptcy. For a time Miller toyed with the idea of trying to import the English-language version of *Plexus* into the United States. He wrote to Huntington Cairns in September 1952 asking for an opinion on whether *Plexus* could pass censorship scrutiny. Cairns was diffident about offering an opinion ("It might present difficulties if I told you that the book was innocuous and the Treasury took a different view."), but he wrote Miller a month later that Arthur Krock, a respected reviewer for *The New York Times*, had read *Plexus* and thought it could be published in the United States with very little editing. Miller wrote back that he did not want to publish *Plexus* in the US because he feared the publicity would hurt June, but he did want the book imported in order to boost his royalties. Miller told Cairns he was supporting himself and his family on royalty revenues that averaged about $5,000 per year. "I start now from zero each month. No dependable income any more."

BEFORE MILLER UNDERTOOK BOOK THREE OF *THE ROSY CRUCIFIXION* he decided to write a book about the books that had shaped his sensibility and outlook on life. The project had been urged on him by his friend Lawrence Powell, the librarian at UCLA, and Miller eagerly took it up, in part because it excited him to revisit and reread the authors he loved, and in part because writing it would give him a respite from *The Rosy Crucifixion*, "this dread book, the hardest task I ever set myself and one which I have avoided for many a year."

Initially, Miller anticipated writing a multivolume work, but as it turned out, *The Books in My Life* was a single volume that runs to 316 pages. Miller began work on it in the last months of 1949 and completed it in December 1950, a remarkable achievement given that he spent much of his time tracking down and rereading hundreds of books. The result is a clear window into Miller's mind and values compressed into his personal survey of many of the most important European writers of the nineteenth and twentieth centuries. It is one of Miller's most accessible and enjoyable books.

Miller regarded the book as an extension of the autobiography he had been writing in *The Rosy Crucifixion*. He states at the outset, "The purpose of this book . . . is to round out the story of my life. It deals with books as vital experience." After saying this, Miller, the man of the street, is quick to say, "If it be knowledge or wisdom one is seeking, then one had better go direct to the source. And the source is not the scholar or philosopher, not the master, saint, or teacher, but life itself—direct experience of life." Nevertheless, he adds, "Books are as much a part of life as trees, stars or dung."

This tension between two forms of knowledge—knowledge gained from direct experience of life and knowledge gained from others' experience as transmitted in books—is a persistent theme of *The Books in My Life*. In his preamble, Miller cautions against reading too much. "One should read less and less, not more and more," he advises, and he laments, "I have undoubtedly read a hundred times more that I should have read for my own good." He urges his readers, "Read as little as possible, not as much as possible." But almost in the same breath he says, "Lend and borrow to the maximum—of both books and money! But especially books, for books represent infinitely more than money . . . When you have possessed a book with mind and spirit, you are enriched." Miller also indirectly affirms the value of reading when he acknowledges the debt that writers owe to their readers: "Without the enthusiastic reader, who is really the author's counterpart and very often his most secret rival, a book would die."

Miller appears to resolve this apparent contradiction in his attitude toward reading by positioning the writer as "reading life" when he puts words on paper. "The writer is, of course, the best of all readers, for in writing, or 'creating', as it is called, he is but reading and transcribing the great message of creation which the Creator in his goodness has made manifest to him . . . Of all artists he is the one who best knows that 'in the beginning was the Word and the Word was with God and the Word *was* God.' "

In proscribing against too much reading, Miller is warning against reading books that do not bring one to the source of life, which is spirit. "The vast majority of books overlap one another," he declares. "Rare are the unique books—less than fifty, perhaps, out of the whole storehouse of literature." But Miller refuses to provide a list of what these books are, although he does attach an appendix listing "The Hundred Books That Influenced Me Most." Miller insists that each individual must discover the books that speak to him. "Each man has to dig his own foundations . . . Whatever the material which vitally affected the form of our culture, each man must decide for himself which elements of it are to enter into and shape his own private destiny."

Herein is found the root of Miller's contempt for formalized education, with its prescribed curriculum based on lists of the "best" books. "We learn nothing from the pedagogues," Miller asserts. "The true educators are the adventurers and wanderers, the men who plunge into the living plasm of history, legend, myth . . ." For Miller, the best writers are exemplars, men and women he regards as "living books" because their words are inseparable from their deeds. Such authors, and their books, are valuable because they point the way to personal freedom. "The struggle of the human being to emancipate himself, that is, to liberate himself from the prison of his own making, that is for me the supreme subject . . . That is why I am powerfully drawn to the men of wisdom, the men who have experienced life to the full and who give life . . . For me the only true revolutionaries are the inspirers and activators, figures like Jesus, Lao-tse, Gautama the Buddha, Akhenaton, Ramakrishna, Krishnamurti. The yardstick I employ is life: how men stand in relation to life."

Who were the authors who influenced Miller, who inflamed his passion for life? With a few exceptions, they were European men who wrote during the latter part of the nineteenth century and the early part of the twentieth century. They were writers dealing with the same historical forces that threatened Miller and made him seek "liberation." The list includes: Emily Brontë, Lewis Carroll, G. K. Chesterton, Joseph Conrad, Daniel Defoe, Rider Haggard, James Joyce, D. H. Lawrence, John Cowper Powys, Herbert Spencer, Jonathan Swift, Alfred Lord Tennyson (English); Balzac, André Breton, Céline, Blaise Cendrars, Alexander Dumas, Élie Faure, André Gide, Jean Giono, Victor Hugo, Marcel Proust, Arthur Rimbaud (French);

Mme. Blavatsky, Dostoevsky, Emma Goldman (Russian); Erich Gut-kind, Hermann Hesse, Count Keyserling, Thomas Mann, Nietzsche, Oswald Spengler, Jacob Wasserman (German); Boccaccio, Cellini (Italian); Knut Hamsun, August Strindberg (Scandinavian); Vincent Van Gogh (Dutch); Maurice Maeterlinck (Belgian); LaoTse, Suzuki (Asian); Krishnamurti (Indian); Petronius, Plutarch, Ancient Greek dramatists (Classical); James Fenimore Cooper, Theodore Dreiser, Emerson, H. L. Mencken, Thoreau, Twain, and Whitman (American). Cervantes, Shakespeare, Tolstoy, and Voltaire are surprising omissions. For some of these writers—Hamsun, Dreiser, Maeterlinck, Rimbaud—Miller cites their entire body of work. For most others, he cites only a single book. The authors to whom Miller extends his highest tributes and proclaims his deepest indebtedness are Blaise Cendrars, Dostoevsky, and Whitman, a fellow Brooklynite.

Swiss-born (birth name Frédéric Louis Sauser), Cendrars led an adventurous, unconventional life that stirred Miller's imagination. After leaving school in Switzerland due to lack of interest in his studies, an attitude that Miller could easily sympathize with, Cendrars went to St. Petersburg to start an apprenticeship with a Swiss watchmaker. It was here that he began to write poetry. He returned to Switzerland to study medicine, then lived briefly in New York before settling in Paris and joining the modernist art movement. He enlisted in the French Foreign Legion in 1914 to fight in World War One and lost his right arm in a battle at Champagne. After his discharge from the army, he became a naturalized French citizen. Though initially known for his poetry, Cendrars gained literary fame after the war for his novels, short stories, and essays. Miller remained deeply thankful to Cendrars for calling attention to *Tropic of Cancer* in a laudatory review published in the French review *Orbes* in 1935. Cendrars was the last person Miller saw on departing Paris in 1939, a chance encounter that made a lasting impression on him. In addition to the chapter on Cendrars in *The Books in My Life*, Miller wrote a book about Cendrars published in French in 1951.

Miller was attracted to Cendrars as one of those "living books" whose adventurous appetite for life saturated his writing. He saw in Cendrars an artist like himself, unafraid to examine life in all its aspects but on a grander scale than Miller had himself experienced. "He is an adventurer in all realms of life," Miller writes. "What interests him is *every* phase of life." There is a sense of boyish hero worship underlying Miller's admiration for the man, as though Cendrars has actually lived out the sort of life that Miller can only imagine. Here he is summarizing Cendrars's career:

> One of the reasons for the great fascination he exerts over me is the resemblance between his voyages and adventures and those which I associate in memory with Sinbad the Sailor or Aladdin of the Wonderful Lamp. The amazing experiences which he attributes to the characters in his books, and which often as not he has shared, have all the qualities of legend as well as the authenticity of legend. Worshipping life and the truth of life, he comes closer than any author of our time to revealing the common source of word and deed. He restores to contemporary life the elements of the heroic, the imaginative and the fabulous. His adventures have led him to nearly every region of the globe, particularly those regarded as dangerous or inaccessible . . . He has consorted with all types, including bandits, murderers, revolutionaries and other varieties of fanatic. He has tried out no less than thirty-six métiers, according to his own words, but, like Balzac, gives the impression of knowing every métier. He was once a juggler, for example—on the English music-hall stage— at the same time that Chaplin was making his debut there: he was a pearl merchant and a smuggler; he was a plantation owner in South America, where he made a fortune three times in succession and lost it even more rapidly than he had made it.

Cendrars excites Miller's admiration because Miller can project onto him his own aesthetic values and then trumpet them loudly without seeming to be self-serving. Much of Miller's "literary criticism," if it can be called that, is in this vein. The authors he praises and holds up as exemplars are always men who afford him a vehicle for advancing his own views on the relationship between life and art. "What a writer learns from Cendrars is to follow his nose, to obey life's commands, to worship no other god but life." This is Miller's own credo. Miller's appreciations of other writers are as much about Henry Miller as they are about their ostensible subjects: more auto-biography, in short. Miller closes his tribute to Cendrars on a humble note. "I bow in reverence. I have not the right to salute you, because I am not your peer. I prefer to remain your devotee, your loving disci-ple, your spiritual brother in der Ewigkert [in perpetuity]."

Miller treats Dostoevsky and Whitman in a long letter he wrote to his Belgian friend Pierre Lesdain, a professor and literary critic. The letter is included as chapter XII of *The Books in My Life*, and dated May 3, May 10, May 20, 1950. The letter ranges over Miller's reading preferences, his ambitions as a writer, and his work habits. At its core is a comparison of Dostoevsky and Whitman, whom he calls "the peaks in modern literature." Miller views them as more than "men of let-ters." They were "deliverers." "The revolutionizing of art which they helped bring about, which they initiated to an extent we are not yet properly aware of, was part and parcel of the greater task of transvalu-ing all human values. Their concern with art was of a different order from that of other celebrated revolutionaries. It was a movement from the center of man's being outward, and the repercussions from that outer sphere (which is still veiled to us) we have yet to hear."

Miller sees Dostoevsky and Whitman wrestling with the major spir-itual problems of the modern age, Dostoevsky with the problem of God and human suffering, Whitman with the related problem of the indi-vidual achieving the cosmic consciousness that can liberate him. Miller's comparison of the two men is one of his most brilliant pieces of literary commentary and is deeply revealing of his own mission as a writer, the mission to awaken his fellow man, especially his fellow Americans.

> The difference between the two, in my eyes at least, is that Whit-man, though the lesser artist, though not as profound, saw bigger than Dostoevsky. He had the cosmic sweep, yes. We speak of him as "the great democrat." Now that particular appellation could never be given to Dostoievsky [*sic*]—not because of his religious, political and social beliefs but because Dostoevsky was more and less than a "democrat ... " No, Dostoevsky was human in that "all

too human" sense of Nietzsche. He wrings our withers when he
unrolls his scroll of life. Whitman is personal by comparison; he
takes in the crowd, the masses, the great swarms of humanity. His
eyes are constantly fixed on the potential, the divine potential,
in man. He talks brotherhood, Dostoevsky talks fellowship. Dostoevsky stirs us to the depths, causes us to shudder and grimace,
to wince, to close our eyes at times. Not Whitman. Whitman has
the faculty of looking at everything, divine or demonic, as part
of the ceaseless Heraclitean stream . . . There is a healing quality
to his vision.

It is this healing quality in Whitman that causes Miller to present
him as a writer and a man who embodies the best that is American,
the values and hopes on which the country was founded and from
which it has strayed. "Whitman is called the great democrat . . . because
he had achieved self-sufficiency." For Miller, as for Whitman, this
self-sufficiency consists merely in the ability to accept the conditions
of life as they are given and to embrace them joyously. Miller
quotes from a Whitman biographer who, in conversation with
Whitman, has managed to capture "the central teaching of his writings and life—namely, that the commonplace is the grandest of all
things—that the exceptional in any line is no finer, better or more
beautiful than the usual, and that what is really wanting is not that we
should possess something we have not at present, but that our eyes
should be opened to see and our hearts to feel what we all have."
Miller comments approvingly, "This view of things strikes me
as essentially American, or to put it another way, as the underlying
promise which inspired not only our best representatives but which
is felt and understood by the so-called 'common man.' And if I am
right, if this broad, easy, genial, simple view of life is reflected (even
dimly) in both the highest and lowest strata of American society, there
is indeed hope for a new race of man to be born on this continent, hope for a new heaven and a new earth." The key, as Miller
quotes Whitman again, is to "find it enough merely to *live* . . . and in
the fact of *life* itself, discover and achieve happiness . . ." Miller adds,
"I would say that it was on this rock—temporarily forgotten—that

Miller on the steps to Anaïs Nin's home, Louveciennes, 1932.
Used with permission of the Anaïs Nin Trust. All rights reserved.

Miller on the Greek island Hydra, 1939. *Used with permission of the Anaïs Nin Trust. All rights reserved.*

Miller at his writing desk on Partington Ridge, 1950s.

Miller painting in his Big Sur studio, 1950s.
Henry Miller Memorial Library.

Henry Miller, watercolorist *Photo by Arthur Knight.*
Henry Miller Memorial Library.

Miller in Carmel Highlands, 1969. *Photo by William Webb.*
Henry Miller Memorial Library.

June Mansfield, the Mara/Mona of the Tropics and *The Rosy Crucifixion*. *Used with permission of the Anaïs Nin Trust. All rights reserved.*

Anaïs Nin, Paris, 1935. *Used with permission of the Anaïs Nin Trust. All rights reserved.*

Anaïs Nin, 1940, the year of Miller's American tour. *Used with permission of the Anaïs Nin Trust. All rights reserved.*

June Lancaster, the mail order bride.
Henry Miller Memorial Library.

Janina Martha Lepska, 1951.
*Photo by William Webb. Henry
Miller Memorial Library.*

Eve Miller, 1950s.
*Photo by Arthur
Knight. Henry Miller
Memorial Library.*

Miller with Renate Gerhardt in Hamburg, 1961. *Special Collections Department, Charles E. Young Research Library, University of California, Los Angeles.*

Miller with Ziva Rodann in Pacific Palisades, California, 1963–64. *Henry Miller Memorial Library.*

Miller, Valentine,
Tony, Lepska, Big
Sur, 1949. *Photo
by Dick Pelatowsky.
University of
Victoria Libraries
Special Collections.*

Henry, Lauretta,
Heinrich, Louise in
Brooklyn, circa 1900.
*Special Collections
Department, Charles
E. Young Research
Library, University of
California, Los Angeles.*

Valentine Miller, age ten, Big Sur. *Photo by Eve Miller. Courtesy Valentine Miller.*

Tony Miller, age eight, Big Sur. *Photo by Eve Miller. Courtesy Valentine Miller.*

Tony, Henry, Valentine, Barbara Sandford, Big Sur, 1954. *Photo by Eve Miller. Henry Miller Memorial Library.*

Henry and Eve in their Partington Ridge bedroom, 1954.
Wynn Bullock, Henry and Eve Miller, 1954 ©1954, 2013 Bullock Photography LLC. All rights reserved.

Henry and Val,
Big Sur, 1956.
Photograph by Morley Baer. © 2012-2013 by the Morley Baer Photography Trust, Santa Fe. All reproduction rights reserved.

Lawrence and Nancy Durrell, Corfu, 1930s.
By kind permission from the Estate of Gerald Durrell.

Emil Schnellock, 1947.
Special Collections, Simpson Library
University of Mary Washington.

Wallace Fowlie.
Houghton Library, Harvard University.

Annette Baxter, circa 1975.
Courtesy of Adrienne Baxter Bell.

James Baxter, circa 1970.
Courtesy of Adrienne Baxter Bell.

Miller visiting Roger Bloom at the Missouri State Penitentiary.
Special Collections Research Center Morris Library, Southern Illinois University.

Henry Miller and Emil White, Big Sur.
Photo by Arthur McEwan. Henry Miller Memorial Library.

Vincent Birge, 1967. *Henry Miller Memorial Library.*

Henry Miller and
Alfred Perlès, Big
Sur, 1954.
Wynn Bullock,
Henry Miller and
Alfred Perlès, 1954
© *1954,2013*
Bullock Photography
LLC. All rights
reserved.

Jack Kahane, founder of
Obelisk Press. *Courtesy of
Juliette Kahane.*

James Laughlin, founder of New Directions.
*©2012 Estate of Rudy Burckhardt/Artists
Rights Society (ARS), New York.*

Huntington Cairns, legal advisor
to US Customs Bureau. *Library
of Congress, Manuscript Division,
Huntington Cairns Papers.*

Michael Hoffman, Agence
Hoffman, Paris. *Courtesy
Georges Hoffman.*

Bern Porter in 1943.
*Mark Melnicove, literary executor, Bern
Porter Estate. Courtesy the Bern Porter
Collection, Bowdoin College Library,
Brunswick, Maine.*

Barney Rosset, founder of Grove
Press. *Photo by Arne Svenson.*

Elmer Gertz, attorney-at-law.
*Special Collections Research Center,
University of Chicago Library.*

America was founded." This view of the key to happiness—finding it enough merely to live—brings Miller back to the transforming role of self-liberation. Or as Whitman put it, "The world will be complete for him who is himself complete."

Miller finished *The Books in My Life* at the end of 1950 and sent the manuscript to Laughlin in January. The two men exchanged suggestions for a title of the book, with Laughlin rejecting *The Quick and the Dead* (which Miller had borrowed from his conversation with Claude in *Plexus*) and *The Plains of Abraham* as off-putting, and offering instead *The Books in My Life*, a title also suggested by Powell. In May, Laughlin wrote Miller that he wanted to visit him in Big Sur to discuss edits to the book, but Miller wrote back asking him not to come. "Has nothing whatever to do with *you*, I hope you understand. I'm in a bad mood, a bad situation, and I don't want to see anyone." A few days later Miller relented and invited Laughlin to come.

The "bad situation" that Miller referred to was his rapidly deteriorating marriage. The arrival in August 1948 of their second child, Henry Tony, only exacerbated the parenting issues that divided Lepska and Miller. Sometime in the following year, Lepska met a man in Big Sur who showed interest in her. His name was Marcel Verzeano. He was a Romanian Jew who had obtained a medical degree in Italy and had worked as a researcher in Paris. He had been married and divorced in Europe, fought in World War Two as a paratrooper, was wounded in Italy, then joined the French underground. He was an adventurer and Renaissance man—a biophysicist who had taught at Harvard, a violinist, an athlete, a singer, charming and good-looking. (The similarities to Blaise Cendrars are remarkable.) He was spending a year in Big Sur before taking up an appointment at the newly formed Brain Research Institute at UCLA and living at Deetjen's Big Sur Inn. As their relationship evolved over a period of a year through meetings at potluck dinners and folk dancing at the Grange Hall, Lepska fell in love. Although Miller probably was aware of their relationship—there were few secrets in the tiny Big Sur community—he said nothing, although in June he wrote to Durrell, "If I did not have my two kids my life would be miserable."

In the summer of 1951 Miller was making plans to visit Europe with Lepska and the children, perhaps in an effort to get her away from Verzeano and try to repair their marriage. The plans were canceled, ostensibly because of difficulties with Lepska's passport, but in reality because Lepska had decided to take the children to the East Coast for a visit with her family. On her way, she stopped in Los Angeles to see Lawrence Powell, who cheerily reported to Miller, "I have never seen her looking so well." Back east, she visited Miller's mother Louise, who was astonished to discover that her son had again become a father. She also confessed to Lepska that she had never read anything written by him. While staying with her parents in New Jersey, Lepska made the decision to leave Miller. She wrote him a long letter explaining her grievances against him and the cumulative effect of her "wounds." Miller wrote her a long answer, but it arrived after she had departed for Los Angeles, and her father sent it back to him unopened. Lepska never saw this letter.

Verzeano was waiting for her in Los Angeles. He asked her to live with him, and she agreed. She then continued on to Partington Ridge to make separation arrangements with Miller. Lepska told Miller she would not seek alimony or child support from him and agreed to share custody of the children. Then, taking the children with her, she joined Verzeano in Long Beach. Miller, heartbroken at the loss of his entire family, begged Lepska to return the children to him, which she did. But their sojourn with him lasted only a few weeks. Miller, unable to manage them even with help, asked Lepska to retrieve them. After the divorce, the two parents shared physical custody of the children according to a schedule that was adjusted to changing circumstances. Tony and Val usually stayed with Miller during the summer and at Christmastime and with Lepska during the school year.

Reflecting many years later on the breakup of her marriage to Miller, Lepska observed that Miller was a different person in private than he was in public. He was more engaged in public, she said, fond of interesting conversations about philosophical issues, the history of civilizations, and mystical topics.

Miller wrote amusingly and movingly about this traumatic event in his life in the collection *Big Sur and the Oranges of Hieronymus Bosch*, published six years later. Knowing that it would be impossible for him to manage two young children, keep up with household chores, and still find time to write, Miller had recruited his friend Walker Winslow to help him parent Tony and Val after Lepska had left and then, at his request, returned the children to him. Winslow was a reformed alcoholic and writer who had first come to Big Sur in 1946 as a friend of Gilbert Neiman. He had stayed at Anderson Creek with Emil White, an arrangement that Winslow's careless personal habits soon made Emil regret. At the beginning of 1951, Winslow was living in Rochester, New York, with his wife Edna and continuing to write. He had proposed writing an article about Miller for the review *Tomorrow*, which had published Miller's work, and was quizzing Miller for the article in their correspondence. By midyear he was separated from his wife and working at the Menninger Foundation in Kansas. He had received an advance from Doubleday to write a book about Karl Menninger's father, but when the deal fell through in August, he wrote Miller that he wanted to return to Big Sur to work on a novel. When he learned of Miller's domestic troubles, he offered to move into Miller's studio, formerly Chez Moricand, and help Miller care for his children. Miller picks up the story as Winslow arrives.

The very next day the fun began. To devote a whole morning to a three-year-old boy full of piss and vinegar is a job for someone with six hands and three pairs of legs. No matter what we decided to play, the jig lasted only a few minutes. Every toy in the place had been taken out, used, and thrown aside in less than an hour. If I suggested that we go for a walk he was too tired. There was an old tricycle he liked to ride, but before the morning was out a wheel had come off and, though I sweated blood, I simply could not make it stay on again. I tried playing ball but his co-ordination wasn't good enough; I almost had to stand on top of him and put the ball in his hands. I got out his building blocks too—several bushel baskets full—and tried, as they say, to have him do something "constructive," but his interest in this pastime lay exclusively in kicking the house, or the bridge, apart after I had built it. That was fun! I tied all his choo-choo cars together, added a few tin cans and other noisemakers to them, and ran about like a zany while he sat and watched me. This bored the shit out of him in no time.

At intervals Walker showed up to see how we were making out. Finally—it couldn't have been more than ten o'clock, if that late—he said: "Go up and work a while. I'll take over. You need a break."

When Val arrived, after school, the difficulties increased. It was nothing but fight, fight, fight. Even if it were nothing more than a rock which one of them had picked up, the other one immediately claimed it. *It's mine, I saw it first! You did not! I did too see it first. Caca pipi head, caca pipi head!* (Their favorite expression.) It now demanded the full time of the two of us to handle the situation. By dinnertime we were always pooped out.

It was the same old story every day. No improvements, no progress. An absolute standstill . . .

One fine day Walker lost his temper. The incident made a deep impression on me. I had never believed it possible for Walker to say so much as a cross word. He was always calm, amiable, yielding, and for patience, well, he had the patience of a saint. With dangerous psychopaths Walker could hold his own. As an attendant in a lunatic asylum he had kept things under control without ever resorting to strap, club or truncheon.

But the kids had found his Achilles heel.

It was in the middle of a long, exasperating morning when he exploded. I was indoors puttering around when he called me out. "You've got to do something," he yelled, his face red as a beet. "These kids are completely out of hand."

At this point in Miller's account, it is easy to imagine the stresses that Lepska had been under, not for weeks, but for years. But to continue:

That evening, after the kids were out of the way, he talked to me quietly and soberly. He made it clear that I was not only punishing myself, but the kids as well. He talked not only as a friend but also as an analyst might talk to a patient. In the course of his talk he opened my eyes to a twist in the situation which I had been blind to. He said that I should endeavor to find out—for my own good—whether my desire to keep the children was based on love for them and concern for their welfare or on a hidden desire to punish my wife.

Walker's words had their effect. I slept on it, thought it over another twenty-four hours, then announced the decision.

"Walker," I said, "I'm throwing in the sponge. You're right. I'll send her a wire to come and fetch them."

Miller wrote to James Laughlin about the pain this decision brought on: "I sent for Lepska to come and get the children, believing finally, after bitter experience, that they would be better cared for, better off in every way with her. I will arrange to see them occasionally; this can be their vacation home; they may enjoy it all the more on that account. It has been a tough struggle, demanding more sacrifice, more surrender, but now I see clear, feel at peace, and hope for the best. I am settling down to writing this week—the decks are clear."

9

EUROPE BECKONS

"All Europe Is Alive & Enthusiastic About My Writing."

MILLER'S DISTRESS OVER THE BREAKUP OF HIS FAMILY WAS PICKED up by friends around the globe. Fred Perlès wrote from London advising Miller to "take it easy . . . don't let anything get you down" and urging him to come to Europe where "you have friends everywhere." James Laughlin consoled Miller for the loss of his children by telling him that caring for them alone would have left him no time to write. Caresse Crosby invited Miller to come live with her—without the children—and help her establish her One World organization in Greece. From New Zealand, George Dibbern, the German adventurer whose *Quest* royalties Miller was helping to recover, suggested Miller bring Tony and Val with him to live on Woody Island, which Dibbern had purchased with the proceeds from a winning lottery ticket. Another invitation came from Albert Maillet, a French admirer who taught English at a lycée in Vienne in the Rhône Valley. Maillet, a Christian mystic who considered Miller to be "a prophet of Christ," had written Miller a devotional letter in 1947 introducing himself. In 1950 he wrote an essay about Miller whose title, "Henry Miller; Superman and Prophet," expresses the extent of Maillet's adulation. He had visited Miller in Big Sur during a trip to America in 1950, after which he wrote to Miller sharing intimate details of his personal life and giving news of his own writing projects. Maillet offered Miller lodging in the home he shared with his wife, Eliane, and three young children and promised childcare for Tony and Val that would free Miller to write.

These offers of rescue failed to cheer Miller. In March he wrote to Durrell: "Now both children are with the mother—temporarily at least. I couldn't cope with the situation single-handed. My friend gave up, the young woman quit after 48 hours of it, and there I was—and locked in, too, by a ten day rain. *Formidable*. I was utterly exhausted. For a new mate I'll have to come to Europe. A Belgian next, or an Italian, I hope. Not an *Anglo-Saxon*."

Instead, relief from Miller's loneliness and depression came out of the blue, in the form of a letter from Eve McClure, a young woman living in Beverly Hills who wrote to Miller to express her admiration for *Tropic of Capricorn*. Eve was the sister of Louise Schatz, the wife of Miller's artistic collaborator on *Into the Night Life*. Lilik and Louise had purchased the copy of *Capricorn* in Paris while en route to their new home in Jerusalem and had mailed it to Eve. Miller responded to Eve's letter and a hasty courtship by mail ensued. After Eve and Miller both wrote to the Schatzes about their correspondence, Lilik wrote enthusiastically to Miller to endorse her. "Eve, Louise's sister has developed a daily letter writing sort of open heart talks to us and beginning with the *Capricorn* we sent her from Paris I watched quite an amazing awakening flame in her which your writing caused—she last speaks of a possibility of coming to see you in Big Sur, she is a good girl + *flexible* intellectually young, healthy, really healthy in body and spirit—not a bad looking dame on top of it as the saying goes—actually I like her very, very much—Has she come? Of course she has some trouble with a man in which business all is finished, going through the finishing touches of the finish now."

At the end of March, during a trip to Long Beach to visit Tony and Val, Miller drove to Beverly Hills to meet Eve. When he returned to Big Sur at the beginning of April, Eve came with him.

Eve McClure was twenty-eight when she met Henry Miller. She was twice divorced and ending a relationship with Gene Mollica, the West Coast distributor of Dana Perfumes, who had afforded her an elegant lifestyle. She was by all accounts a beautiful woman, with dark shoulder-length hair, green eyes, and a full figure. According to her sister Jane, she dressed well and took pride in her appearance but had a tendency to be deceitful. She also had a history of heavy drinking.

Eve had grown up in Berkeley, the middle of three daughters raised by her father, John (called Jack), and her mother, Evelyn Burton. Jack and Evelyn were married in 1915 and lived for a time in Vancouver, where he managed a vaudeville theater. When the Depression hit, he moved his family to the Bay Area to help support his elderly parents. Unable to find work, he began to drink heavily. Evelyn supported the family through this difficult time with her job as a dental nurse. Eventually, Jack found work as an automobile salesman, an unlikely occupation for a man who loved theater, literature, and classical music, and had some success controlling his drinking by joining Alcoholics Anonymous. But emotional crises would trigger relapses and Jack became for Eve and her sisters a weak and ineffectual figure unable to cope with the stresses of life.

After struggling with obesity in high school, Eve went on a starvation diet, lost seventy pounds, and became involved in theater work. Though her skin was freckled, she photographed well and found work as a model. In 1944 she married film director Jack Carr but divorced him after two months to escape an abusive relationship. Then, while performing in Ibsen's *A Doll's House* at the historic Geary Theater in San Francisco, she met the actor Lyle Talbot, whom she subsequently married. Talbot was an older man and, like her father, an alcoholic. After a two-year marriage, she divorced him. By the time she met Miller in 1952, all her relationships with men had been short-lived and dysfunctional.

The suddenness, the reckless impulsivity of Miller's pairing with Eve recalls the pattern of his previous courtships: with June Mansfield, the taxi dancer; with June Lancaster, the dedicated artists' model; with Lepska, the promising graduate student. Each of these partners seemed to bring Miller deliverance from his compulsive search for the ever-elusive ideal mate, the woman who would fill the void created by his despised, inadequate mother. In *Tropic of Capricorn*, the book that drew Eve to him, Miller describes his euphoria at having found and fallen in love with June (Mona/Mara): "One can wait a whole life time for a moment like this. The woman whom you have never hoped to meet now sits before you, and she talks and looks exactly like the person you dreamed about." In the fall of 1944, as

Miller prepared to bring Lepska back to Big Sur, he wrote to Emil White, "I will return with the Polish girl—Lepska. . . She's strong, willing, adventurous. It's real love, a real union. For good. You see, I want to live close with the girl—I look forward to it—a deep, full relationship. We're well matched." And now, as he takes up with Eve, Miller writes to Durrell, "Things have altered radically for me—for the better. . . I've found an 'Eve'. She's been here ten days now, and it was a thorough go from the first. I tell you, I feel like a new man— and about 30 years younger. Moreover, I look it. It's just unbelievable what a change she has wrought in me. Naturally, she's the complete opposite of Lepska." June Lancaster, initially resisting Miller's desper- ate importuning of her to join him in Big Sur, seems to have intuited that Miller was animated by a need that no flesh-and-blood woman could satisfy when she wrote to him in April 1944, "I respect and admire you tremendously for the man and artist you are. Let that suffice. I can not supply the answer to your most important needs."

Miller's mood was ebullient as he settled into his new life with Eve and regrouped. By the end of April he had made arrangements with Lepska to take the children over the summer, and early in May he brought Eve with him to Long Beach for an introductory visit. In July, he wrote contentedly to Durrell, "No writing yet—but painting. And enjoying to the full my new rich life here at Big Sur with my darling Eve." He told Durrell that he hoped to make his oft-post- poned trip to Europe after the children returned to their mother in the fall. He wrote to Nin about his new circumstances and invited her to visit to meet Eve.

In August, Miller received a sobering letter from his old neigh- bor, Jean Wharton, now living in Ojai, California. She had remained friends with Lepska, who had visited her and discussed her separa- tion from Miller. Wharton told Miller that there was a discrepancy between his understanding of Lepska's attitude toward him and what Lepska had expressed to her. She warned Miller against holding onto his bitterness. "I have a premonition, Henry, that unless you free your- self from this bitterness (whether it is 'justified' or not is immaterial) much of the happiness that is yours now will shrivel and die—I see this so clearly that I must say it . . . The whole experience may be a test of the depths of your awareness—your underlying integrity . . . The most searching self-knowledge is necessary for you at this moment."

In September, the children gone, Miller started to work on *Nexus*. He had done no writing since completing *The Books in My Life* more than a year and a half earlier. He was anxious to wrap up *The Rosy Crucifixion* and complete the autobiographical saga that he had begun after his return from Greece. But he dreaded writing *Nexus* because it would thrust him back into the most painful period of his marriage to June, when he reached the nadir of his suffering. In January, after Lepska had left and he was struggling to care for Tony and Val without her, he had written to Durrell, "I know I should yet write *Nexus* and perhaps *Draco and the Ecliptic* too. After that I am ready for the next world." Miller envisioned *Draco and the Ecliptic*—its theme drawn from astrology—as the compression of his search for self-realization into one slim volume. Though he referred to the book frequently in his correspondence, he never wrote it.

While Miller was in a fallow writing period in the early 1950s, his readership and reputation in Europe and America were about to expand significantly through the combined efforts of James Laughlin, his American publisher, and Michael Hoffman, his agent in France. Through the 1930s and '40s, Miller's books were sold primarily in two markets. The banned books published in English by Maurice Girodias through his Obelisk Press and then, after the war, through Éditions du Chêne, were sold exclusively in France, with copies smuggled into Great Britain and the United States by returning visitors and then mailed from false addresses or shipped by Railway Express to bypass the post office. As we have seen, though significant royalties had accumulated in Miller's French account from sales of the banned books, he had difficulty accessing these funds because of the French exchange laws. His royalty account in France was further diminished by devaluations of the franc and by Girodias's bankruptcy.

New Directions titles, on the other hand, though published at frequent intervals in the United States and Great Britain, were not selling. For the year 1951 New Directions reported combined royalties of $391.51 on *The Cosmological Eye*, *The Air-Conditioned Nightmare*, *The Colossus of Maroussi*, *Sunday After the War*, *Wisdom of the Heart*, and *Remember to Remember.* Subtracting the $75/month that New Directions advanced him, Miller ended the year owing his publisher $317. 28.

In 1952 this picture began to change. Hoffman, who had been doggedly pursuing Girodias for back royalties, reported to Miller in January that the rights to Miller's books held by Girodias had been transferred to Hachette, the large book distributor, which had formed a publishing subsidiary, Société Nouvelle des Éditions du Chêne, from Girodias's old imprint. Girodias was not involved in the management of the new entity. Hoffman would argue, successfully, that Hachette's ownership of the rights brought with it an obligation to pay Miller the royalties still owed on those titles, bringing Miller another 3,500,00 francs (about $10,000), but not until March 1955. Hachette also expressed interest in Miller's New Directions titles, which Laughlin had already offered to another French publisher, Gallimard. Gallimard eventually contracted for *Remember to Remember, The Air-Conditioned Nightmare,* and *The Books in My Life,* leaving Hachette to pick up *Sunday After the War* and *The Colossus of Maroussi.* Correa, which in April 1952 published *Plexus* in French subsequently brought out French translations of *The Smile at the Foot of the Ladder, A Devil in Paradise,* and *Big Sur and the Oranges of Hieronymus Bosch.* Hoffman also arranged for the publication of the Tropics in Germany (through Rowohlt Verlag) and Denmark, *Plexus* in Italy through Mondadori, and *Black Spring* in Sweden. Hoffman's efforts on behalf of all of Miller's titles so impressed Laughlin that he agreed to let him represent the New Directions books, as well as the books originally published in France, throughout Europe and South America.

Laughlin was also busy on other fronts. He was in discussions with Victor Weybright, one of the founders of the New American Library, to bring out a selection of Miller's writings, including sixty-eight pages from *Tropic of Capricorn* and three pages from *Tropic of Cancer,* in an inexpensive mass-market paperback. Surprisingly, Miller agreed to the selection of chaste sections from these books. And Girodias gave his permission. Laughlin also made plans to go to Japan to meet with Meredith Weatherby of the Charles Tuttle Company, a publisher's representative, to arrange publication of New Directions titles in Japan. In August, Victor Weybright decided to delay publication of Miller's selected writings because of a Congressional investigation of pornography by the Gathings House Select Committee on Current Pornographic Materials. Weybright's timidity illustrates the extent to which Miller's name was still associated with pornography in the popular mind. The book was eventually issued in 1956 under the title *Nights of Love and Laughter* through the popular New American Library imprint Signet Books. In December, Miller learned from Bob MacGregor, a new editor at New Directions who was taking on many of Laughlin's editing responsibilities, that Rowohlt had offered a $250 advance for the German rights to *Colossus*. (MacGregor, confused by the complexity of Miller's numerous French contracts, asked Miller to prepare a chart that clarified which French publishers held rights to which titles.) By then, Miller was on the verge of taking Eve with him on an extended trip to Europe. The completion of *Nexus* would have to wait.

THOUGH MILLER HAD BEEN DETERMINED TO GET TO EUROPE, he had lacked the funds to make the trip. He had written to Durrell at the end of September, "Not much chance of going to Europe yet. No money. Need lots of cash for such a trip. But I still hope to make it." But by the end of November, the trip was on, and Miller wrote to Bob MacGregor that he planned a long stay. The change in fortune had come in the form of an unexpectedly large payment of royalties owed by Girodias. Eve and Miller left Big Sur on December 27 for Los Angeles and, after a stopover in New York during which Miller visited his mother, arrived in Paris on New Year's Eve. They were met at Gare d'Orsay by Georges Belmont, the translator of *The Smile at the Foot of the Ladder*, and Maurice Nadeau, the editor at Correa, who put them up at his apartment.

For most of January, Miller and Eve remained in Paris, where he was lionized and feted by publishers, his agent, and old friends from the Villa Seurat days such as Hans Reichel and Brassaï. He and Eve were an item in the Paris media, their visit announced in *Samedi-Soir*, *Le Figaro Littéraire*, and *Carréfour* ("An Immortal Returns to Paris," proclaimed the headline). But Miller was not happy with all the attention he was receiving, and he was shocked by the cost of living in France. He wrote to Perlès, who was excitedly trying to arrange a reunion, that he was disappointed with France and already thinking about returning to Big Sur. Perlès begged him to reconsider and to plan for a reunion in Spain, where he and his wife, Anne Barret, would be vacationing in May. Miller lamented to Emil White, who was trying to arrange a short-term rental of Miller's house, that he missed Big Sur and the children. "I've had an awful bellyful of *people*—here. It's hell to be mobbed all the time. The reception (chez Correa) was like an ordeal." His mood did not brighten when he left Paris for the south. "Each day I get more homesick for Big Sur," he wrote from Monte Carlo. "We're apt to pack up and leave any time ... I'm fed up. Too dull, not worth it. And when I think what I could do with the money at home it hurts to see it go here for just bare living. Monte Carlo is very beautiful—but dead." That Miller, who managed to remain cheerful in Big Sur when the wolf was at the door, was complaining of boredom and worrying about money while vacationing in France with his beloved "angel" Eve shows the depths of his gloom. The news that came in mid-February from Michael Hoffman that Miller would have to testify at the upcoming obscenity trial of *Sexus* could only have intensified his dark mood.

Miller seems to have found some relief in Vienne, at the home of Albert Maillet, his French disciple, who had offered him and Eve "a large room with two windows and a comfortable bed, a table and an empty cupboard for your things." Miller was cheered by the company of this "kindred spirit ... a sort of Christ," as he wrote Durrell. But his discontent disposed him to pessimistic predictions about the future of Europe. "I am convinced there will be war before summer is out—it seems absolutely inevitable." He urged Durrell, now living on Cyprus, "to pick a good spot—remote, peaceful—to weather the storm."

In April, Miller and Eve were in Belgium visiting Pierre Lesdain, a professor and critic who was one of Miller's staunchest European admirers and advocates. A letter that Miller wrote to Emil White from Brussels hints at the underlying malaise that was preventing him from enjoying his extended vacation. "Am fed up with doing nothing—especially with food and drink. It's a punishment. And the endless conversation. I certainly could enjoy solitude." It seems out of character that Miller—a bon vivant who enjoyed his table and the company of others, who was famed for his conversation—would be so unhappy with his circumstances, unless one considers how important creative activity was to his sense of well-being. He did not write when he traveled, and he makes no mention of painting either during the trip. He had not been engaged in a sustained period of writing since completing *The Books in My Life* at the end of 1950. It may well be that Miller's expressions of disgust with his travel experiences were the upwellings of a creative atrophy that made it difficult for him simply to relax and enjoy himself.

Early in May, Eve and Miller were back in Paris, where they were joined by Bezalel and Louise Schatz in what must have been a joyous reunion. They planned to travel to Montpellier in the south of France to meet the French surrealist writer Joseph Delteil and his wife, then continue on by car to Spain, where Fred Perlès and Anne Barret would be waiting for them. But Miller still expected war to break out before the end of summer and was ready to depart for America at the first sign of trouble.

Miller fondly recalled his reunion with Perlès in a letter he wrote from Big Sur a year later that was published in 1959 as *Reunion in Barcelona*. More a tribute to Perlès and his salutary influence than a description of their reunion, the letter shows Miller's proclivity for creating on the page a preferred, reimagined reality that conforms to his mythical version of events. Gone are the sour notes about impending war and dulling conversations. Instead, Miller writes that from the moment of his arrival, "I knew I was once again with human beings who spoke my language. From then on, wherever we went in Europe, it was nothing but happy *rencontres* . . . In France, no matter where I found myself, I was at home." This echoes a glossy note Miller had sent from Vienne in March to impress his New Directions editor, Bob MacGregor. "All Europe is alive & enthusiastic about my work. Only America lags . . . As for my trip—it's too full to recount by letter. I enjoy it thoroughly. I can go back now and die in peace."

The reunion with Perlès did seem to revive Miller's spirits. After they had parted, when Miller wrote to Durrell about their time together, his tone was upbeat. "We laughed from the time we met . . . Haven't laughed that way in many a year. And naturally we spoke of you—how much more we would have laughed had you been with us." He closes with, "Keep your pecker up!"

Miller had hoped to travel deeper into the Mediterranean basin, visiting Durrell on Cyprus, then go to Jerusalem with the Schatzes. But money was running low, and Miller dreaded the summer heat of the East. Instead, he and Eve returned to Montpellier with the Delteils to rest before finishing their trip in Great Britain with visits to John Cowper Powys in Wales and another reunion with Perlès in Wells that produced more laughter.

Before Miller left Europe, he received a parting letter from his friend Albert Maillet. He wrote to inform Miller that after his departure from Vienne, Maillet had undergone a mystical experience, an awakening in which he took himself to be a reincarnation of Christ. This revelation coincided with the appearance of a meteor in the sky above Vienne on June 19 at 11 p.m. "When I read about it the next day I had no doubt that it announced my becoming Christ." Maillet then accused Miller of having fallen into error and following the wrong path because of his acceptance of Buddhism. "Your veneration for such men as Buddha and Milarepa is the most nonsensical absurdity which the Devil ever deluded a humankind into . . . Christ is just the opposite and all that is good in you comes from Christ." This farewell letter from a "kindred spirit" adds further to a sense of disturbance about Miller's European trip.

Back in Big Sur in August, Miller reverted to his habitual attitudes about America and Europe in a letter he wrote to Durrell. "We're home almost two weeks now but scarcely adjusted to our 'New World' which I find is even emptier and more poisonous than ever . . . We'll have to get back to the Old World soon—and remain there." It seems that wherever Miller was *not* was where he wanted to be.

MILLER HAD CUSTODY OF TONY AND VAL for the 1953–1954 school year. Prior to the European trip, Lepska had agreed to share custody of the children on alternating years and to leave them in Big Sur during summers. Miller, despite his contempt for the American educational system, had agreed to let Val, now eight years old, attend Big Sur's one-room elementary school with the local children. Tony, who celebrated his fifth birthday in August, was too young to go to school. To keep him amused and away from Miller's writing studio, Eve organized craft classes for the local children, an enterprise that endeared her to the Big Sur community. Miller was still struggling to get *Nexus* under way. In September, Eve's father died in Berkeley.

In November, Eve and Miller were visited briefly by Vincent Birge. Birge was a radio operator who worked for Trans World Airlines on their international flights. On a stopover in Cairo in 1948 he had purchased a copy of *Tropic of Cancer*. The book had a profound effect on Birge, and four years later he wrote Miller a long letter of appreciation. The letter revealed Birge as a sensitive and somewhat isolated young man who had found on the pages of Miller's books a friend who spoke to him more openly and meaningfully than the people in his everyday life. He told Miller that after purchasing the book he had read it twice in his hotel room and had experienced it as a book "which led the reader right into the author's inner self and made of the reader a friend and almost a participant in the living of the writer's life. It was one of those books you 'live' rather than read—revolutionary and iconoclastic—a completely new experience in reading and living and a true revelation. Ever since that time I have been buying and reading your books, whenever and wherever I could obtain them . . ." Birge went on in the letter to express a sense of indebtedness to Miller, and to offer to perform services for him on his frequent trips to Europe, which often brought him to Paris. He told Miller that he was thirty-four years old, was born in Missouri to "poor white trash," and raised in Texas, where his mother now lived. He was now living alone in New York.

Birge was the kind of reader Miller hoped to reach—an ordinary man who was open to the possibility of personal transformation. He wrote back promptly, offering to send Birge a watercolor. Before long, Birge was running errands for Miller in France, sending him copies of the banned books and other obscure titles that Miller requested, and offering to exchange the francs in Miller's royalty account for dollars. He sent Miller a detailed map of Paris showing streets and houses that Miller tacked up on the wall of his studio. As Miller had planned his European trip, Birge offered to obtain free passage on a freighter for him and Eve and suggested that they use his apartment during their stopover in New York. He also sent them a package of treats for their bon voyage party in Big Sur. And so Birge joined the long line of Miller devotees that stretches back through Walker Winslow, Irving Stettner, Bern Porter, George Leite, Judson Crews, Harry Herschkowitz, and Emil White to Richard Osborn in Paris.

Birge and Miller had met briefly in Paris during Miller's stay there, but Birge had been disappointed by his own awkwardness and wanted another opportunity to spend time with Miller. Miller and Eve made him feel welcome during a stay in Big Sur that lasted several days. A grateful Birge wrote them from New York, "I'll never forget how kind you were to me—nor how much I liked your charming home—and of course the *magnificent* country there!" He sent gifts to Tony and Val, records for Miller and Eve. He mentioned a return visit in the spring with his girlfriend, Loraine. Birge would play a significant supporting role in Miller's life for years to come.

On December 29, 1953, at the home of his friend, the artist Ephraim Doner, in the Carmel Highlands, Miller and Eve were married. Eve was twenty-nine, Miller sixty-two.

In February 1954 Miller received a surprise letter from his long-lost daughter Barbara, whom he had abandoned in 1924 when he left Beatrice to take up with June. Barbara, now thirty-four, was living in Pasadena, California, and working as a secretary to an optometrist. She had located Miller by reading a feature article about him that had been published in *Family Circle* magazine when he was still married to Lepska. (The irony of the magazine's title was undoubtedly not lost on Miller.) Anticipating that Miller might decide to avoid her out of fear that reconnecting could lead to legal harassment from Beatrice, Barbara assured Miller that she did not live with her mother, who had her own apartment in Pasadena. "She is a very domineering, aggressive woman as you probably know—and we have entirely different viewpoints about everything. You might like to know I have no intention of letting my mother know I've gotten in touch with you. She wouldn't approve; and anyway it's none of her business."

Miller immediately sent Barbara an emotional reply and urged her to fly to Monterey where he would arrange for her to be met and driven down to Big Sur. He would cover her travel expenses. Barbara wrote back suggesting a summer visit, but then changed her mind. She visited Miller and Eve during a motor trip to San Francisco she took with her married boyfriend, Bo. Miller learned from her that Beatrice had remarried an older man who lost all his money in the stock market crash. That she also told him she had been educated at private schools on Long Island and in Brooklyn probably did not raise her in his estimation.

After this visit, Miller corresponded regularly with Barbara. He suggested that she take up painting, which she did, and encouraged her efforts to obtain a real estate license. He began sending her small sums of money. When she bought a car for her real estate work, she asked him to support the costs of gas and insurance. Over time, Barbara successfully played on Miller's guilt to build dependency. About a year after establishing contact with him, she told Miller she had broken off relations with her mother, implying that he was now the parent who mattered to her. Her letters were now addressed, "Darling Pappy." More requests for money ensued. Their relationship continued in this vein until Miller's death.

In September 1954 Miller received a letter from Perlès informing him that his new London agent, Margaret Crosland, had arranged a contract with Neville Armstrong for Perlès to write a book about his friendship with Miller. He sent Miller an outline of the book, then added the postscript, "Wouldn't it be wonderful if I were in Big Sur now and could do the book there?" Miller wrote back that Eve, who had grown fond of Perlès during their times together in Europe, had immediately suggested that Perlès come for a long stay while the book was being written. Perlès excitedly jumped at the offer but told Miller that his publisher would not advance the $650 needed for round-trip airfare. He also worried about his ability to obtain a visa. As he had done with Moricand seven years before, Miller sent plane fare and acted as the sponsor of Perlès visa application, which was promptly approved, despite Miller's concern that his notoriety might prove a hindrance.

Perlès was scheduled to arrive in Monterey on November 24, Thanksgiving Day. Vincent Birge, who had met Perlès during a TWA trip to London, chauffeured him from Idlewild to La Guardia Airport during a brief stopover in New York. Miller and Eve met Perlès in Monterey and drove him to the Carmel Highlands where they shared Thanksgiving dinner in Ephraim Doner's garden. That night, Miller drove them down to Big Sur. Perlès remained in Big Sur until May and completed the memoir that was published in England later that year as *My Friend Henry Miller*.

Perlès wrote this book to give testimony to his affection for Miller as a man and his admiration for him as a writer. It was intended to dispel the widely held perception of Miller—in America and England—as an outlaw author of dirty books and replace it with a portrait of him as a saintlike, healing figure who through both his example and his writing offered the ordinary man—a man like Perlès—a path to personal salvation. Perlès knew Miller intimately and loved him, and as a writer who could recognize greatness without being able to achieve it, he bowed before what he considered to be Miller's genius. The portrait he made of Miller was devotional, an homage to a man he regarded as living undeservedly without honor in his own country.

That the book had a promotional purpose was evident from the preface, written by Miller himself. For a portrait of Miller written by one of his oldest and dearest friends to be introduced by Miller himself rather than by someone else from Miller's inner circle who knew both author and subject—Anaïs Nin and Lawrence Durrell come immediately to mind—seems blatantly self-serving. Miller, somewhat self-consciously, wrote in the preface that "nothing like a biography, it must be said, has been attempted in this book, nor even a critical evaluation of the subject's work. All that he has endeavored to do, my good friend Alf, is to recount the happy life of shame we all long to lead, if only in dream and reverie." But in fact Alf was attempting to do a great deal more: he wanted to sanctify Miller, and he wanted to persuade him to leave America for Europe.

Perlès begins his account of his friendship with Miller at their first meeting during Miller's 1928 trip to Paris with his wife, June. Perlès had met June the previous year when she had been in Paris

with her lesbian lover Jean Kronski. He had taken an instant dislike
to June. He considered her a "poseuse," the polar opposite of Miller,
who "was both simple and genuine . . . full of childlike enthusiasm."
Perlès met Miller again when he returned alone to Paris in 1930 to
try to become a writer. The story that Perlès tells of Miller's Paris
years conforms closely to Miller's own version of events as related in
Tropic of Cancer and the shorter pieces Miller wrote about his Paris
years such as "Mademoiselle Claude," "Jabberwhorl Cronstadt," and
"The Cosmological Eye." But in Perlès telling, the masks that Miller
placed over his characters are removed and we see them, less distorted
perhaps, through Perlès's more prosaic but more objective eyes. All of
them, including himself, are treated as planets orbiting around Miller,
the sun.

Perlès presents Miller as a man with extraordinary powers of
perception, feeling, and influence. The source of these powers was
Miller's mystical connection with cosmic forces accessible to him
because of his simplicity, his purity of heart, and his detachment from
grasping at life. Miller knew how to give himself to the flow of life,
whichever direction the flow took, and this surrender, in Perlès's view,
made Miller both saintly and completely human. "Miller was pure at
heart," he writes. "Being pure at heart means to be vulnerable, but
vulnerability, on the spiritual plane, is never weakness."

Miller's "psychic magnetism" drew to him a wide range of characters—some aspiring artists like himself, some ordinary workers, trades
people, professionals, others (prostitutes, beggars, cripples) marginalized by circumstances and fate—who found in his nonjudgmental
acceptance and silent empathy a healing power. Perlès had expressed
his gratitude to Miller for this sacred quality in his character in a letter
he wrote shortly before broaching the subject of the book and suggesting that it be completed during a visit to Big Sur. "Joey, I want to
be a Buddhist to understand the significance of your entry into my
life and to interpret it as the karmatic fulfillment of some great deed
I must have achieved in some past life; for I don't have to tell you, at
this late juncture, that you're the best thing that ever happened to me.
I was in the caterpillar stage when I first met you. You haven't 'saved'
my life because one doesn't save a larva's life; it hasn't got one to save.

But your influence has been working on me ever since: I was relying on you as a premature infant does on an incubator. You have changed my mode of life, my attitude towards things, my writing."

Perlès sketches the circle of friends that gathered around Miller at his favorite café haunts in Paris, the Dôme and the Coupole, and at his Villa Seurat studio. Fred Kann, Walter Lowenfels, Michael Fraenkel, Hans Reichel, Brassaï, Wambly Bald, Richard Osborn, Conrad Moricand, and Anaïs Nin all played important roles in Miller's life and his development as a writer, and all became raw material for his books. But not all of them were pleased with Perlès's treatment of them in his memoir of Henry Miller.

Perlès identifies Nin as Miller's most important ally during his Paris years. He imagines them as twin stars in a constellation. "Whenever I think of Henry and Anaïs, the image of Castor and Pollux comes to my mind—the twin stars which, seen from afar, resemble a single star, with a monocle in its eye." He credits her with seeing into the core of Miller. "She recognized the essential Henry Miller at a glance. Her intuition bordered on clairvoyance." But he presents her as subordinate to Miller, acting out of need and dependency. "With her hands and her heart she gave Henry everything . . . Henceforth her whole life was his. She even gave him money . . . She threw herself into his arms and into his mind to be possessed on every plane of her existence. But her gift of herself was a *personal* gift, the gift of one person to another . . . Henry, on the other hand, gave things which strictly speaking didn't belong to him, of which he was only the custodian, as it were. With him, giving did not require the same élan of generosity . . . She needed him more than he needed her."

When Perlès sent the manuscript of *My Friend Henry Miller* to Nin for her review, she did not take kindly to this characterization of her relationship with Miller. She wrote to Perlès and to Miller demanding that Perlès mask her identity by giving her a fictitious name. She objected that the implication of a love affair between her and Miller would injure her husband Hugh and damage her marriage. She may have resented even more the suggestion that she needed Henry more than he needed her when she had championed Miller's writing more strenuously than anyone else, had supported him financially, and had provided to Obelisk Press the funds to print *Tropic of Cancer*. Ten years later, while corresponding with Miller about her soon-to-be-published diary, Nin had not forgotten nor forgiven this slight. She remarked to Miller, "Dear Henry, how do you think I felt the day I read in Fred's book that I loved you *abjectly*?"

Although Perlès and his publisher were adamantly against using a fictitious name in a work of nonfiction, Miller intervened on her behalf, insisting that "human considerations should take place over any other," and Perlès reluctantly divided her into two characters. Anaïs Nin became Miller's literary accomplice and benefactor, and "Liane de Champsaur," a choreographer in a Paris ballet company (Nin had been a dancer at one point in her life) became Miller's lover. Perlès was furious at the compromise, and wrote to Eve, "Tell Henry to write her that she can now sleep in peace - - - with anybody! I'm not going to write to her and I don't want to hear from her either."

Another Miller intimate from the Paris years who was displeased by Perlès's portrait of him was Michael Fraenkel. Fraenkel had sheltered Miller in his Villa Seurat studio during the period when Miller was without a consistent address, had encouraged him to abandon all literary pretense in *Tropic of Cancer* in order to write as he spoke, and had been Miller's correspondent on the voluminous *Hamlet* letters. But Perlès and Miller had preyed on Fraenkel for money and food and delighted in toying with him in a way that went beyond teasing to the verge of bullying. Somewhat smugly, Perlès remarks that "despite the dastardly way in which he [Miller] treated him, he was nevertheless his friend."

Perlès portrays Fraenkel in *My Friend Henry Miller* as pedantic, miserly, and humorless, a fit object for pranks and ridicule. He is described as constantly meditating on death while robed in "a greasy, food-stained brown dressing gown that made him look like an erudite monk of some austere order." Miller and Perlès patiently listen to Fraenkel's endless—and boring—metaphysical discourses in order to sit at his table for a free meal or take the opportunity to pinch francs from his wallet while his back is turned. "It no doubt grieved him," Perlès sarcastically observes, "to provide us with free meals in exchange for the feigned adulation we generously fed him."

Fraenkel, who had already fallen out with Miller over copyright and royalty issues stemming from Fraenkel's publication of the *Hamlet* volume, was not amused when he read Perlès's account of their relationship in the British edition of the book. He wrote to the publisher that he believed the passages in *My Friend Henry Miller* referring to him were slanderous, and forbade the publisher to arrange for a French translation of the book, threatening "to take all appropriate measures." Though Fraenkel did not follow up on his threat, his relationship with Miller was irrevocably poisoned. After his death, Fraenkel's widow, Daphne Gillam, refused to grant permission for Lawrence Durrell to include selections from the *Hamlet* correspondence in an anthology of Miller's writings he was preparing. Although Perlès's intention may only have been to show that the saintly Henry could also be a scoundrel, his willingness to denigrate Miller's intimate friends in order to exalt his subject opens him to the charge of being a sycophant.

Another major figure in Miller's life who was treated unflatteringly by Perlès was June, the Mona/Mara of the Tropics. He places her in a section of the book that deals with Miller's "predilection for the sordid, the diseased, the cancerous." Noting that "there is nothing squalid about Miller—he is the cleanest, the gayest, the most unsordid person alive"—Perlès attributes Miller's fascination with the seamy side of life not to any unwholesomeness but rather to "the attraction of the opposite." Miller's "abject love" for Mona illustrates this need in Miller. "He masochistically wallows in his unholy passion for her." To convey Mona's depravity, Perlès quotes from Miller's description of her in *Tropic of Cancer*. "She was the world's lying machine in microcosm, geared to the same unending, devastating fear which enables men to throw all their energies into the creation of the death apparatus." Perlès wonders why Miller didn't use his extraordinary healing powers to "cure" Mona and concludes that "such as she was, she was perfect—for him, that is. He needed the lying machine, the bag of lies, for his own personal well-being." It doesn't seem to have occurred to Perlès to examine Miller's well-known dysfunctional relationship with his mother to explain his need for a partner who would make his life miserable.

Perlès's American editor, Robert Hill of the John Day Company, was alarmed when he read the portrait of "Mona" in *My Friend Henry Miller*. He feared that Perlès's characterization of her might provide grounds for libel. Perlès dismissed this concern by pointing out that June was now in a mental institution in New York and unlikely ever to see the book. Miller, who had been corresponding with June, knew of her acute condition and had been sending her small sums of money whenever he could, was apparently unconcerned about how the book might affect her should she read it.

After tracking Miller through his Paris years and his brief sojourn in Greece, Perlès's account follows him back to America and his settling in Big Sur. With Miller again in his homeland, Perlès takes up the question of his literary reputation, discusses the continued suppression of his most important works by his countrymen, and wonders whether Miller does not belong in Europe, where his achievements as a writer are appreciated and where he will find the stimulus he needs for his work.

Perlès observes that while Miller's literary reputation—and the sales of his books—expanded rapidly in Europe after the war, he continued to be neglected by both critics and readers in his own country, despite the fact that "his enthusiasm, his exuberance, his child-likeness, are essentially American." Perlès attributes the marginalization of Miller in America to his treatment of his native land. "In his entire bulky work there is not a single flattering reference to his country, let alone England. To people, yes, to individuals in both Britain and America, but never a word of praise for the Anglo-Saxon way of life. And this naturally is resented." Perlès implies that Miller has been ostracized by American officialdom as much for his scathing criticisms of American "civilization" as for his use of obscene language and his graphic descriptions of sex. To underline the gap between the literary merits of Miller's writing and the official American response to it, Perlès builds a section that juxtaposes Judge Goodman's reactions to the Tropics in *Besig v. United States of America* with the estimates offered by eminent critics such as Sir Herbert Read, Ezra Pound, T. S. Eliot, Cyril Connolly, George Orwell, Aldous Huxley, Blaise Cendrars, Edmund Wilson, and Charles Pearce. It is noteworthy that in employing this tactic Perlès relies primarily on appreciations of Miller that have been voiced by Europeans. In bringing his case for Miller's greatness as a writer to its conclusion, he quotes at length from a letter by the Welshman John Cowper Powys, one of Miller's favorite writers.

Powys regards Miller as a writer whose stature places him in the company of Euripides, Aristophanes, Shakespeare, and Goethe. "But as to the *Genius of Henry Miller*, it is one of the most purely *European* in the greatest and deepest sense of that word! It is the true cosmic emotional traditional *Intake* (like eating and drinking and breathing, turned into digesting and absorbing and being inspired) of the old Greek and Latin and *Italian Renaissance aesthetic* civilizations." Powys sees in Miller's core a philosophical attitude toward life that he likens to the Chinese *Tao*, or "Way." Writing from this core, Miller is able to impart to his readers a faith in their own true dispositions, "a trust in fact in Life itself with Death as a *means* to *more Life as well as a rest from all of life's ills* . . . This Taoistic element implies a certain faith and confidence and transparent docility and humility and flowing like water and air unconquerable in a spirit that *apparently yields* but in reality remains *unchangeably itself*"—an attitude toward existence nicely captured by Miller's sobriquet "the Happy Rock."

Perlès concludes his portrait of Miller with a description of the comfortable life that he has built for himself in his Big Sur "paradise." Miller is now "a man who owns a house, a high-fidelity record player, a car, a lovely wife and a couple of exacting dogs," but he is, in Perlès's view, living in a sterile, if beautiful, setting. He closes with two emblematic scenes. In the first, Perlès accompanies Miller to a branch of the Bank of America in Hollywood, where Miller, always unsure of himself when dealing with money, awkwardly cashes a check. Perlès is at pains to describe the bustling activity of the bank, busy with customers making transactions. They leave the bank and enter a nearby bookstore, which is deserted. While Perlès browses, Miller asks the proprietor, whom he knows, if business is good. The proprietor rubs his hands and retorts, "Just had an order for eighteen and a half feet of books . . . Nine and a quarter feet of green books and nine and a quarter feet of red ones." He explains to the bewildered pair that the books were ordered by an interior decorator needing to match the color scheme of a film star's boudoir. So much for American "civilization." Perlès urges Miller to return to Europe to find stimulus for his work. "You can find stimulus in a Paris hovel, in an Italian *trattoria*, in a London basement flat, perhaps even in a Vienna air-raid shelter, but not in Hollywood, not in America. There is something in the American scene that kills the thing in the germ, or corrupts it, or turns it into something else." He parts from Miller with the line "*Je t'attends—à la source.*"

As if in proof of Perlès's argument that Miller needed the stimulus of Europe to write, it was during Perlès's visit that Miller's long writing drought ended and he began work on his next major book, *Big Sur and the Oranges of Hieronymus Bosch*. Though the book would not be completed for another year, by August 1955, three months after Perlès had returned to England, Miller wrote to Laughlin, "The book is growing . . . taking me over. I have now almost 400 pages and the end is not in sight."

In an amusing footnote to the *My Friend Henry Miller* story, Barbara Sandford informed her father in June 1956 that Beatrice had purchased a copy of the book and, having concluded from Perlès's description of his Big Sur lifestyle that Miller was well-off, was considering suing him for unpaid alimony and child support.

PERLÈS'S VISIT USHERED IN A PERIOD OF PRODUCTIVITY AND CONTENTMENT for Miller. At the time that Perlès arrived, Miller's watercolors were being exhibited in New York, first at the Brooklyn Public Library, then at the Esther Gentle Gallery in Manhattan. Nin was invited to speak at the show in Brooklyn. She recorded the evening in her diary and wrote Miller a letter about it as well. She told Miller that seeing his paintings had produced "a marvelous sensation" in her, and remarked their "fantasy and delicacy and sensibility, the richness and airiness of tone, the fluid melting transparencies. They were a joy to behold." She added that the exhibition "broke the sense of eclipse I have had all these years which made me unable to enjoy or read anything of yours, and I am glad of that." She reported that James Laughlin, Kay Boyle, and Abe Rattner attended, but that most of the spectators were more interested in discussing the censorship of Miller's books than in responding to the playfulness and humor of the paintings, a fact which annoyed her and which she tried to alter by reading to them from *The Angel Is My Watermark*. She confronted Laughlin, whom she did not like because he had turned down all her books, over his timidity in not bringing out the Tropics. Laughlin deflected the blame to his lawyers. Miller, obviously pleased by her appreciation and enthusiasm, wrote back that her letter had inspired him to paint several new ones—"the best I ever made." At the end of his letter, he added the news that June had recently been taken to a mental institution in New York.

Miller also took pleasure in helping Perlès research his book. Although the portrait dealt with the years of their friendship, Perlès wanted to understand Miller's background and asked for information about his Brooklyn years. Miller wrote to the editors of *The Brooklyn Daily Citizen* and the *Brooklyn Daily Eagle* to request photographs of the neighborhoods where he grew up. To direct the search, he mentioned streets, stores, schools, churches, and other landmarks. He waxed nostalgic about "the old 14th Ward" and asked if any of the papers' staff might have contact information for any of his boyhood chums, some of whom had shown up as characters in *Tropic of Capricorn* and *The Rosy Crucifixion*. To his delight, he quickly received letters from two of them, Stanley Borowski and Johnny Paul. In a reply, he sketched for Paul his life since leaving Brooklyn in 1930 and enclosed a passage about him from *Plexus* and another about Lester Reardon from *Black Spring*. Life and art were hand in hand.

Miller's finances took an unexpected turn for the better during Perlès's visit. Although he had managed to scrape together Perlès's plane fare, he was without funds, and in February he mailed out another begging letter "to all and sundry," asking friends and supporters to send him a dollar a week until further notice, and promising to repay all loans as soon as he received royalties from Europe. Miller's New Directions royalties for 1954 had totaled only $513, against the $900 he had received in advances. Hoffman had written in January that the outcome of the arbitration with Hachette over Girodias's unpaid royalties was not looking favorable. Hoffman suspected that the umpire had been corrupted. He planned to push the debtors into bankruptcy in order to force a settlement. But then in March came the news that the arbitrator had awarded Miller three million francs (about $10,000).

Hoffman informed Miller that he was now pressing for interest on the long overdue debt. The windfall enabled Miller and Eve to take Perlès on an excursion to Taos, New Mexico, where D. H. Lawrence had once lived and where his widow Frieda made her home.

Perlès's visit was a happy time for all of them. Perlès completed his book, Miller started one, and Eve enjoyed her hostess role. In February, they were visited by Huntington Cairns, who drove down from San Francisco and took them to dinner at Deetjen's. Eve grew very fond of Fred, and he returned the affection. Eve wrote to Durrell, whom she had yet to meet, "How I miss him! He's one of the most delicious (a strange word for it, I'll admit) men I suppose I've ever met. What a riotous 5 months the three of us shared at Big Sur . . . When I think back on those months, sometimes I feel all we did was laugh, and yet I know that's not so. Henry and Fred were both working like hell, and I kept the meals up to par and the wine flowing (which means I worked like hell too!)."

PERLÈS LEFT FOR ENGLAND TOWARD THE END OF MAY, visiting Miller's mother and sister on Decatur Street during a brief stopover in New York. Shortly after his departure, Miller received a letter from Sydney Omarr, a young astrologer who lived in Los Angeles and worked as a news writer for CBS Radio. A devoted reader of Miller's books, Omarr had been struck by the important role that astrology played in Miller's thought and style. He had noted Miller's numerous references to astrology and his frequent use of astrological imagery. He informed Miller that he was working on a book to be called *The Astrology of Henry Miller* and asked Miller if he would cooperate by stating his views on astrology and giving Omarr permission to quote from his works. "I am sure you are probably the most important writer on the American scene today," Omarr told Miller. "Oddly enough, your life and your works are similar to the history of astrology itself."

Miller, though now engrossed in his new book, was intrigued. He wrote back that he would assist Omarr, and asked him to explain his remark about the parallels between astrology and Miller's life. Omarr answered, "To me you are a symbol of the direct tie between literature and astrology, which first became evident during the Renaissance.

Your works too, taken as a whole, compare to the history of astrology
. . . It means, to me, freedom of thought and individuality." Miller
cooperated with Omarr by directing him to correspondents to whom
he had written about astrology, such as Anaïs Nin, Conrad Moricand,
Dane Rudhyar, and Emil Schnellock, and by providing his own commentary on astrology in a foreword to the book.

In the foreword, Miller traced his interest in astrology to his early
Paris years, to "accidental meetings with exciting individuals—such
as [Anaïs Nin's cousin] Eduardo Sanchez, Conrad Moricand, Dane
Rudhyar, Pierce Harwell, Count Hermann Keyserling (through correspondence)." He explains that he is drawn to astrology because
it reveals "that there is a correspondence between macrocosm and
microcosm. In short, that there is a rhythm to the universe, and that
man's own life partakes of this rhythm." Miller claims that he uses
astrology not to plan his life, but as a means to understand his own
character and destiny. "It is not to discover what is going to 'happen'
to us, it is not to forestall the blows of fate, that we should look to
our horoscopes. A chart, when properly read, should enable one to
understand the over-all pattern of one's life."

Miller had had his horoscope read numerous times by different
astrologers, including Moricand, Rudhyar, Harwell, and Omarr. While
in Paris, he had taken up the study of astrology and the occult under
the tutelage of Moricand, and had become a skilled interpreter of
astrological symbols and their correlations. Omarr had remarked to
him in a letter, "Your description of Saturn in the book on Greece
[*The Colossus of Maroussi*] is better than about anything in most astrological texts . . . Your natural understanding of astro-symbolism is fantastic."

One of the most interesting and profound readings of Miller's birth
chart was performed by the eminent astrologer Dane Rudhyar. Miller
had made contact with Rudhyar from Paris in 1939 after reading his
weighty treatise *The Astrology of Personality*, a book recommended to
him by Count Keyserling. In *The Books in My Life*, Miller included
The Astrology of Personality among "the hundred books which influenced me most." Rudhyar's study considered astrology as a tool for
understanding the self. He called it Harmonic Astrology. "Such a type

of astrology provides a basis for the harmonization and integration of the human psyche. It considers the birth-chart as the life-chord of the individual being and destiny it symbolizes; also, we might say, as the true name of this individual being. It realizes that most human beings are living only in parts of themselves, living fragmentary, incomplete and sadly unfulfilled lives. The wholeness that they essentially are, as complete Individuals, is there—potential, archetypal, but expressed or manifested only in bits. This wholeness is the true chord of their individual self-hood; but only a few notes of the chord are sounding at a time, some never vibrate at all, and there is no intensity or fullness in their whole-life performance."

Given this explanation of astrology's significance, it is obvious why Miller, whose main purpose as a writer was to discover and live out the truth of his own being, found in this ancient "science" of cosmic correspondences a ready-made language and a framework that could express and contain his search. Its mysterious origins and intuitive approach to understanding reality accorded well with Miller's temperament as well as with his belief that human history has been devolving in a downward spiral from an ancient race of men who lived on a higher plane of consciousness than modern man. In the foreword, Miller wrote about astrology in terms that echo Rudhyar's words: "What interests me primarily in astrology is its holistic . . . aspect. The man who is whole sees whole, and for him the universe is an ever-expanding universe, that is, a universe more infinite, ever more rewarding to be part of. The life of such a man is complete at every moment. He's a fulfilled individual. Only astrology can reveal to us this potential reality which is man's kingdom—or the garden of fulfillment . . . What I am trying to say is that the study of astrology can help one to the discovery and the acceptance of one's own self."

After his return from Europe in 1940, Miller had remained in contact with Rudhyar and the two men became acquainted while Miller was living in Los Angeles, in Beverly Glen. In October 1945, just before the birth of Miller's daughter Valentine, Rudhyar sent him a reading of his birth chart that must have deepened Miller's belief in the validity of astrology as an analytical tool. "Your mother image and anima function (through which you can reach the collective unconscious and your source of inspiration) are most powerfully and directly stamped and controlled by the Mars function. This might mean a very strong mother complex and 'fixation'; but it would also mean . . . that your ego has felt the need, at once, to work creatively upon the mother-image, has repudiated the physical mother as inadequate, and has built, as soon as it could, a substitute mother-image, the 'ideal woman', connected in the depth of your unconscious with the collective and ancient image of the Great Mother . . . What apparently happened is that she could not, or would not, play in your childhood the part your unconscious imagination had made for her . . . As a result, she stimulated negatively the activity of your unconscious simply by *not fitting* the image you had created for her . . . thus forcing you to transfer your mother image to an 'ideal woman', and soon after to your first mistress 'old enough to be your mother.'" Miller must have felt, reading this interpretation of his chart, that Rudhyar had passed through his horoscope into his childhood home on Decatur Street and become a silent witness to the family dynamic that Miller had described in "Reunion in Brooklyn."

Omarr's book, published in 1959 as *Henry Miller, His World of Urania*, surveys the numerous references to astrology that occur throughout Miller's books—sometimes in the form of imagery, sometimes as extended discursive passages—to show that astrology was a persistent theme in Miller's writing. In some cases, astrology offered the key to understanding Miller's deepest intentions. In *Tropic of Capricorn* (the title refers to Miller's zodiacal sign), Miller considers the date of his birth to have been the first, and most serious, of the many blunders committed by his mother:

> If I were to believe in the stars I should have to believe that I was completely under the reign of Saturn. Everything that happened to me happened too late to mean much to me. It was even so with my birth. Slated for Christmas I was born a half hour too late. It always seemed to me that I was meant to be the sort of individual that one is destined to be by virtue of being born on the 25th day of December. Admiral Dewey was born on that day and so was Jesus Christ . . . perhaps Krishnamurti too, for all I know. Anyway that's the sort of guy I was intended to be. But due

to the fact that my mother had a clutching womb, that she held me in her grip like an octopus, I came out under another configuration—with a bad set up in other words. They say—the astrologers I mean—that it will get better and better for me as I go on; the future, in fact, is supposed to be quite glorious. But what do I care about the future? It would have been better if my mother had tripped on the stairs the morning of the 25th of December and broken her neck. That would have given me a fair start!

In the same book, Miller frequently likens Mona/Mara's profound impact on him to planetary influences. He links the microcosm of their union to the macrocosm of the heavens with surreal flights of language. "We looked out of the black hole of our life into the black hole of the world. The sun was permanently blacked out, as though to aid us in our continuous internecine strife. For Sun we had Mars, for Moon Saturn: we lived permanently in the zenith of the underworld. The earth had ceased to revolve and through the hole in the sky above us there hung the black star which never twinkled. Now and then we had fits of laughter, crazy, batrachian laughter which made the neighbors shudder."

The title that Miller chose for the central work of his career as a writer, *The Rosy Crucifixion*, is rich in occult allusion and esoteric significance as well. As Rudhyar explains, "All the various energies and drivers of the natural life of a plant are harmonized and concentrated within the seed. When the seed germinates in the spring, this is crucifixion—Miller's 'Rosy Crucifixion'!" Rebirth. It was in this work that Miller set out to discover and disclose his essential self, what Rudhyar calls "the seed-pattern of a person's individuality or . . . uniqueness of being" as revealed in the birth chart.

In a letter he wrote to Miller accompanying his horoscope, Rudhyar delved into the meaning of the rosy cross. The image comes from the Rosicrucians, a secret occult society founded in fifteenth century Germany by Christian Rosenkreuz. According to Rudhyar, "The essential symbol of the Rosicrucians is 'the rose that blooms at the center of the cross' i.e. where the vertical crosses the horizontal— the Zenith-Nadir axis, the horizon. In man, it points to the Brachial plexus of the spine which is 'the center behind the heart', perhaps the most sacred in the body, where the 'Tone' of the Self, the change-less vibration of the individual, is centered. It is a spiritual center, not a 'great sympathetic' Chakra." Rudhyar's explanation of the plexus echoes Miller's own reference to this center in his essay on the film *Extase*.

Rudhyar considered Miller's critique of American society as a reaction against its disregard of the cosmic view of man's potential that astrology expresses. "Miller hates to see human beings and society vulgarized and liquefied into sham and amorphous meaningless-ness; into what they really are not! If he criticizes so harshly our U.S. society it is because he sees in it so much that is the glorification of meaninglessness, formlessness, and thus seed-less-ness." Rudhyar's observation is consistent with what Miller had written to Keyserling from Paris in 1938: "the astrological view of man confirms the spiritual viewpoint, in the sense that only he is free who lives out to the utmost his potentialities."

That Miller saw his personal evolution, obsessively pursued in the Tropics and *The Rosy Crucifixion*, as an astrological journey occurring in cosmic time as opposed to historical time, is suggested by the importance he assigned to the unwritten book, *Draco and the Ecliptic*, in which he intended to compress his life story. In a letter to John Cowper Powys written in May 1950, Miller discussed the importance to his writing of occult symbolism and astrology. He wrote, "I have always maintained that writers particularly have a great fecundating source to draw from in the realm of astrology." He mentions Draco. "As for the Dragon . . . years ago, in Paris, I read Frederick Carter's little book, *Symbols of Revelation*, and after reading his words about the occult symbolism of the dragon, I decided that the final book of my 'autobiographical' works (which began with *Tropic of Cancer*) would end with a slim volume to be called *Draco and the Ecliptic*. It has great meaning for me, this title, though I do not as yet know the nature of the contents of this final book." As early as the *Hamlet* cor-respondence, which began in 1935, Miller had written to Michael Fraenkel about the significance of the constellation Draco, the great dragon that encircled the North Pole in its coils. The passage makes clear how Miller applied astrological symbolism to his own personal quest. Omarr included it in *Henry Miller, His World of Urania*: "For the esoteric astrologer a tremendous idea lay behind the myth of the Dragon, which was called the thirteenth House of the Zodiac. For the Chaldeans the Dragon was the first created being; it was through the Dragon in the sky that man gained admittance to the 'heaven beyond heaven' . . . The Dragon which creeps through the fence into Paradise is the same as the sage who liberates himself from the thralls of destiny, the same as the Buddha attaining Nirvana."

This attainment, this liberation, was what Miller sought: to achieve it was to master "the art of living." Miller was writing *The Rosy Crucifixion* in an attempt to free himself from the thrall of his own destiny. He saw in Draco a symbol of escape from personal history and from human history into the "heaven beyond heaven." That he never wrote the book may signify that he never attained the state he sought.

IN JUNE, TONY AND VAL CAME FOR THE SUMMER, AND BECAUSE MILLER was now fully engaged with *Big Sur and the Oranges of Hieronymus Bosch*, this meant even more work for Eve. She wrote to Vincent Birge, who by now had become a member of Miller's inner circle (he was sent a copy of the manuscript of *My Friend Henry Miller*), describing her summer routine.

> The joint's jumping . . . The walls rock and reverberate with the joyful blasts of the little one's tonsils and leaden shoes. Hallelujah! Wish you were here, at the moment. I'm attempting to put up a tree house in that huge oak on the West 40, and can't seem to brace whatever needs bracing, even so . . . it's a handy way of getting rid of superfluous children so why should I kick? However it needs a man's eye . . . and brawn, I'm a sorry substitute now and then. Maybe I can wheedle Harrydick into a helping hand. Henry is like a volcano of work on this new book . . . It pours out like the swollen river after a three year drought. I keep the children occupied all day every day, the program reads like a three ringed circus . . . but as long as they are kept delirious this way, the fighting

and bickering falls off, and Henry keeps on with the book. I think I'll survive the summer . . . although I admit I wonder sometimes if I want to.

The Craft classes are highly successful, I've ten kids this year, and they're turning out one collage, mobile, etc. after another . . . Today they'll work on some clay. Twice a week, all day, this goes. Tues. and Thurs. Wednesday means all day horse-back riding and swimming at the State Park, also Friday. Monday is the town trip. Saturday is beach or neighbor's houses . . . and that leaves me the Sabbath for the more mundane affairs like cleaning the house, washing and ironing their clothes. Henry and I see each other in passing, now and then, we're both so tired at night we fall into bed after the last dog's hung . . . and so it goes.

This letter, written three years into her relationship with Miller, shows the extent to which Eve had become, as Miller's wife, a drudge with no life of her own. She clearly loves the children, she is clearly a creative, devoted stepmother, but her resentment at having a marginalized relationship with her husband is evident. Miller, for his part, seemed thrilled with the arrangement. When the summer had ended and the children were back with Lepska, he wrote to Bezalel Schatz about another upcoming watercolor show, in Japan, where his paintings were being exhibited alongside works by Picasso and Zadkine. He paid tribute to Eve's talent as an artist and savored her equanimity. "Eve made two collages and they are beauties. She has talent, that girl. And she would sell much better than I. People like her work immediately. No more battles with that witch, Lepska. No more grief and anguish. Evie says lunch is ready. Boiled eggs and yogurt. No complaints. Going to town then, will have dinner with Doner, who goes to NY for a month. And love from Evie—but you know that! She gets prettier every day. An angel, really. A 'dancing' angel."

Publishing developments during this period also boosted Miller's spirits. *Sexus*, censored in France but still sold openly, according to Birge who kept Miller apprised, had been seized by the police in Japan, but the Japanese publisher was fighting the censorship. Laughlin was traveling in India and seeking publishing outlets for New Directions titles there. In France, Correa had already expressed interest in the Big Sur book. And although Miller had initially wanted Laughlin to release this book from New Directions' "first look" option because he believed a more commercial publisher might produce more sales, he withdrew the request out of respect for the "sincerity and honesty" of Laughlin's reply, which reminded him that New Directions had been faithful to him and had carried him even though sales of his titles were weak. Also during this period, Schatz was trying to arrange publication of *Tropic of Cancer* and *The Colossus of Maroussi* in Israel, in Hebrew.

But the most significant progress for Miller's reputation and readership in the United States was coming from the New American Library. After a three-year delay caused by the Congressional probe of obscenity in literature, Victor Weybright was ready to bring out a selection of Miller's "chaste" writing with the fetching title *Nights of Love and Laughter*, which had been suggested by Miller (the editors at NAL had suggested *Days of Love and Hunger*). The book was issued in November 1955 in a twenty-five-cent edition of 220,000 copies that placed the work of Henry Miller within the reach of people who purchased inexpensive paperback books in drugstores, train stations, and supermarkets as well as popular bookstores. Widespread reviews were overwhelmingly positive. Miller received a flood of mail from readers wanting to know how to obtain the Tropics. Miller had gone mainstream. Sensing this, Laughlin suggested that the portrait of Conrad Moricand contained in *Big Sur and the Oranges of Hieronymus Bosch* be published separately as an inexpensive pocket book through the NAL Signet imprint. Miller agreed, so long as the section remained in the Big Sur book as well, and fifty thousand copies of *A Devil in Paradise* were issued. Miller was now on hundreds of thousands of nightstands across America.

In January 1956 Miller received word that his mother was ill and dying. The news must have come as a surprise to him. Although he had not seen his mother since 1944, he had had news of her from Lepska, who had visited her with the children in 1951, and from Alfred Perlès, who had stopped by the house on Decatur Street for a short visit with Louise and Lauretta during his return to London the previous May. He reported to Miller, "Both seem to be quite happy;

I asked them if there was anything I or you could do for them, but they're apparently OK and in need of nothing."

Vincent Birge arranged for the Millers to stay at the apartment of his girlfriend Loraine Fowler to help them conserve resources. Miller, Eve, and Birge went together to Louise's house and were dismayed at what they found. (Miller, fearing a scene if Louise discovered he had married again, initially did not let his mother see Eve.) The house was in a state of disrepair, and both women were severely malnourished. Miller learned that the miserly Louise had been forcing them to live on $500 per year while she tried to save every penny.

Miller's immediate problem was to find help for Louise and Lauretta, a nurse for his mother and a caregiver for his sister. He also was worried about the long-term problem of how to care for Lauretta should his mother die, as seemed likely, or become an invalid.

His days were spent nursing his mother, making repairs to the house, running errands, and trying to find help. He was writing regular updates to Emil White that conveyed his sense of despair about the situation. "Atmosphere terribly depressing to me," he wrote. "Mother could recover and live a while—maybe a few years. Or die to-morrow in her sleep. Must find some-one to live (here) with Lauretta in event of mother's death—and even before perhaps." The thought that the crisis might drag on for weeks or months or even years, draining his limited funds and keeping him from his work, made him feel trapped. His sister's condition and future prospects made him "feel like weeping all the time," he told White. In a sign of his desperation, he wrote to Sydney Omarr asking the astrologer to consult his horoscope for clues about the outcome of the crisis.

Omarr wrote back promptly, telling Miller that he had cast a "horary chart" based on the "birth" of Miller's query, and assured Miller that "by the time you receive this, no doubt the problem you wrote me about will have, in effect, solved itself." The key indicator in the chart, Omarr reported, was Mercury. "Mercury, which has been retrograde since January 19, went direct yesterday, February 9th, thus relieving the problem . . . presenting an influence smacking of renewed freedom, lost liberty returned, etc. Mercury rules the 12th house of the chart, representing your 'confinement' in this situation.

Your mother's health is secondary to the actual question, because you really wanted to know when YOU WOULD BE FREE OF THE SITUATION." Omarr went on to report that the chart indicated that the year ahead held travel, variety, and material success for Miller.

Omarr's prediction may have cheered Miller, because on February 14 he reported to White that he had found a nurse to care for his mother at night, though there was "a big row with latter over this. What a scene! I almost had to club her down." Miller expected that his mother, unable to retain food and suffering from dysentery, would not last much longer. But she held out, and he still had no solution to the problem of long-term care for Lauretta. He wrote again to Emil, "The main problem becomes more insuperable as one day succeeds another. I wouldn't care how much money it took, if I could find the person to live with Lauretta. The real answer will have to come from the sky."

Despite the incessant demands of looking after Louise and Lauretta, Miller found time for other activities while in New York that afforded some relief. He and Eve dined with James Laughlin at Bob MacGregor's apartment on a meal that Eve prepared. They went to the theater and sampled restaurants. Miller met with Victor Weybright of the New American Library. He made a recording, *Henry Miller Recalls and Reflects*, with Ben Grauer. And he paid a visit to June, who had been released from the mental institution and was living in her own apartment. Nin heard the tale of this visit some years later and recorded it in her diary. "When Henry's mother died and Henry went to New York, he went to see June. The story I heard made me very sad. June suffered from deforming arthritis. She set a sumptuous table to welcome Henry, good wine and plenty of food, remembering his enjoyment of them. He had a shock at her appearance. She talked as profusely as before, a compulsive talk. Henry was so disturbed that he wanted to leave. Then he realized that June expected him to stay. She pointed to the bed. He began to weep and left hurriedly." As the Millers' stay lengthened, they moved from Loraine Fowler's apartment to Miller's favorite New York haunt, the Hotel Van Rensselaer in the Village.

By the first week in March, Louise's condition had worsened. She was in the hospital, unable to speak, one side paralyzed, her kidneys failing. Her doctor expected her to die any day. But she lasted through most of the month, as Miller's hospital bills mounted, before finally succumbing on March 21. Meanwhile, Miller went frantically from office to office in the city Welfare Department trying, unsuccessfully, to arrange long-term care for Lauretta. Finally, he and Eve decided to bring Lauretta back with them to Big Sur.

Many years later, Miller looked back on the trauma of his mother's death with a sense of grim horror. "That was a trying time for me," he said at the end of his autobiographical memoir *My Life and Times*. "I went to see her every day. But even when dying she was that same determined tyrannical person dictating what I should do and refusing to do anything I asked her to do . . . A weird thing happened when we were burying her. It was a freezing cold day with the snow coming down thick. They couldn't get the coffin angled right to lower it into the grave. It was as if she was still resisting us. Even in the funeral parlor, before that, where she was on view for six days, every time I bent over her one of her eyes would open and stare at me."

It troubled Miller deeply that he had never reconciled with his mother. Toward the end of his life he wrote up a dream he claimed to have had in which after his own death he encounters his mother in Devachan, the temporary dwelling place where souls reside until their return to earth. The mother who appears in this dream is the mother he never had—compassionate, wise, loving. She confesses to him that in her earthly form she was stupid, but now that she inhabits her astral body, she has learned contentment. She parrots the Miller philosophy: "The universe is run by laws; if you break the law you have to pay the penalty . . . You may have noticed we have no schools here. Here one acquires wisdom, not learning. We live according to our instincts and our intuitions. Like that we remain part animal, part human. On earth the function of the brain is greatly exaggerated." The dream world is "the true reality," she tells him. "Down below all is illusion. Only the imagination is real."

In the dream, Miller also seeks his first, idealized love, Cora Seward. He asks his mother if she has seen Cora in Devachan. His mother answers that Cora has probably already returned to earth, which she also wishes to do. This maudlin scene ends with Miller's mother drifting away from him as he calls after her, "Mother, I love you. *I love you!* Do you hear me?"

The role that Miller's mother played in his psyche, the way her influence shaped his relationships with other women and fueled him as a writer, should not be underestimated. Although he had almost no contact with her after leaving Brooklyn for good in 1930, her treatment of him, her aspirations for him, her insistence that he be respectable and conform to society's norms, haunted him as a man and polarized him as a writer. In another short piece he wrote about her as he was nearing his own death, he averred, "It occurred to me that if my mother had been like the mother I dreamed about, perhaps I wouldn't have become a writer after all. I might have become a tailor like my father. I might have become an upstanding pillar of society like she wanted me to be . . . When I finally found the courage to write what I'd been storing up for years, it came pouring out into one long relentless tirade. Beginning with the earliest memories of my mother, I had saved up enough hatred, enough anger, to fill a hundred books."

The Millers departed New York for Big Sur on April 26, with Lauretta in tow. They installed her in the studio at Partington Ridge, and Miller borrowed studio space from neighbor Maud Oakes in order to continue work on *Big Sur and the Oranges of Hieronymus Bosch*. Construction on an additional space to house the children on their visits—they were expected again in June—was started. To Eve's chores was added the responsibility of looking after Lauretta. Miller wrote to Bob MacGregor early in May that the burden of caring for Lauretta had nearly caused Eve to suffer a breakdown. He immediately found space for his sister at a comfortable nursing home in nearby Pacific Grove. Louise had left Lauretta a small estate of $7,000. With the aid of neighbor Giles Healey, Miller found an investment advisor who used these funds to purchase an annuity for Lauretta. But the income from this annuity covered only part of the nursing home costs, and Miller made up the difference from his own income.

AT THE END OF JUNE MILLER REPORTED TO MACGREGOR that he had completed the Big Sur book. "Eve is wrapping it up [typing the manuscript] . . . I think I boiled it down somewhat, only 508 pages now." The Big Sur book was a love letter to Miller's adopted home, a place far removed in space, in ambience, and in spirit from the Brooklyn of his youth and early manhood. Miller rhapsodized over "the timeless quality" of Big Sur, its isolation from the rest of the American continent, its rugged land and seascapes, the independent spirit of its hardy residents, many of them misfits and iconoclasts like himself. He saw in Big Sur "nature smiling at herself in the mirror of eternity."

The book consists of a medley of the usual Miller topics and interests: glimpses of his daily life and routine, profiles of neighbors and other residents, poetic descriptions of the scenery and wildlife, mystical speculations about the laws of the universe mixed with frequent wisdom pronouncements drawn from his life experiences. And there are diatribes against the dominant American culture from which Big Sur offers refuge. The last section of the book, "Paradise Lost," provides an account of the disastrous visit from Conrad Moricand that was also published separately as *A Devil in Paradise*.

Miller observes that people seek out places like Big Sur because they have discovered "that the American way of life is an illusory kind of existence, that the price demanded for the security and abundance it pretends to offer is too great." Miller has found in Big Sur the kind of community that he believes should prevail throughout the country, a community of self-sufficient individuals who interact with one another in a truly democratic spirit. "There being nothing to improve on in the surroundings, the tendency is to set about improving oneself," Miller notes approvingly. In such a community, the individual is free to pursue his most important task, self-fulfillment. "The ideal community, in a sense, would be the loose, fluid aggregation of individuals who elected to be alone and detached in order to be at one with themselves and all that lives and breathes. It would be a god-filled community even if none of its members believed in (a) god." But in most American communities, Miller asserts, "we find only individuals dedicated to 'the good life'."

Against this "status quo," Miller sets the unique and often eccentric individuals who are creating a different kind of life in Big Sur, a life in which one harmonizes one's own personal rhythm with the larger rhythm of the universe, the astrological life. Such a man is Howard Welch, "a plain, handsome ordinary fellow from Missouri" who came to Big Sur in the early 1950s looking for "a place to flop" and found an economic niche collecting his neighbors' garbage in a battered pick-up truck. Howard is "a genuine American type. Tall, lean, muscular, alert, quick-witted, eyes a-twinkle, toes sparkling, slow of speech, musical voice, dry, kindly humor, fond of the banjo, the guitar, the harmonica, capable of working like a fiend if need be, spry as a leprechaun, good-natured, peaceably inclined but quick to flare up if provoked, always minding his own business, always pretending to be less than he is, ever ready to lend a hand, eccentric in attire but in a pleasing, dashing way, scrupulously conscientious, punctilious as well as punctual. Sentimental but not sloppily so, idealistic, slightly cantankerous, neither a follower nor a leader, sociable yet chary of ties, and, where the other sex is concerned, just a trifle difficult to live with. A man to rely on, as a worker, as a helper, as a friend, as a neighbor."

This detailed sketch, which puts on display Miller's powers of observation and his fondness for building a crescendo of detail, hearkens back to other portraits of the American folk-type penned by writers like James Fenimore Cooper, Washington Irving, Walt Whitman, and Mark Twain. Miller seems aware of the bloodlines of this type, "the democratic man our poets sang of but who, alas, is being rapidly exterminated, along with the buffalo, the moose and the elk, the great bear, the eagle, the condor, the mountain lion. The sort of American who never starts a war, never raises a feud, never draws the color line, never tries to lord it over his fellow-man, never yearns for a higher education, never holds a grudge against his neighbor, never treats an artist shabbily, and never turns a beggar away. Often tutored and unlettered, he sometimes has more of the poet and the musician in him, philosopher too, than those who are acclaimed as such. His whole way of life is aesthetic. What marks him as different, sometimes ridiculous, is his sincerity and originality. That he aspires to be none other than himself, is this not the essence of wisdom?"

As Miller fills out the portrait of this ideal American type represented by Howard Welch, Welch comes more and more to resemble Henry Miller, or at least Henry Miller's image of himself: the democratic man "fed up with the scheme of things" who embodies "the ideal material for the making of community."

His treatment of Howard Welch as the archetypal American reveals the extent to which Miller, despite his scathing commentaries on the American way of life, remains at heart a romantic American who believes deeply in the promise of his country but rages that this promise is not being fulfilled. "The American is only an American when he perpetuates the experiment begun by his forefathers," he writes elsewhere in the book. This experiment, Miller believes, has been abandoned for the pursuit of material abundance and comfort. "The great hoax which we are perpetuating every day of our lives is that we are making life easier, more comfortable, more enjoyable, more profitable. We are doing just the contrary. We are making life stale, flat and unprofitable every day in every way. One ugly word covers it all: waste. Our thoughts, our energies, our very lives are being used up to create what is unwise, unnecessary, unhealthy." He quotes Thoreau to bring America back to its roots: "I am convinced that to maintain one's self on this earth is not a hardship, but a pastime, if we will live simply and wisely."

All is not seriousness in Miller's rendering of life in Big Sur. The book is spiced with amusing anecdotes about unwanted visitors, flying saucer sightings, and numerous sketches of neighbors and friends such as Ephraim Doner, Gilbert Neiman, Lilik Schatz, Emil White (to whom the book is dedicated), Lynda Sargent, Jean Page Wharton, and Harrydick Ross, among others. But Miller's central purpose in writing the book is clearly to present Big Sur as a place and a community that fulfills the promise of America—a place where diversity is welcomed, where simplicity is valued, where self-reliance is practiced, where art and artists are admired, where, in brief, Miller's values prevail. Miller's Big Sur is a far cry from the bohemian "cult of sex and anarchy" described by Mildred Brady.

Before Miller sent the manuscript of *Big Sur and the Oranges of Hieronymus Bosch* to New Directions, he had it vetted by some of the subjects who figured prominently in it. Jean Page Wharton wrote him to protest against the treatment he had given Lepska in the section on Moricand, and to warn about its potential to inflict harm on Val through its disturbing imagery of her mother. "The violent things you have written in your powerful style about Lepska shriek out at the reader ... Such writings about the child's mother could implant in Val's mind very horrible pictures that might result in terrible physical disease in Val's own body." Though Miller resented Wharton's editorializing, he had enough respect for her psychological insight and knowledge of his family to take heed. He did not entirely remove his negative remarks about Val's mother, but he toned them down to the point where they could pose no risk to his daughter's mental health.

Another censoring move came from Bob MacGregor, who wrote Miller in August that his depiction of George Leite, coeditor of *Circle*, was libelous and could not be published without a release. Leite had already provided Miller carte blanche in a letter sent the previous year, but because the letter had been written while Leite was a mental patient at Napa State Hospital (Leite had suffered a breakdown after using peyote and Dexedrine sulfate and had also contracted tuberculosis), New Directions' lawyers doubted that it would inoculate the publisher and author against a lawsuit. Miller, who had nothing kind to say about his former disciple anyway, deleted Leite from the book.

ONE OF THE OUTCOMES OF MILLER'S experience in trying to come to the rescue of his astrologer friend Conrad Moricand was his doubt that one human being could come to the aid of another. When Moricand realized that Big Sur was not the right environment for him (he was anything but a "democrat" in Miller's sense of the word) and announced his decision to leave, he chided Miller for his generosity. "What you are doing to me no man has a right to do to another," he protested. Miller was baffled by the accusation, but Moricand went on to explain his resentment. "You invited me to come here, to make this my home for the rest of my days . . . You said I did not need to work, that I could do anything I pleased. And you demanded nothing in return. One can't do that to a fellow-man. It's unjust. It puts me in an unbearable position." Moricand was not being ungrateful; he was telling Miller that he felt burdened by his host's selflessness. Miller drew a lesson from this. "Never, never again, would I make the mistake of trying to solve someone's problems for him. How deceptive to think that by means of a little self-sacrifice one can help another overcome his difficulties! How egotistical!" But Miller did not really believe this, nor did he act upon it. When writing in the Big Sur book about his friendship with Walker Winslow (another man in distress whom Miller had helped), he recounted conversations they held on the subject of mutual aid. Winslow was an alcoholic who had joined Alcoholics Anonymous. His testimony on the healing power of solidarity among alcoholics suffering from addiction caused Miller to rethink his position. He wrote out the substance of their deliberations in the Big Sur book, then withheld it from the final draft, but later included it as a short essay titled "The Hour of Man" in the collection *Stand Still Like the Hummingbird.*

To resolve the question, "Can we really aid another individual, and if so, how?" Miller looked to the teachings of Jesus Christ and the writings of the Jewish philosopher Eric Gutkind. Miller asserted that Jesus taught, through his example and through his parables, that men should aid one another "instinctively and spontaneously when confronted with an issue . . . By responding with a full spirit to any demand which is made upon us we aid our fellow man to help himself . . . The answer, then, is to be ever in readiness, to do the immediate, and to give without stint." According to Gutkind, acting in unison with other human beings brings one into the presence of God. "The absolute unity of all beings which is reached in the gathering together of men who have become completed in their humanity, free from fear, nature and ideology—this is the true 'Tabernacle of the meeting with God', the tabernacle of the present."

Miller had a history of reaching out to men in distress, especially if they were artists or "seekers after truth" like himself. He invited Emil White, a misfit from Central Europe who had retreated to the Yukon to escape World War Two, to join him in Big Sur, then encouraged him to become a painter; he took up the cause of George Dibbern, a pacifist who fled Germany and regarded himself as a citizen of the world; he called attention to the plight of the poet Kenneth Patchen, who suffered from poor health and extreme poverty; he advocated for the Egyptian writer Albert Cossery. So it was in character for him to respond with a generous spirit when a correspondence from Roger Bloom, a forty-four-year-old convict serving a life sentence for armed robbery in the Missouri State Penitentiary, reached him in Big Sur in September 1956.

Bloom had written to Emil White asking how to obtain copies of Miller's books. When Miller responded, Bloom wrote to thank him and to introduce himself. He was serving concurrent sentences imposed by federal and state judges, an eighteen-year federal sentence for armed robbery and a life sentence as an "habitual criminal" under Missouri law. He had been born in Clearfield, Pennsylvania, into a poor family. His father, often unemployed, worked as a wage laborer. At an early age Bloom began to steal in order to help his family put food on the table. He told his parents that he had earned the money, and they didn't question him. When the family home went into foreclosure, Bloom moved to Chicago and took up a life of crime, stealing cars, bootlegging, robbing banks. Prior to the federal and state convictions for which he was serving time in the Missouri State Prison, he had served five other sentences in other prisons for automobile theft and armed robbery (the gun he carried was unloaded, he said). All told, he had spent twenty-eight of his forty-four years in prisons.

Bloom had begun reading Miller in 1947 when he came across the 1942 New Directions anthology *Spearhead*, which contained an excerpt from *Tropic of Capricorn*. When he told his father that he liked Miller's writing, his father gave him copies of the Tropics he had purchased under-the-counter. As they had for so many young men at odds with American society, the books had a transforming effect on Bloom's world outlook. He moved away from self-pity and bitterness and began to work on himself. He wrote to Miller, "Henry, I want to change a lot of things—for me, about me—and through your books I know I'm getting somewhere. One day, please God, I hope I can talk to you."

Miller corresponded with Bloom, encouraging him to have faith in the future, sending him watercolors and books, which of course had to pass the censoring eyes of the warden, E. V. Nash. Soon Miller was corresponding with the warden as well, sending him books and a watercolor, which Nash hung on the wall of his prison office. Nash felt that Bloom was a reformed man and supported his first request for parole, which was heard in 1960. By this time, at Miller's urging, Alfred Perlès, George Dibbern, and Anaïs Nin were also corresponding with Bloom.

Bloom's quest for parole dragged on for ten years, complicated by the dual jurisdictions, turnover of Bloom's lawyers (whose fees Miller paid), and the collapse of two parole plans (Dibbern had offered to

sponsor Bloom's parole to New Zealand but immigration denied
entry; Miller arranged sponsorship in California but was turned down
by the Los Angeles Probation Department). Miller visited Bloom in
prison on three occasions while traveling to and from Europe, met
with the warden and the head of the parole board, and wrote a letter to the governor. Eventually the State of Missouri paroled Bloom
to the federal penitentiary at Leavenworth, Kansas, and in September 1966 the federal parole board freed him. He settled in Chicago,
where, with help from Elmer Gertz, the lawyer who defended *Tropic
of Cancer* in a Chicago obscenity trial, he found work as a barber, then
as a model in print advertising. In November he became engaged to
Gertrude Leikel, a divorcee with a sixteen-year-old son. He wrote to
Miller, "This life I now possess has a meaning all its own. I cannot find
anything to frown about. I glory in each minute I spend awake—and
I breathe a 'prayer of thanks' each morning, for the privilege of being
alive." He closed with, "Keep your pecker up." In August 1968 Bloom
visited Miller and Nin in Los Angeles during a trip to California.

Another distressed soul to whom Miller ministered during this
period was his ex-wife June. In August 1956 Miller was contacted by
Annette Baxter, a young woman from New York who was writing
her doctoral dissertation on Miller and planned to do research in
Miller's papers at UCLA. Miller gave his blessing to the project, and
while Annette and her husband, Jim, were in California they visited
the Millers in Big Sur. A friendship was sparked. While at UCLA,
Annette had read June's letters and had been touched by her plight.
When she returned to New York, she wrote to Miller offering to
look in on June and report to him on her condition. Miller readily
assented and thus began a program to rehabilitate June.

The Baxters visited June at her room in a run-down apartment
house on 95th Street near Riverside Drive that Annette described as
"a hovel." "Hers is a small room, sparsely furnished, and the window
blind seemed to be permanently drawn . . . She uses a community
kitchen and bath." Though living as a recluse without apparent outside contacts or interests, June received them graciously and appeared
comfortable with their presence. The Baxters sent Eve and Miller a
reassuring initial assessment, while noting June's frail condition and

poor appearance. "The fabulous voice of Mona is altogether preserved, with its resonance, its cultivated diction, its subtle inflection; she uses it the way a harpist uses her fingers in handling the two of us. Knowing not at all how much we might know about her, she moved through the conversation with confident finesse, with all her mystery and dignity intact. And her candor, her poise, were so becoming that had we not been well-acquainted with Mona, we might even have failed to credit June with Mona's capacity for guile." However, Annette added, "Her teeth are distressing (the heart condition precludes anesthesia)."

June, barely surviving on her welfare payments and Miller's small gifts, was anxious to find work, but the Baxters advised her that before she looked for a job she needed to fix her rotted teeth. Jim Baxter, a psychiatrist, told June that new techniques in dental surgery made it possible for her to have her teeth extracted without general anesthesia. June arranged to have the work done at a city clinic. Annette told the Millers that she and her husband had doubts about June's ability to find and hold a job. "As we get to know her better we are less and less inclined to be optimistic about the likelihood of a real rehabilitation."

But June surprised them all. By mid-November 1957 June had new teeth. The Baxters celebrated by taking her to a show of Miller's watercolors at the Templeton Gallery on Fifth Avenue. Jim had enough confidence in her to hire her as a night nurse for a patient who had attempted suicide. She took an intern position as a receptionist at the city welfare department and began training to take the Civil Service Exam. Two years later she passed the exam, then took the High School Equivalency Exam. By March 1960 she was working full time for the welfare department and had moved into a pleasant one-room efficiency apartment. The Baxters, who had relocated to Scarsdale, continued to socialize with her, and sent Miller an update after June had spent Thanksgiving with their family. "We can't tell you what a dramatic improvement has taken place on her frame of mind, her appearance, and even her material circumstances. She seems to be managing her full-time job very competently, she has moved to a fine neighborhood and occupies a cheerful one-room apartment . . . Altogether she has accomplished a major feat of self-rehabilitation, in which your unfailing concern has played the most important role.

Compared to the withdrawn creature we first met, she now seems glowing with hope." For Miller, this outcome must have been gratifying confirmation of his belief that there can be an "hour of man" if people act in solidarity.

AS THE SUMMER OF 1956 DREW TO A CLOSE, the emotional and physical tumult of the year began to subside, and Miller could look forward to an open stretch of time in which to work on *Nexus*. The children were returned to their mother in September (Miller wrote to Bob MacGregor, "It's like a tomb here"), Lauretta had settled into the nursing home in Pacific Grove (Miller visited her weekly), construction on the new studio was nearing completion, and the trauma of his mother's death was behind him, though as Eve wrote to Anaïs Nin, "Everything that went with it was devastating to him."

But Miller was unable to make headway with the book, and instead channeled his creative energies into painting and completing a rewrite of *The World of Sex*, which Girodias had agreed to publish in English through his latest imprint, Olympia Press. In February 1957 Miller learned that he had been elected a member of the National Institute of Arts and Letters, but the news did little to cheer him. Writing to Durrell about the honor, he referred to the institute as "our apology for a French Academy."

In fact, a crisis was brewing within Miller. His inability to launch *Nexus* was symptom of a creative malaise brought on by the increasingly untenable circumstances of his Big Sur existence. Miller had idealized the Big Sur lifestyle in *Big Sur and the Oranges of Hieronymus Bosch* and had treated the challenges of living there with his customary humor, but in reality the pressures of his life were making it difficult for him to write and were straining his relationship with Eve. The children were frequently there, some years for the entire school calendar, others during Christmas, Easter, and summer vacations. Though Miller welcomed them and missed them when they were gone, their presence created turmoil in the household. Eve, as Lepska before her, looked after the children and tried to keep them happy without disturbing Miller's work, but this role created stresses on her and her relationship with Miller as she increasingly felt that her own interests and needs were unmet. To this responsibility was now added the burden of Lauretta, whose care made demands on Miller's time and slender income. Then there were the vicissitudes of daily life in Big Sur—the storms, the slides that closed the main highway, the power outages, the constant intrusions by unwanted visitors who made pilgrimages to Miller's door. But perhaps worst of all for Miller the artist was the lack of cultural stimulation in the Big Sur community that Perlès alluded to in his memoir and his letters and that Eve, following their return from the 1953 European trip, felt keenly.

Signs that all was not well in paradise began to appear in Miller's correspondence early in 1957 and recurred with increasing frequency as the months passed and *Nexus* remained stalled. In March he wrote to Durrell, who had just completed *Justine*, the first volume of *The Alexandria Quartet*, and was now living in Sommières with Claude–Marie Forde, also a writer. "If I get a windfall, I would send you the money, or a good part of it, to buy a house for us all to own. I might then be able to make arrangements with my ex-wife to take the children over for a year at a time ... This is supposed to be a great year for me (astrological dope!). Anything can happen. Right now I have 39 dollars. But tomorrow I could have five thousand." In April he picked up Tony and Val for their Easter vacation, and they were back again in June for the summer. He wrote again to Durrell, "Everything hectic here with children ... get no work done at all." He followed this up two weeks later with an even more desperate lament. "Never have I been subjected to more intrusions, more invasions. I am going nuts. I can't even find time to answer my letters regularly. If it continues I am going to quit Big Sur."

But it did continue, and in December Miller wrote a lengthy letter to Durrell and Claude summarizing his dilemma:

> Theoretically I am now working on *Nexus*, last of the trilogy. Actually I haven't done a stroke of work on it for six months. Started it three times in last four years and abandoned it. But I think to tackle it in earnest after first of year and I want this to be the end of the autobiographical series. After that the blue ...

It gets more and more difficult to do any continuous work here. Living on the land, two children, endless visitors, endless chores, no recreation except ping-pong and a half hour's reading a day—no more!—no contact with vital people, no interest in the cultural, or less and less, desirous only of learning how to live easy and relaxed and in the world but not of it, the urge to write recedes.

The strain Miller felt burdened Eve as well. During the fall, when the children were with them again for the school year, she wrote again to Nin:

Henry has taken the two children into town, for shoes and a movie - - - and I can't remember my last "day off". Therefore, full of zim and energy I put the bread to rise, even made a croissant as a special treat for everyone - - - My dedication to Henry [is] overall a dedication to his work, the value of which needs no explaining - - - For to me, there's no difference between the essential Henry, the man, and his creative expression. I'm most definitely "dedicated" "in love with" Henry the man. To give what's needed is the only expression of that love I can offer. There is a certain nourishment that is essential for the tree to keep "giving" its yield. This is where my own personal problems enter into the scheme of things and are often most difficult to work with.

But if Miller the creative writer was losing traction under the increasing stresses of his life in Big Sur, the international Miller publishing factory was thriving. In April 1956 Rowohlt Verlag in Germany had translated *Nights of Love and Laughter* and issued it in an edition of fifty thousand copies. Then in November, Bob MacGregor met with A. S. Frere, chairman of the board of William Heinemann Ltd., a large and prestigious English publishing house. Frere, an admirer of Miller's work, believed that Miller's reputation in England had suffered from a number of poorly edited titles. He proposed bringing out a new title in a quality edition that could reposition Miller in the minds of English reviewers and readers. This edition would be followed by reissues of older titles of the same quality. The Big Sur book was chosen to launch the program, with the understanding that additional titles would be published at the rate of one every eighteen months.

A 1957 censorship trial of *Sexus* in Norway gave Miller wide publicity in Scandinavia and boosted sales of his books there. The Norwegian attorney general charged two booksellers who sold copies of *Sexus* imported from Denmark with selling pornography. Miller was notified of the case by Trygve Hirsch, an attorney representing one of the booksellers. Hirsch asked Miller if he would write a statement for the court explaining why the sex scenes in *Sexus* are necessary to fulfill the artistic purposes of the book. Miller wrote back promptly, a three-page, single-spaced letter declaring his belief "in absolute freedom of expression."

Miller's letter goes beyond a defense of his right to use obscene material in his works to an explanation of his deepest motives and intentions as a writer in order to show that what is deemed obscene must be included in any depiction of reality that pretends to be complete. Miller states that his purpose in writing *The Rosy Crucifixion* "was to tell, no matter how many pages it took, the story of the most crucial period of my life, namely, the seven years preceding my voluntary flight to France." The telling of this story, Miller says, represents "my effort to understand the pattern of my life, its purpose and significance." Miller distinguishes his autobiographical novels from others in the genre. "The difference lies primarily in the understanding and use I have made of 'reality'. To get at the nature of this reality which pervades all life, and which *is* life, I have had to grapple with the metaphysical aspects of suffering, freedom, experience . . . And so, in a fashion quite other than that of realistic novelists and faithful chroniclers, I have made extensive use throughout these books of irruptive onslaughts of the unconscious, such as dream, fantasy, burlesque, Pantagruelian word play, etc., which lend the narrative a chaotic, whimsical, perplexing character—in the minds of many critics. But these 'extravaganza', so to speak, have great significance for me. Especially, need I add, the sexual eruptions. They represent my endeavor, successful or not, to portray the *whole* man." Miller likens his search for self-understanding to the efforts of religious figures to attain a state of grace or awakening in which they see and accept their full humanity. He quotes his friend the astrologer Dane Rudhyar on the Buddha. "In him humanity came to a condition of total and unqualified acceptance of all human experience, to a state of undisturbable wakefulness and lucidity, free from illusion, glamour and uncertainty . . . he dared to contain all reality known to man—to include in his clear conscious- ness the experience of hell as well as heaven."

In the letter, Miller also points out the ironic consequences of efforts to censor human expression. "Censorship works like a boo- merang. It would be better for your countrymen if the Norwegian authorities decided to ban my books. By doing so they would stimu- late the public to make more determined efforts to read these books ... No power on earth can effectively stop the circulation of thought."

Miller's prediction was borne out by events in Norway, as also had happened in France during *l'affaire Miller.* As the trial proceeded— Miller declined an invitation to attend and testify—Hirsch wrote to inform him that publicity stemming from it was stimulating sales of Miller's books, which were prominently displayed in bookstores all over Norway. Nevertheless, in June 1958 the court ruled *Sexus* obscene and sentenced the defendants to fines and two years probation. Miller would have disagreed not with the finding of obscenity but with the ban on it. A year later the convictions were overturned but not the ban.

By 1957 Miller's works were being published and read in transla- tion throughout Europe and Japan. The Tropics, *Black Spring,* and *The Rosy Crucifixion* had been issued in Scandinavia, Germany, and Japan. Rowohlt Verlag had also published *The Smile at the Foot of the Ladder, Time of the Assassins, The Colossus of Maroussi, Remember to Remem- ber,* and *Nights of Love and Laughter. Plexus* had been published in Italy, though the police had confiscated it. *The Air-Conditioned Night- mare, The Smile at the Foot of the Ladder,* and *Time of the Assassins* were brought out in Japan. James Laughlin, traveling in Asia, was attempt- ing to open new markets for Miller's books in India and Burma. There could be no doubt that Henry Miller was an internationally renowned author. Defending the morality of his autobiographical novels, Miller had written to Hirsch: "I have no fear that those who read my works will become depraved or demoralized. Indeed, I possess thousands of letters from readers all over the world which tell the opposite story. Every day I receive letters from people of all ages, all classes of society, who thank me for opening their eyes, thank me for giving them the courage to lead their own lives."

Efforts were also under way to promote Miller's work in the English-speaking countries where he was least read, least appreciated, least understood. Shortly after returning to Big Sur from New York after burying his mother, Miller had received a letter from Eddie Schwartz, an advertising executive from Minneapolis who owned a printing business. He introduced himself as an admirer of Miller's work who wanted to promote the sale of his books. He also offered to do printing for Miller—stationery, brochures, circulars. Within a year, he and Tom Moore, another fan, formed the Henry Miller Literary Society. The society developed a mailing list through which it sent out news about Miller and the release of his books. When *Nights of Love and Laughter* was issued by Signet, the members of the society (about a dozen people) made the rounds of bookstores in Minneapolis urging salespeople to recommend the book to patrons. When the edition had nearly sold out, they returned to the bookstores and bought up the remaining copies in order to fabricate demand for the title that might cause Signet to print more copies. Though the society had a small, mostly local impact (its mailing list topped out with about six hundred names), Miller appreciated their efforts and some years later visited them while returning from a trip to Europe.

Perlès and Durrell also undertook a project to bolster Miller's reputation in England. Both men felt that Miller remained a largely unknown and misunderstood writer in England and, as loyal friends who were also British subjects with their own English readerships, wanted to stimulate interest in him. Perlès had been invited to give a talk about Miller to a gathering of the Institute of Contemporary Arts in London but was unable to attend and sent a letter instead. Perlès pointed out that with Miller's most important books listed on the Index, the list of publications prohibited by the Catholic Church, it was very difficult for readers to get a full sense of his significance. "Due to the absurdly inflexible obscenity and pornography laws in this country and in the States, the ordinary reader is not only unable to get hold of his major works but is led to approach one of our greatest contemporary writers in a spirit of officially-fostered suspicion and distrust. As a result, the *essential* Henry Miller is unknown!" The remedy Perlès suggests—publishing an anthology of uncensorable selections from the banned books—is one that Miller had repeatedly vetoed.

Durrell took another tack. He proposed to Perlès that they carry out and then publish a correspondence about Miller's significance as a writer. Durrell initiated the correspondence with two letters to Perlès, which he copied to Miller. Miller then made a lengthy reply to Durrell that he and Perlès decided to include in the book, which was published in England in 1959 and in the United States in 1961 as *Art and Outrage*. The book contained four letters from Durrell to Perlès, three letters from Perlès to Durrell, and three letters from Miller, one to Durrell and two to Perlès.

In his letters to Perlès, Durrell had taken up the question of Miller's intention in writing the autobiographical novels, and in his reply Miller addresses this question in very much the same language he used in his letter to Trygve Hirsch. "My intention was to do nothing more than tell the story of those years with her [June], what it had done to me, to my soul, if you like. Because it was the damage to the soul, I must tell you, that was the all . . . And so, on the fateful day, in the park department of Queens County, N.Y., I mapped out the whole autobiographical romance—in one sitting. And I have stuck to it amazingly well, considering the pressures this way and that. (The hardest part is coming—*Nexus*—where I must reveal myself for what I was—something less than zero, something worse than the lowest knave.)" He goes on: "The key to my whole work was to be the utter truth . . . whether I *then* knew what later I have come to know absolutely is a question, namely—the words of Jesus, that the truth shall set ye free . . . Yet I do feel that truth is linked to violence. Truth is the naked sword; it cuts clean through. And what is it we are fighting, who love the truth so much? The lie of the world. A perpetual lie."

Miller concludes his letter to Durrell with a hymn to youth, a hymn that informs his attitudes toward parenting (let the kids run free) and education (experience is the only teacher). "At sixty-six I am more rebellious than I was at 16. Now I *know* the whole structure must topple, must be razed. Now I am positive that youth is right—or the child in its innocence. Nothing less will do, will satisfy. The only purpose of knowledge must be certitude, and this certitude must be established through purity, through innocence."

Another project to enlarge Miller's American audience that got under way at this time was an extensive anthology of Miller's writings to be offered under the title *The Henry Miller Reader*. Durrell had been pushing this project for years and had written to Laughlin about it. Miller had received an inquiry from an editor at the Viking Press suggesting an anthology of Miller's writing to be published in the prestigious Viking Portable Library Series. He wrote immediately to Laughlin to sound him out on the proposal. Laughlin was enthused about the prospect of a Henry Miller Reader but understandably resistant to permit another publisher to issue it. "It would be very hard for Bob and myself, for a great many reasons, to turn over the cream of your writing to another publisher." Laughlin proposed that New Directions publish a high-priced hardback book, edited by Durrell, that would include a sampling of Miller's "serious philosophical essays" along with the entire text of *Tropic of Cancer*. Laughlin believed that the censorship climate in the courts was improving and that *Tropic of Cancer* might pass muster if packaged with uncensorable material that positioned Miller as a "serious" writer. But Miller was opposed to this scheme. "I would never dream of permitting the *Tropic of Cancer* to be included in toto in such a book. Nor would I even consent to a trial publication of it on its own—or any of the banned books—unless I was certain in advance that it would not be subject to seizure and suppression. And I refuse to be a scapegoat. I am quite content that these banned books continue to be republished (in English) abroad and in translation. They are all as much alive and sought after now as the first day they were published."

This exchange revealed Laughlin's caution, as well as Miller's reluctance to become involved in a legal battle. The guarantee that he required no one could provide. The dithering over publisher and contents continued for a while but was resolved with a book whose contents were selected and introduced by Durrell, blessed by Anaïs Nin during a visit with the Durrells at Sommières, and published in December 1959 by New Directions.

Durrell organized his selections into simple groups that allowed him to offer the reader a broad sampling of Miller's work. The section subtitled "Places" included essays about Brooklyn, Paris, Dijon, Greece, and Big Sur. "Stories" were drawn from *Plexus, Sunday After the War, Max and the White Phagocytes, The Air-Conditioned Nightmare*, and *Quiet Days in Clichy*. "Literary Essays" showed Miller's skill at penetrating to the essence of writers he admired—D. H. Lawrence, Marcel Proust, James Joyce, Arthur Rimbaud, E. Graham Howe—and connecting their central "message" to his own. "Portraits" of Miller intimates—Anaïs Nin, Hans Reichel, Alfred Perlès, Blaise Cendrars—rounded out the selection. Miller wrote a brief prelude to each of the selections explaining the circumstances in which it was written.

Durrell wrote a short introduction in which he positioned Miller in the literary universe and identified Miller's central intention as a writer. He called Miller "a visionary rather than merely a writer. I suspect that his final place will be among those towering anomalies of authorship like Whitman or Blake who have left us, not simply works of art, but a corpus of ideas which motivate and influence a whole cultural pattern." Clearly influenced by Miller's own declaration of his intention, Durrell praised Miller's unflinching pursuit of the truth, no matter where it led. "It is absolutely veridic and unflinching in its intellectual bravery. It is significant, too, to mention that among the first few great men of the day to acknowledge Miller's greatness was a philosopher, Count Keyserling. I still remember the expression of amazed delight on the face of the author of *Tropic of Cancer* when he unfolded the telegram and read the message: 'I salute a great free spirit.' "

Miller's correspondence with Durrell about his intentions in writing *The Rosy Crucifixion* seems to have provided the stimulus he needed to break through his resistance to tackling *Nexus*, for in April he was finally at work on it in earnest. Eve wrote excitedly to the Durrells, who by now had become an outlet for her concerns about Miller's artistic health, that Miller was hard at work on the book. "I can tell that Henry is about to blast into *Nexus*. He's prepared himself like a surgeon, gone through studio, papers, files, correspondence, thrown everything he could away and is now 'prepared' to start. Up at five each morning, takes a long walk in the dawning, is at his desk by seven. It's marvelous. We're in bed by nine and the routine seems to be rewarding, even to me. The ordeal that the book presents to him you probably understand even more than I can. He's been trying to get at it since 1952, you know."

Early in May, Miller also wrote to Durrell, confirming that the book was under way. "I'm on *Nexus* again, but it's pick and shovel work right now. Breaking the ice. So difficult." He mentions *Draco and the Ecliptic*. "I have in mind to one day write *Draco and the Ecliptic*, long promised. Can only do it when *Nexus* is written. This was to be, and still will be, I hope, a brief, cryptic account of what I believe it's all about—the 'autobiography' I mean. Now and then I get glimpses. I want to be able to review my work, as I once did my whole life (Villa Seurat), as from Devachan. See the pattern, the essence, the significance."

But although Eve was pleased that Miller had finally broken through on *Nexus*, she continued to express her discontent with the status quo of their life in Big Sur. She wanted them to live in France but recognized that his devotion to his children was a major obstacle to the move. She wanted this change in their life as much for Miller as for herself. She had observed the alteration in Miller's mood during Perlès's visit when, in effect, Europe came to Big Sur. Hearing from Durrell that he had visited with Fred during a recent trip to London to collect a literary prize, Eve recalled the joyous times of Fred's visit with them. "Except for the months I spent with Henry in Europe, I've never seen Himself more Himself. The laughter, the rich conversations, the food and wine and joy and sheer nonsense . . . Too good to see Henry so stimulated . . . Henry needs France, or Europe . . . I go 'round and 'round with Henry over this. He's 'in love' in his strange prismatic way with this hunk of paradise he's found . . . He's caught in the web of his love for his children and it's a bit like being on dope. It feels too good to quit . . . I love him deeply, and can somehow feel that to keep him warm, fed content, the farce running as smoothly as possible is my 'role' where he's concerned. The waste, for that's what it honestly is, is like a running sore within me."

Eve had also been corresponding with Nin about Miller's love for his children. Nin, herself childless, considered Miller's love of his children a form of self-love. This observation struck a chord with Eve. "Yes, I have often felt that Henry gives, emotionally, only to his children . . . He is able to give to them, of himself, but not to the woman he loves. It's a strange thing to me . . . What gets blocked off, when and where? (Even though I feel I know.) I met his mother on her deathbed. At 86, dying. She frightened the hell out of me. A real tyrant, cold as ice, and she died without 'recognizing' Henry. This hurt him deeply. I think he's clung to the hope that one day, if only in a glance, the hatred, the rejection, would drop away. The mother image would settle itself. Well, it didn't."

By mid-July, Miller was three hundred pages (of an anticipated twelve hundred) into *Nexus* but still complaining of interruptions that distracted him and stole his time. Eve described one such intrusion in a letter to the Durrells. They were awakened at 2 a.m. by a drunken woman sobbing on their bed and mumbling about the beautiful words in Miller's books. "This is the sort of neurotic youth that beats a path to his bedside," Eve remarks. "It occurs often. Not just once in a while." Miller was growing weary from the struggle to write. "I'm plugging away on *Nexus*," he wrote to Durrell. "Hard sledding. Think it will be my last book. Am about finished as a writer, I think. It's too boring. Let some one else do it, I say."

In October Miller's daughter Barbara came for a three-week visit during which she announced that she wanted to move in with them and become a member of the family. This was too much, even for the ever-hospitable Miller. He wrote sourly to Durrell, "My 37 year old daughter (Barbara) is here for a few days. Thoroughly uninteresting creature—ruined by her mother who still hates my guts. My girl Val is more alive and more mature—*at 12*. I'm saddled with nit-wits and half-wits." Miller gently pointed out to her the impracticality of her joining his already over-crowded household, and Barbara departed with a promise to return for Christmas.

Around this time, Lepska, who had separated from her second husband and wanted to purchase a home in Pacific Palisades, California, offered to sell Miller her share of the Partington Ridge property. Miller needed to raise $3,500 quickly. He had recently been informed by Bob MacGregor that a maquette made by Fernand Léger for an intended illustration in *The Smile at the Foot of the Ladder* was probably quite valuable. Miller had two other Léger maquettes and was interested in selling the lot. Ann Laughlin, James Laughlin's wife, had numerous contacts in the New York art world and offered her help. She suggested that any correspondence Miller had from Léger regarding the maquettes would increase their value. Miller retrieved the documents from the library at UCLA and the entire package was offered to Pierre Matisse, who purchased it for $3,500. Matisse also offered to buy $4,000 of Miller's francs during a trip to France. When negotiations with Lepska over the buyout subsequently broke down, infuriating Miller, he and Eve were suddenly flush with cash. Miller decided to travel to Europe as soon as he had completed *Nexus* and to bring the children with him if Lepska would consent.

The end of the year also brought news of the death of Miller's dearest Brooklyn friend, the painter Emil Schnellock, a man who had supported Miller's artistic aspirations from the outset and had mentored his efforts to become a painter of watercolors. Schnellock had been in poor health since May, when he collapsed from a cerebral spasm. He suffered recurrent heart attacks, was hospitalized, and died on November 18, 1958.

10

FAREWELL TO BIG SUR

"My Saturn Is Really Giving Me Trouble."

"I'M SO EXCITED, I'M ABOUT TO DIE." SO BEGAN EVE MILLER'S LETTER
to the Durrells announcing that Miller had agreed to a return to
France once *Nexus* was completed. For her, the trip was more than a
return visit to the country she had left reluctantly at the beginning of
her relationship with Miller. She hoped that, once there, once Miller
had a deep draught of the culture that had nourished him, once he
was back in physical contact with the writers and artists with whom
he felt kinship, he would decide to remain. She wanted this not only
for herself but also for Miller the writer, and for their relationship.
Her certainty that the life she now shared with Miller in Big Sur was
not sustainable for either of them, and the prospect of a return to
France gave her hope that their marriage might be saved. She concealed her deepest hopes from Miller, but made no secret of them to
the Durrells, or to Anaïs Nin.

Eve obviously felt that the strongest pull that might keep Miller
in Europe was his friendship with Durrell, who was now a permanent resident there. She asked the Durrells for help in finding a place
in their vicinity, and tried to enlist them in her scheme to keep Miller
in France. "Set about finding us a place to rent," she wrote in January. "My dream is to find a place to buy, somewhere in the south of
France ...Then it's up to all of us to keep Henry there ...I feel I must
remain and start living. If we remain here, it's a slow but steady starvation diet, and I'm at the layer of skin and heart." She importuned the
Durrells to aid her campaign. "Think carefully and I imagine you'll

be able to reach Henry with the essence of what I'm trying to get over to him . . . I seemingly cannot. I'm just a wife. (A good one, I might add, and it would be a shame to lose me.)"

To Nin she wrote even more candidly about the deteriorated state of her marriage to Miller. "Henry has at last agreed to a 'trip' to France!! He thinks of it as such, for me, I pray it turns out to be far more than that . . . I've done nothing but dream of this for the past six years . . Henry *needs* France . . . I watch this vital man dissolving. He is another person in Europe . . . I'll never realize my own potential in this country. I've got to breathe, at this point. Start living." Eve then alludes to the emotional neglect that threatens her marriage. "(Henry is unaware of all these hidden dreams and hopes, of course. I doubt he has ever asked me once, in these entire 7 years together, what my hopes and dreams might include!)" But if Miller's indifference to Eve's inner needs was undermining their marriage, where they were living was not the central problem. The change that was needed was in Miller, not in their address.

Miller, for his part, while enthused about seeing the Durrells, was not that sanguine about his return to France. He wrote to Durrell: "My ideal now is Japan." He had no desire to remain long in Paris. "For me it means nothing anymore," he added. But Eve wanted to spend six weeks there. Miller planned to take the children with him on a tour of Scandinavia and the Netherlands while Eve remained alone in Paris. This was surely a sign that each had a different agenda for the trip. However, Miller was not closed to the possibility of relocating his family to Europe. Consideration of the children's needs seemed to be uppermost in his mind. "We made the plane reservation to return from Paris about 20th August, I think. However, if the kids liked it, if we put Val in that 'Ecole d'Humanité' in Switzerland . . . and Tony somewhere else—who knows? But there's their mother to reckon with. And I'm not quitting Big Sur for good—not yet."

Eve excitedly made arrangements for their trip while Miller ploughed ahead on *Nexus*. Through Maurice Nadeau, the editor at Correa, she lined up for two months a large apartment in Paris on the rue Campagne-Première. Durrell had found them an inexpensive cold-water flat in Sommières, where he and Claude had lived before their move to Engances, near Nîmes. He tried to advance Eve's cause when he wrote Miller to tell him about the flat. "If you can give yourself a few months of quiet unpublicized prospecting I'm sure we can unearth you a house to buy and make over, for about 800 to 1,000 pounds; less in the country. No idea how your income rides but am sure you could do just fine here, run a tiny car, and educate the children either in Paris or England." Perlès, always pressing Miller to return to Europe, weighed in with the suggestion that Tony and Val attend Summerhill, A.S. Neill's progressive school in Suffolk.

By the end of March, their travel plans were set and *Nexus* was nearly finished. They would leave for Paris from New York on April 16, stay six weeks in the Paris apartment, then buy a used car and drive south to Sommières. At some point, they expected Perlès to join them. Eve became ecstatic as the date of their departure approached. "I'm singing and jumping and can smell, taste, touch Sommières . . . Just your spirit fills me with fresh inspired hope and the certainty of a more permanent living arrangement," she wrote the Durrells. "That the landlord of the flat has houses for sale . . . it just might all come true, you know? Henry's astrologer sends him the most soaring affirmation in regards everything . . . money, joy, way-of-life, 'new' this's and that's all good better best. I feel like we're on the brink of truly great things." There was a moment of tension when Lepska came to visit the children during the Easter holidays and demanded to know if there was any truth to the article in the French newspaper *Le Figaro* stating that Miller was returning to France to take up permanent residence. "I looked her firmly in the eye, and said Henry never stays anywhere forever," she wrote when reporting the incident to the Durrells.

As Eve typed the manuscript of *Nexus*, she was struck by the parallels between Miller's life in the book's narrative and his life with her. She remarked the similarity in another letter she wrote to the Durrells as they made ready to leave. "The curious thing is that here he is, writing about what *was*, what, 30 years ago? And it's all almost an exact word for word description of what he's living *now*. It ends, you know, as he embarks for Europe for the first time in '28. The slight differences, different wife, 2 children, money, etcetera mean nothing, in relation to the larger thought. He sees it, too. The same desperate need for the nourishment of Europe, is still there . . . and there is no question about it. Even Big Sur can't shake the other deeper needs."

The parallels that Eve detected fed into her desperate hope that Miller would agree to remain in Europe and their marriage would be renewed there. But another parallel was equally, if not more, plausible: that Miller was leaving for Europe because a creative period—and the relationship that sustained it—was coming to an end.

The book that Miller completed just before their departure, the third and final volume of *The Rosy Crucifixion*, delivers his spiritual fare-well to America as he went abroad to Europe for the first time with his second wife. It recounts Miller's suffering and misery in the ménage à trois formed by his marriage to Mona and her lesbian relationship with the psychotic Anastasia Annapolis (Stasia). Miller explores the dynam-ics of this triangle and his reasons for enduring it and finds there the route to his becoming a writer. The suffering, painful as it was, acted upon his life as scourge that stripped away his illusions about who he was and brought him to the core of self from which he could speak with his own voice. The book is thus describing the formation of the seed whose germination constitutes "the rosy crucifixion." This seed Miller transplants to Europe where it can open and take root in a more nourishing soil than his own native land. Mona, in all her mystery and deviousness, like an agent of fate, is the catalyst for this transformation.

The book begins where *Sexus* left off, with Miller barking like a dog in the kennel of his humiliation at the hands of Mona and Sta-sia. "A thousand descriptions could never render the reality of this atmosphere in which we lived and moved," Miller writes. "For here, like the prisoner of Chillon, like the divine Marquis [De Sade], like the mad Strindberg, I lived out my madness. A dead moon which had ceased struggling to present its true face." Miller's suffering is acute because his rival for Mona's love is another woman, and a lunatic. He feels unmanned, impotent, his sense of himself violated. "When a situation gets so bad that no solution seems possible there is left only murder or suicide. Or both. These failing, one becomes a buffoon . . . I was no longer a man; I was a creature returned to a wild state. Perpetual panic, that was my normal state. The more unwanted I was, the closer I stuck. The more I was wounded and humiliated, the more

I craved punishment." Miller has reached a point of despair. "*I had lost the power to love,*" he wails.

In his desolation, Miller speculates on the significance of love as the mysterious force that, emanating from God, permeates all life and matter. "If there is anything which deserves to be called miraculous, is it not love? What other power, what other mysterious force is there which can invest life with such undeniable splendor?" Miller views the energy present throughout the universe as an expression of this love. "Love and energy have always been, always will be. Perhaps in essence they are one and the same . . . Perhaps this mysterious energy which is identified with the life of the universe, which is God in action, as someone has said, perhaps this secret, all-invasive force is but the manifestation of love." Miller concludes that it is the emptiness of living without love, as he now is, that creates in man "this aching for God."

The desolation that Miller feels in his loveless state is mirrored in the world around him, the American milieu. He observes, "Moving amidst my own people I was never impressed by any of their accomplishments; I never felt the presence of any deep religious urge, nor any great esthetic impulse: there was no sublime architecture, no sacred dances, no ritual of any kind. We moved in a swarm, intent on accomplishing one thing—to make life easy. The great bridges, the great dams, the great skyscrapers left me cold. Only Nature could instill a sense of awe. And we were defacing Nature at every turn."

Miller tries various schemes, all unsuccessful, to drive Stasia away so that he can recover Mona as his own. At one point she decides on her own to leave, telling Miller in a moment of lucidity that she finds their situation cruel. Then she changes her mind. Instead, she and Mona secretly make arrangements to leave together for Europe. Miller, who in desperation has taken a job as a gravedigger with the Parks Department, returns home one evening to find the apartment emptied of their belongings. A note from Mona announces, "We sailed this morning on the *Rochambeau*. Didn't have the heart to tell you. Write care of American Express, Paris. Love."

It was this event, this abandonment, that pushed Miller through the barrier to becoming a writer. After receiving a letter from Mona informing him that Stasia had left for North Africa with an Austrian admirer and she had gone to Vienna "with some friends," Miller sat down at his desk in the Parks Department and outlined the book that would become *The Rosy Crucifixion*. "In a mood of utter despair, I sat down at the typewriter to outline the book I told myself I would write one day. My Domesday Book. It was like writing my own epitaph ... As I wrote I laughed and wept." Miller allows himself to hope that the book will be the path to his recovery of Mona's love. Instead, it becomes the seed from which Miller the writer will flower.

Abruptly, Mona returns from Europe without Stasia, who has disappeared into North Africa. (The real Stasia—Jean Kronski—committed suicide at age nineteen while interned at a mental hospital in California.) A relatively stable and tranquil period in her marriage to Miller ensues. With money borrowed from her "admirers," they rent an elegant apartment in an upscale brownstone neighborhood in Brooklyn. At Mona's insistence, Miller quits his job with the Parks Department so as to be free to write. One day she announces that she has been commissioned by a wealthy older gentleman, whom she refers to as "Pop," to write a novel. Pop has agreed to provide her with a generous weekly stipend. All she needs to do is show him pages regularly as proof of her progress. Miller is to ghostwrite this novel.

This setup affords Miller, the author of *Nexus*, opportunity to revisit the early stages of his development as a writer, a period he refers to as his "blissful embryonic state." He gives the reader frequent glimpses into his interests, working methods, distractions, and obsessions, frequently in passages that display his dazzling virtuosity with diction, tone, and imagery. Here he is considering the problem of openings:

> The way in which a book opened—there in itself lay a world. How vastly different, how unique, were the opening pages of the great books! Some authors were like huge birds of prey; they hovered above their creation, casting immense, serrated shadows over their words. Some, like painters, began with delicate, unpremeditated touches, guided by some sure instinct whose purpose would become apparent later in the application of mass and color. Some took you by the hand like dreamers, content

to linger at the edges of dream, and only slowly, tantalizingly permitted themselves to reveal what was obviously inexpressible. There were others who, as if perched in signal towers, derived intense enjoyment from pulling switches, blinking lights; with them everything was delineated sharply and boldly, as though their thoughts were so many trains pulling into the station yard. And then there were those who, either demented or hallucinated, began at random with hoarse cries, jeers and curses, stamping their thoughts not upon but through the page, like machines gone wild. Varied as they were, all these methods of breaking the ice were symptomatic of the personality, not expositions of thought-out techniques. The way a book opened was the way an author walked or talked, the way he looked at life, the way he took courage or concealed his fears.

In another section, faintly self-mocking, he renders his inability to channel his thoughts, to control the free flow of associations that arise from his far-flung interests.

Sometimes I would sit at the machine for hours without writing a line. Fired by an idea, often an irrelevant one, my thoughts would come up too fast to be transcribed. I would be dragged along at a gallop, like a stricken warrior tied to his chariot . . . Pondering over a word like praxis, for example, or pleroma, my mind would wander like a drunken wasp. I might end up in a desperate struggle to recall the name of that Russian composer, the mystic, or Theosophist, who had left unfinished his greatest work. The one of whom someone had written—"he, the Messiah in his own imagination, who had dreamed of leading mankind toward 'the last festival', who had imagined himself God, and everything, including himself, his own creation, who had dreamed by the force of his tones to overthrow the universe, died of a pimple." *Scriabin*, that's who it was. Yes, Scriabin could derail me for days . . . Just looking at a word, as I say. Or a painting, or a book.

For what writer who has ever stared blankly at the emptiness of the white page do these ingenious procrastinations not summon a sympathetic smile?

While Miller plugs away on the book he is writing for Pop, he continues to think about the book he really wants to write, the book about his life with Mona. It will not be a book like other works of literature. Miller intends to pursue his own aesthetic, in which the supreme value will be truth. "Then to hell with literature! *The book of life*, that's what I would write," he vows to himself. This truth of life that Miller intends to discover and reveal begins with inner truth, being true to oneself, to one's sensations, one's memories, one's instincts, one's imagination. It is a mystical truth, not a truth of fact. It is not a truth that can be plotted or arrived at through a system. It is the truth that underlies chaos, the truth of the creative act.

As Miller experiments, giving free rein to his interests and inclinations, as Mona ceases to torment him with her mysterious comings and goings, her web of lies, he grows in confidence and certainty.

> Yes, in my stumbling, bumbling way I was making all manner of discoveries. One of them was that one cannot hide his identity under cover of the third person, nor establish identity solely through the use of the first person singular. Another was—not to think before a blank page . . . To learn to wait, wait patiently, like a bird of prey, even though the flies were biting like mad and the birds chirping insanely . . . Yes, before the Olympian Goethe, before the great Shakespeare, before the divine Dante or the immortal Homer, there was the Voice and the Voice was with every man. Man has never lacked for words. The difficulty arose only when man forced the words to do his bidding. *Be still, and wait the coming of the Lord!* Erase all thought, observe the still movement of the heavens! All is flow and movement, light and shadow.

But the Miller who has arrived at this awareness of the source within himself was not the Miller ghostwriting Mona's novel for Pop. That Miller was still struggling to break free. He looks back on himself. "In some deep, forgotten pit were buried all the thoughts and experiences which I might properly call my own, and which were certainly unique, but which I lacked the courage to resuscitate . . . I was still in the cocoon stage, a worm not yet sufficiently intoxicated with the splendor and magnificence of life . . . Did I fear that once I found that buried treasure which I had hidden away I would never again know peace, never know surcease from toil?"

One day Mona comes home with the news that Pop is so pleased with the pages she is showing him that he has offered to subsidize her for an extended stay in Europe once the novel has been completed. She tells Miller the stipend will be generous enough to allow both of them to travel on it. It remains for Miller to offer his hymn to Europe and his farewell to America, and so bring *The Rosy Crucifixion* to its conclusion.

Miller sees in Europe the link to the long chain of history that binds humanity together. America, he believes, in trying to create a new kind of man—a man without a past, a man dedicated to fact, efficiency, productivity—has lost this connection. Plaintively, he invokes the Europe of his imagining:

"Europe," I concluded to myself, "my dear, my beloved Europe, deceive me not! Even though you be not all that I now imagine, long for, and desperately need, grant me at least the illusion of enjoying this fair contentment which the mention of your name invites. Let your citizens hold me in contempt, let them despise me, if they will, but give me to hear them converse as I have ever imagined them to. Let me drink of these keen, roving minds which disport only in the universal, intellects trained (from the cradle) to mingle poetry with fact and deed, spirits which kindle at the mention of a nuance, and soar and soar, encompassing the most sublime flights, yet touching everything with wit, with malice, with erudition, with the salt and spice of the worldly. Do not, O faithful Europe, do not, I beg you, show me the polished surface of a continent devoted to progress. I want to see your ancient, timeworn visage, with its furrows carved by agelong combat in the arena of thought. I want to see with my own eyes the eagles you have trained to eat from your hand. I come as a pilgrim, a devout pilgrim, who not only believes but *knows* that the invisible face of the moon is glorious, glorious beyond all imagining . . . Accept me, O ancient ones, accept me as a penitent, one not wholly lost but deeply erring, a wanderer who from birth was made to stray from the sight of his brothers and sisters, his guides, his mentors, his comforters."

A few days before sailing on the *Île de France*, Miller goes for a stroll through Brooklyn and tries to summon a favorable thought about America. What comes to mind is a rush of images from the American landscape: the continent itself, not the people who inhabit it.

I tried to think of America as a place I had only heard about. *"Open in the name of the great Jehovah and the Continental Congress!"* And it opened like the door of a hidden vault. There it was, *America*: the Garden of the Gods, the Grand Canyon of Arizona, the Great Smokies, the Painted Desert, Mesa Verde, the Mojave Desert, the Klondike, the Great Divide, the Wabash far away, the great Serpent Mound, the Valley of the Moon, the great Salt Lake, the Monongahela, the Ozarks, the Mother Lode Country, the Blue Grass of Kentucky, the bayous of Louisiana, the Bad Lands of Dakota, Sing Sing, Walla Walla, Ponce de León, Oraibi, Jesse James, the Alamo, the Everglades, the Okefenokee, the Pony Express, Gettysburg, Mt. Shasta, the Tehachapis, Fort Ticonderoga.

He closes with, "Goodbye, Street of Early Sorrows, and may I never set eyes on you again!"

Nexus was first published in October 1959 in Denmark, a country where Miller was widely read and appreciated. Correa issued a French translation in January 1960. The first English edition of the book was published in June 1960 through Girodias's Olympia Press. Writing to his agent Michael Hoffman about the book while he was still working on it, Miller referred to it as "volume 1." Though he contemplated writing a volume 2, and made a number of attempts to complete it, he never went far with it. A few years later, after rereading

volume 1, he wrote to his friend Elmer Gertz, "Now I think it superior to most of the other books I wrote; it's from the center of my
being. Mad, a good part of it. Sublime even, sometimes."

SHORTLY BEFORE MILLER AND EVE LEFT FOR FRANCE, Miller received
a letter from Barney Rosset, the owner of Grove Press and publisher of the quarterly periodical *Evergreen Review*. Rosset offered
Miller a $10,000 advance for the US rights to *Tropic of Cancer* and
Tropic of Capricorn. The advance would be nonrefundable, regardless
of whether either book was ever published. Rosset assured Miller
that Grove Press would assume all risks involved in bringing out and
defending the books. He told Miller that he had first read *Tropic of
Cancer* while a student at Swarthmore College and had written three
papers on it. He enclosed a copy of the unexpurgated edition of *Lady
Chatterley's Lover*, which he had just issued and which had been seized
by the Post Office. Grove was challenging the seizure in federal court.

Though the money and terms must have been tempting to Miller,
he was not encouraging. He wrote back that he doubted the time was
right to try to publish the Tropics, or that the outcome of the Lady
Chatterley trial would pave the way for them. He also told Rosset
that New Directions had right of first refusal on all his US titles. He
urged Rosset to consider publishing works by Blaise Cendrars, Albert
Cossery, and Jean Giono.

Miller then wrote to James Laughlin, seeking his opinion. Laughlin, ever cautious, agreed with Miller that the censorship climate in
America was still not favorable for Miller's banned books and suggested they wait for the outcome of the Lady Chatterley trial. He
thanked Miller for recognizing New Directions' rights and indicated
that, if a respected literary lawyer thought that the Tropics might no
longer be censorable, he would be open to a copublishing venture
with Grove.

There the matter stood for some time. In May Miller had lunch
with Rosset and Girodias in Paris, and not long after that Rosset
wrote Miller again, offering him $2,500 for an option to publish the
books within the next four years, at a time of Miller's choosing. He
dismissed Laughlin's timid "wait and see" attitude. Miller wrote him

back at length from Sommières, elaborating the reasons behind his reluctance to publish the Tropics in America. Superficially, Miller is leery of the notoriety and wealth that would attend a successful publication of the Tropics in America. He fears the further loss of his privacy, already under assault in Big Sur, and the complications of large sums of money. "How could I ever withstand a sensational success, I ask myself. All my efforts in the last few years have been on the direction of simplifying my life. It is not money and fame I need but peace and solitude. As things now stand, it is questionable how much longer I can remain in Big Sur and live the life I choose to live." Miller points out that his banned books are already widely circulated, and his reputation among the readers who really matter to him is secure. All he stands to gain from widespread distribution of the Tropics in the United States is more fame and money, and he wants neither.

But there is a deeper objection underlying his resistance. He holds little hope that the general release of the banned books to the American reading public would further his fundamental purpose as a writer, which is to "inspire and awaken." Miller holds his compatriots in such low esteem that he anticipates being crowned "the King of Smut" should the Tropics become available to all. "I would be given the liberty to thrill, to amuse, to shock, but not to edify or instruct, not to inspire revolt." This prediction is based on Miller's belief that Americans, for all their talk of it, do not understand the meaning of freedom and do not desire it in its true form. "We are moving steadily in the opposite direction of Whitman's democratic vision," he writes to Rosset. "Every decade we surrender more and more of our privileges and rights because we are determined to live in comfort and security at any price." Miller says he has given up all expectation and desire to improve the lives of his readers through his books. "I have come to realize that it is I myself who was awakened, that my hidden purpose in writing the story of my life was to free myself of the devils that possessed me. In short, I have no desire to alter or instruct any one now."

Rosset continued his dogged pursuit of the publishing rights to Miller's banned books and ultimately prevailed when changes in Miller's life circumstances put him in need of large sums of money. In the interval, he kept Miller in play by purchasing the essay "Defense of the Freedom to Read" and a selection from *Nexus* for publication in *Evergreen Review*. But in the long run, the fears Miller harbored about fame and money would turn out to be prophetic.

From the outset of their arrival in Paris in mid-April, Eve and Miller were having different experiences of Europe. Eve was thrilled to be back at last "in civilization," she wrote to the Durrells from the apartment on the rue Campagne-Première. "I breathe—and it's as if I've dropped ten years, a thousand pounds, and shed all the cobwebs of frustration and despair." She raved about their atelier—it even included the services of a maid—and savored visits with several of Miller's friends. And she thought, wishfully as it turned out, that France was having the effect on Miller that she hoped it would, remarking, "The new vitality, the new aliveness. It's already there."

Miller was less enthusiastic. He enjoyed reunion dinners with Brassaï, Abe Rattner, and Beauford Delaney and took pleasure in Tony's quick adaptation to Paris. But in letters to Emil White he voiced many of the same complaints he had made during his 1953 trip with Eve: unwanted appointments and meetings, the high cost of living, too much eating and drinking, no real rest. The weather was cold and dreary, their apartment unheated. "Just like old times," he remarked to Emil. "Only not quite so funny now, what!"

After a brief visit from Durrell, Claude-Marie, and Perlès, who came to Paris to celebrate the Prix du Meilleur Livre Étranger that had been awarded to Durrell's *Justine*, Miller departed with the children for an extended excursion to Scandinavia and the Netherlands. They were accompanied by Gerald Robitaille and his wife, Diane. Robitaille was a French Canadian from Montreal who had first written to Miller in 1950 to announce, "Henry Miller keeps me alive. He's all I need." A correspondence ensued during which Miller soon became Robitaille's "Uncle Henry." Robitaille, a writer, artist, and inventor, moved to Paris with his wife in emulation of Miller's exile. He wrote Miller long self-absorbed letters about his artistic struggles and settled into the role of disciple. During the time that Miller stayed in Paris, Robitaille ferried Tony around the city on his motor scooter.

While Miller and the children were away, Eve received the grim news that her mother had terminal cancer and would probably live no more than six months. This crisis put an end to Eve's hopes that the trip might be prolonged or lead to a permanent stay. Eve's sister, Louise, made immediate plans to travel from Israel to Berkeley to be with their mother and added a stopover in Paris to spend some time with Eve. Eve resigned herself to returning to Big Sur in August, as originally planned.

Complaining of fatigue, Miller cut short his excursion to Scandinavia, eliminating Norway and Sweden and returning from Copenhagen through Amsterdam. He was no sooner back in Paris than he was "itching" to leave. Albert Maillet had invited him to stay as a guest at his home in Die. Miller arranged to be driven there with the children for a stay of about ten days. Eve would remain in Paris until her sister arrived, then drive to Sommières with Perlès in a used Fiat she had purchased. This transaction was made memorable for Miller when the clerk who processed his owner's card told him that she was familiar with his work and asked him to send her his latest book.

Miller appeared to enjoy his stay with Maillet. They set up a ping-pong table in the hallway. The countryside pleased him, and Tony and Val were learning French and getting on well with Maillet's children. He marveled to Emil that large houses in the vicinity could be bought for less than $500. But he showed no inclination to buy one.

In Sommières, Miller's gloom returned. He found himself in a medieval town, in a flat with no hot water, wilting from the muggy heat and unable to swim in the local lakes and rivers because of his perforated eardrums. "Every time I walk out of house here I am stepping into the 14th century. Walls, walls, walls—pressing you flat as you walk. And what types! Wear any damned clothes any old way." He passed the time answering correspondence, playing ping-pong, reading the manuscript of Durrell's *Clea*, and writing an article on Knut Hamsun for a Danish newspaper. Not even the presence of Perlès or his frequent talks with Durrell could bring him out of the doldrums.

The children had been invited to stay for two weeks in a château at Le Chambon owned by Maillet's father-in-law, leaving Miller and Eve free to pursue their own sightseeing interests. But riding in the car on an excursion to the village where Nostradamus was born, Miller suffered a near sunstroke that put him in bed. "I'm panicky now about going out of doors between 10:30 am and 7:30 pm," he complained to Emil. Miller was not blind to the charms of the environs of Sommières, but he was unable to take delight in them. He mentions a visit to "an old Greek settlement called Glanum. Really a gem. What little is intact gives off a perfume, the aroma of antiquity, when the world was small, solid and full of ritual . . . If I ever get my spirits back—I'm in the dumps for weeks now—I may write a little nonsense about it." His letters to Emil reveal that his thoughts are often with Big Sur. He inquires about neighbors and the health of his ailing dog, Pup, wonders if house repairs are being carried out, asks about his correspondence, and worries that there might not be enough money in his bank account to cover Lauretta's expenses. Miller is an unhappy traveler. He rarely mentions Eve, though he does relate that a matador at a bullfight they attended threw his hat to her before dispatching the bull.

At the end of July, as the vacation drew to a close, Miller and Eve retrieved Tony and Val from the château, bringing back with them one of Maillet's daughters, a girl about Val's age. They were joined by Durrell and Claude-Marie's three children. "So there will be great goings on, for the kids." But even the sight of his children having a wonderful time could not lift Miller's spirits. "As for me, I'm in the dumps. Have been ever since I landed in France. Worst vacation ever," he lamented mournfully to Emil. "I have wonderful moments every time I see Durrell. Apart from that it's a nightmare. I just kill time. Sometimes I stay in bed all day. Yet there's nothing wrong with France. I'm wrong for this world, that's all. We don't get along anymore. Life—that's another story. Life's grand. Only I'm not alive anymore." As he closes this letter, he thinks ahead to his return to Big Sur. "Maybe it's good that Pup is still alive. I'll need a friend when I get back. I could about have a mistress for what he's costing me, eh?"

MILLER'S GLOOMY MOOD DID NOT LIFT UPON HIS RETURN TO BIG SUR, and it soon became clear that there were two underlying causes: his deteriorating relationship with Eve and his nagging sense that the completion of *The Rosy Crucifixion* had not brought him the fulfillment he desired. The Durrells, whom both Miller and Eve trusted, became sounding boards for the couple's misery.

Shortly after their arrival, the children were returned to Lepska and Eve began her long and painful vigil with her sister Louise over their mother in Berkeley. Miller was left to fend for himself. He grew more despondent, and wrote to Durrell that he was "going through some sort of crisis . . . Two nights ago I got up in the middle of the night with the firm intent of destroying everything—but it was too big a job . . . Nothing I've done has any value or meaning for me any-more. I'm not an utter failure, but close to it. Time to take a new tack. Years of struggle, labor, patience, perseverance have yielded nothing solid. I'm just where I was at the beginning, which is nowhere."

A few weeks later, Eve wrote to the Durrells giving her perspective on the crisis. She alluded to a change in her relationship with Miller that resulted from "going through several layers of hell these past few weeks . . . Now we live with a certain honesty and reality." Her words imply that she has abandoned her hopes of refashioning her marriage to Miller along lines more tolerable for her. She seems willing to make the neces-sary adjustments in her expectations. "I think everything will probably be o.k.," she writes. "I don't feel it's necessary to let anyone down in this relationship." Eve was prepared to continue her role as stepmother, homemaker, personal assistant and all-around Girl Friday, even as she tended her dying mother. And it was acceptable to her, she claimed, that Miller would do as he pleased. She informed the Durrells that Miller was contemplating a trip to Japan "while these next months are so occu-pied." Miller was consulting his astrologers to determine if the heavens favored such a trip. Eve seemed almost to relish taking on the role of victim. "I do hope he goes. He's lonely when I'm away, misses the chil-dren too—and I feel Japan should be his unique experience somehow . . . That leaves me with house, dog, children's visits, Lauretta, etc. etc. to handle—so he can vacation with freedom—and I can manage that."

But the heavenly signs were not propitious. Miller wrote to the Durrells, "My astrologer has given me the Stop! signal. Must wait till after end of this year. (That bloody Saturn again!) . . . Well, I guess I'll just have to get down to work—*Nexus 2*. No rest for the weary, no peace for the soul."

This crisis for Miller the artist and Miller the man follows a pattern that recurs at every major stage of his career. In the pattern, the death of a relationship accompanies an artistic birth. The two are joined as if partners in a process. In 1924 Miller abandoned his first wife, Beatrice Sylvas Wickens, and his daughter, Barbara, to begin a relationship with his first muse, June Mansfield (Mona), who believed implacably in his talent as a writer. In the early 1930s, as he worked on *Tropic of Cancer*, Nin replaced June as Miller's lover and muse and helped "deliver" Miller's first book. June divorced Miller in Mexico shortly after *Tropic of Cancer* was published. In 1942, back in the United States, his romantic relationship with Nin breaking down, Miller wrote *Sexus*. He then cast about for another companion and helpmate, and found Janina Martha Lepska. Their marriage came to an end as *Plexus* was about to be published. Now that *Nexus* was about to come out, it was Eve's turn to be sacrificed on the altar of Miller's creativity.

Miller himself seems dimly aware of the pattern. As he labors on *Nexus*, volume 2, which is to follow him and Mona on their trip to Paris together in 1928, and waits for the planets to align properly so he can take his oft-postponed trip to Japan, he writes again to Durrell about his feeling that he has failed to fulfill his original intent for *The Rosy Crucifixion*.

> From the very beginning of the trilogy, I was trying to be more simple, more straightforward. I didn't succeed, of course. But the intent was there. What I feel like saying sometimes—when the whole bloody *Crucifixion* comes to an end, is—"Ladies and gentlemen, don't believe a word of it, it was all a hoax. Let me tell you in a few words the story of my tragedy; I can do it in twenty pages."
>
> And what would be the story? That, wanting desperately to become a writer, I became a writer. In the process I sinned. I became so involved with the Holy Ghost that I betrayed my wife, my child, my friends, my country. I fell in love with the medium. I thought— if one makes a stroke on the blackboard that was the thing itself, the reality. I almost fell in love with myself, horrible thought.

Here Miller comes face to face with the issue that absorbed him throughout his writing career: not how to turn language into art but how to turn life into art. He had declared this to be his highest goal in *The Colossus of Maroussi*, following an encounter with an Armenian soothsayer in Athens that had a profound effect on him. As he prepared to leave Greece for America he wrote, "What the way is I have not yet determined, but it seems clear to me that I shall pass from art to life, to exemplify whatever I have mastered through art by my living. To continue writing beyond the point of self-realization seems futile and arresting. The mastery of any form of expression should lead inevitably to the final expression—mastery of life." This mastery was a goal that continually eluded him, despite his efforts. Perhaps Saturn always blocked his way.

Why was Miller seeking escape from the current incarnation of his life crisis through a trip to Japan? The answer may be found in that encounter with the soothsayer in Athens thirty years earlier. The soothsayer told Miller that before his death he would make three trips to the Orient, "where, among other things, I would meet a man who would understand me as no one had and that this meeting was absolutely indispensable for both of us. That on my last visit to the Orient I would never return, neither would I die, but vanish in the light."

Miller broke out of his depression by starting an affair with a young woman, Caryl Hill, who worked as a hostess at Nepenthe, the main Big Sur watering hole where Miller frequently played ping-pong with the locals and where Eve often drank too much. Eve reported to the Durrells that Miller and Caryl had slipped away to San Francisco for a tryst while she was in Berkeley caring for her mother. Caryl was also known to Eve as the live model for her drawing class. Eve acted as though she bore no rancor toward Miller or Caryl over the affair—it is widely reported that Eve had conducted affairs of her own during her marriage to Miller—and even went so far as to prepare dinner for them occasionally. She pretended that Miller's state of mind was all that mattered to her; if he was happy, so was she. "I don't know where it'll all go, but I know that this much to date is damned good for him, and ultimately for me too." Perhaps sarcastically, she blamed Saturn for their troubles. "All Henry's astrologers are in a dither, the letters fly to and from. Something's conjuncting with something-or-other that has all this disturbance gyrating like a cement-mixer." But behind her cavalier front she was grieving. The day she wrote her cheery letter to the Durrells she also wrote a letter to Miller's friend Bob Fink, a chemist, asking him to fill some prescriptions for her mother and to provide her with more medication for her depression. "Alcohol is no help," she wrote, "having given it more than a fair try." In a lighter vein she goes on, "Wish I felt like having a good old-fashioned lay. Something simple like that."

In the new year, after holiday visits from the children, Miller renewed his plans to go to Japan. He intended to have surgery on his eardrums before leaving. The zodiac now favored his prospects, he wrote excitedly to Durrell. "This is my year—1960—so my astrologers tell me. (Quite fabulous, it seems—and on *all* fronts—love, travel, money, everything.) Things have about reached an end (for me) here. Move on!" To Japan. "Astrologically (once again) it's my country. Made for one another (sic). A people of moods. *I'm so fed up with America—even Big Sur.*"

There were positive signs down on earth as well. At the end of September, as New Directions made ready to publish Durrell's *The Henry Miller Reader* in an edition of ten thousand copies, Bob MacGregor reported to Miller that two book clubs had contracted for rights. The Mid-Century Book Club, whose editors included W. H. Auden, Jacques Barzun, and Lionel Trilling, had promised a $4,000 guarantee. The Marlboro Book Club offered $5,500. Heinemann in England had also expressed interest in the anthology.

In January Barney Rosset visited Miller in Big Sur, then wrote him from New York to sweeten his offer for the Tropics. He proposed a $10,000 advance against a $50,000 guarantee, to be paid in full on signing of a contract. He granted Miller the right to choose the publication date. Miller, his life now in transition, gave serious consideration to this offer. He wrote to Laughlin asking for clarification of New Directions' position on the rights. Laughlin called the offer "stupendous," urged Miller to accept it "provided you yourself are satisfied that you want to go ahead with it," but cautioned Miller that he should anticipate a drawn-out court battle because "some judges, and even more so a typical jury, would feel that they [the Tropics] were an attack on the bourgeois order and react accordingly."

Although Rosset assured Miller he was prepared to take on and carry the full burden of any legal consequences from publication of the Tropics, Miller decided to wait.

Early in March, Miller's plans changed. He received an invitation to serve on the jury of the 1960 Cannes Film Festival, held in May, all expenses paid. He decided to accept, and constructed an extensive tour of his European publishers around this junket. He planned to leave in early April, make stops in Hamburg to spend time with Rowohlt, in Die to visit Maillet and pick up the Fiat that Maillet had been storing, drop in on the Durrells, then do his jury duty in Cannes before going to Italy, then possibly Greece on his way to Japan. Eve would remain behind in Big Sur to look after Lauretta, keep up the house, and host the children's visits. Before leaving, he invited Caryl Hill to fly to France in time to meet him in Cannes. Acting again on the advice of his astrologers, he had postponed his ear operation.

Although these ambitious plans did not fully materialize, the trip marked the beginning of Miller's disengagement from Big Sur. He flew to Paris from New York on April 7, remained there a week, then went on to Rome where he joined Alfred Perlès and his wife Anne Barret, who were vacationing there. From Rome he went to Hamburg to meet his German publisher Ledig-Rowohlt. Rowohlt had driven to Sommières the previous July to meet Miller, whom he called "the most lovable author I have," and when he learned that Miller would be in Cannes had invited him to come to Hamburg to promote the German edition of *Black Spring*. During Miller's stay in Hamburg, which lasted about a week, he met Renate Gerhardt, an attractive woman in her late thirties who worked as an editor for Rowohlt Verlag and was in the midst of translating *Nexus*.

During these travels, Miller wrote frequently to Eve, friendly, newsy letters with the greeting "Dear Evie." He told her that he would be in Cannes from May 2 to 21, then planned to visit the Durrells. He complained to her and to Durrell about his lack of privacy—"No matter where I go I'm sought after. Have no life of my own"—and intimated that he might scrap his travel plans and return to Big Sur after seeing Durrell. In mid-May Caryl Hill—"my petite amie from Big Sur"—arrived. A few days later Miller received a letter from Eve requesting a divorce. However, she made it clear that the divorce would be amicable and that she would not exit Miller's life. She told him that the children's welfare was uppermost in her mind and that to minimize the shock to them she would continue to live in the Partington Ridge home in order to look after Miller's various interests—Lauretta, correspondence, business affairs with New Directions—and to provide stability for Tony and Val while Miller traveled. "I think I can be here happily for as long as it seems necessary. You may choose to float about the world for a time, and would need someone in the house in any case. Eventually, should you choose to marry other arrangements would have to be made, but this for now is good enough." Eve also wrote to Lepska informing her of the decision and suggesting summer plans for Tony and Val. Eve did not think the atmosphere in Big Sur was healthy for them—"this zany, increasingly bi-sexual or homo-sexual world here"—and suggested they come for only a part of the summer. She offered to provide Lepska with the funds to take them on a camping trip or a Mexico vacation. Lepska turned down this proposal, but arrangements were made for the children to go to separate summer camps, then come to Big Sur in mid-August.

Miller seemed relieved by Eve's decision. He wrote back from Cannes, "I think all you say is quite right and I'm glad you feel alright about everything. We're still *friends* . . . Certainly I have no bad feelings—how could I?" Eve then informed Miller she had met with an attorney who advised a Nevada divorce based on grounds of "desertion, which is less messy than 'mental cruelty' and whatnot."

Miller, who could be prudish when not dealing with literature, was dismayed by the movies he saw in Cannes. "Films are full of sex, crime, persecution," he wrote to Eve. "Only one jolly one—a Greek film [*Never on Sunday*] with a wonderful actress who plays the part of an amusing whore." But he had lunch with Brassaï and spent evenings in the company of the actor Zachary Scott and his wife, Ruth Ford. When the festival ended, he and Caryl went to Le Ciotat as the guests of the French actor Michel Simon, then paid a visit to the Durrells in Nîmes. From there, he went to Milan to meet his Italian publisher, Giangiacomo Feltrinelli, who was planning to issue a combined edition of the Tropics in Italian. Feltrinelli took him to his château on

Lake Garda, where Miller remained for two weeks. By then he had tired of both travel and Caryl. They returned together to Paris, from where they flew back separately to the United States. At the beginning of July Miller was in Big Sur, at loose ends, uncertain what to do with his time. But soon a siren call from Renate Gerhardt in Hamburg would pull him back to Europe in search of a new home and a new way of life.

ONCE BACK IN CALIFORNIA, MILLER'S RESTLESSNESS DID NOT ABATE. He drove his Cadillac down from Big Sur to Pacific Palisades to be near his children and to give Eve privacy. He watched baseball games and the Democratic Convention on TV. He played ping-pong with Tony. He came down with a cold and while in bed gave thought to resuming work on *Nexus*, volume 2. But he was already contemplating a return to Europe, an open-ended trip in which he would wander from place to place looking for the right spot to set up a European base. He planned to take with him Vincent Birge as driver and "general factotum."

He had begun a correspondence with Renate Gerhardt. Initially, the correspondence was friendly and newsy, but it quickly grew warmer. In July Miller wrote to thank her for a gift of European cigarettes she had sent him and to inform her of his intention to travel again, either to Europe or Japan, leaving in September when Tony and Val would be back in school. He told her that if he came to Europe, he would make a stop in Hamburg-Reinbek "just to say hello again, to shake your hand, thank you for being such a woman as you are—then on, on—like some wandering ghost—on to some new phase of existence—who knows what, who cares?"

Renate's letters at this stage of their budding relationship were warm and empathic. She remarked Eve's loyalty and obvious love for him—"her offer to stay is a tremendously unselfish homage to you!"—and expressed her sympathy that their relationship had unraveled. Renate had been widowed for six years. She told Miller it had taken her five years to recover from her husband's death—"so much did I love him—and this is why I feel I can understand your sadness." As a mother—Renate was raising two teenage boys, Titus and

Ezra—she was impressed by Miller's overriding concern for his children. "It is especially your love, your sometimes frustrated love of your children which I understand best in you, and the way you are concerned about their future lives—it is something strange and beautiful and difficult to have children." She encouraged Miller to continue writing to her.

In Miller's next letter, he frames their relationship in more intimate terms. After affirming his intention to leave soon for either Japan or Europe, he gives her news of his current reading and tells her he is painting watercolors but not yet writing "because I am betwixt and between." This remark is another indication of the importance of a love relationship to Miller's creative powers. He recalls a conversation they held in Hamburg at their first meeting. "Sometimes, when I think of our talks here and there (I think now of that restaurant in the railway station, upstairs, remember?) I wonder what language we *were* talking in. We talked a lot in silences too, don't you think?" He closes with, "Je t'aime bien. J'attends te revoir—où, Dieu le sait mieux que moi."

Before leaving for Paris, Miller sent Renate a more detailed itinerary. He no longer mentions Japan. He plans to stay in Paris for a week, then go to Die to pick up the Fiat that Albert Maillet has been storing for him, then go either to Hamburg or to Lausanne, Switzerland, to visit Georges Simenon. His destinations are vague and expansive. He mentions Spain, Portugal, Corsica, even Egypt. He may go to Vienna, where Emil White will be vacationing. He wonders if Renate might have reason to come to Paris. He tells her that his divorce from Eve will be finalized while he travels and he "shall be free as a bird." Clearly, his plans are beginning to focus on Renate.

Renate also seemed to be pulling him toward her. She wrote him care of Maillet in Die to thank him for sending her a copy of *To Paint Is To Love Again* and to convey her understanding of the autobiographical impulse behind all his writing. "It is your life, your attitude towards life, that makes you a writer," she tells him.

Miller drove directly from Die to Reinbek. Their love flamed up quickly. But Miller stayed with his plan to go to Lausanne and Vienna. When Emil arrived in Hamburg, they went on the road in the Fiat, heading for Switzerland. Miller and Renate exchanged passionate letters. Miller sounds like a love-struck schoolboy. "I miss you so much already," he writes from Gottingen. "All I could think of as we drove along yesterday was you." Renate writes to him at Lausanne in the same vein: "It has almost turned into an obsession with me to try and think of where you might be or what you might be doing at the moment. And I also feel your thoughts seeking me." As he heads for Vienna, Miller has already begun to think of them as a couple. "Somehow I have already (perhaps too audaciously) accepted you as my own, my companion, my help-mate—what you will. It is as if we are already man and wife, and I were taking a brief vacation." He dates the spark of their love to their first encounter at the Hamburg airport in April. "From the very moment you rushed forward to greet me I was taken. Something must happen, it is inevitable. It's only the 'how' of it all that bothers me."

Miller had already begun to think about the complications of form-ing a permanent relationship with Renate. How to do this without upsetting the lives of the children? How to accommodate both of their careers? Miller told Renate from the outset that he could not live in Germany. Would she be willing to take her children out of their school and into a completely new environment in a foreign country? And where might they relocate? Switzerland? Italy? France? Spain? Miller decided to return to Reinbek to spend more time with Renate, to solidify their relationship, to see if they might find a way to join their lives. He asked her to make suggestions, to tell him what *she* wanted. He wondered if she would be willing to come back with him to Big Sur.

Miller spent the next three months in Reinbek, staying at Der Schmiede, a small local inn. Their relationship deepened. In December, while Renate vacationed for three weeks with Titus and Ezra at her parents' home in Buhl, Miller moved into her apartment. He painted watercolors, hung out at Rowohlt Verlag where he played ping-pong with the employees, and wrote impassioned love letters to her. Renate wrote back, assuring him of her love for him. "All other difficulties from now on will be *ours*, and will not intrude just from *one* side; they will be things that have to do with the *two* of us, or the *four* of us or the *six* of us! Imagine that! Crazy to think of it and wonderful at once."

One evening while Renate was still away, an acquaintance of Miller from Rowohlt Verlag wondered if Miller had ever considered writing a play. In a burst of creative frenzy, he dashed off *Just Wild About Harry*, a farce, in less than a week. He wrote to Eve, with whom he was in constant contact, that the inspiration for the play had come from Charlie Chaplin, with whom he had spent several joyous days while staying with Georges Simenon in Lausanne. A few days later, after Renate returned, he wrote to Eve again, telling her that he would soon resume his quest with Vincent Birge for a place to settle, and that when he found it, Renate would join him. "It's decided alright, between Renate and me, that she will join me when I find something. Not easy . . ."

Miller's romantic involvement with Renate Gerhardt led to publishing history. Before going on the road, after conferring with Girodias and Ledig-Rowohlt, Miller decided to accept Barney Rosset's offer for the Tropics. "I was obliged to do this for reasons I'll explain another time," he wrote to Laughlin. It is not hard to imagine the reasons behind his decision. The new life he wished to establish with Renate would require considerable sums of money to sustain. And if he was going to be living in Europe, he would not be subjected to the publicity glare or the threat of prosecution that he feared would accompany the publication of the Tropics in America. Hoffman and Rosset flew into Hamburg to complete the deal, and on February 18, Eve's birthday, Miller signed the contract for both Tropics. Rosset agreed to a $50,000 guarantee, $10,000 paid on the signing, $10,000 a year for four years to be paid on February 18. Miller would receive 50 percent of the guarantee, Hachette 40 percent, and Hoffman 10 percent. Rosset planned to bring the book out in June. He was racing to beat a rival publisher in New York, rumored to be issuing a pirated edition of *Tropic of Cancer* in the belief that the book's copyright was not protected under US law.

Meanwhile, Birge was doing research on possible European locations where Miller and Renate could settle. Miller had also asked Laughlin and Brassaï for suggestions. Criteria for "the spot," as it came to be called, included climate (preferably mild), scenery, schools appropriate for all the children (who spoke different languages), cultural vitality (minus tourists), and a *je ne sais quoi* ambience.

Early in March, Miller and Birge set out from Reinbek, Don Quixote and Sancho Panza in the Fiat Rocinante on a quest for

Miller's mythical home. Over the next four months they would criss-cross Western Europe on an odyssey that exhausted Miller physically, emotionally, and psychically and tested Renate's commitment.

Miller began his search in Switzerland, and was immediately beset by anxiety over his separation from the beloved one. Ten days after they left Reinbek, he wrote her from Locarno in a panic because he found no word from her there on his arrival. "What on earth is wrong? Can you possibly be ill? It is now four p.m. and no answer to my tele-gram as yet. In a few minutes I shall go with Vincent to Lugano—the American Express—to see if any mail is there. Called there this morn-ing—nothing. Drove there twice yesterday—four hours of driving. Came home with that damned belly-ache again." Miller's plaintiveness recalls his early years in Paris, when he used to trudge to the Amer-ican Express office every day, sometimes several times a day, in hopes of finding a letter from June, and with it, a five or ten dollar bill. He told Renate that the Locarno region was not "the spot." "I've done a little exploring around about here. Somehow, despite its extraordinary beauty, wonderful climate, etc. I don't feel it's the place." He noted that there were inexpensive private schools in the area. Yet for some reason, the place fails. He is already feeling desperation. "Sort of desperate now. More so because I get no word from you . . . I just can't believe you haven't written . . . Your silence is like a terrible punishment."

But only hours after writing this, after speaking with Renate on the telephone, his spirits rise. He writes her again, telling her they are heading for Italy—Milan and Venice—and confessing his insecurity. "I do need that little word of reassurance now and then—just three words—'I love you', 'I miss you', 'I need you'." Miller's dependency, his search for the missing mother, is on full display.

During the next several weeks, as Miller raced frantically from Locarno to Milan, to Verona, to Venice, to Nice, to Cannes, to Uzes, to Montpellier, this pattern repeated itself. He despaired of hearing from Renate, and none of the locales he visited resonated with him. In mid-April, from Montpellier, he wrote to Eve that he had signed their divorce papers, adding the note: "Vincent and I both feel that Europe in general is disappointing; it gets worse and worse, more American, more crowded, etc. . . . My Saturn is really giving me trouble . . . Feel blocked, despondent, aimless." But to Renate he wrote, "I know the future is good, brilliant, perhaps." His field of exploration was expanding—he mentioned Cyprus and Malta—in directions that must surely have given Renate pause. She wrote to him in early April, chiding him for the pace of his travels, and hinting at the reason for her limited correspondence. "Don't travel when you are sick, don't travel until it makes you sick. You are driving thru so many countries, never staying long enough to receive your mail . . . Again and again I must say, take your time to find what you really want."

Miller's panicky state led him to fear that France's Algerian crisis might result in civil war, so he retreated from France back to Lausanne. There, his desperation to find a resolution to his search led him to seek the advice of an astrologer, Jacqueline Langmann. Miller, in a letter sent to Renate early in May, called his encounter with this woman "the best intuitive meeting with an astrologer I have ever had." He decided to put to her the question of where to locate. Her answer: Portugal. Based on this recommendation, Miller immediately made plans to go to Lisbon. Exhausted by the driving, Miller arranged to fly. Birge would drive the Fiat, scouting Barcelona, Valencia, Malaga and Gibraltar along the way. So hopeful was Miller that he would find "the spot" in Portugal that he also made arrangements with Eve to fly Tony and Val to New York, where Birge would meet them and escort them to Lisbon. He told her that if Portugal did not work out, Vince would bring the children to Paris instead, then join him on the search. The folly of this plan seemed to elude him.

Miller blamed his distraught state of mind on the zodiac. "All my indecision, frustration, perplexity, setbacks, etc. is indicated in my horoscope at the moment. I will get a few breaks now and then, but these minor aggravations will continue till August most likely. By September, the sky definitely clears." But the chart also indicated a small window of opportunity. "Everything is supposed to be very favorable for me between May 14 to 17th—like a go ahead signal. That's when I arrive in Portugal—we'll see." Renate had also been consulting an astrologer in Hamburg, Dr. Wilhelm Wulff, astrologer to Hitler and Himmler during the war, and Miller wondered what indications for their future she had received from him. He continued to express his agitation over not receiving mail from her. He asked her not to give up.

But Portugal turned out not to be the place either, and Miller, heartbroken, decided to cancel the plans to bring Tony and Val to Europe. Instead, they would go to summer camps. Miller wrote again to Renate from Biarritz early in June. "Coming through Spain I began to realize that I couldn't cope with the situation. By the time I reached here I was almost in a state of collapse . . . I feel utterly lost and helpless and confused. And so guilty, though God knows I did my very utmost. I feel like a complete failure. And your silence tells me that you must feel the same way about me." Writing to Eve about the children's summer plans, Miller sounded even more unhinged. "I seem to have gone to pieces completely. I almost thought I would have to go to a sanitarium. Every setback, every failure to find the place, made me more nervous, more anguished, more helpless. Finally I realized I would have to give up—and that almost knocked me out."

While Miller struggled with his demons in Portugal, Grove Press brought out an edition of thirty thousand copies of *Tropic of Cancer*. The entire edition sold out in days, and within a month Grove had printed another one hundred and thirty thousand copies. The irony of this was not lost on Miller. He wrote to Eve, "How terribly ironic, that just when success (sic) crowns my work, all goes to smithereens."

Miller returned to Reinbek to be with Renate, but their attempt to create a life together was over. Early in July, Miller wrote to Eve about their decision. "All is changed here. Renate and I can see no way to make a life together, in view of all the many problems on both sides. No quarrel, just a serious, realistic consideration of all things combined." The closure restored his equilibrium. "Feel in much better shape, despite everything," he wrote. "I even look good, better than in a long, long while. And, though it all sounds bad—more and more failures—I feel I will pull through, see better days, find a good life yet."

Miller decided to travel on his own for a while before returning to California. He went to Berlin to visit the actress Hildegard Knef and her lover David Cameron, whom he had met in Hamburg when she performed there in *Born Yesterday*. After Berlin he went to Copenhagen to visit his Danish publisher, Hans Reitzel. While there, he met the Italian composer Antonio Bibalo, who had written an opera based on *The Smile at the Foot of the Ladder*. The two men were interviewed by a *Life* reporter, giving a publicity boost to the project. Renate wrote to him in Denmark, telling him of her plans to leave Rowohlt Verlag, move to Berlin, and start her own publishing business. She told Miller she hoped to issue *Just Wild About Harry*, which Rowohlt had turned down, as one of her first titles.

In August, Miller went to Milan to pose for the Italian sculptor Marino Marini, who executed a handsome bronze head of Miller. Then, passing through Reinbek again on his way, he flew to London, connected with Alfred Perlès, and traveled with him to Ireland. As he traveled, he began sending Renate sums of money to help her meet expenses. She wrote to him in London before he flew back to the United States to thank him for these gifts, which she said she found embarrassing. This letter contains a moving assessment of why they had been unable to make a life together.

> I have thought a lot of you, these last 18 months, of you, and of myself being with you, trying to find out, what it was, that made this complete and complex "togetherness" we were both striving at impossible. Impossible to me. What was it, that made me feel terribly alone at important moments, depressed me or revolted me even at times? I guess I know by now. It's the ocean! This terrible wide and deep ocean between you and me, which we were never able to bridge. This ocean, which is also your mother, standing between you and ANY woman you approach, just because even in her last hour she insisted on swallowing a "good by, my dear beloved son." You cannot part with her and therefore never arrive at any other women. The tears you wept about her, here in my room, are still burning in my heart, unforgettable. I wished to be the GUTE FEE [good fairy] and speak them instead of your mother—but that power is not given to me.

Gently, but firmly, Renate hones in on Miller's inability to share himself in a relationship.

> Your innocent words, sometimes! Like: *Renate you must not think that I want to force my way upon you. All I want is to have my way*

for myself! As if there were a MY WAY for two people who want
to live together lovingly! There is no room for a MY WAY, my
beloved Henry! There is only an OUR WAY to which each
partner has to contribute. The terrible error of American couples to think they still can have each *his way*! They do, sure, but
they never become a man and a woman that way . . ."

She ends the letter with a tender lament to the lost potential of
their love.

Henry, my dear Henry, I love you still, as ever, but to make a
man and a wife out of the two of us, it would take many, many
tender and wild nights, which are not given us. It would take
cries of joy to be uttered together, wild cries, and soft groans,
moments where you get lost completely—in the other, in one
another. I had the courage to live up and love up against this terrible ocean, which is also your mother, to dive into it with you,
to dive there for you in order to find you there, on the ground,
all orientation lost, to find you and hold you, tight, tight, tight,
tight—and look, there, we are moving, up, up, together, together
have bridged the ocean and all, there we are, the air, the bright
sky, the sun—a Buddha and his saki.

Miller must have wept as he read these loving and yearning words.
Miller wrote to Renate from New York, telling her, "I feel like my
old self." As the astrologer had foretold in May, the storm of passion
had passed. He reported that he had visited June. "It was a cruel experience, but I'm glad I went. It meant everything to her. She looks so
frightful, so really old, bent, broken, withered, that I didn't know where
the spirit comes from. She has been simply heroic in her comeback . . ."

By the end of October, Miller's life was rearranged. He was living in Pacific Palisades near Lepska and the children, dining with
them daily. Eve had moved in with her Partington Ridge neighbor
Harrydick Ross and was enjoying success with her art. Birge had
settled into Miller's Big Sur home as caretaker. Miller's relationship
with Renate continued, but on different terms.

11

CELEBRITY

"How Marvellous Was the Anonymity of Being
Unknowns, Friends."

THE LIFE THAT AWAITED MILLER ON HIS RETURN FROM EUROPE IN THE
fall of 1961 transformed him from a productive artist who loved
painting and writing into a public figure with a private life more
complicated than he could manage or enjoy. His worst fears about the
consequences of publishing the Tropics in America—loss of privacy,
harassment by public authorities, the burdens of wealth, and, perhaps
worst of all, misunderstanding and misapprehension by American
readers—were about to be realized. Additionally, his physical health
began to deteriorate, and his stubborn resistance to medical treatment
prolonged his discomforts. And for the first time since taking up with
June in 1923, Miller was facing a myriad of personal and professional
issues without the aid and comfort of a helpmate-lover-companion
to assist him with chores, bolster his spirits, and meet his need for love.
Although his celebrity gained him entrée into the glamorous world
of movie stars, film producers, and well-known performing artists,
to intimates like Lawrence Durrell, Anaïs Nin, and Alfred Perlès he
frequently dismissed the privileges that his notoriety brought him for
failing to afford him any real happiness.

When Miller arrived back in the United States, the censorship
pot had already begun to boil. Grove Press had launched the book
in June with a dignified advertising campaign using placements in
highly regarded periodicals and newspapers such as *Saturday Review*
and *The New York Times*. The ads featured glowing testimonials from

"highbrow" critics: Sir Herbert Read, John Ciardi, Norman Cousins, and Karl Shapiro. Anticipating the censorship battle to come, the campaign was designed to position the book as a serious work of literature, a status that would ensure it protection under the First Amendment guarantee of free speech. Book reviews of *Tropic of Cancer*, though not uniformly enthusiastic—*Time* magazine called *Cancer* "a very dirty book indeed" but acknowledged that it was not pornography—treated the book as a legitimate, if flawed, work of art, reinforcing the message of the ad campaign. Sales were spectacular; 68,000 copies of the hardback edition were sold in the first week. The book quickly appeared on *The New York Times* and *New York Herald Tribune* bestseller lists.

But the battle over suppression had begun even before the scheduled June 24 publication date. In October 1960, Dorothy Upham, an American painter traveling in Europe, purchased a copy of *Tropic of Cancer* in Paris and informed the US Customs Bureau that she intended to bring the book into New York on her return, thus provoking a confiscation at Idlewild Airport. Upham challenged the confiscation. Grove jumped into the fray and offered to represent Mrs. Upham in her complaint. They retained Ephraim London to act as her attorney. The ACLU also provided counsel.

While this case was appealed on a jurisdictional question, the US Post Office, which had power to ban obscene material from the mail, on June 10, 1961, confiscated three copies of *Tropic of Cancer*. But four days later, acting on advice from the Justice Department, the Post Office released the book. *The New York Times* reported that lawyers in the Justice Department had concluded that a court battle against *Tropic of Cancer* on grounds of obscenity would probably be lost because the book "was recognized by many critics as having literary merit." Then on August 10, the Customs ban on the book was lifted, also on advice from the Justice Department. Mrs. Upham's copy of the book was returned to her.

These decisions, though favorable, did not put an end to the efforts to suppress the distribution and sale of *Tropic of Cancer* by Grove Press. Nor did they relieve Miller of the stress of a censorship battle he had hoped to avoid. Although the actions by the Post Office and the Customs Bureau indicated a recognition by the Federal government that *Tropic of Cancer* was protected against suppression by the First Amendment, their decisions were administrative, not judicial. Absent a ruling on the question of the obscenity of *Cancer* by the US Supreme Court, local jurisdictions were not constrained from using state and district courts to suppress the book. Bowing to pressure from the censorious in their communities, who were often organized through the national Citizens for Decent Literature, a Catholic group, city and district attorneys, assisted by willing police chiefs, initiated prosecutions against booksellers and distributors carrying the book. These censorship assaults posed an enormous legal and economic threat to Grove, which had assumed the responsibility of defending the book in all the battlegrounds. Grove was fighting a multiheaded monster that could be defeated only through a ruling from the highest court in the land. Grove's legal strategy was built around the goal of pushing a case through the legal labyrinth to the supreme arbiter as quickly as possible, before the tidal wave of litigation could push it into bankruptcy.

Orchestrating this strategy was Charles Rembar, Grove's legal counsel. He drafted a brief that articulates the core argument that would be used by attorneys defending the book from prosecution in all regions of the country. The argument relied on the position advocated by Huntington Cairns from his earliest correspondence with Miller: that the book was immune from censorship because it possessed literary merit and, therefore, social value. Backing up the brief was an affidavit from poet and critic John Ciardi, a reviewer for *Saturday Review*, asserting that *Cancer* was "a valiant and true work of art."

The first court test of the US publication took place in Boston, Massachusetts, in September, the month that Miller returned from his European adventure with Renate Gerhardt. The Massachusetts Obscene Literature Control Commission ("What a title!" Miller remarked) had recommended in July that Attorney General Edward McCormack, nephew of US House of Representatives Speaker John McCormack, initiate a prosecution to ban the book from sale in Massachusetts. The trial judge found the book obscene, and Grove appealed the decision to the Massachusetts Supreme Court. Grove's hope was that this appeal, whatever its outcome, would propel the case to the US Supreme Court where the expected favorable ruling would put an end to litigation over *Cancer* and, by extension, all of Miller's banned books. But though the Massachusetts Supreme Court did eventually overturn the trial court's decision, Attorney General McCormack did not pursue an appeal, and so the path to the US Supreme Court through Massachusetts was closed.

In October, well before the hardcover market for *Tropic of Cancer* had been exhausted, Grove Press was forced to issue a paperback edition of the book by the threat of a pirated paperback being prepared by the Universal Publishing and Distribution Corporation of New York City. Two million copies of the paperback were printed, flooding the market and making the book a target of censorship in local jurisdictions throughout the country. In a short span of time, more than sixty court proceedings were initiated by city, county, and state authorities. Additionally, police departments acting under authority of state obscenity laws confiscated copies of the book from bookstores and intimidated book dealers and their distributors from keeping the book in their inventories. These steps hurt sales of the book, denying Grove the revenue it needed to fight the numerous court cases. By January 1962, "Grove Press estimated that 75 percent of the nation's dealers either never accepted copies or returned them after shipment because of local police action, actual or threatened," noted Earl Hutchinson in his account of Grove's litigation over the book. *Tropic of Cancer* was not on sale in Massachusetts, Rhode Island and many metropolitan areas, including Los Angeles, Chicago, Philadelphia, Miami, Atlanta, Dallas, Houston, Seattle, and Phoenix. Sales of the book were coming chiefly from New York, Washington, San Francisco, and Minneapolis, where foot soldiers from the Henry Miller Literary Society were on active patrol.

The explosion of prosecutions and intimidation following the publication of the paperback had been expected by Rembar. Writing about the legal defense of *Cancer*, he observed that "paperbacks usually arouse the censorious more than hardcover books" because the lower price makes the material easily available to minors. But, he added, "The censor's motivation goes deeper, into a longing to preserve the common man from the ravages of intellect. The intellectual enemy is a small minority, and in any case it is a minority that cannot be saved from its own devil. Sex in literature provided the field on which the struggles recounted in the book took place, but the war was wider. The true censor has objectives beyond the masking of the erotic and the indecent. The end in view is an established principle of suppression, available anywhere in the world of the mind."

Rembar's commentary goes to the heart of Miller's dialectical argument with his country. His anarchistic individualism had inflamed America's terror of experiencing the raw instinctual life into which *Tropic of Cancer* plunged the reader. Miller's book was not a threat to minors; it was a threat to the American way of life.

One of the most aggressive censorship campaigns against *Cancer* was being waged in Cook County Illinois. Chicago's mayor, Richard Daley, a powerful Irish Catholic politician, declared that he had been shocked by the book and ordered a probe. The *Chicago Tribune* responded by purging the book from its bestsellers list. Police in Chicago and several of its north and northwest suburbs began removing copies of the book from bookstands, intimidating booksellers, and in some instances arresting clerks for selling copies of the book.

Guided by Rembar, Grove was retaining teams of lawyers to defend the book and its sellers in numerous jurisdictions, continuing to hope for a case that would travel quickly to the US Supreme Court and extinguish the wildfire of litigation. Rembar retained Elmer Gertz, a noted civil libertarian and friend of Mayor Daley, to take the lead in defending the book in Illinois. Gertz became involved in a suit initiated by the ACLU to restrain the Chicago police from confiscating the book. Like Huntington Cairns, Gertz was a lawyer with a deep respect for literature. He had written a book about Frank Harris, a former customer of Heinrich Miller's tailor shop. As he prepared for the trial scheduled to begin in January 1962, Gertz began reading Miller's work. Just before the trial opened, Miller sent him words of encouragement. Alluding to astrological readings he had received, Miller wrote, "You know, one way or another, the book will eventually win out. That too is written in the stars. One has to have infinite patience, especially in dealing with imbeciles, eh what?"

Gertz wrote back to thank him, and his letter revealed a man of widespread interests and strong human sympathies. He quickly followed up with an order of several titles by and about Miller, and enclosed a check. He told Miller that at the upcoming trial before Judge Samuel Epstein in the Superior Court of Cook County he would be seeking a declaratory judgment that *Tropic of Cancer* is not obscene. He made it clear that he was trying to set the stage for an appeals process based on constitutional law that could carry the case to the US Supreme Court. Miller, sensing immediately that his cause was in capable hands, told Gertz, "If you win this fight you will have accomplished a very big thing—for writers *and* readers. I think the time is ripe—and I have a hunch you are the man to do it." From this initial exchange a friendship was born that lasted until Miller's death.

At the trial, Gertz called Richard Ellmann, a noted Joyce scholar who taught at Northwestern University, Hoke Norris, the literary editor of the *Chicago Sun-Times*, Frank Ball, the sales supervisor of book distributor McFadden Publications, and Barney Rosset to testify. He gave Miller a positive portrait of Judge Epstein. "It is very fortunate that we have a judge who, despite an innate prudery, is an honorable man through and through, who will decide on what he thinks the law and facts are, even if it hurts him . . . The Judge personally is opposed to censorship. At the same time, he thinks that two or three passages in *Tropic of Cancer* are inexcusable."

In February, Judge Epstein ruled that the book is not obscene and enjoined the Chicago Police Commission and the Police Chiefs of Chicago and its suburbs from interfering with its sale. To commemorate the decision, Miller sent Gertz an inscribed copy. Mayor Daley, responding to pressure from the Catholic community, ordered Chicago's counsel to appeal the decision. Simultaneously, a Los Angeles jury convicted Bradley Smith of a misdemeanor for selling *Tropic of Cancer*. Los Angeles attorney Stanley Fleishman was retained to handle Smith's appeal. Grove Press now had two cases tracking toward the US Supreme Court.

Miller, meanwhile, was struggling to maintain order in his personal life and find time to work on *Nexus*, volume 2. He wrote to Gertz in February, "I have my own trials." Large royalty payments from Grove, New Directions (sales of Miller's titles had spiked due to the publicity about *Cancer*), and European publishers were creating a whole new set of problems for Miller. Prior to signing his contract with Grove, Miller's main financial worry had been too little income to cover his expenses. Now, suddenly, the problem was *too much* money. Eve was still keeping track of his finances, and he went to Big Sur in January to meet with his accountant and business advisor to ascertain his tax liabilities. Meetings with lawyers followed at which he was advised to set up trust funds for his children.

Renate Gerhardt had also begun to make financial demands on Miller. While still traveling in Europe he had been sending her small sums to help cover her living expenses. In October 1961 she had informed him that she planned to move to Berlin where she would start her own *verlag*. She believed she had a financial backer. Hildegard Knef was helping her find a suitable apartment. Renate wondered if Miller might join her there, and offered a tempting invitation. "If I could see that it were no danger for your good spirits, then I would say let's go there together—me printing, you writing NEXUS and having a good time together, with talks, guests, no guests, walks, meals, etc. But I am afraid that the same old story would start all over again." Miller, though pleased at this sign of love from her, had no intention of going to Berlin, which he regarded as a "hot spot" where war might once again break out. He cautioned Renate, who had been born in Berlin, against relocating there.

In November, Renate cabled Miller for $1,000—"no catastrophe"—and Miller promptly complied, though he became annoyed when no letter of explanation followed the request. In December, facing a tonsillectomy, she cabled for another $1,000. Miller arranged for Rosset to forward her the money. He wrote her: "No need to explain to me what the money was for—that you needed it is enough . . . All I want to hear from you ever is that you are well, happy, and still have a spot of affection for me in your heart." In January, when he wrote her again to inquire about the outcome of her surgery, he gave her encouragement to ask for money whenever she needed it, no doubt leading her to believe that he now considered himself her benefactor. "And how are you fixed financially?" he asked. "Do you need some more of the filthy lucre? Just say the word." Gerhardt wrote back asking him for $1,500 to help her start her publishing company. Miller's deep need for emotional attachment to a woman had now fastened on Gerhardt, and he was willing to pay to have this need met. Complying with her requests, requests he had encouraged, opened a spigot of financial assistance that would flow for several years and drain Miller emotionally as well as financially.

Miller was also experiencing health problems at this time. Pain in his hips—worn down from years of walking the streets of New York and Paris—had sent him to a doctor in November. He reported to Eve that the doctor had detected deterioration of both hip joints and a cyst on his left hip that would require an operation to remove. But Miller dreaded invasive surgery and postponed the procedure. His doctor suggested he limit his walking, and exercise by swimming and bicycling. During the Christmas holidays, he came down with a severe case of the flu, canceled his plans to go to Big Sur with the children, and stayed in bed for two weeks.

In March, Miller made ready to go to Europe again for a brief visit. Barney Rosset had invited Miller to serve as a juror for the Formentor Prize, an award of $10,000 given annually to an influential author of any nationality. The jury convened at Cape Formentor on the Spanish island of Mallorca. Miller arranged to travel through New York to London, where he would spend time with Perlès, then on to Paris, where he would meet up with Renate and take her with him to Mallorca. Then he planned to return with her to Berlin for a short stay there. On his way to New York, he detoured to Jefferson City, Missouri, to visit Roger Bloom at the State Penitentiary. He was flush with cash, expecting a $5,000 royalty from New Directions, a $27,000 royalty from Grove, a $2,700 advance from Dutton Co. for publication of his correspondence with Durrell, in addition to payments from Hoffman for his European royalties. Before leaving, he instructed Eve to comply with any requests for money from his daughter Barbara, who had asked if he would help her purchase an investment property in Pasadena. Barbara and Renate were not the only beneficiaries of Miller's largesse with money. He was sending Antonio Bibalo, the composer of the opera based on *The Smile at the Foot of the Ladder*, $100 per month and was paying $500 per month in alimony and child support to Lepska. He also continued to send a small check to June every month. In May, Walker Winslow asked him for a loan of $500, which Miller provided, and in June, Gerald Robitaille asked Miller to send him "more than $100." Miller turned him down, infuriating Robitaille.

While in Mallorca, Miller became ill again with the flu. A Spanish doctor who treated him detected a heart problem, prescribed medica tion for him, and urged him to see a specialist when he returned to the United States. In May, Gertz wrote to Miller in Paris to inform him that Chicago's appeal of Judge Epstein's ruling had deliberately been filed with the wrong court as a delaying tactic that would permit the Chicago police to continue suppressing the book. Gertz succeeded in getting the appeal moved directly to the Illinois Supreme Court.

Miller returned to the United States at the beginning of June. On his way back to California he stopped in Minneapolis to meet members of the Henry Miller Literary Society. Elmer Gertz came up from Chicago to join the gathering. Miller wrote about this visit in the Society Newsletter and paid tribute to Gertz with the enco- mium, "I hope we shall see him sitting on the Supreme Court bench, where he belongs." During this stopover, Miller was interviewed by Audrey Booth at the University of Minnesota radio station KUOM. He called it, "Probably the best interview I have ever had." Before returning to Los Angeles, Miller paid another visit to Roger Bloom.

During this period Miller was in frequent contact with Anaïs Nin, who was working with her literary agent, Gunther Stuhlmann, to edit a selection of Miller's correspondence with her. Nin was in discus- sions with New Directions as the potential publisher of the letters. Nin, fiercely guarding her privacy, wanted only Miller's side of the correspondence to be published. Ever since Perlès's portrait of her in *My Friend Henry Miller*, Nin had been distrustful of Miller and fearful that the extent of her relationship with him would become public knowledge. She had written to Wilbur Smith, a librarian at UCLA, requesting the return of her letters to Miller, which he had deposited there. And she had also asked Miller for assistance in their recovery. So sensitive was she about her strained relations with Perlès and Miller that she asked Roger Bloom, who was corresponding with all three of them, "never to mention anything about me to either Henry or Fred."

Miller, for his part, was at pains to maintain good relations with Nin, his earliest benefactor. He wrote her in July that he would ask Smith if her letters could be returned. He assured her that even if UCLA would not return the letters, she would be able to control who had access to them and who could publish them. He repeated his offer that she receive all royalties from any publication of his letters to her, in effect making her a gift of them. He also offered to help her financially if she were in need. "I would give anything to annihilate this fear, suspicion, doubt, or whatever it is that plagues you . . . Certainly toward *you* I have never had anything but the best feelings." Miller followed up this letter by sending Nin a check for $2,500, which she accepted.

Nin came to Pacific Palisades from her home in Silver Lake, another suburb of Los Angeles, to thank him. She had not seen him since her 1947 visit to Big Sur. She recorded their meeting in her diary. The entry affords a vivid portrait of Miller at this critical stage of his life, traveling the new road of "success."

I let Rupert [Pole] drive me to a typical, ordinary little California house, cream colored, with neat lawn—his ex-wife's home, his children's home. When Henry opened the door there was the Negroid warmth of his voice and the shock of his ageing. It was no longer the pink skinned, clean, clear face. He was not fat, but there was the slight tremor and the slackness of seventy. The eyelid falling over the right eye slightly—giving to his left eye more fixity by contrast. This eye gave me a strange uneasiness. It was an indication of my own ageing—because this time, even while softened by the voice, and the sentimentality, and the past, I saw the slyness, the deep lack of feeling I had not observed before. . .

But I felt grieved at his ageing. He talked about his children. They came in. They looked like a million other Californian teenagers. . . His son came in to ask him to pay for some shorts which would be delivered. Made to order. "He dresses better than I do," said Henry admiringly. "And my daughter came home the other day with a poem by Rimbaud to translate.

I never thought my children would be reading and translating Rimbaud." I can see why Eve complained he loved his children more than he loved her. Because Henry has remained one of them—has more affinity with them than with adults.

In August, Miller traveled to Edinburgh to participate in the International Writers Conference. He appeared on a panel chaired by Mary McCarthy. The discussion topic was—what else?—censorship. Other panel members included James Baldwin, William Burroughs, and Norman Mailer. Burroughs, whose novel *Naked Lunch* was about to be published by Grove Press, was one of the stars of the conference. McCarthy introduced Miller by saying that he was one of the two most interesting writers of the twentieth century, the other being Burroughs. Strange company for Miller, who abhorred drugs. Lawrence Durrell was on another panel, and when the conference ended they went to Paris together.

Miller remained in Europe until the end of October. From Paris he went to Copenhagen to visit his Danish publisher Hans Reitzel and to see Antonio Bibalo, who was hospitalized with tuberculosis. Miller then flew from Copenhagen to Munich to stay as the guest of Hildegard Knef at her home on Lake Starnberg. Renate briefly joined him there. In company with "Herr Munzer," an actor friend of Knef, Miller traveled through the countryside of Bavaria, sightseeing mad King Ludwig's castles and marveling at the scenery. He and Munzer also made an excursion to Salzburg, where Miller toured one of Mozart's houses. While in Munich, he met George Dibbern's wife, whom he had helped during the war with care packages, and one of her daughters. By mid-October he was in Berlin staying with Renate and working with her on the translation of *Just Wild About Harry*. He left Europe on October 29 and made a stop in Chicago to see Elmer Gertz before returning to Pacific Palisades.

The summer had brought several significant developments in the *Cancer* censorship wars. Sales of the book had benefited from the rapid proliferation of well-publicized court cases. Rosset had written Miller in July that hardcover sales of the book were finished, after one hundred thousand copies sold at $7.50. Miller had heard that half a million copies of the paperback book had been sold in New York City alone. But Grove estimated that, due to the relentless pressure from censors, "75 percent of the nation's book dealers either never accepted copies or returned them after shipment because of local police action, actual or threatened."

There had also been two major court actions. As was often the case with legal tussles over *Tropic of Cancer*, the results were contradictory. In July the Massachusetts Supreme Court, on a 4–3 vote, reversed the decision of the trial judge in Boston who had declared the book obscene, "and became the first high court to hold that *Tropic of Cancer* might lawfully be published in the United States." Charles Rembar was especially pleased that the court's opinion "gave explicit recognition to the social-value test—the first judicial opinion to do so." Gertz agreed with Rembar that the decision was probably a turning point in judicial attitudes toward the book. He wrote to Miller in Europe, "I think the mature opinion has been formed that it is wrong to censor anything with literary value."

But almost simultaneously, a Brooklyn court took aim not only at the book and its publisher but also at Miller. The district attorney, Edward Silver, charged Miller, Rosset, and three distributors of the book with violating a New York state obscenity statute. Although the violation was a misdemeanor, the penalty following conviction could include up to three years in prison in addition to a fine. The charge encompassed two counts: one for writing and publishing the book, a second for entering into a conspiracy to do it. What was especially remarkable about the charges was the allegation that the conspiracy had taken place between January 1, 1961, and June 30, 1962. The court appeared to be ignorant of the fact that the book had been written in Paris in the early 1930s. When Miller failed to appear in court to enter a plea, the court issued a warrant for his arrest.

Rembar and Gertz disagreed over whether Miller should appear to enter his plea. Rembar, because he represented Grove Press, advised Miller to appear. Grove was concerned that publicity portraying Miller as a fugitive from justice might prejudice judges in other cases that were pending, incite more litigation, and hurt sales of the book. Gertz, though also retained by Grove, wanted to protect Miller.

He felt that because the charges were based on an obvious falsehood, the court's motives were not to be trusted. Perhaps its real motive was to humiliate the native son who had often portrayed his life in Brooklyn as debauched. He wrote to Miller, "It is clear that the prosecution is fraudulent and malicious. What reason is there to suppose that they would not subject you to some other such embarrassing result?"

The threat of extradition hung over Miller for some time, though the court never took the steps to bring the matter to a California court. Grove's lawyers employed various delaying tactics to keep the Brooklyn authorities at bay. But the threat was just the sort of public harassment that Miller dreaded would accompany the publication of the Tropics. His main defense against this worry was astrology. He wrote to Nin in February, "Now the Brooklyn authorities are after me again—trying to extradite me. Another mess. I count on my horoscope—which says prison is not for me. I'm charged with a *felony* this time—imagine it!"

By November 1962 over a million paperback copies of *Cancer* had been sold. Back in Pacific Palisades, Miller was beset by financial worries. His tax advisors were recommending that he purchase a house and make donations of watercolors and manuscripts to reduce his taxable income. He had begun thinking about buying a home in Pacific Palisades while in Berlin, in the belief that it would give his children more security. He envisioned living in the house with Lepska and the children, an arrangement that would require a large house with his own wing for privacy. But writing to Renate about his circumstances, he worried about the tensions that might arise from cohabiting with his former wife and their children. "I'm also a bit disturbed about sharing a home with Lepska—how we can both live our own lives, arrange our affairs, without treading on one another's toes. Am going into this, as you know, for the children's sake. But it's a bit of a sacrifice." Lepska dispelled any reservations Miller might have had about joint occupancy of a larger house when she sold her home on Las Lomas Avenue. Miller immediately began house hunting in Pacific Palisades, and by mid-December had put down a $5,000 deposit on a two-story house with a pool. The house would need extensive renovations to accommodate its motley occupants.

Facing large tax bills from the exploding sales of *Cancer* and the substantial costs of buying and maintaining a large home in one of Los Angeles's most desirable communities, Miller worried about his ability to continue sending money to Renate Gerhardt. Renate had been regularly cabling him requests for funds to keep her fledgling publishing enterprise, Gerhardt Verlag, afloat—$2,000 in July, another request in November, followed by another in December. With each appeal her pleas became more desperate. Her employees had been let go, she was operating the business from her home, and her printer was refusing to deliver books she hoped to sell during the Christmas season until his bill had been paid. Miller, never one to plan ahead where business matters were concerned, was caught in a squeeze. "Money!" he exclaimed in one letter to her. "I'm getting pinched for cash if I go through with deal to buy house I have in mind . . . I'm worried about you—how I can come to your aid should you need more cash in a hurry." Nevertheless he assured her he would always find a way. "However much I may need cash I can always scrape up what you need—unless it's an extraordinary amount."

Further complicating his business affairs at this time, Miller signed contracts to sell film rights to *Tropic of Cancer* and *The Smile at the Foot of the Ladder*. The complexity of the *Cancer* film deal required him to form his own corporation, Rellim. Rellim then partnered with producers Elliott Kastner and Stan Shpetner to form a third entity that entered into an agreement with Joseph Levine's Embassy Pictures, the financier, to produce the picture. Miller had to spend $1,500 to form the corporation and pay his lawyers. The film was scheduled to go into production in the spring. Bernie Wolfe, a friend of Miller, would write the script. Miller stood to make $100,000 if the film was produced. The film contract with producer Patricia Hardesty for *Smile* was simpler. She planned to make an art film, also in France, and hoped to interest Marcel Marceau, the internationally famous mime, in the role of Auguste.

The one bright spot in all these dealings and business maneuvers was that Elmer Gertz, learning of Miller's need to donate watercolors, offered to act as a middleman in the transactions, finding donees among universities, museums, and art institutions willing to accept the paintings, and making sure the gifts were properly documented to qualify as charitable donations under the tax code. Gertz did not charge Miller for these services. He also warned Miller about doing business with Levine. He told Miller that he had performed legal services for Levine when the producer was attempting to make a film about Clarence Darrow, but bills he submitted were never paid.

As the year drew to a close, Miller was in a disconsolate mood due to the state of his finances and his personal life. He was wanted by a court in Brooklyn, he was facing enormous tax bills and living expenses, he was preparing to live under the same roof with an ex-wife with whom he was often at odds, he was leaking money to a lover in Germany who rarely had time to write to him except to ask for more, and he was in physical pain. Worst of all, he had no time or energy to write, and the one activity that always gave him joy and release—painting—he now was forced to do to reduce his tax burden. He wrote to Renate, "The future looks so bleak, so austere, so empty, so futile for me. I could weep—but I won't." Plaintively he added, "I have no one to turn to for love, comfort, consolation." On New Year's Eve he wrote to Nin, who had sent him a Christmas card congratulating him on his success, that his application for a home loan had been turned down by one company because of his literary reputation. "This 'success' means nothing, is just one big headache," he told her bitterly.

THE KNOT OF PERSONAL AND FINANCIAL PROBLEMS THAT MILLER struggled with persisted and intensified during the next year. Renate wrote him at the beginning of January, "I need—and need desperately—$6,000 to cover the minimum costs up to the first income that can keep me going." She reported that her dismissed employees were spreading the rumor that she was bankrupt. Miller scrambled to secure the funds, then finding himself short of the down payment he needed to make on his newly purchased home, he asked Durrell to loan him $5,000. Durrell wrote back that he didn't have the money to give, but Hoffman came to the rescue with a large remittance from the English publisher John Calder, who was preparing to issue *Tropic of Cancer* in England. Renate continued to ask Miller regularly for large infusions of cash: $2,000 in March, $2,000 in May, $2,000 in June.

In spite of all the demands and distractions, Miller was still trying to write *Nexus*, volume. 2. He wrote to Gertz in mid-January that he had completed about one hundred pages of the book and hoped to finish it before April, when he anticipated going to Paris for the filming of *Tropic of Cancer*. He decided to go up to Big Sur for several weeks to escape the extensive and costly renovations that Lepska was supervising at the new house.

Miller remained in Big Sur for three weeks, and when he returned he was in better spirits, although the Brooklyn authorities were again pushing him to appear in court and Rembar was advising him to go. (Stanley Fleishman, who was handling Bradley Smith's appeal in California, advised Miller not to go to Brooklyn and proposed some delaying tactics to Rembar.) Miller was hopeful that his new environment would enable him to make headway on *Nexus*. He wrote to Nin that he was happy in his new house. "Lovely place, this new home. Have a good pool, too. Feel I can work here—at last." In addition to working on *Nexus*, Miller was collaborating with Bernie Wolfe on the screenplay for the *Cancer* film and churning out watercolors like a factory worker, then sending them off to Gertz who placed them with donees. By the end of March he had produced 60 paintings worth $15,000 in tax deductions. It was a great irony that Miller's watercolors, which he had often bartered for living necessities in Big Sur when his book sales brought in very little money, were now being used to shelter his royalties. What had been a creative delight for him—using color, water, and paper to create works of art that he exhibited in galleries and gave in thanks to people who had helped him—had now become a chore imposed on him by a tax advisor. He wrote to Eve, "I'm getting better and better at it—but for what end, I ask myself? I seem to give them all away—don't have a damned one for myself."

The strain of keeping all these balls in the air simultaneously wore Miller down emotionally and physically. Interruptions constantly halted his work on *Nexus*, frustrating him. When Renate cabled him for money at the end of March and he did not have the funds on hand to send her, he blacked out. He wrote to Gertz, "I rush, rush every day, to do what must be done. Last night I gave out utterly. Too much work, too much pushing. And too many problems, of all sorts."

In May Miller stretched his sacrosciatic muscle, an injury that caused him considerable pain and made it difficult for him to walk. Then the producers of the *Cancer* film had a falling-out and filming was postponed.

But not all the news was bad. Miller's work was continuing to reach the public. New Directions had issued *Stand Still Like the Hummingbird*, a new collection of Miller's shorter pieces (the title essay had been published in *Esquire*). In February they brought out *Just Wild About Harry*, and Bob MacGregor was actively seeking theatrical producers to stage the play. He succeeded in interesting Herbert Machiz, a producer and director, who arranged to present the play in July at the Spoleto Festival in Italy. Another performance was scheduled for the Edinburgh Festival in August. In January, Miller learned that Antonio Bibalo had completed his opera based on *Smile*. The opera was scheduled to be performed in Hamburg the following year. Dutton and Company published the Durrell-Miller correspon dence in February, and in April John Calder brought out a hardcover edition of *Tropic of Cancer* in England. The book sold 40,000 copies the first day. No prosecution of either the publisher or booksellers in England ensued. Perlès wrote excitedly to Miller, "Joey, you're a hero in England." Hardcover sales of *Cancer* in Germany climbed to fifty thousand, a staggering number for that country. And in May, Gertz reported to Miller that the Wisconsin Supreme Court, by a 4-3 vote, had ruled that *Tropic of Cancer* is not obscene. Two state Supreme Courts had now ruled favorably on the book. Decisions were pending in New York, Illinois, and California. Also in May, the Ankrum Gallery in Los Angeles put on a show of Miller's watercolors to help establish valuation for the Internal Revenue Service. Miller had by then completed eighty-five new paintings. The show was a success, with paintings selling at prices equal to or higher than his standard valuation of $250. Unfortunately, Miller's crippled muscle prevented him from attending.

Despite his many "trials," Miller's life at this time was not without its compensations. The sensational qualities of his reputation gave him easy access to the world of Hollywood, a realm he entered with a mixture of scorn and curiosity. It is not surprising that a man of Miller's temperament and appetites would be drawn into the orbit of motion picture luminaries. Miller enjoyed pleasure and beautiful women, both of which were plentiful and within easy reach. He was living in a community, Pacific Palisades, inhabited by movie stars. He was famous for writing books about sex. He had two film projects "in development." And he had made the acquaintance of Joe Gray, a marginal Hollywood player who became for Miller in Los Angeles what Emil White had been in Big Sur, a devoted friend and willing pander. He had met Gray at the home of a mutual friend in October 1961. Gray was Jewish, an ex-boxer whose nose had been flattened in the ring. Plastic surgery had made him handsome, and when he came to Los Angeles from New York to join his brother Mack in the movie business, he found easy pickings among the aspiring starlets. Gray toted Miller with him to Hollywood parties and brought to his doorstep hopeful young actresses wide-eyed at the opportunity to meet the notorious author of *Tropic of Cancer* and *The World of Sex*. After Gray's sudden death in 1971, Miller wrote an affectionate portrait that placed him among the gallery of libidinous rogues populating the Tropics. Here Miller presents his version of a scene from a Hollywood party and its aftermath.

In the beginning of our friendship he used to haul me to Hollywood parties. What dull affairs! But Joe would always say, "Wait a minute, there'll be some hot-looking dames come in before the night's over . . ." As the night wore on he was handing out his cards like laundry tickets. It was amazing how many girls kept his card and telephoned him a day or two later. By that time Joe had of course, forgotten their names.

"Wanda?" he would repeat. " Oh yes, you're the blonde girl, aren't you?"

"No," she might say. "I'm the short fat girl with dark hair."

"Then fuck you!" he would reply, and hang up.

Miller's Tinseltown escapades were not merely exaggerated fantasies he invented for satirical effect. He *was* going to Hollywood parties and romancing starlets. Writing to Renate in June after cabling her another $2,000, Miller described an evening spent at Tony Curtis's house among the marquee names of the movie industry.

I had a marvelous night of it last Saturday at Tony Curtis'
(movie star) birthday party. Met his charming young wife (18)
Christine Kaufman, German, with whom I spoke French almost
the entire evening. I also met and had wonderful talks with
David Niven, Henry Fonda, Jack Lemmon (and his beautiful
wife! Felicia Farr), Frederic March, Ernie Kovacs' widow (Edie
Adams, another interesting creature), Rosalind Russell and
Mike Romanoff, among others. One of the best, most exciting,
intelligent soirees in Hollywood I ever attended. Kirk Douglas
was there too, but I passed him up—no favorite of mine.

In this letter Miller also told Renate that he now believed he
would never finish *Nexus,* volume 2, and that because of the problems with the producers of the *Cancer* film he would probably not go
to Europe that year.

In September, Miller began what he called "a light romance" with
Ziva Rodann, a thirty-year-old Israeli starlet living in Beverly Hills.
The romance started, as it had with June Lancaster in 1944 and Eve
McClure in 1952, with a letter. Rodann wrote Miller to express her
appreciation for the pleasure she had received from reading one of his
books, *The Colossus of Maroussi.* Miller promptly wrote back, sent her
copies of some of his other books, and gave her his telephone number.
He took her to see a production of *'Tis a Pity She's a Whore,* one of
his favorite plays, at UCLA. Before the month was over, Rodann was
writing him love letters and asking him to arrange a photo session for
her with Miller's friend Leon Shamroy, a prominent cinematographer.
Miller gave her money, explained astrology to her, and asked Sydney
Omarr to cast her horoscope. Omarr warned him against too deep an
involvement with Rodann. "I sense that care must be taken, with regard
to this relationship, lest some kind of adverse publicity results and brings
notoriety to her and unravels much that is currently swinging in your
favor . . . She is more 'sober' in this relationship than you are, because
her effect on you is so intense, dynamic, stirring up Fifth House juices,
revitalizing you." Omarr recognized Miller's need for the stimulus of
passion, especially at this stage of his life, and the vulnerability this need
created, already so evident in his relationship with Renate Gerhardt.

Before long, Miller was in misery over this relationship too, chiding Rodann for "billing and cooing" by phone, then putting him off with "call me tomorrow" when he tried to arrange dates. Her flightiness both tormented and entrapped him, in a pattern reminiscent of his life with June. "I am the fool who always loves, who sees gold where there is only straw," he wrote to her despondently. The romance in their relationship was short-lived, Miller tiring of her coyness, Rodann moving to New York, but they continued to correspond as friends for several years. In a reversal, Miller asked her for money in 1968, but she wrote back that she had none to give him.

Despite Miller's protestations of impending insolvency, Renate continued to cable requests for money to keep her publishing enterprise afloat. His responses to her are often a mixture of reprimand and capitulation. In July, responding to a request for $2,000, Miller sent her $1,000, then explained that he would be able to send another $1,000 if he sold a story to *Playboy*. He tried to close the tap. "I've done all I could for you, my dear Renate. I doubt if I can do much more, under the circumstances - - - if I had what I have given away these last two years I would be sitting pretty. You got most of it."

In August, after Renate again cabled for money, Miller wrote her forlornly, "I have nothing to give anymore. I have been bled dry—and you are the greatest sinner of all, unfortunately." He told her that he had given his last $5,000 to Bernie Wolfe, who was suing Rellim and the *Cancer* producers over nonpayment of his screenplay fee. He closed the letter with a pathetically revealing remark. "Now I suppose I'll never hear from you again . . . I remain ever yours—impotent but devoted." Miller's choice of the word "impotent" suggests how he linked his ability to be Gerhardt's financial benefactor with his virility, and how vulnerable this psychic connection made him to exploitation. Renate, in a bid to keep Miller in play, wrote back that the astrologer Wulff has assured her that all her forthcoming titles will be a success, that she is on the verge of "making it."

At the end of August, Miller received an unexpected remittance from Hoffman, immediately cabled Renate the balance of her last request, and left the door open for her to expect more should she need it. He ended this letter, "So you still love me? I can scarcely believe it." But in September, after meeting with his accountant and learning that he faced large estimated tax payments, he was again firm that he could give no more.

No matter how much royalties I receive these next six months or so I will have to disburse from ten to twelve thousand dollars; in January a few thousand dollars more, and in April a good deal more. At the moment I have less than $1500 in the bank. In addition to all this, I must also donate watercolors and mss. and other documents to the tune of $20,000. In the last two years I made about $150,000 and you see what I have left. I'm virtually on the edge of bankruptcy. All this means that, no matter how desperate your situation may get, I won't be able to give you another cent.

But this financial report did not deter Renate. In December she wrote Miller that she had seen Ledig-Rowohlt at the Frankfurt Book Fair and had learned from him that there were three hundred and fifty thousand marks in Miller's *Cancer* account. She urged Miller to live part of the year in Europe to protect his European income from currency fluctuations and US taxes. Miller continued his pattern of adamant refusal followed by yielding for several more years. All told, he gave Renate over $60,000.

Many years later, Miller wrote about his love affair with Renate in *Joey*, volume three of the *Book of Friends*. As is often the case with Miller's "autobiographical" writings, the version of events presented on the published page is at variance with the reality evidenced in his private correspondence. He renders his fruitless search with Vincent Birge as a merry journey; mail from Renate awaits him at every stopover. Blame for the failure of their relationship is placed on Renate's astrologer Wulff, who, Miller has learned, warned Renate that "a life with me would be disastrous." Miller makes no mention of the financial support he gave Renate following his return to California.

Over the summer of 1963, there were two more significant developments in *Cancer's* legal wars. In July, the California Supreme Court ruled in a civil case brought against the Los Angeles City Attorney by the bookseller Jake Zeitlin that *Tropic of Cancer* was constitutionally protected because it was not obscene. But in the same month, the New York Supreme Court ruled that the book was obscene, thus intensifying pressure on the US Supreme Court to resolve the contradictory findings. The New York court's decision gave renewed impetus to Brooklyn's case against Miller and Grove, and prevented Grove from shipping copies of the book from New York.

As he often did in December, the month of his birth, the month of dreary gatherings of his Brooklyn family for Christmas, Miller ended the year in a depressed mood, and again wrote to Anaïs Nin. "I'm in a terrible mood—really depressed, discouraged, no desire to do anything—but suppose it will blow off, like the fog, before too long—It's always this way at X'mas for me. Maybe a little worse this year, that's all. I didn't send out any cards nor give any gifts—not even to the children. That's a step in the right direction, I feel."

The new year brought changes in Miller's domestic circumstances and a final resolution of the court disputes over *Tropic of Cancer.* In January 1964 Miller enrolled Tony, who had been attending the local public high school, at the Army and Navy Academy in Carlsbad, a transfer that Tony had requested and Miller approved because "It will lift him out of the poisonous atmosphere here." Miller's home life had been further complicated that month when Lepska remarried and her new husband moved in. In February, Val, who had decided not to attend college, despite being accepted at the University of Oregon, married Ralph Day and soon left for an extended honeymoon in the southern United States and Europe. Miller reported to Renate that Tony returned for the wedding, which was attended by over one hundred people, "most of them strangers to me," a remark that made Miller sound like a visitor in his own home.

The Brooklyn court was continuing to press Miller to appear, renewing threats of extradition if he refused. To mollify the court, he signed an affidavit for Rembar that he would not leave the country until the matter was settled. Reflecting his bitter mood at the numerous harassments that besieged him, he printed up new letterhead with the motto "The time of the hyena is upon us" written across the bottom.

To his great relief, Lepska and her husband moved to Altadena in April, leaving him temporarily alone in the large house, a circumstance he enjoyed. His injured muscle was now healed, allowing him to ride his bicycle again. He continued to socialize with the Hollywood upper class, writing to Eve that he was "hungover" from a party at the home of David Selznick and Jennifer Jones, where he met Dorothy McGuire and learned from George Cukor that "Ava Gardner is a great fan of mine." With Val and Lepska gone, Miller was in the hunt for a personal assistant to serve as secretary, cook, and chauffeur. Probably because he was recovering his privacy, his spirits lifted, despite the continuing financial and legal problems. He wrote gaily to Renate, whose financial troubles he optimistically believed to be over ("I have had it confirmed astrologically"), "Must tell you that often, on dropping into bed after a late night out, I am laughing out loud. When I go to one of these Hollywood parties—many of them quite wonderful —I start looking for the best, the liveliest chicks, and I hug and kiss them right in front of everyone, explaining that since I am so very old no one can object to my strange behavior. And what a response I get. (Telephone calls, telegrams, invitations—all of which I forget.)" This picture of Henry Miller as amorous buffoon cavorting with starlets like some randy satyr no doubt fed popular perceptions of him as a sex-obsessed old man. *Playboy* eagerly latched onto this image and published an interview with him by Bernie Wolfe in its September issue.

In June, Miller heard from Gertz that the censorship climate in Chicago had worsened. He told Miller, "We are in desperate need of some new decisions by the United States Supreme Court and these are likely to be handed down some time this month." Two weeks later, the Illinois Supreme Court reversed Judge Epstein, and Gertz quickly went to New York to work with Rembar on an appeal to the US Supreme Court.

The resolution of the legal question whether *Tropic of Cancer* is obscene came later that month, from a case in Florida not expected to reach the US Supreme Court. And it was made in anticlimactic fashion, in the wake of a decision on another case, *Jacobellis v. Ohio*. Nico Jacobellis was the manager of a movie theater in Cleveland Heights. He had been arrested and convicted of violating an Ohio obscenity statute for exhibiting a French film, Louis Malle's *The Lovers*. In overturning the conviction, the US Supreme Court opined that a work could be denied First Amendment protection only if found to be "utterly without redeeming social significance." The court then applied this standard to the Florida conviction of a bookseller arrested for selling *Tropic of Cancer* and on June 22, 1964, by a 5–4 vote, reversed the decision against the book. Gertz told Miller, "This means, as we interpret it, that *Tropics* may be sold anywhere in the United States." Rembar noted wryly, "*Tropic of Cancer* was saved on a review that had no briefs, no argument, and not even an opinion that the book could call its own—by a decision from which nearly half the court held aloof" (four Supreme Court Justices had voted not to review the case).

Miller wrote to Gertz that his astrologer Jacqueline Langmann had predicted this outcome before Rosset had published the book. "It's in the stars that *Cancer* won't fail—I told Barney this when he published it . . . When the book is fully published in this country that will be the death of it." He then congratulated Gertz, and told him that sales of *Cancer* in Germany and in England had reached one hundred thousand. *Tropic of Capricorn*, which Grove had issued in September 1962, was also selling strongly.

Miller had now reached two high plateaus of accomplishment as a writer: He had completed the task he set himself in 1927 to tell the story of his "rosy crucifixion" (though he had abandoned *Nexus,* volume 2, that project may have been driven by a reluctance to part with his central saga as a writer), and he had seen all sanctions lifted against the book that had made him famous throughout the world. Was he fulfilled? Was he a "success"? In the eyes of the world, and of his adoring friend Alfred Perlès—"Joey, you're a hero"—he was. But Miller judged himself by a higher standard, and by that standard he was not yet fulfilled, he was not "a success." From the time he had completed *The Colossus of Maroussi*, Miller had held that the goal of an artist should be to pass beyond mastery of his medium to mastery of the art of living. But it must have been clear to Miller that he had still to do this. He had felt a letdown after completing *The Rosy Crucifixion*, had written to Durrell that he considered himself a failure, the completion of his autobiography "a hoax." And following the breakup of his marriage to Eve he had been in search of himself, wandering Europe like the same homeless nomad who had restlessly prowled the streets of Paris in the 1930s. Since agreeing to publish *Tropic of Cancer* in America, he had been at the mercy of both internal and external forces beyond his control, subject to his inner need to find the (nonexistent) ideal woman and to the legal statutes of a society he had no wish to join. Perhaps this is why he wrote to Elmer Gertz on his seventy-second birthday, "I seem to be living everybody else's life but my own."

Miller realized his true position, and being the writer he was, turned his satiric eye on himself yet again in a letter he wrote in October 1965 to his friend Georges Belmont, who had asked him to describe his new life in Pacific Palisades. Miller sent off the following reply, which Belmont had published in France. It offers a portrait of Miller in celebrity.

When I moved down here from Big Sur, and only a few people knew my whereabouts, my life was relatively calm. But that didn't last long. Here is how it goes now . . .

Every week I receive at least a dozen unasked for books to review, about a similar number of manuscripts, usually from unknown individuals, all of whom ask me not only to read their work but to comment on it, give them advice, and intercede with publishers for them. Every week I get two or three requests to read from my work, lecture, or just talk to students in one college or another throughout the country. Every week someone asks if he or she can come for just a few moments and photograph me—or will I sit for a painting. Requests to talk over the radio or appear on television are all too frequent. Then there are the people who would like me to collaborate with them on one project or another, from amateur theatrical productions to juvenile delinquency programs. From all over Europe, Asia and Africa come visitors—writers, sociologists or religious fanatics who would like to discuss their views with me over a cup of coffee. All during the day and late into the night the telephone rings; fortunately, I seldom answer it. In fact, I hardly hear it ring any more. Between times come invitations for dinner, lunch, sometimes breakfast. And last but not least are the letters which pour in, some addressed to Big Sur, some to my publishers, some simply to Henry Miller—California. Among them are always a few asking for money, usually from young writers or painters who would like to spend six months or a year abroad so that they may work in peace and in an ambiance more conducive to work than here. Occasionally people write to ask if they can send *me* money, or help me in any way, as cook, chauffeur, secretary or what...

My routine is to get up when I feel like it, swim in the pool if the weather permits, take a spin on my bike for an hour, play ping pong if I can find a "customer," then paint a few water colors, and wonder if next day I may be able to make a fresh start on a long abandoned book.

If it's a Wednesday I watch the wrestling bouts for two hours in the evening; other nights I search the TV program in hopes of finding an old movie (1930 to 1940 vintage preferably). If there is a Japanese film showing I will travel 25 or 30 miles to see it. About midnight I retire and read in bed for a half hour to an hour; I never read during the day...

Now and then I also assist my son with his home work, that is if it is a subject I can cope with... Now it is Camus' *The Stranger.* He tells me he doesn't see much point to the story. Neither do I. However, this morning, reading the newspaper, to my amazement I read that a young student killed two men wantonly—after reading this same book. So maybe he had a point, Camus!

In this community of ours, and wherever the hand of "progress" prevails, the hydra-headed enemy reveals itself by means of the telephone, the radio, the TV, the automobile, the freeways, race riots, smog, insecticides, technology, space travel, alcohol, tobacco, poisoned foodstuffs, advertisements and a general lack of anything to worry about except cancer, heart trouble, arthritis, neurosis, psychosis, taxation, multiple insurance policies, murder, rape, arson, this war and the next, the atom bomb, Red China, red herrings and Communism in any form, shape, or manner, whether overt or concealed, benevolent or malevolent, true or false, etcetera.

So you see, life in the Palisades is not much different from life anywhere in the western world.

Miller lived for sixteen years after the Supreme Court's decision on *Cancer*. He settled into the life of a literary celebrity, giving interviews, appearing in films, socializing with the Hollywood elite. Several times he returned to Paris: once for the filming of Robert Snyder's documentary *The Henry Miller Odyssey*, a second time to attend the opening of a watercolor show in Paris and to visit Durrell, a third time to serve as a consultant on the oft-postponed movie version of *Tropic of Cancer*. The film, misconceived and miscast with a drunken Rip Torn portraying Miller as an alcoholic, received poor reviews, an "X" rating, and quickly disappeared. Miller continued writing, three slender volumes of reminiscences about friends, but painting became his main creative activity. He rode his bike, played ping pong (some times with nude starlets), and swam in his heated pool.

He endured the inevitable shocks and disappointments: the death of Eve in 1966 from alcoholism, of Lauretta in 1969 from cancer, Val's divorce after a year and a half of marriage, Tony's bitter experience as an enlistee in the Army Medical Corps during the Vietnam War. He made a foolish marriage to a young Japanese singer he had met in a piano bar who agreed to become his wife to avoid being deported. The marriage lasted only three years, although ten years elapsed before they finally divorced. His health continued to decline, and in 1973 he lost the sight in his right eye following a ten-hour surgery to remove a blood clot that threatened his life. In 1977, Anaïs Nin, with whom he had become fully reconciled, died.

Miller was sustained in his last years of life by a passionate but platonic love affair with a beautiful young actress with the bewitching name Brenda Venus, and by his continuing friendships with Alfred Perlès and Larry Durrell. Durrell, who had also been plagued by the penalties of celebrity following the international success of *The Alexandria Quartet*, wrote to Miller in 1967 the poignant words that summed up the lost purity of their early lives as writers: "But how marvellous was the anonymity of being unknowns, friends."

12

The Henry Miller Legacy

"The Greatest Contribution Literature Can Make"

When Henry Miller launched his career as a writer with the autobiographical "novel" *Tropic of Cancer*, he fired a shot across the bow of literary tradition with the declaration "Everything that was literature has fallen from me . . . This then? This is not a book. This is libel, slander, defamation of character . . . a gob of spit in the face of Art, a kick in the pants to God, Man, Destiny, Time, Love, Beauty." He had uttered similar sentiments in his correspondence with Emil Schnellock when he wrote, "I start tomorrow on the Paris book: first person, uncensored, formless—fuck everything!" Critics and reviewers of Miller's work quickly picked up on his rebellious attitude, and soon branded him an "outlaw" writer and "desperado." This reputation has stayed with Miller until today. He remains something of an outlaw, shunned by much of academia, excluded from the American literary pantheon by most commentators, omitted from anthologies of 20th century American literature, rarely taught. But he continues to have readers and advocates, and *Tropic of Cancer* remains on lists of the one hundred best American novels of the twentieth century. He has left us a significant legacy, which, as he predicted, has largely been ignored. But as Erica Jong remarked in her 1993 tribute to Miller, *The Devil at Large*, we ignore him at our peril.

Much as Miller claimed to have repudiated the tradition, his writing bears the marks of many influences: American, European, Eastern, Classical. He is a writer whose roots go deep and wide into the soil of human thought and expression. And Miller has enriched the soil that nurtured him, transmitting his discoveries and innovations to artists who followed him: the Beats, Norman Mailer, Philip Roth, Cormac McCarthy, Bob Dylan and yes, even the Beatles. So, although Miller from the outset brazenly declared himself to be an iconoclast and outsider, a rejecter of tradition, in the very act of doing this he was identifying himself with a tradition, the tradition of counterpoint and opposition that includes Voltaire, Swift, Thoreau, Twain, and Thorstein Veblen, among others—and he was adding his voice to it.

If the course of Miller's career can be likened to a river, many tributary streams, some literary, some personal, fed its channel. As Miller's first biographer Jay Martin has noted, "Miller's memory of literary tradition has fed his imagination and generated the energy for his work as much as personal experience did . . . As he was abundantly receptive to literary materials, his work would be powerfully expressive of tradition."

Although Miller had no formal education beyond high school, during his formative years as a writer he read eclectically across a wide variety of texts. As we have seen, so important were his readings to his development as a writer that he devoted an entire book to revealing his literary sources. In the appendix to *The Books in My Life*, Miller provided a list of "The Hundred Books That Influenced Me Most." While he listed the books alphabetically, even a cursory scanning of the titles discloses major groupings. In their form and subject matter, these groupings define the boundaries of Miller's style and thematic concerns.

The largest grouping includes works of fiction by writers as diverse as Emily Brontë, Blaise Cendrars, Joseph Conrad, James Fenimore Cooper, Dostoevsky, Knut Hamsun, James Joyce, Thomas Mann, Marcel Proust, Rabelais, and Mark Twain. These writers are for the most part a gallery of some of the major nineteenth and twentieth century practitioners of the literary form, the novel, that Miller struggled to adapt to his own interests and themes, then broke away from with the "formless" fictive autobiography that distinguished him from his contemporaries and baffled and offended many of his critics.

Dostoevsky had the greatest impact on Miller's thinking about the novel. Maria Bloshteyn, in her study of Dostoevsky's influence on Miller, believes that Miller concluded from his immersion in the writing of Dostoevsky during the 1920s that Dostoevsky had exhausted the possibilities of the traditional novel and that a new literary form was needed to express the condition and sensibility of modern man. "According to Miller," Bloshteyn states, "Dostoevsky enabled new writers to discard literature, in all its staid conventions and formalities, and to create a different kind of writing, more intimately entwined with life itself." In *Nexus*, Miller puts into the mouth of the character John Stymer his own view of the significance of Dostoevsky.

> As I see it, with Dostoevski's death the world entered upon a complete new phase of existence. Dostoevski summed up the modern age much as Dante did the Middle Ages. The modern age—a misnomer by the way—was just a transition period, a breathing spell, in which man could adjust himself to the death of the soul. Already we're leading a sort of grotesque lunar life. The beliefs, hopes, principles, convictions that sustained our civilization are gone. And they won't be resuscitated. Take that on faith for the time being. No, henceforth and for a long time to come we're going to live in the mind. That means destruction ... self-destruction. If you ask me why I can only say—because man was not made to live by mind alone. Man was meant to live with his whole being. But the nature of this being is lost, forgotten, buried. The purpose of life on earth is to discover one's true being—and to live up to it ... All that we have stifled, you, me, all of us, ever since civilization began, has got to be lived out. We've got to recognize ourselves for what we are. And what are we but the end product of a tree that is no longer capable of bearing fruit. We've got to go underground, therefore, like seed, so that something new, something different, may come forth.

Speaking for himself in *The Books in My Life*, Miller recalled the powerful impression Dostoevsky made on him as a young man struggling to find his way in New York. "I have often made mention of the celebrated photograph of Dostoevsky which I used to stare at years ago—it hung in the window of a bookshop on Second Avenue in

New York. That will always be for me the real Dostoevsky. It is the man of the people, the man who suffered for them and with them."

Another major grouping consists of works on Eastern philosophy, occultism and mysticism, works that stirred the religious impulse that is overtly or implicitly expressed in much of Miller's writing. The works include Madame Blavatsky's *The Secret Doctrine*, Balzac's *Seraphita* and *Louis Lambert*, the *Tao Teh Ch'ing* of LaoTse, *The Gospel of Ramakrishna*, *The Centuries* by Nostradamus, Dane Rudhyar's *Astrology of Personality*, A. P. Sinnett's *Esoteric Buddhism*, and *Zen Buddhism* by Suzuki. In his 1964 *Playboy* interview, Miller acknowledged these formative sources. "I make no secret of the fact that I have been much influenced by Taoistic writing and Oriental philosophy in general," Miller told interviewer Bernard Wolfe. Several commentators have pointed out that Miller's quest for self-understanding and self-realization—the central themes of his work—makes him essentially a religious writer and that recognizing him as such would go a long way toward clearing up critical misconceptions of him as a renegade author notable primarily for challenging our sexual taboos. In his recent study of the origins and manifestations of the religious impulse in Miller's writing Thomas Nesbit wrote, "Henry Miller constructed a religious universe in which self-liberation remained his ultimate goal. Building upon the traditions of Christian writers such as William Blake, Miller saw religion, art, and sex as three kindred vehicles to achieve emancipation. The sexual dimension of his oeuvre should be seen within this greater project."

An Indian commentator, Nandyal Raganath, traced Miller's insistence on the central role of sexuality in human life to "the influence of ancient Indian thought . . . Like ancient Indians, he too believed that sex was neither immoral nor moral, but it was amoral; and what was fundamental and justified in life was also justified in art."

Miller also saw himself as primarily a religious writer. He told his French translator Georges Belmont in 1972:

> Fundamentally I am a religious man without a religion. I believe in the existence of a Supreme Intelligence . . . call it God if you like. I believe there is a bond between myself and this God who is bound with the cosmos. But I also believe it to be a fact that

we shall never *know*, we shall never penetrate into the mystery of life. That's a thing you've got to accept, and in that sense I am religious . . . The important thing is that man should never lose sight of his link with the universe. Life is a miracle. For me, everything is mystery and miracle.

A related influence was American transcendentalism as expressed in the writings of Emerson, Thoreau, and Whitman. Miller includes Emerson's *Representative Men* (kin of D. H. Lawrence's "aristocratic spirits" and Miller's "exemplars"), Thoreau's *Civil Disobedience* and Whitman's *Leaves of Grass* on his list of one hundred. Karl Orend, among others, has pointed out Miller's blending of the Hindu philosophy of the East and the idealism of the New England transcendentalists. "Henry Miller was essentially a Hindu writer, who came to practice Buddhism as a way of life . . . Hinduism is the center-pin of American transcendentalism, just as Buddhism is of the Beat generation. Hinduism was a major influence on writers who influenced Henry Miller, such as Walt Whitman, Henry David Thoreau and Ralph Waldo Emerson."

From the transcendentalists, Miller absorbed a belief in the potential divinity of man, a divinity realized when man finds his connection to the eternal flow of cosmic energy that surrounds him and submits to it. In *The Books in My Life*, Miller reserved his highest praise for Whitman, whom he considered a fully emancipated human being and one of only a few Americans—Thoreau was another—to have fulfilled the promise of the New Land by creating a new kind of man. "Whitman's outlook is not American, anymore than it is Chinese, Hindu or European," Miller wrote in a short essay on Whitman. "It is the unique view of an emancipated individual, expressed in the broadest American idiom, understandable to men of all languages." These words could be applied to Miller's own writing. If Miller can be said to have modeled himself on another writer, that writer is the seer and prophet Walt Whitman. While holding up Whitman as one of his "exemplars," Miller quotes a passage from him that, as he says, "expresses my own view of life."

A fitly born and bred race, growing up in right conditions of outdoor as much as indoor harmony, activity and development, would probably, from and in those conditions, find it enough merely *to live*—and would, in their relations to the sky, air, water, trees, etc., and to the countless common shows, and in the fact of *life* itself, discover and achieve happiness—with Being suffused night and day by wholesome ecstasy, surpassing all the pleasures that wealth, amusement, and even gratified intellect, erudition, or the sense of art, can give.

Approvingly, Miller asserts, "I would say that it was on this rock—temporarily forgotten—that America was founded."

Three other groupings suggest themselves from Miller's list. Though Miller was not a philosopher, he looked at human history and its impact on the individual human being from a broad philosophical perspective. Four major European thinkers shaped his attitudes: Oswald Spengler, Friedrich Nietzsche, Élie Faure and Erich Gutkind. Spengler's *Decline of the West*, with its thesis that human cultures pass through cycles of birth, growth, decay, and death followed by rebirth has obvious echoes in the morbid atmosphere of *Tropic of Cancer* ("the cancer of time is eating us away"). Spengler's pronouncement that from the ashes of a dying society a new culture will be born, brought into being by a few isolated visionaries, is reflected in Miller's conviction that he was living in a dying civilization in need of a new kind of literature for a new kind of man. Similarly, Miller found inspiration from Nietzsche's dismissal of conventional religion and morality, and his belief in the possible emergence of an "ubermensch," a more highly evolved human being, comparable perhaps to Emerson's "representative man" and Miller's "exemplar." Erich Gutkind, another German philosopher, wrote a book called *The Absolute Collective* that Miller returned to frequently and recommended to friends like Durrell. The subtitle of this book, "A Philosophical Attempt to Overcome Our Broken State," suggests its significance for Miller. Gutkind addressed the absence of God in modern life by declaring that God would appear to man if he ceased hiding from the world by using God to try to explain it. The absolute collective was the unity of God, world and man: "the absolute unity of all beings which is reached in the gathering together of men who have become completed in their humanity, free from fear, nature and ideology." Faure's *History of Art*, by showing that it was possible to understand human history through the prism of art, gave substance to Miller's view that artists like himself were the true creators of civilization.

Much of Miller's writing is noted for its humor and savage satirical thrusts against conventional social attitudes and behavior, especially sexual behavior. In many of his works, especially the autobiographical "novels," Miller's view of himself, his friends, his lovers, is essentially comic. Nearly all his characters are lost, ineffectual, morally adrift, at the mercy of their instincts—in modern parlance, "clueless." The lineage of Miller's humor can be traced to works such as Boccaccio's *Decameron* and *The Satyricon* of Petronius, in addition to Swift's *Gulliver's Travels* and Mark Twain's *Adventures of Huckleberry Finn*. Twain undoubtedly impressed Miller with the comic possibilities of the tall tale, which so many of the garrulously narrated scenes and situations in the autobiographies resemble. And perhaps Miller saw in the image of Gulliver, bound to the earth by a swarm of tiny men, a metaphor of his own condition in American society.

Miller identified with artists and especially with people he considered "artists of life," exemplars like D. H. Lawrence, Whitman, Jesus, St. Francis of Assisi. Through biography and autobiography the struggles, sufferings, and achievements of such exemplary individuals are revealed. The stories of these isolated figures who had the courage to walk the lonely path of self-realization motivated Miller as a man and as a writer to embark on his own identity quest. His list of influential books contains numerous accounts of these inspirational figures, including *The Story of My Misfortunes* by Pierre Abelard, *Diary of a Lost One* (Anonymous), *Journey to the End of the Night* by Louis-Ferdinand Céline, *Conversations with Goethe,* by Johann Peter Eckermann, *Dostoevsky,* by André Gide, G. K. Chesterton's *St. Francis of Assisi, Interlinear to Cabeza de Vaca* by Haniel Long (for which Miller wrote the preface), Nijinsky's *Diary,* William Blake's *Circle of Destiny,* Marcel Proust's *Remembrance of Things Past,* Herbert Spencer's *Autobiography, Krishnamurti,* by Carlo Suares, Van Gogh's *Letters to Theo.* Miller's debt to these works is evident in his choice of autobiography and personal essay as his primary means of expression.

There remain on the list works of fancy and imagination that comport with Miller's eagerness to incorporate fantasy, myth, and the irrational in his own writing. Miller experimented with a variety of literary styles and voices as part of his endless exploration of himself and his search for appropriate means of expression. He disdained "realism" and "naturalism" as inhibitors of his imagination. He professed that from his early days as a reader he was drawn to books that activated a sense of wonder: myths, legends, adventures, nonsense. In this vein Miller lists *The Arabian Nights*, Greek myths and legends, Hans Christian Andersen's *Fairy Tales*, *Alice in Wonderland*, *Robinson Crusoe* (another "autobiography"), Grimm's *Fairy Tales*, H. Rider Haggard's *She*, Francois Rabelais's *Gargantua and Pantagruel*, Sir Walter Scott's *Ivanhoe*, and Tennyson's *Idylls of the King*. One commentator, Bertrand Mathieu, has detected in Miller's self-appointed role as seer and illuminator of reality an identification with the Greek myth of Orpheus, whose lyre could charm gods, men, and beasts. Mathieu saw Miller developing over the course of his career an "Orphic personality" and found parallels between the adventures of Orpheus and Miller's travels in Greece, as recounted in *The Colossus of Maroussi*.

This review of the most notable books from Miller's personal library reveals the extent to which his own writing was grounded in the forms, styles, and subject matter of a broad literary tradition. But Miller was not a derivative writer, though he admits that when he started out in the 1920s he was trying to write like his idol, the Norwegian novelist Knut Hamsun. Since his aim as a writer was not to please a reading audience but to become himself, he strove for his own unique voice. But this voice inevitably resonated with voices from the past that he had absorbed through his focused but wide-ranging reading. Miller acknowledged this debt in his 1964 interview with Bernard Wolfe. "We all show influences and derivations. We can't avoid using or being used. When it comes time to express yourself, what you put forth should be done consciously, without thought of influences. But all this is in your blood already, in the very stream of your being."

Miller summed up the role of literary influences on him midway through *The Books in My Life*:

What were the subjects which made me seek the authors I love, which permitted me to be influenced, which formed my style, my character, my approach to life? Broadly these: the love of life itself, the pursuit of truth, wisdom and understanding, mystery, the power of language, the antiquity and the glory of man, eternality, the purpose of existence, the oneness of everything, self-liberation, the brotherhood of man, the meaning of love, the relation of sex to love, the enjoyment of sex, humor, oddities and eccentricities in all life's aspects, travel, adventure, discovery, prophecy, magic (white and black), art, games, confessions, revelations, mysticism, more particularly the mystics themselves, the varieties of faith and worship, the marvelous in all realms and under all aspects, for "there is only the marvelous and nothing but the marvelous."

He adds, "But the struggle of the individual to emancipate himself, that is to liberate himself from the prison of his own making, that is for me the supreme subject."

Complementing books as a formative and sustaining influence on Miller's writing were people: childhood friends, wives and lovers, literary allies, devotees. Though Miller lived in the relative isolation of Big Sur for a major portion of his writing career, he was not a solitary man but enjoyed the company of others, carried on a staggering correspondence with friends, fellow writers, well-wishers, and followers, and filled his books with stories of people he had encountered from all walks of life. Many commentators and readers have remarked on the natural, conversational style of much of Miller's prose, a style that creates the illusion that Miller is simply having a talk with the reader, perhaps over a cup of coffee or a glass of wine in a café. This conversational style has its roots in letters Miller wrote to personal friends in Brooklyn during the period when he was working in his father's tailor shop. Miller dates his origins as a writer to these letters to friends. "I owe my beginnings as a writer to the fact that long ago when I worked in my father's tailor shop, I had lots of spare time and I wrote letters, letters galore, long letters—20, 30, 40 pages. To friends . . . Letter writing, I think, gave me my natural style."

If letters to friends put Miller on the path to becoming a writer, it was his second wife, June Mansfield (Smith), who propelled him down it, insisting that he give up his nine-to-five job as the employment manager for Western Union and devote himself full-time to writing while she supported them with scams, gold digging, and waitressing. And it was June who pushed him to Paris in 1930, where he found himself as a writer. Although June was then supplanted as Miller's muse by Anaïs Nin, Miller never forgot his debt to her. He inquired after her well-being, sent her small sums of money regularly, visited her on his occasional trips to New York, and arranged for his friends Annette and Jim Baxter to help her become self-sufficient following her struggles with physical and mental illness. Miller made his relationship with June the central work of his life. "If you read the books you read what a life I had," he told Roger Jones during an interview in 1977, when he was eighty-four years old. "How I relied on my wife June to keep me alive. Was I lucky! One chance in a thousand. This was an exceptional woman. An extraordinary woman."

Once in Paris, it was letter writing to a friend—his boyhood chum, the painter Emil Schnellock—that opened the door to his breakout novel, *Tropic of Cancer*. Miller wrote Emil frequently describing his life in Paris, the city itself, his attempts to finish the manuscript of *Crazy Cock* that he had brought with him. The voice that he developed in these letters to Emil became the voice of *Cancer's* narrator. And numerous passages from these letters were lifted wholesale and placed in the novel. George Wickes, editor of *Letters to Emil*, observed, "His long, rambling letters to his old friend about everything he experienced led him to the style he had been avoiding in his formal, structured, 'literary' endeavors."

At this important point in Miller's development as a writer, the early 1930s, several people entered his life to give him moral and physical support as he struggled to create and then obtain publication for his books. Alfred Perlès, who became a devoted and lifelong friend, bumped into Miller at a Paris café not long after Miller, penniless, had settled in Paris. Perlès, like Miller, was an outcast writer, a Bohemian living on the margins of society, scarred by his experiences as an Austrian soldier during World War One. He worked for the *International Tribune* and could afford a room in a shabby hotel, which he shared with Miller, who wrote there while Perlès was at work. Perlès also obtained a proofreading job for Miller at the *Tribune*, one of Miller's rare concessions to employment. Perlès became in Paris what Emil White was later to become in Big Sur, a buddy, a foil—Perlès had no pretensions that he could match Miller as a writer—an ally whose devotion was unwavering.

While many writers base the characters in their fiction on people they know, Miller was unique in veiling these connections very thinly. Nearly all the characters in the Tropics and *The Rosy Crucifixion* have been identified by scholars. Miller made up names for them to avoid lawsuits for libel and slander. This process of "masking" his friends began with *Tropic of Cancer*.

Another Paris rescuer was Richard Osborn, a lawyer who worked in the Paris office of the National City Bank, and whom Miller also met in a café. Osborn had his own literary aspirations, so he invited Miller to bunk with him at his upscale apartment near the Eiffel Tower. Miller, loyal to those who had helped him, kept up a correspondence with Osborn for years and arranged for publication of one of his poems.

Around this same time Miller met another expatriate American writer living in Paris, Michael Fraenkel. Fraenkel had earned an independent income from a book distribution business he operated in America and had come to Paris to pursue his interest in writing about his favorite subject, the spiritual death of modern man. Miller was introduced to Fraenkel by their mutual friend Walter Lowenfels, who intuited that the two men shared a philosophical outlook. After an introductory lunch that Perlès also attended, Fraenkel offered Miller sleeping space on the floor of his apartment at 18 Villa Seurat. The two men sparred with each other during long philosophical discussions to which Perlès was a bewildered but amused witness. When Miller showed Fraenkel the manuscript of the novel *Crazy Cock*, Fraenkel threw it on the floor in disgust and told Miller that he had no talent for writing "literary" novels and should abandon that approach in order to "write as you talk, write as you live."

The most important figure to come to Miller's aid at this critical juncture of his career was Anaïs Nin. Nin and Miller quickly struck up a literary friendship that evolved into a love affair. Miller sent her pages of the *Cancer* manuscript, which she read and enthusiastically critiqued. When the book was finished, she helped Miller get it published through Jack Kahane's Obelisk Press and wrote the preface. Nin subsequently subsidized an apartment in Clichy where Miller and Perlès took up residence and continued to support Miller financially when he moved to Villa Seurat. Nin also introduced Miller to Conrad Moricand, who tutored Miller in the occult mysteries of astrology, read his horoscope, and gave Miller his translations of esoteric teachings held at the Bibliothèque Nationale. Through Moricand, Miller was introduced to the writings of Aleister Crowley, a contemporary leader of the Rosicrucian Order.

Nin was the only member of the Villa Seurat Circle who did not appear as a character in *Tropic of Cancer*. Miller kept his promise to her not to exploit their relationship in his writing, though he did write a flattering portrait of her published as "Une Être Étoilique." After a chill during the forties and fifties, their friendship resumed when Miller settled in Pacific Palisades and Nin lived in the Silver Lake district of Los Angeles.

The publication of *Tropic of Cancer* brought Lawrence Durrell into Miller's life. Durrell, then living on Corfu, borrowed a copy of the novel from a neighbor and wrote immediately to Miller to express his admiration. "It strikes me as being the only really man-size piece of work which this century can really boast of," Durrell exclaimed, initiating a personal and literary friendship that lasted until Miller's death. Durrell came to Paris in 1937 with his wife Nancy to sit at the master's feet. Durrell, Miller, and Perlès referred to themselves as "The Three Musketeers" and kept up a jovial long-distance friendship that sustained them all through the many ups and downs in their personal lives and careers. As Perlès paid tribute to Miller with the memoir *My Friend Henry Miller*, Durrell did likewise as the editor of *The Henry Miller Reader*. "The Three Musketeers" also linked arms for *Art and Outrage*.

Over the years, following Miller's successful debut in Paris, as he wrote in relative obscurity and struggled with poverty in Big Sur, he continued to attract admirers and allies who promoted his work and helped him with survival: Gilbert Neiman, Emil White, Bern Porter, George Leite, Judson Crews, Vincent Birge in California; Kathryn Winslow, Walker Winslow's former wife, who operated a gallery in Chicago selling Miller's work; Eddie Schwartz and Tom Moore, who started the Henry Miller Literary Society in Minneapolis. James Laughlin's commitment as Miller's first American publisher was unmatched, though Miller at times failed to appreciate it. Michael Hoffman, Miller's agent in France, vigorously pursued Miller's foreign royalties. Barney Rosset, rolling the dice against censorship in the United States, brought Miller fame and wealth, privileges that Miller tolerated rather than enjoyed. In the last stages of his life, his health declining, Miller had the support and friendship of Joe Gray, his Santa Barbara publisher Noel Young, Brenda Venus, his last "lover," and Connie Perry, a high school friend of Val who served as his personal assistant and secretary.

WHAT TODAY IS MILLER'S STANDING AS A WRITER IN THE WORLD OF letters and with the general reading public? Miller's work has from the outset polarized critics and commentators, who have found it difficult to classify him or to measure him against contemporaries and forerunners. His more mystical and philosophical writings, doggedly issued over the years by New Directions, found few readers and only faint critical praise. The more highly regarded banned books, when finally issued in the United States, became bestsellers, but readers were drawn more by Miller's sensationalistic treatment of sex—his obscenity—than by the message behind it. Miller dismissed this narrow focus on only one aspect of his writing. "I employed obscenity as naturally as I would any other way of speaking," he told George Wickes. "It was like breathing, it was part of my whole rhythm. There were moments when you were obscene, and then there were other moments. I don't think obscenity is the most important element by any means. But it's a very important one, and it must not be denied, overlooked, or suppressed."

Ezra Pound set the tone of the discussion with his famous double-edged remark as he passed *Tropic of Cancer* along to James Laughlin: "Here is a dirty book worth reading."

Admirers of Miller's work have praised his vitality, his enthusiasm for life, his candor, his human voice, his frequently brilliant flights of language, his assaults on the conformity and mechanization of modern life. Detractors have called him an outlaw, a renegade, a desperado, a buffoon, an egoist, a misogynist, a pornographer and have faulted his style for being long-winded and repetitive, his philosophy for being muddled and simplistic. He has probably polarized opinion more than any other twentieth-century American writer, yet he is scarcely taught in undergraduate and graduate English programs at major colleges and universities across the country.* He has been excluded from anthologies of twentieth-century American literature, to the detriment of both his reputation and the literacy of college students.

Perhaps the best way to come to terms with Miller is to accept his own assessment of himself as a writer. In *The Books in My Life*, after Miller summarizes the influences that shaped him, he declares his central purpose to be self-liberation. Miller restated this core mission numerous times in interviews that he granted during the "celebrity" period that followed publication of the banned books. In an interview with Audrey Booth that took place in Minneapolis in 1962, Miller stressed the highly personal nature of his writing.

> All my books are entirely personal, subjective, biased and preju-
> diced . . . I don't profess ever to be saying what's true or what is,
> you know, only what I see, what I feel. The only thing one can
> do is follow himself, do you see; dig in, discover what he is, and
> who he is, and reveal himself.

This determination to reveal himself fully explains the variety— and the unevenness—of the voices, modes, styles, and subjects found in Miller's work, and his willingness to blend them all together in an apparently formless arrangement. If the central theme of all his books is the self, it follows that Miller will take up and examine all aspects of the human being: the physical man of the senses, the instinctual man in the grip of unconscious forces and drives, the spiritual man who yearns for harmony, union, connectedness with his fellow man and the cosmos, and the intellectual man, the rational man who must use his mind to navigate his relationship to society, to try to understand it and come to terms with it.

---

*For the results of an informal survey of college-level English departments, see Appendix D.

Each of these aspects of man is given extensive treatment in Miller's writing. The sensual man delights in food, in wine, in painting, in music, in gathering impressions on long walks through city streets or rugged countryside, in sexuality; the instinctual Miller is released in surrealistic dream sequences like "Into the Night Life" and in bursts of "automatic writing" that make no sense to the conscious mind but invite the reader to join him on a fantastic voyage; the spiritual, mystical Miller seeks God and the eternal life, "the life everlasting," that is found when man is able to realize the fullness of the present moment. The rational, intellectual Miller enjoys spirited conversation, reads widely and deeply, respects art and artists, and revolts violently against the social forces of conformity and repression that threaten to prevent each individual from embarking on the journey of self-discovery that will allow him to fulfill his unique human destiny.

Viewing Miller simultaneously from these multiple perspectives may be the best way to bring him into focus and to position him among other twentieth-century artists. Those commentators, like Karl Shapiro, who called Miller a "wisdom writer" or, like Thomas Nesbit and George Warren Polley, a "religious writer," may have come closest to the mark, but Miller's complexity, his seeming boundlessness, makes placing him in a single category problematic. Miller strove to be unique, and perhaps the very difficulty critics have had in locating him is proof that he succeeded.

Miller was aware of his own amorphousness, as he revealed in a 1956 interview with Rochelle Girson that was published in *Saturday Review*.

I don't consider myself a realist at all because I employ every device. I use dream sequences frequently and fantasy and humor and surrealistic things, everything and anything which will deepen and heighten this thing called reality, because what people call reality is not reality in my mind. I am not only telling the truth; I am telling the whole truth, which is in your whole being and not just the surface, do you see? We are many things; we are a great universe. Just to describe the acts, our sexual life, our conflicts that are external, that's nothing. There's the inner force, which is so much more important.

What has been Henry Miller's impact on the culture of America? Before the US publication of the Tropics by Grove Press in the early 1960s, Miller had a small but devoted readership that fed on the reflective essays, short narratives and highly personalized portraits of selected fellow artists that New Directions steadily supplied. James Laughlin once estimated that Miller had fewer than five thousand readers in America. Readers hungry for the "complete" Miller, the Miller who sought to reveal all aspects of himself in a single volume had to find a way to get their hands on a smuggled copy of one of his banned books.

The publication of the Tropics exploded Miller's audience. Millions of copies were in circulation, and discussions of their merits proliferated in all America's social arenas: courts and legislatures, schools and universities, the popular press, radio, television, and film. Miller had penetrated the culture. His main thrust was his treatment of sexuality, and he was quickly labeled "The King of Smut" by cruder minds. But Miller's impact on the 1960s went far beyond the sexual revolution we longingly associate with that period. While it may be impossible to establish cause and effect in matters of cultural influence, it is surely arguable that Miller's message of liberation, and the multiple dimensions of life to which it applied, rippled through the various social and intellectual movements that define that period.

Morris Dickstein, in his study of the culture of the 1960s, *Gates of Eden*, observed that "for the culture of the sixties the watchword was *liberation*: the shackles of tradition and circumstance were to be thrown off, society was to be molded to the shape of human possibility." This impulse toward liberation—the central credo of Miller's work—found release in a wide range of social movements that appear to echo many of the tenets of Miller's thought and style of expression. In addition to the sexual revolution and the liberalizing of acceptable forms of literary expression, the sixties experienced the civil rights movement (an obvious political counterpart of Miller's belief in the dignity of the individual), the human potential movement, the hippie movement, the emergence of provocative, socially conscious lyrics in popular music, and the protests against the Vietnam War. All of these movements are consonant with the themes, messages, and arguments found throughout Miller's work. Miller's footprints are visible in the protest literature of the Beats, in the sordid depths of William Burroughs, in the surreal lyrics of Bob Dylan and John Lennon, in the dropout ethos of Ken Kesey and his merry prank-sters, in the self-actualization psychology of Abraham Maslow, in the literary techniques of the New Journalism as practiced by Tom Wolfe and Truman Capote, in the sexual ravings of Norman Mailer, in the self-referential fiction of Philip Roth, in the utopian hippie ideal of community living, in the pacifism of conscientious objectors who either refused to serve in the Vietnam War or deserted their country. If Miller did not influence the 1960s, then at least it can be said that he anticipated them by thirty years.

The noisiest controversy provoked by the publication of Miller's banned books swirled around his rendering of sexuality, and his "posi-tioning" of women in their sexual role. Kate Millett famously attacked Miller in *Sexual Politics* as a misogynist—"Miller is a compendium of American sexual neuroses, and his value lies not in freeing us from such afflictions, but in having the honesty to express and dramatize them"—and Norman Mailer in *The Prisoner of Sex*, followed later by Erica Jong in *The Devil at Large*, just as famously defended him. Miller himself deplored in his readers what he saw as the exclusivity of their focus on the sexuality in his autobiographical novels and their mis-understanding of its significance. Miller tried to educate his reading public about the meaning for him of sexuality in an interview pub-lished in the "gentleman's magazine" *Esquire* in 1966.

> I don't think it was ever my aim to make sex itself an important issue. It was always the *total liberation* of oneself that I was concerned with, not just sexual liberation alone. What we never get at is the most important goal in life. It's what I call spiritual liberation, and that's a religious thing . . . At bottom, it's really like awakening in the true sense, yes, awakening, *spiritual awakening, spiritual liberation.*

But Miller had opened floodgates that had been repressing American sexuality since the Puritans had reduced it to an unpleasant but necessary duty. The new tolerance for freedom of sexual expression was quickly co-opted by the predatory forces of commercial exploitation and spread rapidly through other forms of public discourse—advertising, television, film, fashion, "romance" literature. Six years after his *Esquire* interview, Miller threw up his hands in disgust. "More and more I've grown disgusted with my readers," he told Digby Diehl in a *Los Angeles Times* interview. "I revealed everything about myself, and I find that they're interested in this sensational life. But I was trying to give them more than that."

What, finally, has Miller given us? He has given us the greatest gift, himself—unconcealed, unashamed, unadorned, unapologetic. His work, as Hugo Manning perceived, is a love letter to the reader. "It is a long and intermittent letter that Henry Miller is writing to this one or that one, or to mankind in general. It is the long open letter of a man who is revealing various forms of himself with ease and grace." Or, as Miller himself put it during a 1966 interview published in *Mademoiselle*, "The greatest contribution literature can make is to free people sufficiently so that they are able to love."

Miller began his career writing letters to friends. At the end of his life, his powers failing, his interest in writing abating, he produced three slender volumes of reminiscences. Their title: *Book of Friends*.

Miller died in Pacific Palisades, California, on June 7, 1980, at the age of eighty-eight years, in the arms of his friend Bill Pickerill.

Appendix A
"Notes on H. M."

by June Lancaster

June Lancaster lived briefly with Miller during the summer of 1944. She made these notes about her host and sent them to Bern Porter the following year. Miller remembered June as "The Mail Order Bride" in *Reflections*, edited by Twinka Thiebaud and published in 1981.

Loves good food—buys only the best. Took great delight in filling & emptying the pantry—has a passion for using & discarding. Takes special interest in the preparation of food. Likes to eat on time. Ravenously hungry after work. Drank wine usually only with meals. Sent his grocery lists to friends as souvenirs. These were scribbled over with addendum such as color notes, memos for friends, personal reminders, fragments of ideas & philosophical side glances, etc. Always an excellent host—was always perturbed if guests arrived and he did not have sufficient food & wine to offer them.

Immaculately clean & orderly. Has a place for everything—always neatly folds his clothes and hangs them up. Intensely dislikes insects and all vermin. Liked the cats. Petted them while soliloquizing. Fed them exceptionally well. Loves corduroys, plaid shirts, patches and ties. (Delighted in the fact he had stolen some beauties from a painter friend who had seemingly hundreds of ties molding away on racks.)

Thoughtful to compliment others on their work or appearance, especially if one was wearing some particularly interesting article of clothing that delighted him. Equally thoughtful to give his just criticism.

Very thoughtful of others & highly appreciative of any small (or large) favor shown him. Exceedingly generous. Gives everything away. Claims a small Chinese God brings him money whenever he touches it.

Very friendly & social—usually reserved unless he has the floor, then he speaks enthusiastically with a marvelous sense of humor, accentuating his remarks with gestures & grimaces. Often he claims, "I should have been a clown!"

He enjoys having someone read to him. Smokes moderately. Takes a nap during the day. Does eye exercises regularly at bedtime. Commenting on the fine presentation of his body & especially the diminutive size of his navel, "Certainly," he exclaimed. "I was born with a gold spoon in my mouth!"

Has developed the masculine, feminine & child nature in himself. Exceedingly sensitive. Can be exceedingly compassionate & again as formidable as a judge from Heaven or Hell.

Seemed to undergo a metamorphosis of physical appearance throughout the day.

Soliloquized during his painting sessions expressing phrases such as, "Tell us something we don't know!" Often admired his paintings with the exclamation, "Marvelous! What a beauty!"

Have never heard him discredit anything he has ever done creatively in painting or writing. He attacks everything with reverence, even drudgework of a domestic nature. Believes everything should be done with joy & ease.

Whatever he starts he finishes. Determines to overcome all obstacles. Takes great interest in solving new problems regardless of how trivial.

Happy, robust disposition; sagacious, energetic & intolerant with anything (man or beast) hinting of sluggishness. He seems to illuminate everything with his attention.

Believes there are only two real kinds of artists: genius and childlike primitives. "The rest, I should like to mow down with a machine gun," he says. (With gestures!)

Addicted to decorating the backs of his letters with all manner of addenda. Takes a walk after breakfast before sitting down to write.

Appendix B
HOROSCOPE OF HENRY MILLER

"An Angel Surrounded by Flames"
by Conrad Moricand

IN JULY 1936, AT THE REQUEST OF ANAÏS NIN, CONRAD MORICAND charted Henry Miller's horoscope and wrote an explication of its meaning. The horoscope reading was based on Miller's date, time, and place of birth, and a sample of his handwriting, all furnished by Nin. Moricand had yet to meet Miller. Miller was deeply impressed by Moricand's penetration of his character through the horoscope and wrote him to express his appreciation. Moricand wrote the horoscope in French; the translation is by Miller.

HENRY MILLER — BORN DECEMBER 26TH 1891 12:30 NOON NEW YORK CITY
The opulence of this theme with its innumerable facets is somewhat dramatic, to say the least. For if there is observable a truly impressive accumulation of intellectual and emotional riches, it is nonetheless rather difficult to envisage the manner and the way in which these manifold qualities may express themselves. The influence of an individual and his effect upon the world depend not so much on his intellectual and emotional gifts as upon his ability to give expression to them. One is confronted, in this chart, with a veritable congestion of faculties and feelings, the only outlet or channel for which would appear to be the career of a writer.

The image which this chart evokes, is that of some great sea-monster which plunges tirelessly, and with the suppleness of a shark to the nethermost depths of the sea in order to continually bring back to the surface the trophies of an unknown world. The dynamism, the propulsive force, the suppleness of this marine monster are indicated by Aries and Taurus, which cover the ascendant. The powerful jaws of the "shark," capable of crushing anything, together with the insatiable voracity, are indicated by the double conjunction of Mars-Uranus and the Moon in the Seventh House. The abysmal depths are suggested by the position of the Sun and Mercury (in the first degrees of Capricorn) at the precise place in the Zodiac where the Sun now reaches its lowest declination in the Southern Hemisphere. We shall now study the different aspects of this sea monster, its behavior, and the waters in which it swims.

The Ascendant, in Aries, gives the clue to the temperament, and especially the behavior, of this individual in the world. The emblem for this constellation is that of a man exposing his breast to the spears of the enemy, which is to say an extraordinary courage and love of danger for the sake of domination. Domination, in this particular case, expressed rather on the intellectual plane and tinged with a religious flavor not devoid of mysticism and metaphysical leanings, as is clearly indicated by the conjunction of the Sun and Mercury, near the Meridian, in the Ninth House. The subject will always seek to escape and to elude others, as well as to surpass himself, by liberating himself from all limitation and conventions.

The virtues of Aries are ardor, contempt for danger, and enthusiasm; the defects are tyranny, recklessness and fanaticism. A nature which is impetuous, ambitious, enterprising, and which expresses itself through action. Obstacles are disregarded, unrecognized, one might say. Obstacles when encountered are overthrown, and if unsuccessful, the individual becomes furious. A type which seeks much more to assert himself than to please. An assurance, which is absolute, almost brutal: accompanied often by great insolence. The hand is quick to strike, and the energy and will are like iron. An almost continuous state of ebullience, of inward stir and fury. Never satisfied with himself or with anything: the appetites never appeased. An intelligence which is powerful and dynamic, striving always to push every intellectual experiment to its last limits. Is fond of change, or romantic or sentimental adventures, but dogmatic too, seeking certitude, and revealing a capacity at the same time for making quick decisions and irrevocable conclusions. Where there is danger he is the first. Likes to play with difficulties, and to create them too. Aries is the type which fears nothing, except to lose his life. The Ascendant, situated in the first degree of Aries, seems to promise all the elements for success: utility, adroitness, promptitude. Insatiable appetite. Avidity. "The pursuit of the prey."

Taurus, also covered by the Ascendant, only adds to the above characteristics tenacity, obstinacy and perseverance, assuring the subject not only a control over himself but over others. Attenuating the dynamic quality of Aries, and permitting also quick alternations of speed and rhythm, Taurus, when the moment is favorable, enables the individual to proceed with slowness and caution, and thus attain his goal with certainty.

Whereas Aries and Taurus delineate the character of the native, the Seventh House, which embraces Libra and Scorpio, indicate more particularly the way in which the subject meets the world. We made mention earlier of the powerful jaws and insatiable voracity of the shark, by reason of the vise-like conjunction of Mars-Uranus and the Moon in this house. The double aspect here presented, with Uranus found in exaltation, signifies not only the element of violence but an uncommon tenacity. It gives, moreover, great ardor to the feelings and sentiments, as well as indicating their need of independence. In such a conjunction there is not only a powerful magnetism, but magic too—sorcery, one might say, if the triplicity of Fire were not deficient. What magnetism there is, consequently, remains static, passive, so to speak. It is a magnetism which is centrifugal rather than centripetal. A torpedo which explodes only when it hits the target.

This is the horoscope of a rebel, an insurgent, an uncompromising non-conformist. The emotional nature is restless and erratic, suffering perpetually from the restrictions and limitations which life imposes upon it. Gifted with a remarkable intuition. The hallucinated look of a visionary.

Mars, situated in its domicile, Scorpio, makes the emotional nature passionate, instinctive and deliberately implacable. It tends to make the subject move in a world of the real, the material, the tangible. The fundamental nature of Scorpio is reptilian. It is a symbol or procreative force, of intra-atomic energy, fecundating power, sex. It is a principle of life and of death. Desire manifests itself brusquely, without bargaining or reckoning, and always with fatal significance. Extreme and contradictory moods. The conjugation of Sun and Mercury in Capricorn at last take us to the "austral depths" which we mentioned previously. The depths, furthermore, are reinforced by Saturn in the Sixth House and Neptune in the Second, which orients the mind towards introspection, be it via the desires or via the subconscious. In this domain everything works out well, both as regards the inner life of the subject and the outside world.

The Goat (Capricorn) is the creature which scales the heights while browsing. It gains the summits with gaze riveted to the earth. Capricorn symbolizes the Earth, its ponderability, its secrets, its fatality.

The Earth always resists. The resistance varies, depending upon the nature of the other elements with which it may come in contact. Fire hardens Earth, but Earth extinguishes Fire. Air disintegrates Earth and reduces it to dust, but Earth needs Water in order to be decomposed. Only water can penetrate Earth and fecundate it, with the aid of Fire and Air. Earth is hard, elastic or soft. Water, in permeating it, lays it bare and reveals the structural scaffolding: Rock. The Earth, so rich in secrets, yields slowly and reluctantly. Earth is the heaviest of the elements. It is the beginning and the end of all things, and bears the imprint of fatality.

Mercury in conjunction with the Sun in Capricorn indicates a profound and heavy spirit with a predilection for the mysterious and the contemplative. The mind is directed inward rather than outward. Death is more fascinating to this type of mind than life. It is a mind which lights up the depths. Detects immediately the weak point in everything. The mind, in contradiction to the feelings, is reticent, timorous and dubious of itself when a decision must be taken. The cerebral activity is slow, laborious, painful. Indefatigable worker. Profits by everything to enrich and to progress. A tenacity which overcomes all obstacles through concentration, will power and patience.

In this connection it should be remarked, however, that the Sun squared with Saturn, opposing the analytic spirit to the synthetic, gives a keen sense of the relativity of all things: a natural propensity for humor, which is none other, as Keyserling has well said, than "a divine irony vis-à-vis oneself." All the more so, in this case, since the Sun is situated in the Ninth House, the realm of the spiritual. Let it not be forgotten that laughter is a divine attribute. It occurs whenever we approach the sense of the infinite and compare this subtle sense with its common counterpart.

The chances for happiness, which are considerable, are more apt to be realized to the intellectual plane, and in all forms of mental activity, than in the love life, which is controlled by Venus in the Tenth House. On this level there are noticeable indeed strange inhibitory complexes both of a cerebral and subconscious origin, which are likely to prevent a full liberation and which may be regarded as the ransom demanded of this rich and tormented spirit.

Jupiter, the ruling planet (and very well aspected in its domicile, Pisces), indicates that happiness is to be attained only by a perfect balancing of these two opposing forces: the centrifugal dynamism of the emotions and the centripetal concentration of the mind. Saturn placed in the Sixth House, Libra, only accentuates this configuration, for Saturn is here seen in its role as arbiter and unifier, the symbol of the middle way. Libra indeed is the indication of the existence of conflicting forces, in action and reaction. Libra always oscillates between two forces, seeking to restore equilibrium.

The symbol of Pisces and of Neptune is Jupiter, which is here represented in its domicile (Pisces) and which, because of the multiplicity of its aspects seems adequately to express and sum up the factors of this chart. The emblem of Jupiter is that of an angel surrounded by flames.

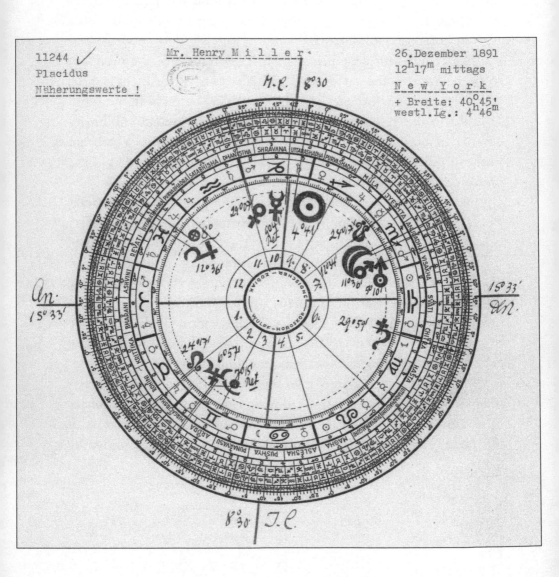

Appendix C
"O LAKE OF LIGHT"

Risen from the milky sward
I saw the one I love with flower
And on her breast an unborn moon

O wondrous moon! O lake of light!
The grass so green is turning white
O moon, O wondrous lake of light!

Milk of fire upon her tongue
Drew birds of jade and betel gum
Run river run!

The world of late grown small
Now achieves its just dimension
The one I love grown big with flower
Wheels within the lunar hour
Birds of jade in milky fire
Mitigate the heart's desire

Then run, river, run, as runs the sun
For none are born except the one
That lies upon the breast undone

The moon unborn is chill as night

The heart is like a lake of light
Flower, moon, milk of fire
These together do conspire

Take wing, strange birds, take wing!

—Henry Miller

Appendix D
ACADEMIC SURVEY FINDINGS

BETWEEN AUGUST 25, 2010, AND OCTOBER 14, 2010, I SURVEYED BY email four-year college and university English departments at selected academic institutions in the fifty United States to determine if works by Henry Miller are being taught in graduate and/or undergraduate English classes. Emails were sent to professors teaching genre, topical, or survey courses in twentieth-century American literature that include the period of Miller's major output, 1930 to 1960. Following is a listing, by state, of the institutions surveyed and my findings. A discussion incorporating significant comments from respondents follows.

State	E-Mails Sent	Replies	Teach HM	Titles
Alabama (3)	9	3	0	
Alaska (2)	3	1	0	
Arizona (2)	3	1	1 (2011)	*Undecided*
Arkansas (4)	6	2	0	
California (31)	78	43	4	*Tropic of Cancer; Black Spring; Stand Still Like the Hummingbird*
Colorado (2)	4	1	0	
Connecticut (5)	12	9	1	*The Colossus of Maroussi*
Delaware (1)	2	1	0	
Florida (3)	14	6	1	*The Air-Conditioned Nightmare*

State	E–Mails Sent	Replies	Teach HM	Titles
Georgia (3)	6	3	0	
Hawaii (2)	2	1	0	
Idaho (2)	4	2	0	
Illinois (8)	16	10	1	*Tropic of Cancer; Tropic of Capricorn; Black Spring; The Colossus of Maroussi*
Indiana (5)	10	5	0	
Iowa (3)	4	3	2	*Tropic of Cancer; Tropic of Capricorn;* "Walt Whitman" from *Stand Still Like the Hummingbird*
Kansas (2)	5	3	0	
Kentucky (3)	10	6	1	*Tropic of Cancer*
Louisiana (4)	8	6	1	*Tropic of Cancer; Black Spring*
Maine (4)	7	3	0	
Maryland (5)	12	10	0	
Massachusetts (11)	24	14	2	*Tropic of Cancer; The Colossus of Maroussi; The Air-Conditioned Nightmare*
Michigan (4)	7	3	1	*Tropic of Cancer*
Minnesota (2)	3	3	0	
Mississippi (3)	6	3	0	
Missouri (3)	5	1	0	
Montana (2)	3	3	0	
Nebraska (2)	10	6	0	
Nevada (2)	6	2	1	*Tropic of Cancer*
New Hampshire (2)	1	1	0	
New Jersey (4)	10	7	1	*Tropic of Cancer; Black Spring*
New Mexico (2)	4	3	0	
New York (7)	22	14	3	*Tropic of Cancer; Black Spring; The Colossus of Maroussi; The Air-Conditioned Nightmare*

State	E-Mails Sent	Replies	Teach HM	Titles
N. Carolina (5)	12	6	1	*The Air-Conditioned Nightmare*
North Dakota (1)	1	0	0	
Ohio (10)	20	13	3	*Tropic of Cancer; Tropic of Capricorn; The Air-Conditioned Nightmare*
Oklahoma (2)	7	3	0	
Oregon (2)	5	4	1	*Black Spring; Stand Still Like the Hummingbird*
Pennsylvania (10)	18	13	1	*Tropic of Cancer*
Rhode Island (2)	5	1	1	*Black Spring*
South Carolina (2)	3	2	0	
South Dakota (1)	2	1	0	
Tennessee (4)	7	3	0	
Texas (3)	8	4	1	*Tropic of Cancer; The Air-Conditioned Nightmare*
Utah (3)	10	6	0	
Vermont (2)	1	1	0	
Virginia (4)	8	5	0	
Washington (2)	17	6	0	
West Virginia (1)	1	0	0	
Wisconsin (3)	5	3	0	
Wyoming (1)	2	1	1	*Tropic of Cancer; Tropic of Capricorn*
Totals (196)	**444**	**250**	**28**	***Tropic of Cancer: 19*** ***Black Spring: 6*** ***Colossus: 5*** ***Nightmare: 5*** ***Tropic of Capricorn: 4*** ***Hummingbird: 3***

The response rate to my informal email survey was over 50 percent, indicating a high level of interest and cooperation from the academic community in my question: "Do you assign works by Henry Miller in your courses on twentieth-century American literature, and if so, which works?" Many respondents went beyond a simple "yes" or "no" answer, and offered explanations, apologies, personal anecdotes around Miller and his circle, and encouragement for the biography. But the final tally confirms what my own experience as a graduate student and English teacher had led me to suspect: Henry Miller is an American author, many would say an important American author, who is rarely taught in major colleges and universities across the United States, despite the facts of his prodigious output, relentless dedication to the highest aims of literature, and acknowledged (by many respected critics) stature as one of the most important and influential authors of the last century.

Why?

Following are some explanations that were offered by respondents to the survey.

"His works are sui generis in so many ways that they don't fit into the predominant paradigms used to explain literature in the thirties."

"I do not assign works by Miller in my American Literature courses. In large part, this is a reflection of the fact that I was myself never introduced to Miller, either as an undergraduate or a graduate student."

"About a decade ago I taught Tropic of Cancer *a number of times with great pleasure and success. . . . As you doubtless know, my younger colleagues never go near Miller: they deem him —his treatment of women, etc.—politically incorrect. Perhaps their timidity has affected me. I hope not."*

"There is a huge problem of availability with Miller. It would be interesting to teach him in courses that included the 1930s (excerpts from the Tropics) and in post-war American literature (from The Air-Conditioned Nightmare *alongside* On the Road*) for instance. But he isn't in the textbooks and there aren't any texts or parts of texts online."*

"*Your inquiry prompted me to examine the lit anthologies on my shelf and not one includes Miller. And I've read Miller, loved his work, but I do not read him in an academic setting. I read him on my own.*"

"*I do imagine that for many there is no small amount of anxiety about potential backlash against teaching sexually frank works in class.*"

"*My university is in a conservative area . . . and Miller's texts would be controversial to teach when others are available. The outcry against Miller would be more stressful than I would find worthwhile.*"

"*I am a large fan of Miller and try to pitch a Miller class once a year to no avail . . . It may be some reservation about the perceived superfluous sexuality and what not, but I truly think it is mostly because I am a lecturer not on the tenure track. It is standard practice in most universities to leave the upper division class pitching to the tenured faculty.*"

"*Since the canon exploded into smithereens, there is an infinity of possible choices for any given reading list; and Miller doesn't come to mind as an urgent read, especially for ideologues of various stripes under the totalitarian regime of 'identity scholarship'.*"

"*I feel such writers as Bukowski, Miller, Céline, Anaïs Nin to be part of an oxymoronic 'Alternative Canon', writers who may not be regularly found in 'canonical' anthologies, but who will always be read, always have their followings, even perhaps always have their 'schools', their 'disciples', always be as important as, or perhaps more important than, the conventionally 'canonized' writers. And they don't really 'need' to be read in literature classes, because they don't really need to be 'taught' in order to be understood and enjoyed.*"

"*I have scarcely heard his name mentioned in thirty years.*"

"*I read some Henry Miller many years ago, but have never assigned any of his works to a class. Actually, if you have any recommendations for reading/teaching, I'd be happy to pick him up again.*"

"*Miller was so influential, it's hard to think of his books not being taught, but the truth is I don't think they are, certainly not to my knowledge here at Stanford. Maybe that's not such a bad thing—to discover Miller is to feel oneself caught up in defiance, subversion, outrageous unrespectable frankness and revolutionary humor. Can you sustain these feelings if they are blessed by sober institutional authority? Is that not a sort of counter-subversion? Just a thought*" (*Tobias Wolff*).

Karl Orend, a noted Miller scholar who writes from Europe, took up the question of Miller's neglect by American academia in an essay published in *The Chronicle of Higher Education* (vol. 50, no. 18, January 2004) and titled "Making a Place for Henry Miller in the American Classroom." Orend addressed several of the politically charged explanations for Miller's ostracism—his alleged misogyny, argued by Kate Millett, defended by Norman Mailer; his anti-Semitism, easily refuted by his close relationships with Jews such as Bezalel Schatz, Ephraim Doner, and two of his wives, as well as by his oft-expressed admiration for Jewish writers and thinkers such as Isaac Bashevis Singer and Erich Gutkind, not to mention his fondness for the bread he found in Jewish delicatessens; the absence of "politically correct" ethnic themes and concerns for minority groups—Blacks, Asians, gays—now fashionable in academic circles. But beyond these rationales for dismissing Miller, Orend found a deeper explanation: that Miller was essentially a European writer largely ignored in America because of a fearful insularity rooted in America's cultural insecurity and terror of sexuality. "That colleges neglect Miller is due to a fundamental misunderstanding of his work and the context of his achievement. He was not, at heart, an American writer, but rather a European writer, heavily influenced by Hindu and Buddhist thought, as arguably were his predecessors Ralph Waldo Emerson and Walt Whitman."

I can't agree with Orend that Miller was not an American writer—nearly all of Miller's work is based on his experiences as an American living in America—but I do agree with him that it is fear of his message that, in effect, continues to censor him from American readers. Miller criticized America harshly and mocked its sexual mores, but he did this from the position of a man who deeply loved the "idea" of America, and felt that this idea, exemplified by Whitman, had been betrayed by the ruling political and business interests. America's reaction to Miller has been defensive, and continues to be. If you don't like the message, then destroy the messenger.

But there is another view of Miller's continuing exile, suggested in Tobias Wolff's response. That it is as it should be. Miller wrote for his own salvation and the salvation of readers who wanted to be saved—from emptiness, from spiritual death. Those readers find him, are nourished by him, and pass the message along. Perhaps Miller is favored to be excluded from the canon.

Miller wrote and had published over fifty books. His voluminous correspondence was collected in editions of letters to Emil Schnellock, Lawrence Durrell, Anaïs Nin, Wallace Fowlie, James Laughlin, J. Rives Childs, Joseph Delteil, Elmer Gertz, Brenda Venus, and Hoki Tokuda. His watercolors were exhibited in Paris, London, Stockholm, Tokyo, New York, Washington, DC, Chicago, Los Angeles, and Santa Barbara. They now are offered for sale by dealers for five figure sums. He appeared in films and was interviewed on television and radio and in numerous magazine articles. The censorship battles over his banned books shook the American legal system to its foundations and roiled public discourse.

How can America's great intellectual centers continue to neglect and ignore an artist who is so uniquely American, who gave himself so completely to his work, and who became such a powerful conduit of modern thought?

List of Institutions Surveyed

Alabama
        Auburn University
        University of Alabama – Birmingham
        University of Alabama – Tuscaloosa
Alaska
        University of Alaska – Anchorage
        University of Alaska – Fairbanks
Arizona
        Arizona State University
        University of Arizona
Arkansas
        Arkansas State University

University of Arkansas – Fayetteville
University of Arkansas – Little Rock
University of the Ozarks
California
         Cal Poly San Luis Obispo
         California State University – Bakersfield
         California State University – Channel Islands
         California State University – Chico
         California State University – Dominguez Hills
         California State University – East Bay
         California State University – Fresno
         California State University – Fullerton
         California State University – Long Beach
         California State University – Los Angeles
         California State University – Monterey Bay
         California State University – Northridge
         California State University – Sacramento
         California State University – San Bernardino
         California State University – San Marcos
         California State University – Stanislaus
         Occidental College
         San Diego State University
         San Francisco State University
         San Jose State University
         Sonoma State University
         Stanford University
         University of California – Berkeley
         University of California – Davis
         University of California – Irvine
         University of California – Los Angeles
         University of California – Riverside
         University of California – San Diego
         University of California – Santa Barbara
         University of California – Santa Cruz
         University of Southern California
Colorado
         Colorado State University
         University of Colorado – Boulder
Connecticut
         Connecticut College
         Trinity College

University of Connecticut
Wesleyan University
Yale University

Delaware

University of Delaware

Florida

Florida State University
University of Florida
University of Miami

Georgia

Georgia State University
Georgia University of Technology
University of Georgia

Hawaii

University of Hawaii – Hilo
University of Hawaii – Honolulu

Idaho

Boise State University
University of Idaho

Illinois

DePaul University
Marquette University
Northwestern University
Southern Illinois University – Carbondale
Southern Illinois University – Edwardsville
University of Chicago
University of Illinois – Chicago
University of Illinois – Urbana

Indiana

Ball State University
Notre Dame
Purdue University
Indiana State University
Indiana University

Iowa

Grinnell College
Iowa State University
University of Iowa

Kansas

Kansas State University
University of Kansas

Kentucky
  Morehead State University
  University of Kentucky
  University of Louisville
Louisiana
  Louisiana State University – Baton Rouge
  Louisiana State University – Shreveport
  Tulane University
  University of Louisiana
Maine
  Bates College
  Bowdoin College
  Colby College
  University of Maine
Maryland
  Goucher College
  Johns Hopkins University
  Loyola University Maryland
  University of Maryland – Baltimore County
  University of Maryland – College Park
Massachusetts
  Amherst College
  Boston College
  Boston University
  Harvard University
  Massachusetts Institute of Technology
  Mount Holyoke College
  Smith College
  Tufts University
  University of Massachusetts – Amherst
  University of Massachusetts – Boston
  University of Massachusetts – Lowell
Michigan
  Michigan State University
  University of Michigan
  Wayne State University
  Western Michigan University
Minnesota
  Carleton College
  University of Minnesota
Mississippi

Mississippi State University
University of Mississippi
University of Southern Mississippi

Missouri

Missouri State University
University of Missouri
Washington University

Montana

Montana State University
University of Montana

Nebraska

University of Nebraska – Lincoln
University of Nebraska – Omaha

Nevada

University of Nevada – Las Vegas
University of Nevada – Reno

New Hampshire

Dartmouth College
University of New Hampshire

New Jersey

Princeton University
Rutgers University – Camden
Rutgers University – New Brunswick
Seton Hall University

New Mexico

New Mexico State University
University of New Mexico

New York

Barnard College
City College of New York
Columbia University
Fordham University
SUNY – Albany
SUNY – Buffalo
SUNY – Stony Brook

North Carolina

Duke University
North Carolina State University
University of North Carolina – Chapel Hill
University of North Carolina – Charlotte
University of North Carolina – Greensboro

North Dakota
>   University of North Dakota

Ohio
>   Denison University
>   Kent State University
>   Kenyon College
>   Oberlin College
>   Miami University
>   Ohio State University
>   Ohio University
>   University of Cincinnati
>   University of Toledo
>   Wright State University

Oklahoma
>   Oklahoma State University
>   University of Oklahoma

Oregon
>   Oregon State University
>   University of Oregon

Pennsylvania
>   Bryn Mawr College
>   Bucknell University
>   Dickinson College
>   Haverford College
>   Lehigh University
>   Pennsylvania State University
>   Seton Hall University
>   University of Pennsylvania
>   University of Pittsburgh
>   Villanova University

Rhode Island
>   Brown University
>   University of Rhode Island

South Carolina
>   Clemson University
>   University of South Carolina

South Dakota
>   University of South Dakota

Tennessee
>   Vanderbilt University
>   University of Memphis

University of Tennessee – Chattanooga
University of Tennessee – Knoxville
Texas
Baylor University
Texas A&M
University of Texas
Utah
Boise State University
Brigham Young University
University of Utah
Vermont
Middlebury College
University of Vermont
Virginia
George Mason University
University of Richmond
University of Virginia
Washington & Lee University
Washington
University of Washington
Washington State University
West Virginia
West Virginia State University
Wisconsin
University of Wisconsin – Madison
University of Wisconsin – Milwaukee
Wyoming
University of Wyoming

ACKNOWLEDGMENTS

I am indebted to many people whose assistance, support, generosity, and encouragement strengthened my commitment to give readers a fresh perspective on Henry Miller. When I began the project in 2007, my first source was Lepska Warren, Miller's wife during the early years of his Big Sur adventure and mother of his children Valentine and Tony. Over the course of six months, she received me in her home in Santa Barbara and graciously answered my many questions about her life before, during, and after her marriage to Miller. I can only hope that I have followed her example for candor and fairness in my treatment of Miller. Valentine and Tony, who fiercely guard their father's reputation and legacy, challenged me to be truthful and accurate, and shared with me intimate details about their family life with Miller, Lepska, and Eve. Eve's sister Jane Howell read the finished manuscript and gave it her blessing, along with vital information about Eve's personal history. Toby Rowland-Jones of Big Sur arranged my interview with Bob Nash, one of Miller's neighbors and cronies on Partington Ridge, and then introduced me to Ada Banks, the current owner of Miller's former home. Ada gave me a tour of the house and served tea on the patio where Miller spent many hours with family and friends. I am grateful to them all.

Biographies of important historical and literary figures would be practically impossible to write without the curatorial and research services provided by libraries and their staffs. I did not fully appreciate how these professionals keep the flame of knowledge burning until

I wrote this book. I am obliged to many libraries and researchers in North America for their assistance in identifying, locating, and copying documents essential to a full and coherent narrative of Miller's life. Martha Davidson investigated the Huntington Cairns Papers at the Library of Congress and sent me key documents; Jean Cannon recovered Miller's correspondence to Barbara Sandford, Emil White, and Renate Gerhardt from the Harry Ransom Center, University of Texas at Austin; Shelley Cox retrieved Eve Miller's confessional and revealing letters from the Morris Library at Southern Illinois University, Carbondale; Lynn Shirey searched the New Directions records at the Houghton Library at Harvard University looking for correspondence from Lepska, Eve, and Miller. Additionally, I received valuable assistance from the library staffs at the University of Victoria, Southern Illinois University at Carbondale, Bowdoin College, the University of Chicago, Harvard University, the Library of Congress, the University of Mary Washington, and the Henry Miller Memorial Library in Big Sur (thank you, Keely and Magnus!). Without exception, these professionals offered help that was both cheerful and alert. I owe special thanks to Robert Montoya, Lilace Hatayama, and all the staff at the Special Collections Department, Charles E. Young Research Library, University of California at Los Angeles, where the bulk of Miller's papers as well as the papers of Anaïs Nin are housed. I could not have written *The Unknown Henry Miller* without their tireless assistance and interest.

For a first-time author, nothing is more welcome than encouragement and criticism from seasoned writers and readers who know and love literature. I was fortunate to have sat next to the well-known author Myra MacPherson at a dinner party in Palm Springs just as I was beginning my search for a publisher. Myra gave me valuable editorial feedback on my writing and then provided me with entrée to her literary agent, Dan Green. Will Schwalbe, the former editor-in-chief of Hyperion Books, shared with me his knowledge of the publishing world, recommended publishers I should approach, and opened doors for me. Robert Archer, a colleague from my early years as an English teacher whose taste and judgment I respect, gave the completed manuscript a close read and offered many astute comments about its style and structure. My friend Jonathan Wight gave me valuable legal advice on my publishing contract. My editor at Skyhorse/ Arcade, Cal Barksdale, has been from his first contact with my submission responsive, kind, and helpful in guiding me through the steps of the publishing process.

Finally, I wish to thank my companion of twenty-seven years, Mimi Baer, herself a lover of books, who encouraged me to write this biography, cheered me through the long process of research and composition, and rejoiced with me in the pleasure of its completion and publication.

1944–1947, edited and with a Preface by Gunther Stuhlmann. Copyright © 1971 by Anaïs Nin. Harcourt Brace Jovanovich, Publishers. From *The Diary of Anaïs Nin. Volume Five. 1947–1955*, edited and with a Preface by Gunther Stuhlmann. Copyright © 1974 by Anaïs Nin. Harcourt Brace Jovanovich, Publishers. From *The Diary of Anaïs Nin. Volume Six. 1955–1966*, edited and with a Preface by Gunther Stuhlmann. Copyright © 1966, 1976 by Anaïs Nin. Harcourt Brace Jovanovich, Publishers. From Miller-Anaïs Nin Correspondence. Anaïs Nin Papers. Special Collections Department, Charles E. Young Research Library. University of California, Los Angeles. All text extracts used with permission of the Anaïs Nin Trust. All rights reserved.

By James Laughlin, from PREVIOUSLY UNPUBLISHED MATERIAL, copyright © 2012 by New Directions Publishing Corp. Reprinted by permission of New Directions Publishing Corp. By Durrell-Miller, from THE DURRELL-MILLER LETTERS 1935–1980, copyright © 1963 by Lawrence Durrell and Henry Miller, copyright © 1988 by Barbara Sylvas Miller, Henry Tony Miller and Valentine Lepska Miller. Reprinted by permission of New Directions Publishing Corp. By Henry Miller, from ALLER RETOUR NEW YORK, copyright © 1991 by Barbara Sylvas Miller, Henry Tony Miller, and Valentine Miller, copyright © 1991 by New Directions Publishing Corp. Reprinted by permission of New Directions Publishing Corp. By Henry Miller, from BIG SUR AND THE ORANGES OF HIERONYMUS BOSCH, copyright © 1957 by new Directions Publishing Corp. Reprinted by permission of New Directions Publishing Corp. By Henry Miller, from LETTERS TO EMIL, copyright © 1944, 1945, 1950, 1968 by Henry Miller, copyright © 1989 by Barbara Sylvas Miller, Henry Tony Miller, and Valentine Lepska Miller, copyright © 1989 by George Wickes. Reprinted by permission of New Directions Publishing Corp. By Henry Miller, from REMEMBER TO REMEMBER, copyright © 1961 by Henry Miller. Reprinted by permission of New Directions Publishing Corp. By Henry Miller, from STAND STILL LIKE THE HUMMING-BIRD, copyright © 1962 by Henry Miller. Reprinted by permission of New Directions Publishing Corp. By Henry Miller, from SUNDAY AFTER THE WAR, copyright © 1944 by Henry Miller.

By Eve McClure Miller, from Letters to Lawrence Durrell, Letters to Vincent Birge, Letters to Roger Bloom. Lawrence Durrell Collection. Special Collections Research Center, Morris Library, Southern Illinois University Carbondale. Copyright © 2011 by Jane Howell. Reprinted by permission of Jane Howell. By Eve McClure Miller, Letters to Henry Miller, Letters to Lepska Verzeano, Letters to Bob Fink. Henry Miller Collection. Special Collections Department, Charles E. Young Research Library. University of California, Los Angeles. Copyright © 2011 by Jane Howell. Reprinted by permission of Jane Howell. By Eve McClure Miller, from Letters to Anaïs Nin. Anaïs Nin Papers. Special Collections Department, Charles E. Young Research Library. University of California, Los Angeles. Copyright © 2011 by Jane Howell. Reprinted by permission of Jane Howell. By Eve McClure Miller, from Letters to New Directions. New Directions Corp. Publishing Records. Houghton Library, Harvard University. Copyright © 2011 by Jane Howell. Reprinted by permission of Jane Howell.

By Henry Miller, Letters to Emil White. Harry Ransom Research Center, The University of Texas at Austin. Copyright © 2012 by George Boroczi, Henry Tony Miller, and Valentine Lepska Miller. Reprinted by permission of George Boroczi, Henry Tony Miller, and Valentine Lepska Miller. By Henry Miller, Letters to Barbara Sandford. Harry Ransom Research Center, The University of Texas at Austin. Copyright © 2012 by George Boroczi, Henry Tony Miller, and Valentine Lepska Miller. Reprinted by permission of George Boroczi, Henry Tony Miller, and Valentine Lepska Miller. Letters to Renate Gerhardt. Alexander Miller Collection. Harry Ransom Research Center, The University of Texas at Austin. Copyright © 2012 by George Boroczi, Henry Tony Miller, and Valentine Lepska Miller. Reprinted by permission of George Boroczi, Henry Tony Miller, and Valentine Lepska Miller.

By Henry Miller, from Huntington Cairns Papers. MSS 14746. Library of Congress, Washington, D.C. Copyright © 2012 by George Boroczi, Henry Tony Miller, and Valentine Lepska Miller. Reprinted by permission of George Boroczi, Henry Tony Miller, and Valentine Lepska Miller.

A NOTE ON SOURCES

MY ACCOUNT OF MILLER'S LIFE HAS BEEN BUILT UP PRIMARILY FROM
two sources: Miller's extensive correspondence with friends, family
members, admirers, lovers, wives, publishers, agents, and lawyers; and
Miller's own account of his life as it is presented in his autobiographical novels and essays. From these sources a portrait of Miller the man
and Miller the literary artist has emerged. I have also drawn from the
diaries of Anaïs Nin for insight into Miller's life-changing relationship with her. Extensive interviews with Miller's third wife Lepska
Warren provided valuable information about their life together in
Big Sur. Correspondence by Miller's fourth wife Eve McClure gives
added dimension to his domestic life during the Big Sur years. For
the chronological sequence of events in Miller's life I have relied
on Mary Dearborn's biography of Miller, *The Happiest Man Alive*,
published in 1991. An indispensable resource for Miller's publishing
history is *Henry Miller: A Bibliography of Primary Sources*, edited by
Roger Jackson and Lawrence Shifreen. Also of help to the researcher
tracking the critical reaction to Miller is Shifreen's *Henry Miller: A
Bibliography of Secondary Sources* (1979).

The bulk of Miller's correspondence is held by the Special
Collections Department at UCLA, which also holds the papers of
Anaïs Nin, as well as a small collection of Lawrence Durrell's papers.

A much larger collection of Durrell material that includes correspondence from Eve McClure can be found at the Special Collections Research Center, Southern Illinois University, Carbondale. Miller's letters to Roger Bloom can also be found there. Miller's letters to his Big Sur factotum Emil White are in the the Harry Ransom Center at the University of Texas as are his letters to his German editor and translator Renate Gerhardt as well as his letters to his daughter Barbara Sandford. Much of Miller's correspondence with Emil Schnellock, Anaïs Nin, Lawrence Durrell, James Laughlin, Wallace Fowlie, and Elmer Gertz has been published. These letters reveal the many facets of Miller's complex personality and testify to the extraordinary loyalty he received from his closest friends.

In documenting this book, I chose not to add note citations for specific references within sources but instead to list the sources used for each chapter. However, following are selected notes intended to supplement or explain some information given in the text.

NOTES

Chapter One
The Paris Years
1 **In the spring of 1939**: Miller dated his letter to Cairns April 30, 1939. He wrote in his own hand at the top, "Hunt! This is not for publication. For you personally. If I'm killed then OK.—do as you like. Henry."

Chapter Three
Adrift in America
47 **Another writing project**: The account of *Opus Pistorum* and Miller's relationship with Barnet Ruder and Gershon Legman is given extensive treatment by Roger Jackson in *Henry Miller: A Bibliography of Primary Sources*.

57 **Today I said to him**: Nin's diary entry is dated February 13, 1941. The passage quoted here was not included in her published diary of that year.

Chapter Four
Settling in Big Sur
77 **The Happy Rock**: Miller coined this image in a letter to Emil Schnellock written August 25, 1938: "You live like a happy rock in the midst of the ocean: you are fixed while everything about you is in turbulent motion."

Chapter Five
A Writer in Big Sur
92 **Miller's idol, the French writer Blaise Cendrars**: Cendrars's review appeared in the summer 1935 issue of *Orbes* under the title "Un écrivain américain nous est né." Miller was deeply touched when Cendrars visited him at his Villa Seurat studio after reading *Tropic of Cancer*.

92 **It is a flowing, swelling prose**: Orwell's swipe at "the flat cautious statements and snack-bar dialects that are now in fashion" may have been aimed at the clipped prose style of Ernest Hemingway, a writer Miller detested.

93 **But the existence of a body of favorable criticism**: The most sympathetic and penetrating critical responses to Miller were written during World War Two. In the 1960s, when his Paris books were issued in the United States and the feminist movement was building, he came under attack for being a misogynist because of his often degrading characterizations of women. No one seemed to notice that most of the men in his books, including his own persona, were equally degraded. The misogyny charge was leveled at Miller again in a "review" of Frederick Turner's *Henry Miller and the Making of "Tropic of Cancer"* that appeared in the January 29, 2012, issue of *The New York Times Book Review* under Jeanette Winterson's byline.

98 **In the essay "Of Art and the Future"**: One cannot help but wonder about Miller's reaction were he alive today to read news accounts of life in China and India, where the materialist values of capitalism are being eagerly absorbed by billions of people.

103 **"before hopping a boat to England"**: See "Via Dieppe-Newhaven" in *The Cosmological Eye* for Miller's account of the episode that soured him on the English.

Chapter Six
Marriage and Family

105 **Janina Martha Lepska:** Janina uses Lepska as her first name.

108 **I have a young wife**: Lepska was born on March 23, 1923.

116 **"anti-Semitic propagandist"**: The charge that Miller was anti-Semitic has been repeated numerous times, most recently by Jeanette Winterson in her "review" of Turner's book. To anyone familiar with the facts of Miller's life, the charge is ludicrous. Many of Miller's most intimate and trusted friends, lovers, and professional associates were Jews. A partial list: his second wife, June; his Paris cronies Michael Fraenkel and Walter Lowenfels; his French publishers Jack Kahane and Maurice Girodias; his French agent Michael Hoffman; his traveling companion Abraham Rattner; his close friend and factotum Emil White; his artistic collaborator and brother-in-law Bezalel Schatz; his Big Sur neighbor the artist Ephraim Doner;

the felon Roger Bloom; the attorney Elmer Gertz who defended *Tropic of Cancer* in the Illinois courts; Joe Gray; the Israeli starlet Ziva Rodann.

Chapter Seven
A Year of Crisis

138 **"Joey"**: Miller and Perlès used this nickname for each other. Joey was the name of one of Miller's close childhood friends in Brooklyn.

146 **"As though the chief object of existence were to forget"**: It is not hard to imagine Miller's disgust were he alive today to witness our mass addiction to all sorts of portable electronic devices that disengage us from ourselves and from the physical world around us.

149 **"a little self-governing community"**: The similarity between Miller's description of the Hedgerow Theatre and the compact for the government of America's first truly democratic community, Providence, Rhode Island, founded by the Puritan divine Roger Williams in 1636, is striking. Williams wrote, "We whose names are hereunder written, being desirous to inhabit the town of Providence, do promise to submit ourselves, in active or passive obedience, to all such orders or agreements as shall be made for public good of the body, in an orderly way, by the major consent of the present inhabitants, masters of families incorporated together into a township, and others whom they shall admit unto the same, *only in civil things* [i.e. without regard to religious beliefs]." The compact was signed by thirteen people who had followed Williams to Rhode Island to escape the tyranny of the Massachusetts Bay Colony. Miller's embrace of pure democracy is in a direct line of descent from Williams.

Chapter Eight
The Rosy Crucifixion

168 **hoping to cash in on the real estate boom**: The episode resulted in Miller's humiliation for sleeping on a bench in a public park, alluded to in *The Smile at the Foot of the Ladder*.

168 **Claude**: Unlike most characters in Miller's autobiographical books, Claude is entirely fictional, the voice of the enlightened Miller commenting retrospectively on his earlier self.

170 ***The Books in My Life***: A gateway into Miller's mind and values that can prepare the reader for the linguistic and sexual pyrotechnics of the Tropics, *Black Spring*, and *The Rosy Crucifixion*.

Chapter Nine
Europe Beckons

192 **a long letter of appreciation**: Hundreds of letters of appreciation from readers around the world may be found in the Henry Miller Collection at UCLA. Miller's writing had a profound effect on many people by bringing them to their own spiritual awakening. Some, like Alfred Perlès, Richard Osborn, Emil White, Bern Porter, George Leite, Judson Crews, Walker Winslow, and Vincent Birge, served him from a sense of devotion to his message and example. Others, like Joseph Janson of Chicago, sent him food and clothing during his years of poverty in Big Sur.

201 **"unconquerable in a spirit that *apparently yields* but in reality remains *unchangeable itself*"**: This image of Miller was captured in the metaphor "The Happy Rock," borrowed by Bern Porter for the title of his book of tributes to Miller.

206 **"the birth-chart as the life-chord of the individual being"**: Rudhyar's use of musical imagery derives from his background as a composer.

224 **"The Baxters, who had relocated to Scarsdale"**: Annette and Jim Baxter died in a fire at their Scarsdale summer home on September 18, 1983.

Chapter Ten
Farewell to Big Sur

249 **reunion dinners with Brassaï**: For an account of the Miller–Brassaï friendship, see Brassaï's *Henry Miller The Paris Years*. New York: Arcade Publishing, 1995.

259 **"Je t'aime bien . . . "**: *I love you very much. I look forward to seeing you—where, God knows better than I.*

Chapter Eleven
Celebrity

276 **"I let Rupert drive me . . ."**: Rupert Pole was Nin's second husband. However, she remained married to Hugo Guiler. She lived with Rupert on the West Coast, Hugo on the East Coast.

Chapter Twelve
The Henry Miller Legacy

295 **Bob Dylan**: In a March 1966 *Playboy* interview, Dylan said, "I like Henry Miller. I think he's the greatest American writer."

SOURCES

Chapter One
The Paris Years

Breton, André. *Surrealist Manifesto*, <http://en.wikipedia.org/wiki/Surrealism>.

Dearborn, Mary. *The Happiest Man Alive*. New York: Simon & Schuster, 1991.

Kahane, Jack. *Memoirs of a Booklegger*. London and New York: Michael Joseph, 1939.

Miller, Henry. *Aller Retour New York*. New York: New Directions, 1991.

———. *Black Spring*. New York: Grove Press, 1963.

———. *The Cosmological Eye*. New York: New Directions, 1939.

———. *Letters to Emil*. Edited by George Wickes. New York: New Directions, 1989.

———. *Tropic of Cancer*. New York: Grove Press, 1961.

———. *Tropic of Capricorn*. New York: Grove Press, 1961.

Miller–Huntington Cairns Correspondence. Huntington Cairns Papers. MSS. 14746 Library of Congress, Washington, DC.

Miller-Durrell Correspondence. Henry Miller Collection. Special Collections Department, Charles E. Young Research Library. University of California, Los Angeles.

Miller–Anaïs Nin Correspondence. Henry Miller Collection. Special Collections Department, Charles E. Young Research Library. University of California, Los Angeles.

Miller–Anaïs Nin Correspondence. Anaïs Nin Papers. Special Collections Department, Charles E. Young Research Library. University of California, Los Angeles.

Miller–Richard Osborn Correspondence. Henry Miller Collection. Special Collections Department, Charles E. Young Research Library. University of California, Los Angeles.

Miller–Emil Schnellock Correspondence. Henry Miller Collection. Special Collections Department, Charles E. Young Research Library. University of California, Los Angeles.

Shifreen, Lawrence, and Roger Jackson, eds. *Henry Miller: A Bibliography of Primary Sources*. Ann Arbor, MI: Roger Jackson; Glen Arm, MD: Lawrence Shifreen, 1993. Privately published.

Spingarn, Joel. "Huntington Cairns, Federal Censor," *The American Mercury*, vol. 69 (Summer 1949).

Stuhlmann, Gunther, ed. *Henry Miller. Letters to Anaïs Nin*. New York: G. P. Putnam's Sons, 1965.

———. *A Literate Passion. Letters of Anaïs Nin & Henry Miller 1932–1953*. San Diego; New York; London: Harcourt Brace, 1987.

Wickes, George, ed. *Henry Miller. Letters to Emil*. New York: New Directions, 1989.

———. *Lawrence Durrell & Henry Miller. A Private Correspondence*. New York: E. P. Dutton, 1964.

Chapter Two

Interlude in Greece

Dearborn, Mary. *The Happiest Man Alive*. New York: Simon & Schuster, 1991.

Miller, Henry. *The Colossus of Maroussi*. New York: New Directions, 1958.

Miller-Durrell Correspondence. Henry Miller Collection. Special Collections Department, Charles E. Young Research Library. University of California, Los Angeles.

Miller–Anaïs Nin Correspondence. Henry Miller Collection. Special Collections Department, Charles E. Young Research Library. University of California, Los Angeles.

Miller–Anaïs Nin Correspondence. Anaïs Nin Papers. Special Collections Department, Charles E. Young Research Library. University of California, Los Angeles.

Stuhlmann, Gunther, ed. *Henry Miller. Letters to Anaïs Nin*. New York: G. P. Putnam's Sons, 1965.

———. *A Literate Passion. Letters of Anaïs Nin & Henry Miller 1932–1953*. San Diego; New York; London: Harcourt Brace, 1987.

Wickes, George, ed. *Lawrence Durrell & Henry Miller. A Private Correspondence*. New York: E. P. Dutton, 1964.

Chapter Three
Adrift in America

Dearborn, Mary. *The Happiest Man Alive*. New York: Simon & Schuster, 1991.

Jackson, Roger. "*Opus Pistorum* and Henry Miller." *Henry Miller. A Bibliography of Primary Sources*. Lawrence J. Shifreen & Roger Jackson, eds. Ann Arbor, MI: Roger Jackson; Glen Arm, MD: Lawrence J. Shifreen, 1993. Privately published.

Laughlin, James. "Henry Miller," *We Moderns/Gotham Book Mart 1920–1940*. New York, Schoen, 1940.

Merrill, Knud. "All the Animals in the Zoo." *The Happy Rock*. Edited by Bern Porter. Berkeley: Packard Press, 1945.

Miller, Henry. *The Air-Conditioned Nightmare*. New York: New Directions, 1970.

———. "Another Open Letter," *New Republic* 109 (December 6, 1943).

———. Notebook of American Tour. Henry Miller Collection. Special Collections Department, Charles E. Young Research Library. University of California, Los Angeles.

———. "Reunion in Brooklyn." *Sunday After the War*. New York: New Directions, 1944.

———. *The Wisdom of the Heart*. New York: New Directions, 1941.

Miller–Huntington Cairns Correspondence. Huntington Cairns Papers. MSS. 14746. Library of Congress, Washington, DC.

Miller–Colt Press Correspondence. Henry Miller Collection. Special Collections Department, Charles E. Young Research Library. University of California, Los Angeles.

Miller–John Dudley Correspondence. Henry Miller Collection. Special Collections Department, Charles E. Young Research Library. University of California, Los Angeles.

Miller–Family Correspondence. Henry Miller Collection. Special Collections Department, Charles E. Young Research Library. University of California, Los Angeles.

Miller–Bernadine Fritz Correspondence. Bernadine Fritz Papers. Special Collections Department, Charles E. Young Research Library. University of California, Los Angeles.

Miller–Eleanor Howard Correspondence. George Howard Papers. Special Collections Department, Charles E. Young Research Library. University of California, Los Angeles.

Miller–Sevasty Koutsaftis Correspondence. Henry Miller Collection. Special Collections Department, Charles E. Young Research Library. University of California, Los Angeles.

Miller–James Laughlin Correspondence. Henry Miller Collection. Special Collections Department, Charles E.Young Research Library. University of California, Los Angeles.

Miller–Gilbert Neiman Correspondence. Henry Miller Collection. Special Collections Department, Charles E. Young Research Library. University of California, Los Angeles.

Miller–Anaïs Nin Correspondence. Anaïs Nin Diary. Anaïs Nin Papers. Special Collections Department, Charles E. Young Research Library. University of California, Los Angeles.

Miller–Abe Rattner Correspondence. Henry Miller Collection. Special Collections Department, Charles E.Young Research Library. University of California, Los Angeles.

Miller–Emil Schnellock Correspondence. Henry Miller Collection. Special Collections Department, Charles E.Young Research Library. University of California, Los Angeles.

Miller–John Slocum Correspondence. Henry Miller Collection. Special Collections Department, Charles E.Young Research Library. University of California, Los Angeles.

Stuhlmann, Gunther, ed. *Henry Miller. Letters to Anaïs Nin.* New York: G. P. Putnam's Sons, 1965.

———. *A Literate Passion. Letters of Anaïs Nin & Henry Miller 1932–1953.* San Diego; New York; London: Harcourt Brace, 1987.

Wickes, George, ed. *Henry Miller and James Laughlin. Selected Letters.* New York; London: W. W. Norton, 1996.

Widmer, Kingsley. *Henry Miller.* New York: Twayne Publishers, 1963.

Chapter Four
Settling in Big Sur

Anderson, Wendell. *Judson Crews and His Poetry.* Carson, CA: Dumont Press, 1994.

Crews, Judson. *The Brave Wild Coast. A Year with Henry Miller.* Los Angeles: Dumont Press, 1997.

Henson, Paul and Usner, Donald. *The Natural History of Big Sur.* Berkeley: University of California Press, 1993.

Humphrey, Joanne Fenton. *Emil White of Big Sur.* Chagrin Falls, OH: Windjammer Adventure Publishing, 1997.

Miller, Henry. *Black Spring.* New York: Grove Press, 1963.

———. "Another Open Letter," *New Republic,* 19 (December 6, 1943).

———. "A Preface to *The Stranger*," *What's Doing,* III (May 1948).

———. *Reflections.* Twinka Thiebaud, ed. Santa Barbara, CA: Capra Press, 1981.

Miller–Huntington Cairns Correspondence. Huntington Cairns Papers. MSS. 14746. Library of Congress. Washington, DC.

Miller, Henry, and Fowlie, Wallace. *Letters of Henry Miller and Wallace Fowlie (1943–1972)*. New York: Grove Press, Inc., 1975.

Miller–Wallace Fowlie Correspondence. Henry Miller Collection. Special Collections Department, Charles E. Young Research Library. University of California, Los Angeles.

Miller–Harry Herschkowitz Correspondence. Henry Miller Collection. Special Collections Department, Charles E. Young Research Library. University of California, Los Angeles.

Miller–June Lancaster Correspondence. Henry Miller Collection. Special Collections Department, Charles E. Young Research Library. University of California, Los Angeles.

Miller–George Leite Correspondence. Henry Miller Collection. Special Collections Department, Charles E. Young Research Library. University of California, Los Angeles.

Miller–New Directions Correspondence. Henry Miller Collection. Special Collections Department, Charles E. Young Research Library. University of California, Los Angeles.

Miller–Anaïs Nin Correspondence. Anaïs Nin Papers. Special Collections Department, Charles E. Young Research Library. University of California, Los Angeles.

Miller–Anaïs Nin Correspondence. Henry Miller Collection. Special Collections Department, Charles E. Young Research Library. University of California, Los Angeles.

Miller–Bern Porter Correspondence. Henry Miller Collection. Special Collections Department, Charles E. Young Research Library. University of California, Los Angeles.

Miller–Emil White Correspondence. Henry Miller Collection. Special Collections Department, Charles E. Young Research Library. University of California, Los Angeles.

Norman, Jeff. *Images of America: Big Sur*. San Francisco, CA: Arcadia Publishing, 2004.

Porter, Bern. Interview by Phil Nurenberg. *Bern Porter: His Experiences with Henry Miller, Albert Einstein* . . . Ellensburg, WA: Vagabond Press, [1983?].

Schevill, James. *Where to Go, What to Do, When You Are Bern Porter*. Gardiner, ME: Tilbury House Publishers, 1992.

Stuhlmann, Gunther, ed. *Henry Miller. Letters to Anaïs Nin*. New York: G. P. Putnam's Sons, 1965.

———. *A Literate Passion. Letters of Anaïs Nin & Henry Miller 1932–1953*. San Diego; New York; London: Harcourt Brace, 1987.

Wall, Rosalind Sharpe. *A Wild Coast and Lonely. Big Sur Pioneers*. San Carlos, CA: Wide World Publishing/Tetra, 1989.

Wickes, George, ed. *Henry Miller and James Laughlin. Selected Letters*. New York; London: W. W. Norton, 1996.

Chapter Five
A Writer in Big Sur

Cendrars, Blaise. "Un Écrivain américain nous est né," *Orbes*, Summer 1935.

Chiaromonte, Nicola. "The Return of Henry Miller," *New Republic*, 3 (December 4, 1944).

Dearborn, Mary. *The Happiest Man Alive*. New York: Simon & Schuster, 1991.

Fowlie, Wallace. "Shadow of Doom: An Essay on Henry Miller," *Accent*, 5 (Autumn 1944).

Kazin, Alfred. *On Native Grounds: An Interpretation of Modern American Prose Literature*. Cornwall, N.Y.: Cornwall Press, 1942.

Miller, Henry. "Murder the Murderer." *Remember to Remember*. New York: New Directions, 1961.

——. *Sunday After the War*. New York: New Directions, 1944.

Miller, Henry, and Fowlie, Wallace. *Letters of Henry Miller and Wallace Fowlie (1943–1972)*. New York: Grove Press, 1975.

Miller–Huntington Cairns Correspondence. Huntington Cairns Papers. MSS. 14746. Library of Congress, Washington, DC.

Miller–Caresse Crosby Correspondence. Henry Miller Collection. Special Collections Department, Charles E. Young Research Library. University of California, Los Angeles.

Miller-Durrell Correspondence. Henry Miller Collection. Special Collections Department, Charles E. Young Research Library. University of California, Los Angeles.

Miller–Wallace Fowlie Correspondence. Henry Miller Collection. Special Collections Department, Charles E. Young Research Library. University of California, Los Angeles.

Miller–George Leite Correspondence. Henry Miller Collection. Special Collections Department, Charles E. Young Research Library. University of California, Los Angeles.

Miller–New Directions Correspondence. Henry Miller Collection. Special Collections Department, Charles E. Young Research Library. University of California, Los Angeles.

Miller–Bern Porter Correspondence. Henry Miller Collection. Special Collections Department, Charles E. Young Research Library. University of California, Los Angeles.

Miller–Lawrence Powell Correspondence. Henry Miller Collection. Special Collections Department, Charles E. Young Research Library. University of California, Los Angeles.

Miller–Emil Schnellock Correspondence. Henry Miller Collection. Special Collections Department, Charles E. Young Research Library. University of California, Los Angeles.

Miller–John Slocum Correspondence. Henry Miller Collection. Special Collections Department, Charles E. Young Research Library. University of California, Los Angeles.

Miller–Emil White Correspondence. Henry Miller Collection. Special Collections Department, Charles E. Young Research Library. University of California, Los Angeles.

Moore, Nicholas. *Henry Miller.* London: Opus Press, 1943.

Muller, Herbert J. "The World of Henry Miller," *Henry Miller and the Critics.* Edited by George Wickes. Carbondale and Edwardsville: Southern Illinois University Press, 1963.

Orwell, George. "Inside the Whale." *Henry Miller and the Critics.* Edited by George Wickes. Carbondale and Edwardsville: Southern Illinois University Press, 1963.

Rahv, Philip. "The Artist as Desperado," *New Republic* 104 (April 21, 1941).

Read, Herbert. "Henry Miller." *Henry Miller and the Critics.* Edited by George Wickes. Carbondale and Edwardsville: Southern Illinois University Press, 1963.

Rosenfeld, Paul. "The Traditions and Henry Miller," *Nation* 149 (November 4, 1939).

Wickes, George, ed. *Henry Miller and James Laughlin. Selected Letters.* New York; London: W. W. Norton, 1996.

———. *Lawrence Durrell & Henry Miller. A Private Correspondence.* New York: E. P. Dutton, 1964.

Wilson, Edmund. "Sunday After the War," *The New Yorker* 20 (October 21, 1944).

———. "Twilight of the Expatriates," *New Republic* 94 (March 9, 1938).

Chapter Six
Marriage and Family

Dearborn, Mary. *The Happiest Man Alive.* New York: Simon & Schuster, 1991.

Federal Bureau of Investigation. "Henry Miller." File #14106 MEM. May 1, 1945.

"Kahn, Albert E.," *Contemporary Authors*. Volume 118. Detroit: Gale Research, 1981.

Kahn, Albert. "Odyssey of a Stool-Pigeon," *New Currents* 3 (January 1945).

Miller, Henry. "Quest." *Books Tangent To Circle*. Waldwick, NJ: Bern Porter, 1959.

———. "Obscenity and the Law of Reflection." *Remember to Remember*. New York: New Directions, 1961.

———. *Semblance of a Devoted Past*. Berkeley: Bern Porter, 1945.

———. *The Time of the Assassins*. New York: New Directions, 1962.

Miller–George Dibbern Correspondence. Henry Miller Collection. Special Collections Department, Charles E. Young Research Library. University of California, Los Angeles.

Miller–Huntington Cairns Correspondence. Huntington Cairns Papers. MSS. 14746. Library of Congress, Washington, DC.

Miller–Judson Crews Correspondence. Henry Miller Collection. Special Collections Department, Charles E. Young Research Library. University of California, Los Angeles.

Miller–Durrell Correspondence. Henry Miller Collection. Special Collections Department, Charles E. Young Research Library. University of California, Los Angeles.

Miller, Henry and Fowlie, Wallace. *Letters of Henry Miller and Wallace Fowlie (1943–1972)*. New York: Grove Press, 1975.

Miller–Wallace Fowlie Correspondence. Henry Miller Collection. Special Collections Department, Charles E. Young Research Library. University of California, Los Angeles.

Miller–Michael Hoffman Correspondence. Henry Miller Collection. Special Collections Department, Charles E. Young Research Library. University of California, Los Angeles.

Miller–George Leite Correspondence. Henry Miller Collection. Special Collections Department, Charles E. Young Research Library. University of California, Los Angeles.

Miller–New Directions Correspondence. Henry Miller Collection. Special Collections Department, Charles E. Young Research Library. University of California, Los Angeles.

Miller–Alfred Perlès Correspondence. Henry Miller Collection. Special Collections Department, Charles E. Young Research Library. University of California, Los Angeles.

Miller–Bern Porter Correspondence. Henry Miller Collection. Special Collections Department, Charles E. Young Research Library. University of California, Los Angeles.

Miller–Lawrence Powell Correspondence. Henry Miller Collection. Special Collections Department, Charles E. Young Research Library. University of California, Los Angeles.

Miller–Russell & Volkening Correspondence. Henry Miller Collection. Special Collections Department, Charles E. Young Research Library. University of California, Los Angeles.

Miller–Emil Schnellock Correspondence. Henry Miller Collection. Special Collections Department, Charles E. Young Research Library. University of California, Los Angeles.

Miller–Paul Weiss Correspondence. Henry Miller Collection. Special Collections Department, Charles E. Young Research Library. University of California, Los Angeles.

Pucciani, Oreste. Letter to Lawrence Clark Powell. November 8, 1949. MS. Henry Miller Collection. Special Collections Department, Charles E. Young Research Library. University of California, Los Angeles.

Senate Committee on the Judiciary. *Communist Activity in Mass Communications. Hearings Before the Subcommittee to Investigate the Administration of the Internal Security Act.* Eighty-Fifth Congress, second session. Washington: US Government. Printing Office, 1958–59.

Shifreen, Lawrence, and Roger Jackson, eds. *Henry Miller: A Bibliography of Primary Sources.* Ann Arbor, MI; Glen Arm, MD: Roger Jackson and Lawrence Shifreen, 1993. Privately published.

Stuhlmann, Gunther, ed. *Henry Miller. Letters to Anaïs Nin.* New York: G. P. Putnam's Sons, 1965.

———. *A Literate Passion. Letters of Anaïs Nin & Henry Miller 1932–1953.* San Diego; New York; London: Harcourt Brace & Company, 1987.

Warren, Lepska. Interview by Arthur Hoyle. Santa Barbara, California. December 1, 2007–July 5, 2008.

Wickes, George, ed. *Lawrence Durrell & Henry Miller. A Private Correspondence.* New York: E. P. Dutton, Inc., 1964.

———. *Henry Miller and James Laughlin. Selected Letters.* New York; London: W. W. Norton, 1996.

———. *Henry Miller. Letters To Emil.* New York: New Directions, 1989.

Chapter Seven
A Year of Crisis

Baradinsky, Oscar, ed. *Of, By and About Henry Miller.* New York: Alicat Bookshop Press, 1947.

Brady, Mildred. "The New Cult of Sex and Anarchy," *Harper's* 194 (April 1947).

Chafee, Zechariah, Jr. *Government and Mass Communications*, vol. 1. Chicago: University of Chicago Press, 1947.

Bufano, Beniamino. "Genesis of the Night Life," *What's Doing*, [June–July 1947].

Fowlie, Wallace. "Shadow of Doom: An Essay on Henry Miller," *Accent* 5 (Autumn 1944).

Freemantle, Anne. "Expatriate's End," *Commonweal* 47 (December 12, 1947).

Glicksberg, Charles I. "A Milder Miller," *Southwest Review* 33 (Summer 1948).

Jackson, J. H. "The Last Expatriate," *Time* 51 (June 28, 1948).

Miller, Henry. *A Devil in Paradise*. New York: New Directions, 1956.

———. *Remember to Remember*. New York: New Directions, 1961.

———. *The Smile at the Foot of the Ladder*. New York: New Directions, 1974.

Miller–Huntington Cairns Correspondence. Huntington Cairns Papers. MSS. 14746. Library of Congress, Washington, DC.

Miller–June Corbett Correspondence. Henry Miller Collection. Special Collections Department, Charles E. Young Research Library. University of California, Los Angeles.

Miller–George Dibbern Correspondence. Henry Miller Collection. Special Collections Department, Charles E. Young Research Library. University of California, Los Angeles.

Miller-Durrell Correspondence. Henry Miller Collection. Special Collections Department, Charles E. Young Research Library. University of California, Los Angeles.

Miller–Michael Hoffman Correspondence. Henry Miller Collection. Special Collections Department, Charles E. Young Research Library. University of California, Los Angeles.

Miller–George Leite Correspondence. Henry Miller Collection. Special Collections Department, Charles E. Young Research Library. University of California, Los Angeles.

Miller–New Directions Correspondence. Henry Miller Collection. Special Collections Department, Charles E. Young Research Library. University of California, Los Angeles.

Miller-Nin Correspondence. Henry Miller Collection. Special Collections Department, Charles E. Young Research Library. University of California, Los Angeles.

Miller-Nin Correspondence. Anaïs Nin Papers. Special Collections Department, Charles E. Young Research Library. University of California, Los Angeles.

Miller–Alfred Perlès Correspondence. Henry Miller Collection. Special Collections Department, Charles E.Young Research Library. University of California, Los Angeles.

Miller–Emil Schnellock Correspondence. Henry Miller Collection. Special Collections Department, Charles E.Young Research Library. University of California, Los Angeles.

Miller–Irving Stettner Correspondence. Henry Miller Collection. Special Collections Department, Charles E.Young Research Library. University of California, Los Angeles.

Miller–Alan Watts Correspondence. Henry Miller Collection. Special Collections Department, Charles E.Young Research Library. University of California, Los Angeles.

Miller–Walker Winslow Correspondence. Henry Miller Collection. Special Collections Department, Charles E.Young Research Library. University of California, Los Angeles.

Mosher, Clint. "Group Establishes Cult of Hatred in Carmel Mountains," *San Francisco Examiner* 186 (May 3[4?], 1947).

———. "Emma Goldman Inspired Carmel Hate Cult Chief," *San Francisco Examiner* 156 (May 5, 1947).

———. " 'Colony of Hate' Barker an Important Figure," *San Francisco Examiner* 156 (May 6, 1947).

———. "Carmel Shuts Its Doors to Miller Cult," *San Francisco Examiner* 156 (May 7, 1947).

Nin, Anaïs. *The Diary of Anaïs Nin. Vol. 4, 1944–1947*, Edited by Gunther Stuhlmann. New York: Swallow Press, 1966–1980.

Orend, Karl. *The Brotherhood of Fools and Simpletons*. Paris: Alyscamps Press, 2005.

Rolo, Charles J. "Notes on the avant-garde," *Tomorrow* 7 (March 1948).

Smith, Harrison. "The New Coast of Bohemia," *Saturday Review* 30 (August 16, 1947).

Stettner, Irving. *Beggars in Paradise*. Paris; London: Stroker-Carrefour Alyscamps, 1995.

Stuhlmann, Gunther, ed. *A Literate Passion. Letters of Anaïs Nin & Henry Miller 1932–1953*. San Diego; New York; London: Harcourt Brace, 1987.

Warren, Lepska. Interview by Arthur Hoyle. Santa Barbara, California. December 1, 2007–July 5, 2008.

West, Herbert Faulkner. "The Strange Case of Henry Miller." In Herbert Faulkner West, ed., *The Mind on the Wing: A Book for Readers and Collectors*. New York: Coward-McCann, 1947.

Wickes, George, ed. *Henry Miller and James Laughlin*. New York; London: W. W. Norton, 1996.

Chapter Eight
The Rosy Crucifixion

Besig v. United States. No. 13227. United States Court of Appeals, Ninth Circuit. October 23, 1953.

Durrell, Lawrence. "Studies in Genius:VIII–Henry Miller," *Horizon* 20 (July 1949).

Miller, Henry. *Big Sur and the Oranges of Hieronymus Bosch*. New York: New Directions, 1957.

———. *The Books in My Life*. New York: New Directions, 1969.

———. *Plexus*. New York: Grove Press, 1965.

———. *Sexus*. New York: Grove Press, 1965.

Miller–Durrell Correspondence. Henry Miller Collection. Special Collections Department, Charles E. Young Research Library. University of California, Los Angeles.

Miller, Henry and Fowlie, Wallace. *Letters of Henry Miller and Wallace Fowlie (1943–1972)*. New York: Grove Press, 1975.

Miller–Huntington Cairns Correspondence. Huntington Cairns Papers. MSS.14746. Library of Congress, Washington, DC.

Miller–Wallace Fowlie Correspondence. Henry Miller Collection. Special Collections Department, Charles E.Young Research Library. University of California, Los Angeles.

Miller–Michael Hoffman Correspondence. Henry Miller Collection. Special Collections Department, Charles E. Young Research Library. University of California, Los Angeles.

Miller–Pierre Lesdain Correspondence. Henry Miller Collection. Special Collections Department, Charles E.Young Research Library. University of California, Los Angeles.

Miller–New Directions Correspondence. Henry Miller Collection. Special Collections Department, Charles E.Young Research Library. University of California, Los Angeles.

Miller–George Olshausen Correspondence. Henry Miller Collection. Special Collections Department, Charles E.Young Research Library. University of California, Los Angeles.

Miller–Alfred Perlès Correspondence. Henry Miller Collection. Special Collections Department, Charles E. Young Research Library. University of California, Los Angeles.

Miller–Lawrence Powell Correspondence. Henry Miller Collection. Special Collections Department, Charles E.Young Research Library. University of California, Los Angeles.

Miller–Walker Winslow Correspondence. Henry Miller Collection. Special Collections Department, Charles E. Young Research Library. University of California, Los Angeles.

Saroyan, Chesley. "*The Rosy Crucifixion*: A Review," *Points*, October–November 1949.

United States v. Two Obscene Books. No. 25449. United States District Court for the Northern District of California, Southern Division. September 17, 1951.

Warren, Lepska. Interview by Arthur Hoyle. Santa Barbara, California. December 1, 2007–July 5, 2008.

Wickes, George, ed. *Lawrence Durrell & Henry Miller. A Private Correspondence.* New York: E. P. Dutton, Inc., 1964.

———. *Henry Miller and James Laughlin. Selected Letters.* New York; London: W. W. Norton, 1996.

Chapter Nine
Europe Beckons

Annette Baxter–Miller Correspondence. Henry Miller Collection. Special Collections Department, Charles E. Young Research Library. University of California, Los Angeles.

Roger Bloom–Miller Correspondence. Henry Miller Collection. Special Collections Department, Charles E. Young Research Library. University of California, Los Angeles.

Carter, Frederick. *Symbols of Revelation.* London: A. Fitzadam, [1931?].

Dearborn, Mary. *The Happiest Man Alive.* New York: Simon & Schuster, 1991.

Durrell, Lawrence, ed. *The Henry Miller Reader.* New York: New Directions, 1959.

Fitzpatrick, Elayne Wareing. *Doing It With the Cosmos. Henry Miller's Big Sur Struggle for Love Beyond Sex.* Xlibris Corporation, 2001.

Michael Fraenkel–Miller Correspondence. Henry Miller Collection. Special Collections Department, Charles E. Young Research Library. University of California, Los Angeles.

Howell, Jane. Email interview by Arthur Hoyle. May 17, 2010–July 17, 2010.

MacNiven, Ian, ed. *The Durrell-Miller Letters, 1935–80.* New York: New Directions, 1988.

Maillet, Albert. "Henry Miller, Superman and Prophet." *Henry Miller: Between Heaven and Hell.* Edited by Emil White. Big Sur, CA: Emil White, 1961. Privately printed.

Eve Miller–Vincent Birge Correspondence. Vincent Birge Papers. Special Collections Research Center. Southern Illinois University, Carbondale.

Eve Miller–Durrell Correspondence. Lawrence Durrell Collection. Special Collections Research Center. Southern Illinois University, Carbondale.

Eve Miller–Anaïs Nin Correspondence. Anaïs Nin Papers. Special Collections Department, Charles E. Young Research Library. University of California, Los Angeles.

Eve Miller–Vincent Birge Correspondence. Lawrence Durrell Collection. Special Collections Research Center. Southern Illinois University, Carbondale.

Miller, Henry. *Big Sur and the Oranges of Hieronymus Bosch*. New York: New Directions, 1957.

———. "Four Letters of Henry Miller to Count Keyserling," *International Henry Miller Letter*, No. 5 (August 1963).

———. "The Hour of Man." *Stand Still Like the Hummingbird*. New York: New Directions, 1962.

———. *My Life and Times*. New York: Playboy Press, 1972.

———. "Reunion in Barcelona." *The Intimate Henry Miller*. New York: New American Library, 1959.

———. *Sextet*. Santa Barbara: Capra Press, 1977.

———. *Tropic of Capricorn*. New York: Grove Press, 1961.

Miller–Vincent Birge Correspondence. Henry Miller Collection. Special Collections Department, Charles E. Young Research Library. University of California, Los Angeles.

Miller–Roger Bloom Correspondence. Roger Bloom Collection. Special Collections Research Center. Southern Illinois University, Carbondale.

Miller–Caresse Crosby Correspondence. Henry Miller Collection. Special Collections Department, Charles E. Young Research Library. University of California, Los Angeles.

Miller–George Dibbern Correspondence. Henry Miller Collection. Special Collections Department, Charles E. Young Research Library. University of California, Los Angeles.

Miller–Durrell Correspondence. Henry Miller Collection. Special Collections Department, Charles E. Young Research Library. University of California, Los Angeles.

Miller–Giles Healey Correspondence. Henry Miller Collection. Special Collections Department, Charles E. Young Research Library. University of California, Los Angeles.

Miller–Trygve Hirsch Correspondence. Henry Miller Collection. Special Collections Department, Charles E. Young Research Library. University of California, Los Angeles.

Miller–Michael Hoffman Correspondence. Henry Miller Collection. Special Collections Department, Charles E. Young Research Library. University of California, Los Angeles.

Miller–June Lancaster Correspondence. Henry Miller Collection. Special Collections Department, Charles E. Young Research Library. University of California, Los Angeles.

Miller–Albert Maillet Correspondence. Henry Miller Collection. Special Collections Department, Charles E. Young Research Library. University of California, Los Angeles.

Miller–New Directions Correspondence. Henry Miller Collection. Special Collections Department, Charles E. Young Research Library. University of California, Los Angeles.

Miller–Nin Correspondence. Henry Miller Collection. University of California, Los Angeles.

Miller–Alfred Perlès Correspondence. Henry Miller Collection. Special Collections Department, Charles E. Young Research Library. University of California, Los Angeles.

Miller–Alfred Perlès Correspondence. Anaïs Nin Papers. Special Collections Department, Charles E. Young Research Library. University of California, Los Angeles.

Miller–Powys Correspondence. Henry Miller Collection. Special Collections Department, Charles E. Young Research Library. University of California, Los Angeles.

Miller–Barbara Sandford Correspondence. Henry Miller Collection. University of California, Los Angeles.

Miller–Barbara Sandford Correspondence. Barbara Sandford Collection. Harry Ransom Center. University of Texas, Austin.

Miller–Bezalel Schatz Correspondence. Henry Miller Collection. Special Collections Department, Charles E. Young Research Library. University of California, Los Angeles.

Miller–Edward Schwartz Correspondence. Henry Miller Collection. Special Collections Department, Charles E. Young Research Library. University of California, Los Angeles.

Miller–Jean Wharton Correspondence. Henry Miller Collection. Special Collections Department, Charles E. Young Research Library. University of California, Los Angeles.

Miller–Emil White Correspondence. Emil White Correspondence. Harry Ransom Center. University of Texas, Austin.

Nin, Anaïs. *The Diary of Anaïs Nin*. Edited and with an introduction by Gunther Stuhlmann. Vol. 5. New York: Swallow Press, 1966–1980.

Nin, Anaïs. *The Diary of Anaïs Nin*. Edited and with an introduction by Gunther Stuhlmann. Vol. 6. New York: Swallow Press, 1966–1980.

Omarr, Sydney. *Henry Miller: His World of Urania*. London: Villiers Publications, 1960.

Sydney Omarr–Miller Correspondence. Henry Miller Collection. Special Collections Department, Charles E. Young Research Library. University of California, Los Angeles.

Perlès, Alfred. *Art and Outrage. A Correspondence about Henry Miller between Alfred Perlès and Lawrence Durrell/with an intermission by Henry Miller*. London: Village Press, 1973.

———. *My Friend Henry Miller*. New York: John Day Company, 1956.

Dane Rudhyar–Miller Correspondence. Henry Miller Collection. Special Collections Department, Charles E. Young Research Library. University of California, Los Angeles.

Rudhyar, Dane. *The Astrology of Personality; a reformulation of astrological concepts and ideals, in terms of contemporary psychology and philosophy*. The Hague: Servire/Wassenaar, 1963.

———. Untitled essay, September 10, 1955. Rudhyar–Miller Correspondence. Henry Miller Collection, University of California, Los Angeles.

Wickes, George, ed. *Lawrence Durrell & Henry Miller. A Private Correspondence*. New York: E. P. Dutton, 1964.

———. *Henry Miller and James Laughlin. Selected Letters*. New York; London: W. W. Norton, 1996.

Chapter 10
Farewell to Big Sur

Birge, Vincent. "Travels with Henry: Searching for Shangri-La." *Henry Miller: A Book of Tributes*. Edited by Craig Standish. Orlando, FL: Standish-Books, a Division of C.P.S., INK., 1994

Fitzpatrick, Elayne Waring. *Doing It With the Cosmos. Henry Miller's Big Sur Struggle for Love Beyond Sex*. Xlibris Corporation, 2001.

Gerhardt-Miller Correspondence. Henry Miller Collection. Special Collections Department, Charles E. Young Research Library. University of California, Los Angeles.

Gertz, Elmer, and Felice Flannery Lewis, eds. *Henry Miller: Years of Trial and Triumph, 1962–1964. The Correspondence of Henry Miller and Elmer Gertz*. Carbondale: Southern Illinois University Press, 1978.

Howell, Jane. Email interviews by Arthur Hoyle. May 17, 2010–July 16, 2010.

MacNiven, Ian, ed. *The Durrell-Miller Letters, 1935–1980*. New York: New Directions, 1988.

Eve Miller–Durrell Correspondence. Lawrence Durrell Collection. Special Collections Research Center. Southern Illinois University, Carbondale.

Eve Miller–New Directions Correspondence. New Directions Corp. Publishing Records. Houghton Library, Harvard University.

Eve Miller–Nin Correspondence. Anaïs Nin Papers. Special Collections Department, Charles E. Young Research Library. University of California, Los Angeles.

Miller, Henry. *The Colossus of Maroussi*. New York: New Directions, 1941.

———. *Joey. Volume III Book of Friends*. Santa Barbara, CA: Capra Press, 1979.

———. *Nexus*. New York: Grove Press, 1965

Miller–Vincent Birge Correspondence. Henry Miller Collection. Special Collections Department, Charles E. Young Research Library. University of California, Los Angeles.

Miller-Durrell Correspondence. Henry Miller Collection. Special Collections Department, Charles E. Young Research Library. University of California, Los Angeles.

Miller-Gerhardt Correspondence. Alexander B. Miller Collection. Harry Ransom Center. University of Texas, Austin.

Miller–Grove Press Correspondence. Henry Miller Collection. Special Collections Department, Charles E. Young Research Library. University of California, Los Angeles.

Miller–Eve Miller Correspondence. Henry Miller Collection. Special Collections Department, Charles E. Young Research Library. University of California, Los Angeles.

Miller–New Directions Correspondence. Henry Miller Collection. Special Collections Department, Charles E. Young Research Library. University of California, Los Angeles.

Miller–Gerald Robitaille Correspondence. Henry Miller Collection. Special Collections Department, Charles E. Young Research Library. University of California, Los Angeles.

Miller–Emil White Correspondence. Emil White Correspondence. Harry Ransom Center. University of Texas, Austin.

Alfred Perlès–Miller Correspondence. Henry Miller Collection. Special Collections Department, Charles E. Young Research Library. University of California, Los Angeles.

Wickes, George, ed. *Lawrence Durrell & Henry Miller. A Private Correspondence*. New York: E. P. Dutton, 1964.

———. *Henry Miller and James Laughlin. Selected Letters*. New York; London: W. W. Norton 1996.

Chapter 11
Celebrity

Miller–Roger Bloom Correspondence. Henry Miller Collection. Special Collections Department, Charles E. Young Research Library. University of California, Los Angeles.

Bonn, Thomas. *Heavy Traffic and High Culture: New American Library as Literary Gatekeeper in the Paperback Revolution*. Carbondale: Southern Illinois University Press, 1989.

———. *Undercover: An Illustrated History of Mass Market Paperbacks*. New York: Penguin Books, 1982.

Dearborn, Mary. *The Happiest Man Alive*. New York: Simon & Schuster, 1991.

Gerhardt-Miller Correspondence. Henry Miller Collection. Special Collections Department, Charles E. Young Research Library. University of California, Los Angeles.

Gertz, Elmer, and Felice Flannery Lewis, eds. *Henry Miller: Years of Trial and Triumph, 1962–1964. The Correspondence of Henry Miller and Elmer Gertz*. Carbondale: Southern Illinois University Press, 1978.

Hutchinson, E. R. *Tropic of Cancer on Trial: A Case History of Censorship*. New York: Grove Press, 1968.

MacNiven, Ian, ed. *The Durrell-Miller Letters, 1935–1980*. New York: New Directions, 1988.

Miller, Henry. *Joey*. Vol. III, *Book of Friends*. Santa Barbara, CA: Capra Press, 1979.

Miller–Georges Belmont Correspondence. Henry Miller Collection. Special Collections Department, Charles E. Young Research Library. University of California, Los Angeles.

Miller-Durrell Correspondence. Henry Miller Collection. Special Collections Department, Charles E. Young Research Library. University of California, Los Angeles.

Miller-Gerhardt Correspondence. Alexander B. Miller Collection of Henry Miller, 1936-2007. Harry Ransom Center. University of Texas, Austin.

Miller–Grove Press Correspondence. Henry Miller Collection. Special Collections Department, Charles E. Young Research Library. University of California, Los Angeles.

Miller–Michael Hoffman Correspondence. Henry Miller Collection. Special Collections Department, Charles E. Young Research Library. University of California, Los Angeles.

Miller–Eve Miller Correspondence. Henry Miller Collection. Special Collections Department, Charles E. Young Research Library. University of California, Los Angeles.

Miller–New Directions Correspondence. Henry Miller Collection. Special Collections Department, Charles E. Young Research Library. University of California, Los Angeles.

Miller–Anaïs Nin Correspondence. Anaïs Nin Papers; Henry Miller Collection. University of California, Los Angeles.

Miller–Sydney Omarr Correspondence. Henry Miller Collection. Special Collections Department, Charles E. Young Research Library. University of California, Los Angeles.

Miller–Alfred Perlès Correspondence. Henry Miller Collection. Special Collections Department, Charles E. Young Research Library. University of California, Los Angeles.

Miller–Gerald Robitaille Correspondence. Henry Miller Collection. Special Collections Department, Charles E. Young Research Library. University of California, Los Angeles.

Miller–Ziva Rodann Correspondence. Henry Miller Collection. Special Collections Department, Charles E. Young Research Library. University of California, Los Angeles.

Miller–Emil White Correspondence. Emil White Correspondence. Harry Ransom Center. University of Texas, Austin.

Miller–Walker Winslow Correspondence. Henry Miller Collection. Special Collections Department, Charles E. Young Research Library. University of California, Los Angeles.

Miller, Henry. *My Bike & Other Friends*. Santa Barbara, CA: Capra Press, 1978.

Nin, Anaïs. Diary, Aug. 8, 1962. Anaïs Nin Papers. University of California, Los Angeles.

Rembar, Charles. *The End of Obscenity: The Trials of Lady Chatterley, Tropic of Cancer and Fanny Hill*. New York: Random House, 1968; London: Andre Deutsch, 1969.

Schwartz, Edward, and Thomas Moore, eds. *Henry Miller Literary Society Newsletter*. Minneapolis: Ad Art Advertising, 1959–1962.

Tropic of Cancer. Directed by Joseph Strick. Performed by Rip Torn, Ellen Burstyn. Paramount Pictures, 1970.

Wickes, George, ed. *Henry Miller and James Laughlin. Selected Letters*. New York: W. W. Norton, 1996.

———. *Lawrence Durrell & Henry Miller. A Private Correspondence*. New York: E. P. Dutton, 1964.

Chapter 12
The Henry Miller Legacy

Belmont, Georges. *Henry Miller in Conversation with Georges Belmont*. Chicago: Quadrangle Books, 1972.

Berthoff, Warner. *A Literature Without Qualities: American Writing Since 1945*. Berkeley; Los Angeles; London: University of California Press, 1979.

Bloshteyn, Maria. *The Making of a Counter-Culture Icon: Henry Miller's Dostoevsky*. Toronto; Buffalo: University of Toronto Press, 2007.

Booth, Audrey Jane. "Interview with Henry Miller." In Frank Kersnowski, ed. *Conversations with Henry Miller*. Jackson: University of Mississippi Press, 1994.

Brown, James Dale. *Henry Miller*. New York: Ungar Publishing Company, 1986.

Dearborn, Mary. *The Happiest Man Alive*. New York: Simon & Schuster, 1991.

Dickstein, Morris. *Gates of Eden: American Culture in the Sixties*. New York: Basic Books, 1977.

Diehl, Digby. "Q & A: Henry Miller." In Frank Kersnowski, ed. *Conversations with Henry Miller*. Jackson: University of Mississippi Press, 1994.

Drury, David. "Sex Goes Public: A Talk with Henry Miller." In Frank Kersnowski, ed. *Conversations with Henry Miller*. Jackson: University of Mississippi Press, 1994.

Ellis, Richard. "Disseminating Desire—Grove Press and the End(s) of Obscenity." In Gary Day and Clive Bloom, eds. *Perspectives on Pornography*. London: MacMillan Press, 1988.

Fraenkel, Michael. "The Genesis of *Tropic of Cancer*." In Bern Porter, ed. *The Happy Rock: A Book About Henry Miller*. Berkeley, CA: Bern Porter, 1945.

Girson, Rochelle. "Interview." In Frank Kersnowski, ed. *Conversations with Henry Miller*. Jackson: University of Mississippi Press, 1994.

Jones, Roger. "Henry Miller at Eighty-Four." In Frank Kersnowski, ed. *Conversations with Henry Miller*. Jackson: University of Mississippi Press, 1994.

Jong, Erica. *The Devil at Large*. New York: Turtle Bay Books, 1993.

Mailer, Norman. *Genius and Lust*. New York: Grove Press, 1976.

———. *The Prisoner of Sex*. Boston: Little, Brown, 1971.

Manning, Hugo. "The Wider Purpose of Henry Miller." *Anaïs: An International Journal*, vol. 8, 1990.

Martin, Jay. "Remember to Remember: Henry Miller and Literary Tradition," *CLIO* 7 (1977).

Mathieu, Bertrand. "Henry Miller as Orphic Poet and Seer." In Ronald Gottesman, ed. *Critical Essays on Henry Miller*. New York: G. K. Hall, 1992.

Miller, Henry. *The Books in My Life*. New York: New Directions, 1969.

———. "Interview," *Mademoiselle* 64 (December 1966).

———. *Letters to Emil*. George Wickes, ed. New York: New Directions, 1989.

———. *Nexus*. New York: Grove Press, 1965.

———. *Tropic of Cancer*. New York: Grove Press, 1961.

————. "Walt Whitman." *Stand Still Like the Hummingbird*. New York: New Directions, 1962.

Miller–Michael Fraenkel Correspondence. Henry Miller Collection. University of California, Los Angeles.

Miller–Richard Osborn Correspondence. Henry Miller Collection. University of California, Los Angeles.

Millett, Kate. *Sexual Politics*. New York: Doubleday, 1970.

Mitchell, Edward, ed. *Henry Miller; Three Decades of Criticism*. New York: New York University Press, 1971.

Nesbit, Thomas. *Henry Miller and Religion*. New York & London: Routledge, 2007.

Orend, Karl. *Sex and Society Through the Eyes of Henry Miller*. Paris: Alyscamps Press 2006.

Peerenboom, Randall. "Living Beyond the Bounds: Henry Miller and the Quest for Daoist Realization." In Roger T. Ames, ed. *Wandering at Ease in the Zhuangzi*. Albany, NY: State University of New York Press, 1998.

Polley, George Warren. "The Art of Religious Writing: Henry Miller as Religious Writer." *South Dakota Review* 7 (Autumn 1969).

Ranganath, Nandyal. *The Oriental Element in Henry Miller*. Doctoral Dissertation. Andhra University, Waltair, 1982.

Shapiro, Karl. "The Greatest Living Author." In Karl Shapiro, *In Defense of Ignorance*. New York: Random House, 1952.

Stuhlmann, Gunther, ed. *A Literate Passion: Letters of Anaïs Nin & Henry Miller 1932–1953*. San Diego; New York; London: Harcourt Brace, 1987.

Wickes, George, ed. *Lawrence Durrell & Henry Miller: A Private Correspondence*. New York: E. P. Dutton, 1964.

————. "Interview with Henry Miller." In Frank Kersnowski, ed. *Conversations with Henry Miller*. Jackson: University of Mississippi Press, 1994.

————. *Henry Miller and the Critics*. Carbondale: Southern Illinois University Press, 1963.

Williams, John. "Henry Miller: The Success of Failure." *Virginia Quarterly Review*, 44 (Spring 1968).

Winslow, Kathryn. *Henry Miller: Full of Life*. Los Angeles: Jeremy P. Tarcher, Inc., 1986.

Wolfe, Bernard. "Playboy Interview: Henry Miller," *Playboy* 11 (September 1964).

INDEX